Golden Ages, Dark Ages

# Golden Ages, Dark Ages

Imagining the Past in Anthropology
and History

EDITED BY

## Jay O'Brien
and
## William Roseberry

UNIVERSITY OF CALIFORNIA PRESS
Berkeley    Los Angeles    Oxford

University of California Press
Berkeley and Los Angeles, California

University of California Press
Oxford, England

Library of Congress Cataloging-in-Publication Data

Golden ages, dark ages : imagining the past in anthropology and
  history / edited by Jay O'Brien and William Roseberry.
      p.   cm.
  Includes bibliographical references and index.
  ISBN 0-520-07018-6
  1. Anthropology—Methodology.  2. Ethnohistory.  3. Economic
anthropology.  I. O'Brien, Jay.  II. Roseberry, William, 1950–   .
GN33.G64   1991
301—dc20                                                        90-24806
                                                                   CIP

Printed in the United States of America

1   2   3   4   5   6   7   8   9

The paper used in this publication meets the minimum requirements of American National
Standard for Information Sciences—Permanence of Paper for Printed Library Materials, ANSI
Z39.48-1984 ⊗

*To Blanche dePuy O'Brien and the memory of John J. O'Brien, Jr.*
*(1923–1990) for lessons in critical imagination*

# CONTENTS

# PREFACE

This book began as something other than what it has become. When we organized a symposium on "The Construction of Natural Economy" for the Annual Meeting of the American Anthropological Association a few years ago, our original goal was to criticize oppositional models in anthropology by collecting a series of historical reconstructions that took apparently primordial social forms (peasant households, forms of community, ethnicity, and the like) and placed the emergence of those forms within modern history. Such a project necessarily involves a multistranded critique of the romantic search for cultural authenticity, of the imposition of naturalized oppositional categories upon more complex social-historical experiences, and of the reading of cultural difference in historical terms. As is evident from our Introduction and several essays in this volume (see especially the chapters written by Roseberry, Painter, Lennihan, and O'Brien), such themes retain a central place in the present book.

As we began moving from symposium papers toward a book, however, some interesting changes began to occur. First, we contacted additional authors (Rebel, Spaulding and Kapteijns, Swedenburg, Smith, Sider, and di Leonardo) who, beyond simply "rounding out" the book, changed its basic shape. Most importantly, their papers helped us extend our critique of naturalized oppositional categories in two directions—toward an examination of the manner in which some of our most basic concepts (of gender, ethnicity, and the like) are infused with naturalistic constructions, and toward a consideration of the politically charged contexts in which such oppositions are constructed by historical actors and by intellectuals. Second, our many attempts to write an Introduction for the volume engaged the new and revised versions of essays for the volume, the critical commentaries of our contributors and colleagues, and recent stimulating contributions to the convergence of anthropology and history. In all of these engagements, a book and argument have emerged that no single individual could have foreseen at the outset. This is truly a collaborative product.

We begin, then, by thanking our contributors, with special thanks to Hermann Rebel, Gavin Smith, Gerald Sider, and Micaela di Leonardo for their careful readings of various drafts of the Introduction. We also thank Jane Guyer and Ann Stoler for their contributions to the original symposium, and Henry Bernstein for his perceptive and challenging comments on the original papers. Among the other colleagues who have offered criticism and encouragement, especially on the Introduction but more generally on the project as a whole, are Ann Binder, Kim Clark, Lindsay DuBois, Ellen Gruenbaum, William Kelly, Nicole Polier, George Saunders, and Jane Schneider as well as the participants in Jay O'Brien's Anthropology and History Seminar at Lawrence University. At the University of California Press, Stanley Holwitz has been a knowledgeable and encouraging colleague, in addition to understanding the problems and delays associated with producing an edited book. Jane Schneider and an anonymous reviewer provided especially helpful critical commentary on the manuscript.

# Introduction

*William Roseberry and Jay O'Brien*

It is by now a cliché to claim that the world is characterized by radical cultural differences and contrasts. Even as the world comes to resemble a "global village," we still find places and people who seem strikingly unmodern, who live and think in ways that may unsettle a Western sensibility. Anthropologists often serve as professional interpreters of such cultural difference, but like the educated public to whom they represent other modes of being, they may misleadingly frame that difference in *historical* terms. Tourists and anthropologists alike may talk of travel to distant lands in terms of visits to our own past. The global village characterized by rapid communications and cultural homogeneity is presented (at least implicitly) as "modern"—part of our present and future—while the world of cultural difference and heterogeneity is viewed as representative of a more traditional, perhaps more authentic, set of human pasts.

Such a view, at once popular and academic, ignores the extent to which the various social and cultural forms and practices encountered in the present are themselves the products of modern social, political, and cultural processes. It ignores the *possibility* that such processes have simultaneously created the cultural homogeneity we assume to be modern and the cultural heterogeneity we project upon the past. It is easy to view a variety of markers of cultural difference as the legacies of traditional modes of life. That they may be: the modern world presents a rich array of cultural symbols carrying ancient pedigrees. We suggest in this book, however, that the modern transformation has involved the constant creation of new expressions of cultural difference as well as fundamental redefinitions of old ones. Consequently, in our view, treating such difference as if it indicated the persistence of traditional cultures into the modern world is likely to miss precisely those features that make those cultural expressions important aspects of people's current lives.

*1*

In recent years, several studies have stressed the invention or construction of cultural and political traditions. Benedict Anderson's *Imagined Communities* (1983) explores the construction of nationalism in the modern world; Hobsbawm and Ranger's *The Invention of Tradition* (1983) explores the creation of a variety of political traditions and ceremonies, especially in the late nineteenth and twentieth centuries. Common to such inventions is the projection of modern practices and associations into a deep past, dressing up those practices and associations with the clothing of custom, primordial loyalties, and ancient rites. Social actors impose, in short, a naturalized and archaic set of symbols upon modern social relations and processes.

The present book fits well within this "new tradition" of anthropological and historical work, but we extend the focus to include the traditionalist complicity of anthropologists and historians themselves. That is, we contend that some of the basic concepts used by anthropologists and historians to talk about (or "construct") cultural others or the past are themselves the ideological products of the construction of the modern "Western" world. Indeed, this book is intended as a fundamental challenge to the very terms in which we conceive the past, especially but not exclusively in its relationship to cultural diversity.

I

The defects of the historical projection upon cultural diversity reflect deeply rooted problems in the discipline of anthropology itself, indeed in the larger system of social thought of which it is a part. Comparative and historical understanding in general is often embedded in a variety of oppositional models taken to represent past and present. Whether expressed in terms of primitive versus civilized, traditional versus modern, folk versus urban, natural economy versus market economy, community versus contract, underdeveloped versus developed, or other polar pairs, such models represent deductive constructs intended to present historical change as a transition from one abstract pole to the other. The pole representing the past is often based upon naturalistic assumptions. Historical analysis then proceeds by sorting the mixed elements of any concrete reality into those left over from the past and those belonging to the emergent future. The analytic division of Third World societies into "traditional" and "modern" sectors is a familiar example of this procedure. The sectors are generally defined on the basis of assessments of the relative modernity of existing features of production, exchange, social organization, and so forth, without any rigorous attempt to account for the supposed sectors or their past and present interconnection. Rather than reconstructing social, political, and cultural changes in the past, this exercise reproduces a pseudohistorical process immanent in the categories themselves and derived from implicit evolutionist assumptions. Actual societies sharing temporal space are radically disconnected in thought and assigned to different abstract evolutionary stages or epochs, according to how many "modern" traits they possess.

At one level, our objection is unsurprising. Readers are already familiar with the criticisms of modernization theorists and their use of evolutionistic oppositions between tradition and modernity (see, e.g., Frank 1969). We raise again the problem of oppositional models because their use has been more pervasive and influential than the early critics realized. In the first place, oppositional constructions are also popular among critics of Western civilization and thought. Indeed, several recent authors have resorted to oppositional models in an attempt to avoid the positivist assumptions and preoccupations of Western social science. One tendency, represented by anthropologists such as Marshall Sahlins (1972) and Michael Taussig (1980), opposes use-value economies to exchange-value economies, or natural economy to commodity economy, tending to celebrate and romanticize the former. The distinction is firmly grounded in the work of Marx and the German Historical School of the nineteenth century. Sahlins is using the opposition to construct a noncapitalist economics—a model of nonmaximizing, nonaccumulating economics having a use-value orientation and based on household provisioning; Taussig is trying to illuminate the politics of peasants first encountering the introduction of capitalist relations of production. In both cases, however, the attempt to construct a noncapitalist economics or an anticapitalist discourse founders on the unrecognized use of capitalist categories, or categories designed to illuminate Western, capitalist life, to analyze non-Western economics and politics. "Natural economy" or "use value" says more about what the economy is not (it is not capitalist) than what it is. Likewise, the politics of natural economy only make sense in the presumed first encounter with commodity economy. In both cases, paradoxically enough, the categories of a later epoch are used to illuminate an earlier one as part of a proclaimed attempt to avoid the imposition of Western categories. This ignores or underestimates the extent to which the cultural forms the authors examine are themselves, in part, the products of colonial and postcolonial experience that continue to dress themselves in the ceremonial garb of hallowed tradition.

The essays in this book offer a variety of challenges to this sort of oppositional critical theory. Sahlins's project, for example, fits well within and depends upon a body of theoretical work on peasantries. Most models of peasantries assert the centrality of the household as a combined unit of production and consumption, as—in Galeski's (1972) words—a combination of enterprise and domestic economy. In the classic statements of household economy, the linkage between the household and natural economy was explicit. For example, A. V. Chayanov saw his model of the peasant household as a model of "our economic past" (1966 [1925]:2), a past in which human economic activity is dominated by the requirement of satisfying the needs of each single production unit, which is, at the same time, a consumer unit. Therefore, budgeting here is to a high degree *qualitative*: for each family need, there has to be provided in each economic unit the qualitatively corresponding product *in natura*. (Ibid.:4).

Although more recent students of peasantries might not explicitly invoke such crudely naturalistic assumptions, they often take the household and household economy as a historical base line. For example, Louise Tilly and Joan Scott (1978) begin their study of the transformations of "women, work, and family" in modern Europe with an assertion of the importance of family economy in town and countryside in early modern Europe, and much of their understanding of the participation of women and men in processes of proletarianization, and the effects of such processes on them, depends upon their initial model of family economy. Yet the extent to which the early modern family economy might itself have been the product of earlier and concurrent changes, as Roseberry's chapter in this volume argues for England, is not considered.

In his model of the protoindustrial family economy, Hans Medick explicitly connects it with an earlier, peasant economy. The new feature in protoindustrial households, according to Medick, was that they are no longer removed from extensive exchange networks, that they had lost their "autarky." He sees the form and organization of the household, however, as resting upon an older, agricultural, self-sufficient base.

> In the peasant household the regulation of production and consumption was primarily geared to its own subsistence and its needs to maintain selfsufficiency. This regulation by no means excluded relationships of "limited exchange." In the "ganzes Haus" of the rural industrial producer this unity of the producing workshop and the consuming household lost its relative autarky. Generative reproduction among the landless and land-poor industrial producers was no longer tied to the "social reproduction" of a relatively inflexible rural property structure. Production, consumption, and generative reproduction increasingly broke away from their agrarian base. They came to be entirely determined by the market, but, at the same time, they preserved the structural and functional connection that was provided by the family. The social mode of the "ganzes Haus" still formed an effective socio-economic structural model, after its agrarian self-subsistence base had largely disappeared.
>
> For even under these new conditions, the household remained tied to the structural and functional prerequisites of the traditional "family economy." (Medick 1981:40)

In his careful analysis of early modern commercial production within households, Medick approached but then retreated from a fundamental rethinking of the naturalistic assumptions that pervade models of family economy. Instead of pointing to the paradoxical "symbiosis between the 'stone-age economy' and merchant or putting-out capital" (ibid.:50), he might have questioned the model of stone-age economy itself and explored in more detail the connection between, in this case, merchant and putting-out capital and the social *construction* of "family economy." Unfortunately, he remained wedded to the historical assumptions of natural economy and used them to interpret the values and economic strategies of producers within proto-industrial households. What we are proposing, in contrast, is a view that connects household economy and merchant capital not simply as a paradox-ical symbiosis but as a constitutive and perhaps defining feature. In doing so, we begin to question the naturalistic assumptions regarding use-value orientations and nonaccumulation strategies that have been imputed to peasant and protoindustrial households.

The first three chapters in this book attempt the sort of historical recon-struction suggested here. Roseberry explores the emergence of apparently independent household production units with the enclosures in early modern England, arguing that we need to look beyond the apparent continuity of household forms and examine the changing social, economic, and cultural contexts of household production, the erosion of a "hidden economy" in the open fields. Rebel analyzes the political invocation of classicist images of the *oikos* in early modern Austria in the construction of a model of the peasant household and the absolutist state (see as well Rebel 1983). Moving beyond forms of household production, Painter explores the construction and recon-struction of reciprocal forms of labor exchange in highland Peru during the colonial and postcolonial eras, paying close attention to the changing posi-tions of peasant producers within regional and extraregional processes of economic expansion and contraction. Taken together and in conjunction with other recent studies (see Gudmundson 1986; Roseberry 1983, 1986; Stoler 1985), these essays suggest the possibility that fundamental aspects of "family economy" might be the product of early modern and modern social, political, and cultural processes and that our models of family economy might be the product of political and ideological discourses derived from the more recent past in which fundamental features and preoccupations of the present are projected upon a naturalized past. Our point here is not that household production units as such were invented in modern times. We seek to suggest rather that more recent "family economies" differ profoundly from similar forms found in the past. Family economies encountered in the capi-talist present cannot be taken as useful guides to the family economies of noncapitalist pasts, and the naturalistic assumptions with which past family economies are studied cannot be simplistically applied to the family econ-omies of the capitalist present.

With this point, we move beyond a consideration of the "modern" con-struction of "traditional" social forms toward an examination of the politics of natural economy itself. A sophisticated treatment of such politics can be found in the work of Michael Taussig. In *The Devil and Commodity Fetishism in South America* (1980), he elaborates an opposition between use value and exchange-value economies and explores the nature of the cultural and political response of peasants to the initial introduction of capitalist relations. Capitalist relations are, in turn, seen as characterized by exchange value; noncapitalist relations of various sorts are seen as characterized by use value. Taussig is especially interested in the use of devil imagery by peasants and others to respond to the social relations introduced with a capitalist economy. He explores this problem in two settings: the Cauca Valley of Colombia and the tin mines of the Bolivian Andes. In both cases, the metaphorical opposition is imposed on a complex social and cultural process. In the Cauca Valley, Taussig uses the concept of a "peasant mode of production" to characterize a population of escaped slaves and their descendants, who have attempted to maintain their independence and who have used commodity production as part of that attempt. Taussig might have paid more attention to this in his account: the social history of the peasant producers of the Cauca Valley clearly belies the naturalized opposition with which Taussig seeks to understand them. Nonetheless, his treatment of the Cauca Valley is much more detailed and careful than is his analysis of devil imagery and the propitiation of spirits in the mines of Bolivia. There we encounter metaphorical history. We read analyses of cosmological systems among Aymara peasants (based on the ethnographic work of Bastien [1978] and the Buechlers [1971] among altiplano peasants) that are then imposed upon tin miners with the extraordinary statement, "Miners either come directly from [peasant] life or have a background in its dictates and sentiments" (Taussig 1980:214). This is manifestly untrue, or at least it is not true in the simplistic way Taussig has presented it. Many of the descendants of peasants who have ended up in the tin mines come not from the altiplano but from the Cochabamba Valley, where a mestizo peasantry developed in the colonial period, and where a vibrant commercial peasant economy competed with hacienda production in the eighteenth century. Social differentiation and impoverishment by the late nineteenth and early twentieth centuries began to push the children of many peasant households out of the valley and into the mines (see Larson 1988:305–319). Reference to cosmology and images of reciprocity among altiplano peasants does not begin to grasp the complex social experience of the ethnically different peasants who actually entered the mines.

Moreover, tin miners in Bolivia are among the most militant workers in South America. Yet they continue to build images of Hahuari (the "devil" in the mines) and their union has insisted on the right to maintain the images and engage in propitiation rites as part of a conscious and oppositional political strategy (see Nash 1979). It is a strategy that involves the explicit use of images from a precolonial past and that offers a political critique in cultural terms. That is, markers of ethnic identity are consciously used in political struggles. But the cultural process that informs such ethnic politics should not be understood solely, or even primarily, in epochal terms. Use of a metaphorical opposition between use value and exchange value to understand that strategy carries us several steps away from the actual activity and thought of the actors. It reduces that activity to the terms of a (Western) model that can be easily consumed by a sophisticated (Western) anthropological audience.[1]

At issue here are the social construction and politics of cultural difference—in this case, of ethnicity. While Taussig attempts to enclose such differences within an oppositional historical (or epochal) model that sees a more authentic set of human pasts confronting an evil capitalist present, several essays in this volume place the construction and politics of a variety of cultural forms (ethnicity, gender, and "the community") in a different light. Concepts of ethnicity are most directly addressed in the essays by di Leonardo and O'Brien, with important support and elaboration in the contributions of Spaulding and Kapteijns, Swedenburg, Smith, and Sider. O'Brien shows that what appear to be primordial ethnic distinctions in Sudan reflect the condensation of much more complex social and cultural processes as a variety of populations—from West African Hausa and Fulani migrants to White Nile villagers—came to adopt or modify certain ethnic identities as they occupied distinct niches within a segmented labor market. As they did so, the fundamental principles on the basis of which ethnic identities and relations between them were organized were transformed. Di Leonardo's examination of recent American inventions of ethnic and gender constructions extends our understanding of such constructions by placing them within ongoing intellectual and political disputes. This political dimension is elaborated in different ways in the various contributions to this volume, especially in Smith's exploration of the construction of "community" within ongoing land-recuperation campaigns in Peru, and Swedenburg's study of the construction of Palestinian nationalism within a situation of Israeli occupation and domination.

In an especially suggestive comment, Sider (this volume) observes that "gender," "ethnicity," and "the domestic" emerge as modes of marking difference, and that these modes can become "frameworks for judgments and critiques of domination." We shall elaborate on this insight in the following section. For now we wish to concentrate on the indicated connection between the political construction of naturalized communities (of gender, ethnicity, nationhood), and the intellectual construction of such images within our basic concepts. Spaulding and Kapteijns demonstrate this connection with their careful exploration of the work of historians such as H. A. MacMichael, J. S. Trimingham, and P. M. Holt. Di Leonardo's important critique of sociologists such as Robert Bellah and his associates and of historians such as Carroll Smith-Rosenberg brings us from sixteenth- and seventeenth-century

Europe or nineteenth- and twentieth-century Sudan to the American present, demonstrating and criticizing the use of naturalized images of the Other within current political debates.

Such usages should be seen as a collaborative product of history and anthropology, which have effectively served as boundary-maintaining disciplines responsible for reporting on those who are not like "us." Anthropology may represent the Other in terms of cultural distance and history may represent the Other in terms of temporal distance, but the terms of representation are often largely interchangeable, mixing the cultural and the temporal. The concern with the present in the construction of specific pasts entails preoccupation with measuring the distance between "them" and "us" and cataloging the dimensions of that difference, whatever the relative valences assigned (see also Alonso 1988). Edward Said (1978) has argued that the knowledge resulting from such practices is inevitably tied to power. Through conquest, Europe gained the ability to define an object simultaneously of domination and of knowledge called "the Orient" (which somehow included Chinese Confucians and Algerian Muslims), which Orientalists could then examine for clues to the fatal flaws that made Orientals losers and the West the winner in the race to civilization. With the Orient, or the non-Western world in general, constituted as an array of neatly bounded units, their difference became an intrinsic characteristic fully contained within them.

Although recent postmodernist authors in anthropology seem to offer a similar critique of anthropological images of discrete cultures and "pure products," they may simultaneously and paradoxically depend on the construction of an Other based on radical cultural difference. Such a construction is central to Marcus and Fischer's resurrection of cultural relativism as "cultural critique" and underlies their criticism of Said (1986:2; cf. Ortner 1984:143). Their posing of the problem presupposes the radical separation between "us" and "them" that Said criticizes, and transforms it to a problem of crossing boundaries between autonomous cultural objects. They therefore remain within the same hermeneutical current in contemporary anthropology—particularly in its Geertzian form—to which most historians attempting to overcome their discipline's long neglect of culture have tended to turn. The erection of a form of historical relativism on the foundation of cultural relativism places stress on the otherness of a distant "them" from an unproblematic "us." As Rebel (1989:123) has expressed it:

> By stressing alterity, cultural [or historical] relativism places in the path of analysis an obstructive sense of internal cultural homogeneity that not only fails to examine those points where cultures engage each other out of separate histories but also, secondly, forecloses on the question of the depth to which analysis can go in understanding experience and of the precise ways by which experience enters historical-cultural processes.

Such an approach ignores the power relations that made possible and operate at the very core of the ethnographic project of representing the Other, and neglects a more considered examination of the historical construction of cultural difference within unequal fields of power. In an analysis that is central to this book's argument, Gerald Sider observes:

> It is ordinarily thought that the expansion and consolidation of a colonial political economy (or indeed of modern state power) destroys or undermines prior cultural distinctiveness, or generates distinctions in the context of seeking to divide and conquer. But ethnic group formation in the colonial context—the creation of cultures and peoples—is not so much a product of divide-and-conquer policies as of a much more complex, less specifically planned, and far more resistance-permeated process that we might call "create and incorporate." In this process the developing social and cultural distinctiveness is often' crucial to the expansion and consolidation of the colonial frontier. (1987:17)

It might appear that, having criticized others for looking at the past through the concerns of the present, we are guilty of the same sins in our own concern with modern usages and constructions. Indeed, we seem to be concerned with the past primarily in relation to, or as a construction of, the present. Where we differ most profoundly with the scholars whose work we have criticized is in our conceptualization of the past and present and the relationship between them, as well as in our understanding of cultural difference and the pertinence of historical metaphors to express such difference. In his critique of the tendency to treat cultures and societies as autonomous entities, Eric Wolf (1982:6–7) vividly captures what we find wrong with prevailing modes of representing cultural and historical distance:

> By turning names into things we create false models of reality. By endowing nations, societies, or cultures with the qualities of internally homogeneous and externally distinctive and bounded objects, we create a model of the world as a global pool hall in which the entities spin off each other like so many hard and round billiard balls. Thus it becomes easy to sort the world into differently colored balls, to declare that "East is East, and West is West, and never the twain shall meet." . . . Names thus become things, and things marked with an X can be targets of war.

There is, of course, much more than cultural distance involved in placing an X on a particular culture for the purpose of aiming bombs. Virtue, too, is on the side of those who have the power to decide where the X will be placed. The history of the origins of the modern world often takes the form of a moral relay race, as Wolf puts it (1982:5), in which each runner passes the torch of civilization and virtue on to the next, from the ancient Greeks to the contemporary American guardians of Western civilization. This kind of history tells us how the good guys won out at each stage over the bad guys and paved the way for our "modern," "civilized" way of life.

Oppositional modeling of the sort we have been discussing need not, however, endorse such a political reading of the civilizational process. Indeed, most of the scholars we have been discussing start with liberal or radical sentiments, and their sympathies clearly lie with those without civilizational virtue, those who "live and die in unredeemed time" (Thompson 1978*b*:296). Nevertheless, they have tended to accept the terms used to describe that supposed civilizational process and invert their meanings, endorsing the "traditional" and rejecting the "modern." Within such a framework, dissent from existing forms of domination—both at the level of social action and in social analysis—can occur only on the basis of a reversal of the polarities of prevailing oppositional models: romantic primitivism or crude nationalism.

For concepts of peasant households, of gender, of ethnicity, and of nation, then, we suggest a critical perspective similar to Karl Marx's observation concerning eighteenth-century ideologies of the individual. Complaining that philosophers and political economists took the lone individual as the point of departure for their historical speculations, Marx observed that they saw the individual

> as an ideal, whose existence they project into the past. Not as historic result but as history's point of departure. As the Natural Individual appropriate to their notion of human nature, not arising historically, but posited by nature. (Marx 1973 [1857]:83)

In this book we argue that various naturalized social forms have played a role similar to this in social and cultural analysis; gender, ethnicity, household, community, and so on have been taken as history's points of departure, as fixed units, rather than as the changing results of social and political processes. The chapters of this book seek to show these social forms as the products of particular processes operating in specific social fields.

To view these forms as "historic result" rather than "history's point of departure" is to outline a wide array of historical and anthropological projects. For example, upon showing that certain aspects of peasant household economy in sixteenth-century England are created within early modern or modern economic, social, and political processes, it would be inappropriate to assert that "household economy" is therefore a simple product of the modern world. Rather, each of these essays shows that a form of household economy, or a particular ethnic configuration, or a specific notion of community emerges at particular conjunctures, within particular fields of power, and within particularly complex and uneven sedimentations of the past and the present. Our understanding of the household economy of sixteenth-century

England requires an examination of open-field agriculture, the complex relations between manors and villages in late feudal and early modern England, the demographic crisis of the fourteenth century, the commercial expansion of the sixteenth century, the enclosures, the emerging three-tiered structure of landlord, tenant farmer, and rural laborer, and the expansion of domestic manufacture in the countryside. Our understanding of reciprocal forms of labor exchange in Puno, Peru requires an examination of pre-Hispanic economic, social, political, and cultural forms of work and labor appropriation, the uneven effects of nearly three centuries of Spanish rule, the nineteenth-century expansion of wool exports and its differential effects on rural villages, the collapse of wool exports, and the construction of a highland labor reserve. Our understanding of the ideology of community in Huasicancha, Peru in the 1960s requires an exploration of the shifting relations between the village and Hacienda Tucle, the complex strategies of villagers to use and lay claim to hacienda land, the migration of villagers to urban areas, the establishment of enterprises through which villagers and migrants could make claims on each other's labor and resources, and the expression of these claims within an ongoing process of contention and struggle. And so on, for each of the processes explored in this book. This is not merely an effort to achieve fuller and more richly textured empirical accounts. It is fundamentally a question of theory in which the denaturalization of central forms forces us to pose a new set of questions.

Although the book is unified by a general critique of anthropological and historical uses of naturalized oppositions, then, the argument is necessarily carried in examinations of specific processes and problems, each of which suggests a new set of problems or a new direction for scholarly work. Our intention in this book is not simply to invert the conventional wisdom, to assert that the "natural" should be seen as "historical"—or the "traditional" as "modern." Such a project would preserve the prevailing terms of discourse and simply change the positions of some of their objects. Rather, we contend that there have been a variety of *modern tracks toward the traditional*, that with the construction of different household econom*ies*, different ethnic-it*ies*, and so on, the (combined and uneven) development of the modern world has created worlds of social, economic, and cultural difference.

In this respect, Painter's and Lennihan's essays offer truly radical perspectives. Painter's suggestion that what appears capitalist and what appears peasant, what modern and what traditional, depends on the moment in various cycles of growth and decline that one examines the Puno countryside in Peru, should give our more confident theorists pause. Likewise, Lennihan's suggestion that the theoretical movement from one form of labor contract to another in northern Nigeria is not necessarily a chronological movement, or that the chronological movement cannot be read from the present-day distribution of forms and that the forms can be combined and recombined, can disappear and reappear, in response to prevailing social conditions, undermines received assumptions.

## II

The essays in this book represent attempts to place apparently traditional social forms within modern history. That is, they place these forms within social, economic, and political processes associated with the making of the "modern" world, and within a set of intellectual and political discourses about "modernity." Taken as a whole, they embrace a tension between "real history" on the one hand, and the historical commentaries and texts of social actors and intellectuals on the other. The tension is contained within the concept of history itself, in its reference to actual pasts, to the process by which "we" come to acquire knowledge of pasts, and to the images, concepts, words, and texts with which we communicate that knowledge. In our view, "historical" work must embrace all three meanings: attempts to restrict history to "what actually happened" result in gross forms of positivism and empiricism; attempts to restrict history to historians' discourses result in a bloodless nihilism and the neglect of the historical meanings of important categories of social actors.

In the preceding pages we have considered the relationship between oppositional models and the actual pasts of peasantries and ethnic formations. We turn now to an examination of the models as social, political, and ideological constructions. Many of the essays in this book deal with the formation of imagined communities formed in opposition to other such imagined communities in contexts of political contention or struggle. Images of and symbols from the past weigh heavily in such groups, and in many cases the creation of a fundamentally new community is presented as simple continuity from the past. Differences and conflicts between "us" and "them" are presented as natural or at least long-standing and traditional. Even when an imagined community is presented as new, it seeks legitimacy by assigning its opposition to a discredited past. It would be premature to attempt to generalize a formula for such processes, but we see in the cases analyzed here some broad themes that bear more general consideration.

We group these themes in terms of three broadly conceived issues: the *context* of inequality and contestation; the *process* of struggle and the place of naturalized and oppositional historical images within it; and the *production* of the historical images themselves. Swedenburg draws upon Gramsci's distinction between hegemonic and subaltern cultural forms to make a corresponding distinction between hegemonic and subaltern views of history in order to understand important differences between historical visions created by the agents of a dominant class seeking to legitimate their power and stifle opposi-

tion and visions created by subordinate groups struggling against that power. We think that this provides a useful framework for thinking about the
imagined pasts presented in this book, as long as the distinction between the
"hegemonic" and "subaltern" does not become a new vehicle for producing
dichotomous historical models, with a distinction between a necessarily "inauthentic" hegemonic history and an "authentic" subaltern or people's history. The problems here are multiple, first because neither the hegemonic
nor the subaltern forms a homogeneous bloc. Rather, the individuals and
groups we label hegemonic and subaltern have important *internal* differences—different interests, lived experiences, projects, struggles, and so on.
Much of the process by which an apparently coherent set of historical and
cultural images is created involves an internal struggle, as Smith's essay
makes clear. Swedenburg's case, in which the counterhegemonic is not,
strictly speaking, the subaltern, provides another important example.

Our cases also make clear that the hegemonic and subaltern do not exist
in isolation from each other. As Jackson Lears insists, "the line between
dominant and subordinate cultures is a permeable membrane, not an impenetrable barrier" (Lears 1985:574). We need to move, then, from discussions of hegemony to studies of complexly determined *hegemonic processes*, from
the Gramsci of *State and Civil Society* or *The Modern Prince* to the Gramsci of the
*Notes on Italian History* (Gramsci 1971 [1929–35]).

It is in terms of such processes that we propose to think about the cases
presented here, and it is also in terms of such processes that Lears's reference
to a "permeable membrane" becomes important. Part of what makes that
membrane permeable is the existence of a common discursive framework.
Indeed, a central feature of any hegemonic formation, and a kind of measure
of its success, is the ability to frame the terms of discussion and debate, to
shape a language in which basic relationships, movements, and problems can
be talked about. Certain terms and associations are acceptable; others are so
unacceptable they cannot even be thought. Such terms are never fixed but
are themselves the objects and means of debate and contention, and the very
process of contention may change the terms or their associated meanings. We
see this most clearly in the language of gender, ethnicity, community, and
history in the chapters that follow.

A subordinate movement needs to present itself in terms that its members
and opponents can understand. The establishment of a kind of legitimacy
often requires that the group and its context be placed within preexisting and
accepted frameworks. For example, the group may be presented as a kind of
community, and communities are valued; that community may be seen to
hold a central if neglected place in the history of the larger society; the community's struggle may be presented as a democratic struggle and therefore
fully in keeping with the society's core values; indeed, it can be argued that
the struggle rediscovers and reinvigorates certain lost values and traditions

for society as a whole. Even as the movement adopts preexisting terms of argument, however, its use of those terms in new contexts and in the presentation of new demands stretches and transforms the terms themselves, especially as the movement enjoys some success. Di Leonardo's chapter clearly demonstrates this process. She suggests that the success women and minorities in the United States had in legitimating their claims to civil rights, economic opportunities, and so on, altered the ideological terms in which their claims could be opposed. This gave rise to the generalization of "interest groups" as categories whose rights could be infringed, the formation of a variety of white ethnic groups, modeled in important ways on minority groups, to defend various white "communities" against "reverse discrimination," and the redefinition of antifeminist agendas in terms of reconceived "women's rights."

Here we have one case of struggle between hegemonic and subaltern images that has resulted in a transformation in the terms of political contention as dominant groups seek to absorb victories by subordinate groups in order to reestablish cultural hegemony. The histories of all the contending parties then are rewritten accordingly, as di Leonardo shows, in such a way as to relativize the suffering of oppressed groups and obfuscate the identity of the agents and beneficiaries of their oppression. In this rewriting, white ethnics in the United States, alas, suffer discrimination just like other ethnics. Not incidentally, prejudice and discrimination become naturalized in the process—enduring if disturbing tendencies of all communities to look down their noses at and discriminate against other communities.

Thus, the terms of contention naturalize difference and competition in general and in many particulars. Ethnic loyalties are presented as primordial and inescapable—or, in more liberal versions, as capable of being transcended only very gradually through the civilizational process. Not all naturalized differences are relativized in this way. Gender in particular tends to be left as a fundamental category of human difference, but the terms in which this difference is constructed change in accordance with shifts in the overall process of contention.

The cases analyzed in these chapters indicate that although all historical images are actively constructed, the agency and conditions of their construction vary considerably. As illustrated by Rebel, Kapteijns and Spaulding, and Swedenburg, dominant powers may undertake or sponsor deliberate and sometimes coordinated programs of invention of national traditions and other ideological images, sometimes involving social scientists or other academics. It seldom happens, however, that we find an easy or obvious relationship between a process of political and economic domination and a cultural process in which corresponding hegemonic images are constructed. For one thing, the process of establishing political power involves a series of contests, compromises, and *ad hoc* arrangements that may become "permanent." At the time, actors will have a set of images of themselves and of their allies and opponents, images that are themselves contingent historical products and subject to change in the context of the encounter itself or in latter-day interpretations of that encounter. The civilizing mission may become the black legend; the heathen may become the noble savage. What is most interesting about many of these images and encounters is their contingent character, their lack of system. Indeed, one of the characteristics of a hegemonic discourse may be the ability to *create* apparent systemic coherence.

For example, in Sudan under British colonialism specific historical images seem to evolve more or less unconsciously as the outcomes of political and economic policies. Certainly British policy in Sudan was shaped by Orientalist notions about the people they ruled, but the images of particular Sudanese communities which the British came to hold—and which their Sudanese successors in power largely confirmed—emerged informally out of British experience of the varied responses by those communities to colonial policies. Orientalist attitudes taught British colonial authorities to look for some ethnic groups that might be fierce fighters, others that would be hard workers, and still others that would be lazy creatures suitable for only the most menial of tasks under supervision. When they found hard workers, they wanted to know their ethnic identity in order to find out where to get more like them. When they had to resort to less desirable types, they designed policies directed specifically at them which might motivate them to work harder. Gradually, an ethnically segmented labor force emerged in which the type and style of participation of each ethnic group was explained by reference to their supposed traditions. Discrepancies were treated, tautologically, as exceptions—degenerate Arabs or Arabized Africans and so on.

In other cases, hegemonic images may represent attempts to appropriate or incorporate the cultural practices and historical visions of subaltern groups. These attempts are seldom separate from ongoing processes of political domination or struggle and are especially important in state formation and consolidation, in which constructed nationalisms (Anderson's [1983] "imagined communities") figure prominently. Here we see writers, folklorists, government agencies, and the like attempting to create a hegemonic cultural or historical understanding as a basis for defining the national community and legitimating their position within it, perhaps as guardians of the community's traditions. Examples include the folklore movement of early-nineteenth-century central Europe, or the competing visions of Palestinian peasants in the Israeli state and the Palestinian nationalist movement, or the construction of a "Mexican" peasantry as part of the institutionalization of a revolution (Lomnitz 1987). In such cases, the authorship of historical images is often clear. We can point to the Grimms or to the creation of a National Institute for Anthropology and History. Even in such cases, however, the images are not simply constructed out of thin air. They must connect with, and seem to arise from, "history" or "tradition": the Grimms must deal with what Old Marie told them, even as they rewrite passages for their middle-class readers (Rebel 1988). In this tension between authenticity and incorporation arises the *necessity* of multiple authorship, and in multiple authorship lies the possibility of contention or struggle over the images themselves.

Here too we can locate particular authors and actors, as in a variety of ethnic movements and subaltern, "counterhegemonic" nationalisms. On occasion we may be able to witness or reconstruct the formation of parties, the writing of texts that rediscover or reinterpret aspects of the past. But authorship need not take such organized and literate forms. We find it as well in the complaints of the Huasicanchinos (Smith's essay), in which a disparate collection of city, town, and village dwellers, petty traders and herders, all with backgrounds in Huasicancha, come to define themselves as an indigenous community, a definition that is "written" in contentious community meetings in the context of an ongoing struggle with an encroaching hacienda and a repressive state. The definition involves the creative use of political definitions available within the state (the recognition of *Comunidades Indigenas*) and issues that were part of more generalized disputes between haciendas and villages throughout the highlands (see also Smith 1989).

But we also see in the construction of these naturalized images much more diffuse, nonsystematic authorships. This is especially evident in di Leonardo's contribution, in which several authors and actors have contributed to the construction of naturalized images of women's culture and white ethnicity, and in which authors and actors built upon images already available from other processes of ethnic construction and contention. Sider's careful and systematic reading and presentation of two women's memoirs is especially important here (see also Sider 1986). Certainly, the minister who gave an old woman writing materials and suggested she write her autobiography had some idea of "a past" that needed to be preserved. But the story itself reflects images individually constructed out of one person's experience. Her descendant, writing many years later, is doing something similar. The social isolation these people lived in seems crucial here. We see perceptive and intelligent individuals producing politically important and effective historical visions without someone formally undertaking either to codify or to glorify the past. Such visions may grow out of individual and family histories that represent similar experiences of isolation. When such experiences are widespread and become the focus of struggle, these visions may become more broadly social and cultural as they are acknowledged as such and activated in struggle. That is, they may become *cultural* images, rather than remaining individual visions, as they become *politicized*.

## III

There is much in our discussion here that is preliminary and tentative. We offer these observations and propositions as a framework within which to think about the potential wider significance of the particular analyses presented in the following essays and as a starting point for further work on these issues. We think that these analyses offer a new perspective that can serve as a basis for building upon one of Marx's insights, which has been more often invoked than examined. Human beings, he observed,

> make their own history, but not of their own free will; not under circumstances they themselves have chosen but under the given and inherited circumstances with which they are directly confronted. The tradition of the dead generations weighs like a nightmare on the minds of the living. And, just when they appear to be engaged in the revolutionary transformation of themselves and their material surroundings, in the creation of something which does not yet exist, precisely in such epochs of revolutionary crisis they timidly conjure up the spirits of the past to help them; they borrow names, slogans and costumes so as to stage the new world-historical scene in this venerable disguise and borrowed language. (1974 [1852]:146)

Without entering here into a discussion of Marx's text, we nevertheless wish to suggest some implications for the present project. Most clearly, these studies suggest that the "tradition of the dead generations" never figures in such struggles merely as a dead weight but is actively reworked in each new context. Such struggles, however, need not appear revolutionary or epoch-making in order to result in significant shifts in dominant historical images. Important actors in the process may not even be conscious of themselves as participants in a struggle or of their role in producing politicized cultural images. But most crucially, it seems to us, the cases presented here make the very notion of culture historically problematic; we need to know more about particular traditions, particular dead generations, particular nightmares, and particular living minds. Individual visions and class interests become cultural images when they are appropriated as the traditions of imagined communities activated in political struggle. White ethnicities reemerge in reaction to the late-twentieth-century struggles of oppressed minorities in the United States. Colonial Sudanese ethnic identities crystallize around contested niches in an expanding capitalist labor market. We need to know more about such processes, their contexts, and their agents.

To answer such questions, even to ask them, requires that we move beyond the simplistic invocation of oppositional models. When we encounter such models in the work of social scientists, we need to examine their unstated assumptions and their own history within a set of modernist preoccupations. When we encounter them in the cultural and political models of social actors, we need to pay more attention to the processes of their construction within ongoing processes of contention and struggle, the uneasy relationship between the simple constructions and more complex experiences, and the tensions and contradictions they simultaneously express and conceal.

The essays in this book offer provisional steps toward such a critical anthropological and historical project. They remind us that metaphorical oppositions give us *imagined* pasts. We are not arguing that such images of difference are merely fictions or that we uniquely possess the keys to finding out "what really happened" in the past. Many of the essays in this book demonstrate an active concern for "real history" (cf. Marx and Engels 1970 [1846]; Thompson 1978*b*:37–50), but we make no appeal to a privileged epistemology that finally reveals the Truth—either about the past or about cultural diversity. Rather, we are motivated by a firm sense that we (including "they") are bound up together in a unified set of social, political, and cultural processes and struggles that have produced the present and over which we, in concert, must take control if we are to shape a future free of domination. This aspiration, rather than epistemological privilege, is our starting point in the reconstructive endeavor to which this book is devoted.[2]

## NOTES

1. For further comments and criticisms on this book, as well as a remarkable response by Taussig, see da Matta (1986); Gregory (1986); McEachern and Mayer (1986); Post (1986); Trouillot (1986); Turner (1986); and Taussig (1987). See as well Roseberry (1989:218–222).

2. As this book was going to press, we encountered two other sources that contribute to this reconstructive endeavor. First is Edwin Wilmsen's (1989) magisterial reanalysis of "foraging" societies of the Kalahari, placing their formation within an unfolding regional political economy in southern Africa, showing that "foragers" came to occupy an ethnic niche within a segmented labor market. Wilmsen's work is situated within a critique of the same oppositional constructions with which we are concerned in this volume, and extends the critique to an alternative historical reconstruction of one of the classic objects of anthropological knowledge. A special issue of *Anthropological Quarterly* edited by James Brow offers a series of important papers that elaborate quite nicely on the political construction of images of community (*see* Brow 1990*a*, 1990*b*; Swedenburg 1990; Crain 1990; Church 1990).

# ONE

# Potatoes, Sacks, and Enclosures in Early Modern England

*William Roseberry*

Despite its title, this essay deals not with potatoes but with peasants. It draws its initial inspiration from Marx's famous commentary on the French peasantry of the mid-nineteenth century:

> The small peasant proprietors form an immense mass, the members of which live in the same situation but do not enter into manifold relationships with each other. Their mode of operation isolates them instead of bringing them into mutual intercourse. . . . Their place of operation, the smallholding, permits no division of labour in its cultivation, no application of science and therefore no diversity of development, variety of talent, or wealth of social relationships. Each individual peasant family is almost self-sufficient; it directly produces the greater part of its means of life more through exchange with nature than through intercourse with society. The smallholding, the peasant, and the family; next door, another smallholding, another peasant, another family. A bunch of these make up a village, and a bunch of villages makes up a department. Thus the great mass of the French nation is formed by the simple addition of isomorphous magnitudes, much as potatoes in a sack form a sack of potatoes. (Marx 1974 [1852]:238–239)

One of the first tests one might apply in evaluating the degree of orthodoxy in a Marxist is whether or not this passage has been memorized. Does he or she apply this "model" universally, or does the author see that Marx was talking about a specific peasantry at a specific historical conjuncture? It is clear from a reading of *The Eighteenth Brumaire of Louis Bonaparte* and *Class Struggles in France* that Marx situates the smallholding peasantry in terms of their emergence in the aftermath of the French Revolution. He examines their politics in terms of their relationships with merchant capital and the taxing power of the state, as well as the symbolic position of Paris in both relationships.

Even if we adopt a more historically specific and sensitive interpretation, however, the passage remains problematic. It is interesting to note how many of the terms basic to most social scientific—including non-Marxist—definitions of peasantries can be found in the passage:
 —"small peasant proprietors";
 —"Their place of operation, the smallholding";
 —"individual peasant family is almost self-sufficient";
 —"the smallholding, the peasant, the family."

These terms serve to remind us that Marxist and non-Marxist scholars, despite numerous and important theoretical and political differences, share certain assumptions about peasantries: such producers are seen to participate in a household economy that is virtually self-sufficient and certainly precapitalist.

While many peasantries fit within such a definition, problems arise when the assumptions are applied transhistorically. Although Marx was careful to show that the peasants he saw in France were a historical product, and a fairly recent one at that, other scholars have attempted to place family economy in a primordial past. One might recall, for example, A. V. Chayanov's explicit reference to his analysis of the peasant household as a model of "our economic past" (1966 [1925]:2). He, in turn, explicitly associates himself with the German Historical School, which calls to mind his contemporary, Karl Bucher. In his *Industrial Evolution*, after an analysis of the presumed noneconomic life of primitive peoples, he proposed a three-step historical model from independent domestic economy to town economy to national economy (Bucher 1967 [1900]; cf. Kocke 1979). A more recent literature, firmly rooted in German historicism, takes the self-sufficient household as historical starting point as well. It is not often remembered that Polanyi posited "householding" as a third economic principle in addition to reciprocity and redistribution (1944:53). In his model of a domestic mode of production, Marshall Sahlins (1972) takes the isolated household as primordial, drawing explicitly on Bucher as he does so. More recently, Hans Medick has posited the persistence of a "family economy" among peasants and artisans in early modern Europe, drawing explicit inspiration from Chayanov's analysis of peasants (Medick 1981).

Whatever one thinks about the presumed primordial character of family economy, this remarkable similarity in the historical vision of much of Marxist and non-Marxist thinking regarding peasants is worthy of note. The precapitalist, nearly self-sufficient household is taken as a historical starting point. Among the assumptions that go along with this historical vision, we might list the following:

1. Household production may be seen as a form inherited from the past, "maintained" or "reproduced" under capitalist conditions;
2. Although households are not seen as part of a natural economy, the

unity of enterprise and home may be seen to lead to an orientation
toward reproduction rather than accumulation;

3. Family economy may be seen as a bulwark of antibourgeois values;
4. Family economy may be seen as not subject to, or as resistant to, the
   laws of commodity economy or capitalist development.

This essay subjects the family-economy model to a historical critique by
examining rural transformations in early modern England.[1] It will be argued
that "England" saw a movement from a more community-based form of
production characteristic of late feudalism to a more household-based form
of production in the early modern period. However much this may look like a
classic (and in many circles discarded) argument, its crucial difference deserves emphasis. It is inadequate to state the problem either as a movement
from community-based to household-based forms or vice versa. What matters are changing *relations* of community and household within particular historical epochs and modes of production. There is a long-standing dispute in
European studies regarding whether primordial agrarian forms were based
on communities or households—that is, whether production was communal
or "in severalty." Both sides tend to miss the point. Both view "individual"
and "community" through a nineteenth-century—that is, bourgeois—lens,
defining them as essences rather than relations.

One recent well-known example is Alan Macfarlane's *The Origins of English Individualism* (1978), which argues for the antiquity of individualism in
England by means of an examination of property holding and land transfers
within and between households. Unfortunately, the book does not mention
agricultural field systems or the debate about the relative antiquity of the
open-field system, which is crucial for the resolution of such an argument.
But Macfarlane's basic problem is that he pursues his argument as if household and community and individual were unproblematic categories, as if
they were not themselves embedded in, and products of, a history. To say
that individual decisions were mediated by a community does not necessarily
mean that individuals and households did not pursue particular (and
perhaps particularistic) strategies. And to say that individual households
were basic production units and were able to pursue certain strategies is not
to place them in league with Iowa farmers. The *meanings* of individual and
community differ according to—and even within—modes of production, and
these distinct definitions cannot be understood without reference to the forms
of struggle that occur within particular modes.[2]

## THE FEUDAL BACKGROUND

In accounts of peasant agriculture during the feudal era, it is common to
stress that the basic unit of production was the household. Certainly all the
evidence of manorial charters and rent rolls indicates household organiza-

tion, and the fundamental household organization of production will not be challenged here. I argue, however, that scholars have moved too quickly from a formulaic reference to the household as unit of production to a series of latter-day and inappropriate assumptions about the nature of the households, their relationships with other households, their place within social and political networks and so on. Orvar Lofgren (1984) has suggested that historians have been too dependent on the nature of their data (i.e., its organization by households) and have overemphasized the importance of the household. He is most interested in productive relations that do not show up so easily in sources of evidence and therefore constitute a "hidden economy"— hidden perhaps from the subjects themselves, hidden certainly from historians who try to reconstruct those subjects' lives. In what follows, then, I accept the household as basic unit of production but explore the implications of one aspect of the "hidden economy."

My argument concerns the old open-field regions of England—the swath that cuts from the northeast through the Midlands to a broad southern base—which constituted the agricultural heart of feudal polities. I am concerned here with the development and fate of the classic three-field rotation system and strip cultivation, along with many variations on this theme. Household plots were not compact but were scattered in strips throughout the three fields. The use of the three fields in each year and season, and the timing of, for example, the harvest, tearing down of hedges, letting beasts on the stubble, and so on, depended on decisions made by the village rather than households. While the household served as the basic unit of production, then, basic production decisions were mediated by a community. Such communities should not be romanticized: they were communities of unequals. Village agriculture was characterized by differentiation throughout the feudal period—between free tenants and villeins, husbands (tenants with full holdings) and cotters, and so on. Decisions made in the name of the community could be taken by privileged individuals who served as community and manorial officers. It is to be expected that they looked out for private interests to the extent that this was possible. Nevertheless, open-field agriculture and strip cultivation imposed strong limits upon private initiative despite differentiation. Accumulation possibilities were restricted in such a system, in part because of the physical requirements of classic strip cultivation and the collaborative practices that these imposed, and in part because of the community ideology that at once allowed individuals to pursue private aims in the name of the community and restricted their ability to fully realize such aims. Although one could point to the household as a basic unit of production, then, a concept of a domestic mode of production or a family economy would be most inappropriate here. While production was not communal, the community constituted an important relation of production.[3]

During the 1960s and 1970s, historians debated the relative antiquity of the open-field system. It was traditionally thought that the system was ancient and, given its geography, a characteristic of the "primitive" Germanic community. A more recent revisionist thought stresses that documentary evidence for the system in its fully developed form comes only in the twelfth and thirteenth centuries and on into the early modern period. Joan Thirsk, the person who introduced the argument to England, posits an original individualized production, with partible inheritance, with the gradual emergence of the various aspects of common-field practice as population pressure increased. As the classic open-field system emerged, there would be a concomitant move toward impartible inheritance (Thirsk 1964, 1966; Titow 1965; Hoffman 1975; Dodgshon 1975). It is not necessary to get into the details of this debate, which was marred by an unfortunate argument over a primordial communal or individualized form of production. If we avoid the ideological debate and concentrate on an early situation in which households lived and farmed and grazed their animals in communities but in which the more formal, rigidified aspects of a three-field rotation were a relatively late development, we come to some interesting conclusions.

The evidence for a three-field rotation comes in community charters, in which a variety of rights and duties vis-à-vis manors is spelled out: what is owed to the lord by individual tenants, what lands are held by the lord and what lands by the tenants, access to commons, how basic decisions are to be taken, and so on. These charters were the product of the twelfth and thirteenth centuries and could be seen by both the manor and the members of the community as advantageous. Indeed, even the mark communities, taken by Maurer and, following him, Engels and Marx as evidence of primordial community, were the products of this era.

Charters take rather different shapes in "England" and "France." In Hilton's comparison (1973), the differences relate to a community enfranchisement movement and the demise of serfdom in France but to the reimposition of labor dues and the strengthening of serfdom in England. In Brenner's interpretation (1976, 1982), this difference was due to the greater class organizational strength of the peasantry in France than in England, which in turn was related to a weak French state as opposed to a strong central state in England.

Brenner is correct to view the differences, and the social forms themselves, in terms of struggle, but he is wrong to express this as a class struggle or to envision a class organizational strength for the French peasantry. The nature of the struggle was that it, or rather *they*, were localized between individual manors and individual communities. They centered on the definitions of custom, and charters spelled out custom. The spelling out of custom, with constant reference to practices dating from time immemorial, necessarily involved acts of invention. Custom was a subject for dispute, and the custom that finally appeared in a charter reflected the relative strength of contending parties. "Ancient" duties were imposed if the manor was strong enough to make them stick; "ancient" rights were granted if the community was strong enough to press such claims. Differences in the types of charters that might emerge could be due to regional variation; in some cases "French" and "English" differences might be seen. But much of the variation must also be explained in terms of local relationships and events. For example, was the village subject to a single manor or several? Did the manor exercise control over neighboring villages as well? And so on. Different customs reflect the variable weight of relations between manors and villages. This is one reason why generalization about basic social relations in feudal Europe is so difficult. Such relationships were spelled out in local charters, and there were almost as many sorts of customs and dues as there were manors and communities.

While it is important to stress struggle, then, it is improper to assess that struggle in the terms of the nineteenth and twentieth centuries. One must turn from class to community and see the feudal peasant community as a *form and product of struggle.* By struggle we do not refer simply to the more obvious instances of rebellion, such as the well-known risings in fourteenth-century Flanders, Catalonia, France (the Jacquerie and the Tuchin movements), and England (see Hilton 1973). These actions were certainly important, but we would consider feudal society to be remarkably stable and free of contention if we limited our scope to these more visible and violent expressions. We need also to consider movements such as crusades and heresies (ibid.), as well as a variety of "silent struggles" (Bloch 1966:167–180): ecclesiastical organizations that could serve as "fronts" for communal action, and more secular forms such as contention over village governance, enfranchisement, and custumals.

Although these struggles cannot be understood outside the relationship between classes, objectively defined in terms of their position within a mode of production, contentious relations were resolved, or not resolved, through communities. Communities were not class organizations; indeed, class organization was impossible under feudalism. The village community could be seen as the form through which the peasantry, or, more properly, a segment of the peasantry, expressed its interests. It could also be the form through which the lord guarded his interests and administered the manor. The well-known slogan runs: "The manor could be strong only where the village community was strong" (Homans 1953:40). The community, then, was a product of class relations, but it was not a class organization.

This is one reason why the literature on the antiquity of the open-field system is so important. If we reject the view of strip cultivation as a primordial characteristic of Germanic communities, we can begin to see a developing relationship between the household form of production and the mediating community as a relation of production. This in turn should draw our attention back to those wealthy households who controlled community decisions but saw their accumulation possibilities limited by open-field agriculture. If the community limited their maneuver in relation to their fellows, it was a form of struggle that allowed them to protect their interests in relation to the manor. Individualized contention and struggle would have been as unthinkable in the twelfth and thirteenth centuries as class struggle.

We might now briefly consider the changes that occurred in the context of the fourteenth- and fifteenth-century crisis of feudalism. This period of high mortality produced a crisis for tenants that necessarily became a crisis of incomes for manors. Many writers, overlooking the death and desolation, stress the structural strength of the peasantry vis-à-vis the lords during this period. The fifteenth century is seen as the golden age of the English peasantry. Indeed it was, for those who survived. The period was characterized by extraordinary spatial and social mobility as peasants abandoned manors and went elsewhere to seek better deals (or to escape disease). Younger sons could gain tenancies as entire families failed and tenancies were vacated. Tenants could occupy multiple tenancies. On some manors, there was a complete turnover of peasant families (for good local studies see Hilton 1954; Howell 1983; Dyer 1980). The nature of tenure changed. Serfdom was dropped for individuals in order to attract or keep tenants. Tenancies, even for the privileged, were often changed from copyhold by custom of the manor to copyhold by the will of the lord. "Custom," which had been fought for in earlier centuries, was rejected. During this period of flux, it no longer necessarily served peasant interests. It was always double-edged. If custom offered protection, it also assured domination. During a period of mobility when protection was not needed, domination was rejected.

The crisis period represented, then, a period of dramatic structural change. The change was indicated, first and most obviously, in the persons who were occupying tenures. It also changed the nature of the relationship between classes. Serfdom disappeared, and peasant households were able to press for more advantageous leases and lower rents. Lords withdrew from direct management and depended upon rents drawn from tenants. Among the peasantry, the devastation that accompanied and made possible the structural changes had differential effects. The crisis period precipitated the emergence of a relatively privileged group of peasants freed from feudal obligations and occupying several tenures (see Hilton 1954 for a description of this process in Leicestershire; Dyer 1980 for the Bishopric of Worcester). When these tenants are considered in connection with tenants of the old demesne lands, who often had no background in the peasantry and who rented land in a single block if possible, we see the creation of a group of people separate from the peasantry but resident in the village. During the period of economic contraction there could be little outlet for their endeavors, but they constituted a new group in a position to take advantage of any changes that might occur in the market.

Another structural fact stands out about this whole period of mobility and enfranchisement in England. Individual freedom was won by households rather than communities, in contrast with the earlier enfranchisement movement on the Continent. The community, though still a product of struggle, was less and less a form of struggle. The terms of contention had shifted downward in the social structure to the household and/or individual. Even so, the community still mattered, not only as a product of struggle but as an organizational form in agricultural production. It still set limits on individual maneuver and accumulation and still offered guarantees to cotters and others. Wealthy peasants who had found in the community a set of limits and a form of protection now saw in the community only a set of limits. Thus the period of crisis and mobility was also characterized by stirrings within village communities, as individuals exchanged and consolidated strips and removed plots from village rotation schemes and their concomitant community obligations. We enter here upon the history of enclosures.

## EARLY MODERN ENCLOSURES

The enclosures are still in contention. Aside from the struggles and contemporary commentary that occurred during enclosures, one continues to encounter sharp divisions among recent historians. Consider, for example, the difference in perspective between an E. P. Thompson ("Enclosure was a plain enough case of class robbery, played according to fair rules of property and law laid down by a Parliament of property-owners and lawyers" [Thompson 1963:218]) and an Eric Kerridge ("To assert that capitalism throve on unjust expropriations is a monstrous and malicious slander. Security of property and tenure answered capitalism's first and most heartfelt need. Where insecurity reigned, it was because of the absence, not of the advent or presence of capitalism" [Kerridge 1969:93]). There are essentially two rather extreme views, with much variation on both ends. The first, taking its inspiration in part from Marx's description of primitive accumulation, stresses enclosure as expropriation and claims that as a result of the enclosure movements English peasants were stripped of their connection with the land. The second sees enclosure as agricultural improvement and denies that it was associated with expropriation. Rather, according to this view, a smallholder class continues to exist in England, and even if there was a significant decline in their numbers in early modern England, enclosures were not at fault. Smallholders were most at risk during periods when enclosures were not widespread and for "economic" rather than "political" reasons.

In a practice that is widespread in hegemonic academic discourses, the second group of historians often presents the theoretical opposition in chronological terms. The expropriation view is seen to belong to an older, careless, and politically charged historiography, while the nonexpropriation view is placed in a more recent, modern, neutral historiography. Aside from the fact that this view ignores the social and political conditions of scholarly work in the mid to late twentieth century, it also underestimates the extent to which both views have been simultaneously present—when the enclosures were actually occurring, in the early twentieth century, and at present. Indeed, many of the latter-day nonexpropriation arguments were anticipated in 1912 by Gonner (1912).

Aside from the fact that the arguments can never be resolved because of the sharp political differences represented by the two extremes, discussion has been hindered by a lack of specification regarding the process of enclosure and the broad social, economic, and political movements of which they were a part. The nonexpropriation authors have an interest in limiting the definition as much as possible—separating periods characterized by enclosure from periods not characterized by enclosure, separating economic processes from political, and so on. To the extent that expropriation authors accept these definitions, or are persuaded to get into an argument about the impact of "enclosures" narrowly defined, their attention is drawn away from the complex of transformations that deserves critical analysis.

In this essay, I adopt a broader definition of "enclosure" as the whole complex of "improvements" associated with the elimination of common privileges and constraints and the introduction of individual privileges and constraints. This could entail the conversion from open to closed fields, the consolidation of strips into compact plots and the elimination of three-field rotation, the elimination of common privileges over pasture, waste, and so on, and the conversion of former common to individual use. Parliamentary enclosures of the late eighteenth and early nineteenth centuries did this as a package for an entire village. Earlier enclosures were more often partial or piecemeal, as particular individuals would exchange and consolidate strips and remove their lands from village rotations or as village strips would be consolidated but commons would remain, and so on. Such a definition encompasses a number of different processes and can hardly be considered narrow. Even so, this essay takes an even broader approach to the "enclosure movements," which refers to the entire complex of transformations in English agriculture during the early modern period, including those periods during which enclosures per se were not predominant. The actual enclosure and the fate of the small farmers in the succeeding decades must be considered together. One cannot simply concentrate on the legal treatment of such farmers in the text of the actual enclosure agreement.

The enclosure movements can be divided into two broadly defined periods: (1) a "long sixteenth century," roughly 1460 to 1640; and (2) a "long eighteenth century," roughly 1660 to 1830. Clearly, if our interest was the English Civil War, this not-so-clever dismantling of the seventeenth century would be inappropriate. Further, recent writers have placed greater stress on the seventeenth century as a century of enclosure. Nonetheless, it can be argued that the early-seventeenth-century enclosures can be understood as a continuation of the movements that had characterized the sixteenth century. Further, the complicated transformations of the hundred years that followed the Civil War serve as prelude to the parliamentary enclosures of 1760 to 1830.

The long sixteenth century witnessed many kinds of enclosure, locally pursued, which have often been lumped together under the inadequate label, "enclosure by agreement." The last seventy years of the long eighteenth century witnessed the more centralized and uniform process of parliamentary enclosure. Because of this period's closeness to our own, and because parliamentary enclosures left documents (enclosure acts, enclosure awards, and the like) for latter-day historians, this is the period that has always captured the popular imagination.

Historians generally agree, however, that the earlier periods were crucial: at least half, and perhaps a good deal more than half, of the countryside, including the Midlands, had been enclosed by the end of the seventeenth century (Kerridge 1968:24; McCloskey 1975:124, 125; Hoskins 1951:16, 17; Wordie 1983). In what follows, despite the present lack of reference to actual localities, the analysis concerns the transformations that occurred in the old open-field areas—the triangle that is narrow in the northeast, broad in the south, and encompasses the Midlands.

### The Long Sixteenth Century

By the end of the fifteenth century, a number of circumstances and movements contributed to a recovery from the crisis of the fourteenth and fifteenth centuries. The victory and accession of Henry VII in 1485 marked the beginning of the restoration of internal order after more than a century of war and internal strife—although plots and rebellions were to plague the Tudors. In addition there was a quickening of economic life throughout Western Europe that was associated with the restoration of old trade links and the creation of new ones as a "world-economy" was established (Wallerstein 1974; Braudel 1984; Kriedte 1983). Population grew, increasing demand for land and grain. At the same time, the recovery of the textile trade increased demand for wool. A long cycle of economic expansion had begun.

During this period, the first enclosure movement became a public problem. The problem became apparent in a number of ways. It was raised by prominent individuals complaining of engrossment, conversion from arable to pasture, depopulation, and the disappearance of villages. In addition, England witnessed a series of local rebellions that arose from situations of rural discontent provoked by enclosure even if they were not directed solely at enclosure. The Crown also saw enclosure as a problem and promoted several measures opposing the conversion of arable to pasture, the tearing down of cottages, the building of hedges, or the depopulation of villages. The Statutes themselves were not randomly distributed. Some were responses to disturbances; others were passed during periods of dearth, when conversion of arable to pasture was seen as a major problem (Thirsk 1967:229). Acts were insufficient, however, and were difficult to enforce. Despite official opposition, enclosures continued. The Crown therefore appointed occasional commissions of inquiry to report on the progress of enclosure. Later legislation also encouraged and rewarded informers. Nonetheless, by the end of the sixteenth century, official opinion was beginning to shift. The early Stuarts appointed commissions and brought charges against enclosers, but they were no longer required, as the early statutes had mandated, to restore arable or tear down hedges. Violators were now required to pay a fine, and by the 1630s the commissions under Charles I appeared to be little more than "odious financial engines" (Tawney 1912:391).

Who promoted such radical changes in the countryside even as official policy forbade it? Two broadly defined groups deserve attention: landlords and their tenants. Landowners on the whole experienced the sixteenth century as a time of crisis. Rents were fixed in a period of inflation; fines and fees were low; yet landlords were expected to maintain a noble life-style in the face of declining income. Their holdings were "all honour and no profit" (Tawney 1941:9). Yet landlords were not an undifferentiated group. It is now common to distinguish between "court" and "country" lords, the former content to depend on rural incomes and a variety of urban and court activities and perquisites, the latter actively improving their properties, becoming major sheepmasters, innovating in mining and manufacture, modifying leases, and benefiting from the profits of enclosure.[4]

The sixteenth century also witnessed the rise of the gentry (Tawney 1941), relatively new and more modest landowning and renting families, neither peasant nor noble. They were squires and knights, men of local influence who might have come from families that held lesser titles for generations or from families that might, only a few generations earlier, have been yeomen or husbands. This too was a differentiated group. The gentry included many improvers—agriculturalists who leased land and accomplished enclosure, consolidated plots, and turned farms into capitalist enterprises. Indeed, reference to the sixteenth-century gentry generally calls up this image. Yet the gentry also included many who earned their wealth elsewhere—in trade, the law, or court service—and who acquired land as a source of status. For them land was a secure investment with a steady source of income to pass on to their widows and heirs. The rack-renting gentry must therefore be counterpoised with the patriarchal squire, concerned for "his" tenants (see Everitt 1967:458–462).

The class change of the sixteenth century was one that did not correspond to status distinctions derived from an earlier order. A new class of entrepreneurial landowners (and manufacturers and traders) was emerging, composed of elements of an old aristocratic order that was still in place. Although some lords took an active part in the enclosing and improving of their estates, however, the basic structural relationship that had emerged from late feudalism was one in which the landlord was a rentier, content to live on fixed and customary rents. The entrepreneurial lord had to actively upset the established balance. Tenants, among whom might be included gentry who were leasing old demesne farms or whole manors, were often the active force in agricultural improvement.

Discussion of tenants should not be limited to gentry, however. We should also consider another active group: the yeomen, descendants of peasant copyholders who held two, three or more farms and who might enter into private agreements to exchange strips and consolidate their farms. The structural position of the group was created in the fourteenth- and fifteenth-century crisis, when peasants were able to alter substantially the terms of their leases and occupy more than one tenure. If the sixteenth century produced the rise of the gentry, it also produced the rise of the yeoman, who paid low rents, accumulated resources, bought more farms (sometimes entire manors), rented others, and enclosed and improved their properties (Hoskins 1950:154–159; Tawney 1912). Although such persons had roots in a peasantry, they were not themselves peasants: they hired rural laborers, subcontracted farms, and accumulated the resources for sons or grandsons to style themselves as gentry.

Further consideration of the activity of the improvers must take into account a long-standing debate about the consequences of the enclosure movement. The basic argument can be quickly summarized. Marx saw the sixteenth-century enclosures as part of capitalism's "blood and dirt" phase, emphasizing the expropriation of cultivators from the soil (1977 [1867]: part 8). There is also a wide literature, especially from the early twentieth century and most notably from R. H. Tawney (1912), that has stressed the expropriation of the mass of peasants and the rise of a yeomanry. Eric Kerridge (1969), however, in an explicit critique of Tawney, contends that no expropriation occurred and that peasants were protected in law and courts. It is important to note that Kerridge accomplishes this by narrowing the field of debate. He is not interested in the peasantry as a whole, including squatters on the waste, subtenants, cotters, lessees—in short, the whole mass of differentially situated rural cultivators. Because squatters and cotters had no firm legal right to village lands, their expulsion is not of great concern. Tawney, in contrast, was concerned with the various types of peasantry and their fate. He saw the loss of access on the part of those with less firm rights to land as the loss by a class to a right to livelihood.

Kerridge concentrates his attention on the copyholders and makes his reinterpretation of their fate speak to Tawney's analysis of a much more broadly defined group of producers. Kerridge points out that Tawney wrongfully lumps together copyholders by custom of the manor and copyholders at the will of the lord, with the former occupying old customary land and the latter occupying demesne land that had been let out as lords abandoned demesne cultivation. Copyholders at the will of the lord were not protected by custom and could therefore be thrown off their lands as the lord attempted to improve lands directly or by renting them out to an enterprising tenant. Tawney, by blurring this distinction, exaggerated the expropriation of copyholders. Although copyholders at the will of the lord did lose their tenancies, copyholders by custom of the manor were more favorably situated, their rights were affirmed in court, and they were not evicted. This is an important correction, one that makes possible a more subtle interpretation of the meaning of sixteenth-century enclosures, but one that is marred in Kerridge's treatment by an ideological argument.

It is important to remember, however, that the distinction between copyhold by custom and copyhold at the will of the lord may not be so clear as Kerridge suggests. During the fifteenth century, some copyholders by custom had abandoned custom during a period when they needed no protection and took their tenancies at the will of the lord. During a century when protection was again needed, tenants and lords struggled over the very definition of tenure. Recognition by courts of copyhold by custom or at will was not a simple declaration of unproblematic rights but a balancing of competing claims, with decisions resting upon the relative strength of contending parties (see Hoskins 1957:102–112 for a description of such disputes in one Leicestershire locality). The confusion of a historian like Tawney, then, may be in large part a reflection of a confused and conflictful social situation.

It is also important to recognize that the distinction between two forms of copyhold is one of a bundle of legal distinctions that Kerridge treats as firm but which were in fact all jumbled up. One of the *consequences* of enclosure was a legal revolution in property and rights. What had been a complex of rights and obligations became disentangled. Some of the former rights gained legal recognition; many did not. Those rural cultivators who were able to get their rights recognized (e.g., free tenants and copyholders by custom) benefited; others did not. Kerridge is taking the *results* of the movement and using them as *tools* to analyze the movement itself, contravening the most basic procedures of historical reconstruction.

Nonetheless, one should not lay too much stress on the expropriation of tenants in this period. It is true that in the fifteenth and early sixteenth centuries, as lands were turned to sheep walks, villages and cottages were torn down and some tenants were wrongfully evicted. As we move into the sixteenth century, however, the weight of public opinion and state protection is against such enclosers. In addition, the incentive to turn to pasture began to fade by the middle of the sixteenth century. Although sheep provided meat as well as wool, enclosure was just as likely to be associated with agricultural improvement, with convertible husbandry, and it no longer produced the dramatic phenomenon of deserted villages. How, then, to account for the reported displacement of people in the countryside?

We should remember that copyholders and freeholders were relatively privileged tenants. Copyholders with firm rights to their tenures were the descendants of the newcomers of the fourteenth and fifteenth centuries, holding medium-sized farms and, in some cases, several farms. On the estates of the Bishopric of Worcester, the number of tenants tended to remain stable in the late fifteenth and early sixteenth centuries, and the size of tenures tended to increase. Indeed, of four people in Warwickshire investigated by the enclosure commissioners in 1517 for depopulation, two were customary tenants. Yet this was a period in which population was beginning to increase. If the numbers of the tenant population were relatively stable, the general population increase can be accounted for by the increase of nontenants—cottagers, laborers, and the like (Dyer 1980:242, 243, 312–315).

If we look to the established tenants for a process of expropriation that gave rise to a proletariat, then, our attention will be misplaced. A form of expropriation did take place, but middle-level and wealthy peasants were protected and in many cases thrived. Indeed, although the land market was extraordinarily strong in the late sixteenth and early seventeenth centuries, there probably was not a great demand for peasant property. Rising gentry and yeomen, as well as those large landlords who were doing well, were more interested in acquiring whole manors or demesne lands. And much land of this sort was for sale, not only from landlords in financial straits but more importantly from the Crown and confiscated monastic lands (Habakkuk 1965:656, 657).

Whence, then, the displaced population? One source was the group of tenants who did not enjoy secure tenure, especially those who held at will on the old demesne lands as the lord attempted to reverse the parcelization of the demesne and lease it out as a whole (or sell it, or take direct control over it). Likewise, subtenants of customary tenants were in a precarious position, especially if the tenant decided to consolidate his farms and improve them. Cottagers on the waste, who cultivated no land but took advantage of the common, likewise enjoyed no rights as property rights were rigidified during the enclosure movement. Yet another section would be composed of those who retained rights to land and cultivated it but who, with the progress of partial enclosure, found their rights to common diminished and had to seek additional sources of livelihood. If we were following Eric Kerridge, none of these people would merit our attention. They had no rights and therefore lost no rights. Yet in a real sense they were expropriated. In the open-field village, they could expect to gain a livelihood, whether or not their right to a livelihood was legally recognized. As lords cleared the demesne or wastes by right of unity of possession, or as tenants took control over holdings that had been sublet, or as tenants who enjoyed legal rights agreed to extinguish common rights, all of the less-privileged groups who had expected a livelihood under the old system were displaced.

What happened to them? Those who retained some rights to land might stay in the village, work their land, take up cottage by-employments, and resort to occasional or seasonal wage labor. Others left, to be classified and arrested as vagrants (Tawney 1912:268–275; Beier 1974), to settle in expanding urban centers, or, commonly, to settle elsewhere in the countryside. One possibility was to move from enclosed to open villages. More important was a move away from densely settled open-field regions into forest areas, within the West Midlands themselves and elsewhere. There they would settle as squatters in regions with relatively few husbands. They would build cottages, farm a little land if they could secure it, raise cattle and sheep on the wastes, work seasonally for wages, and engage in cottage manufacturing. It has been estimated that one-quarter of England's cottage population and one-half of the cottage population in the Midlands were engaged in woolen manufacture in this period: spinning wool, knitting stockings. Forest by-employments were more diversified: woodwork, ironwork, pottery, and the like (Everitt 1967; 1966: 56–73; Thirsk 1961).

During the sixteenth century, the numbers of such laborers increased, and laborers' social conditions worsened. While wages increased threefold from 1500 to 1640, prices increased sixfold, resulting in a 50 percent decrease in real wages (Everitt 1967:435). The situation was advantageous to landlords and secure tenants, grossly disadvantageous to those who depended on wages. By the end of the seventeenth century, Gregory King estimated that 23 percent of England's population could be classified as "labouring people and our servants" and 24 percent as "cottagers and paupers" (Coleman 1955–56). King's figures were educated guesses and their reliability is subject to continuing debate. Nonetheless, as M. D. George noted and Coleman seconded, "perhaps the most startling thing . . . is that to his contemporaries there was nothing surprising in his figures" (cited in ibid.:283).

Both for the tenant secure on a holding in an enclosed village and for the rural laborer, the locus of activity and the effective locus of decision making was increasingly the household. This was true even in open-field villages, which maintained a community shell but in which a good bit of strip consolidation and improvement was accomplished. The shift in focus began in the crisis period of feudalism, as the lord was removed from direct management and as tenant populations and conditions of tenure were substantially altered. It accelerated in the sixteenth century with economic expansion. Except in those areas that were converted to sheep walks by lords, the quickening pace of activity did not necessarily place tenants in danger. In fact, a significant portion of the tenantry enjoyed greater security of tenure than they had under feudalism as copyhold became virtually identical with freehold. The security of tenure, however, was won not by communities but by individuals. The focus on householding reached its extreme in those villages that were fully enclosed, but significant strides could be made even within the open-field system.[5]

The great paradox of the enclosure movements in the long sixteenth century was that it displaced one group of peasants and confirmed another group with more secure rights to land. For both, the household had become "an island unto itself" (Thirsk 1967:255). It should be remembered that this movement was simultaneous with market expansion and with the increasing investment of merchant capital in rural domestic manufacture. The household economy of early modern England was not removed from the market, and it did not represent an antimarket principle. Rather, it was intimately involved with market expansion and in some respects a product of it.

It is in this light that we can turn once again to the fate of the middle-level peasant in the sixteenth century. If we concentrate less on the expropriation of peasants by landlords and more on the fate of yardlanders and halfyardlanders in villages that were experiencing profound transformations in the midst of commercial expansion, a more complex picture will emerge. Margaret Spufford has compared the experience of middle-level peasants in three villages in early modern Cambridge. The processes differed in each village, but middle-level farmers were generally threatened. Of special interest was the village of Chippenham, on the chalklands, where yardlanders and half-yardlanders suffered especially severe losses in the late sixteenth and seventeenth centuries. There it appeared that the middle-level peasants were especially vulnerable to the expansive activities of yeomen, to whom they were indebted (Spufford 1974:65–68).

"Family economy" was therefore emerging in an expanding commercial economy and could experience markedly different fates—depending on ecological variation, the presence or absence of a powerful lord, the extent of freeholding, the degree of insertion in the market, and so on. For both the peasant and the laborer, involvement with the market presented opportunities for enrichment and impoverishment. The household economy, acting in a differentiated commercial environment that had produced it in the first place, could potentially undermine itself. A more complete analysis of that potential requires a discussion of later movements and trends.

## The Long Eighteenth Century

In considering the long eighteenth century, we will examine two periods: (1) from 1660 to 1760, or from the Restoration to the Parliamentary Enclosure Acts; and (2) from 1760 to 1830. After a brief summary of significant trends during the two periods, we will consider the overall impact of the eighteenth century on the English peasantry.

It has been suggested that in contrast with the late sixteenth and early seventeenth centuries, which may have witnessed a "rise of the gentry," the late seventeenth and early eighteenth centuries witnessed a "rise of the aristocracy" (Habakkuk 1940). A number of factors contributed to the accumulation of land in larger estates. Although the period experienced commercial and colonial expansion, the agricultural sector was relatively stagnant. The high grain prices of the long sixteenth century had come to an end; the late seventeenth and early eighteenth centuries experienced not only a general decrease in prices but a series of severe fluctuations. Furthermore, landowners were subject to heavy taxation, 20 percent of rentals, now more efficiently assessed and collected. Finally, in the especially severe years from 1690 to 1720, rents remained stable. For the smaller or middle-level gentry, especially if their properties were heavily mortgaged, their positions were precarious; some were forced to sell. Purchasers included larger landlords, who were in a better position to survive the lean years, and merchants who were attempting to establish an estate (ibid.; Habakkuk 1965).

Landlords experiencing a period of retrenchment faced limited but important options. Those with entailed estates could not sell a portion of the estate without entering into a formal agreement with the heir and other beneficiaries. They could, however, improve their estates in a variety of ways. They could, for example, restructure their leases, converting from leases for lives to leases for years, increasing entry fines, and the like. Most of the protective obstacles to such restructuring had been swept away as a result of the Civil War. In addition, they could consolidate tenancies and let out larger farms. Such a movement did not necessarily depend upon the improving spirit of the landlord. The aristocratic ideal still required supreme indifference to money. Yet the increased costs of maintaining that ideal forced many an improvident landlord into debt. Because the estate was to be protected for the heir, and because entail limited the options open to the lord, it was not uncommon for lords to turn their estates over to trustees who would do the managing and improving for them (Mingay 1963:48, 49, 67–70, 125–130).

If the period was not a good one for middle-level gentry and small tenants, it was also not a good one for more modest freeholders, from husbands to yeomen. They were subject to the same decline in prices and heavy taxation, and their children may have been attracted by increasing opportunities in towns and cities. Those peasants who, in the face of these difficulties, decided to sell their holdings had little difficulty in finding buyers. Unlike the situation that prevailed a century before, large landowners were now interested in accumulating peasant property. Local landlords in pursuit of improvement bought out neighboring freeholders in order to create consolidated blocks that could be leased out. In addition, while the landholding strategy of previous centuries was to accumulate land in a variety of settings, the new strategy was to build up a compact estate, allowing for more efficient management— not to mention space for a park surrounding the hall so that the lord's view would not be obstructed by cottages or their inhabitants (Habakkuk 1965; Johnson 1909).

It is difficult to estimate the statistical impact of this movement, in part because most estimates depend on Gregory King's disputed figures from the close of the seventeenth century as a starting point (F. M. L. Thompson 1966; Cooper 1967; Beckett 1977). It may be sufficient to state that the one hundred years after the Restoration were years in which peasants, both tenants and owner-occupiers, were threatened and displaced. In some cases, displacement accompanied enclosure, as enclosure by private agreement continued apace except during the war years from 1690 to 1715. It was a movement that affected relatively wealthy and relatively poor peasants alike, for the commercial expansion that had made small-scale accumulation possible had been checked.

By about 1750, conditions had changed. Prices increased for grain and livestock in response to demographic growth and diversification. Increased manufacture in towns and cities, as well as in villages throughout the agricultural zones (e.g., woolens in the West Riding, hosiery in the East Midlands), expanded the population of cottagers who might have seasonal connections with agriculture as well as villagers who had no connection at all. Growth and diversification increased demand for food as well as industrial crops, and all farmers, small and large, were in a position to respond to the more favorable circumstances. Small farmers close to urban areas were favorably situated to provide fresh meat, milk, and vegetables to growing markets. In general, however, the large landlord was in a better position to respond to the new developments, and there was a tendency for large owners to accumulate yet more land and for large tenants to replace small (see Chambers and Mingay 1966; Mingay 1963:90–92 et passim; Thirsk 1957: 197–198: Tate 1967:80–87).

During this period, a new form of enclosure, by private act of Parliament, became more popular. Over four thousand enclosure acts were passed between 1750 and 1850, affecting over six million acres, and they were bunched in two periods: the 1760s and 1770s, and between 1793 and 1815. The first period produced close to nine hundred acts; the second approximately two-thousand. As in earlier centuries, the movement was most profoundly felt in the Midlands (Chambers and Mingay 1966:77,78; cf. Blum 1981).

The procedure for enclosure by act was as follows (Tate 1967: chaps. 9, 10). A group of landowners (generally including the landlord and not limited to persons resident in the village) in a parish presented a petition to the House of Commons complaining of the deleterious effects of intermixture of strips and requesting permission to bring a bill authorizing enclosure. After permission was granted and a bill drawn up and read, it was submitted to a committee, generally composed of House members from the county involved or neighboring counties. Few then or since have been willing to suggest that committee members were disinterested. The committee was to consider the merits of enclosure as well as any opposition and report back to the House with its recommendation. Part of the report was an assessment of the degree of support or opposition, but support was not weighed in terms of the numbers of villagers for or against enclosure but in terms of the relative weight of property held in the village. Thus a certain number of acres would be judged in favor, a certain number against, or a certain assessed value in favor, a certain value against. It was entirely possible for most of the population of the village to be opposed to enclosure while the overwhelming majority of the acres represented supported enclosure, just as it was possible for most of the support to come from nonresident landowners. Upon being passed by the House of Commons, the bill would then be sent to the Lords for amendment and approval, after which royal assent was required.

Upon completion of this process, an enclosure commission, to be compensated by the landowners and beneficiaries of enclosure, would be appointed to accomplish the distribution. Commissioners could serve on a number of enclosures simultaneously and were appointed to represent certain interests (e.g., the landlord's, the tithe owner's). They were responsible for determining the extent and nature of rights held by landowners in the parish, surveying the land, and accomplishing a redistribution that would extinguish common rights and compensate with property all those who were giving up common rights. Upon enclosure, all owners were expected to hedge their property within a short time.

What effect did this movement have on small farmers and rural laborers? In a classic but disputed account that overemphasizes the extent of open fields in the eighteenth century and thus overemphasizes the importance of the enclosure acts, the Hammonds (1970:73) contend that "enclosure was fatal to three classes: the small farmer, the cottager, and the squatter." Despite the flaws in their analysis, the Hammonds did draw scholarly attention for the first time to the differential impact of enclosures on these three groups.

*Of the small farmer*, the Hammonds suggest that even in those cases in which farmers received fair shares (and they contend that smallholders' rights were not zealously protected), the costs of enclosure, of paying the commissioners, and of hedging their plots were prohibitive. They were forced to sell their land and migrate to English cities or America or become day laborers (ibid.:73–75). Here two key points have been contested (Gonner 1912; Chambers and Mingay 1966: chap. 4; Mingay 1968; Tate 1967). First, it is argued that however unfair the system itself may have been, however much Parliament may have been a "committee of landlords," the actual work of the commissioners was generally fair. All customary rights that could be established were recognized and compensated, and smallholders did not lose their rights in the actual enclosure. Second, it is suggested that the costs of enclosure and hedging were somewhat less than had been supposed and therefore not the burden that the Hammonds had suggested (Tate 1952–53). Thus the enclosure itself did not represent an expropriation of the small-holder and did not present an immediate threat to his existence. In fact, if the evidence from land-tax assessments is to be believed, the number of smallholders remained stable and even increased over the course of the Par-liamentary enclosure period (Davies 1927).

Faced with this evidence, we might ask when the major decline in the numbers of smallholders occurred. Certainly a major period of crisis oc-curred during the century following the Restoration, that is, *before* the Par-liamentary enclosures, as stressed in Habakkuk's classic account (1965). Mingay, in agreeing with this conclusion, also offers a useful analysis of trends in terms of economic cycles. Thus, the periods of heavy enclosure corresponded to periods of high prices, which were beneficial to the large farmer but would also allow the small farmer to more easily meet the costs of enclosure (Mingay 1968).

A number of questions may be raised about the assumption of the stability of the small farmer, however. First, much of the reasoning is based upon statistics comparing land tenure in England as a whole over wide periods of time. In the process, small farmers are defined as farmers with between twen-ty and one hundred acres, which takes us well beyond most definitions of peasants. In considering this group, Mingay examines two sorts of data: the number of small farmers across time, and the percentage of land controlled by small farmers. Unfortunately, the first statistic is not placed in the context of a rapidly expanding population, which would make the actual diminution that much more dramatic. The second statistic can obscure a great deal of differentiation and accumulation within the broadly defined "small farmer" category. In addition, Mingay makes no attempt to compare the fate of small farmers regionally. Thus the localization of relatively small farmers in the north and the virtual disappearance of smallholding in the Midlands is not treated as a problem. As we begin to turn our attention to local situations, the poverty of this macro-level approach for an understanding of the dynam-ics of small-scale agriculture in the context of enclosure becomes more readily apparent.[6]

If we set aside the rare attempts to demonstrate a vibrancy for small farmers in early modern England, we note a more common tendency in the revisionist literature. This tendency accepts the historical disappearance of the small farmer as a class but directs its attention to the timing of this disappearance. Unfortunately, as crucial as this question is for an understanding of English agrarian history, many authors come to it in an apparent attempt to demonstrate that the enclosures were not "at fault," that no expropriation, in the strict sense, took place. If it can be shown that enclosure was but one of a series of causes for the disappearance of a peasantry, and probably not the immediately precipitating factor at that, then a major stain can be thought to have been removed from the history of English capitalism. Few would be so crude as to disavow interest in "all the hazards of this fleshly world" (Kerridge 1969:65), but many historians are interested in showing that the hazards that affected the English peasantry were due to the operation of economic laws rather than the political machinations of expropriators.

To this, two points must be made. The first is that the separation of the economic and political in this way is false and that economic laws do not operate in a vacuum but in a context of class relations and contention. Thus our attention should not be directed solely to the actual distribution of land in an enclosure award but to the entire historical movement of which the redistribution was a part. The pressures placed upon small farmers in the century following the Restoration, the redistribution of land with enclosure, and the fate of the small farmer in the decades following enclosure must be treated as a whole. If the small farmer receives an enclosed plot during a period of rising prices but has difficulty paying debts and maintaining the farm during subsequent periods of falling prices, it makes little sense to separate a "political" enclosure from an "economic" recession. Preenclosure agriculture, with access to commons, would have offered a series of protections to the small farmer during a recession. The "political" extinction of those protections had a definite "economic" effect.

But this point, which requires no emphasis for those influenced by Marxist assumptions, would not be accepted by those who make such a distinction in the first place. The second point requires a more thorough examination of the enclosure itself, and it therefore takes the form of a question: Did the conversion of common right to private right represent a form of expropriation—legal and with "compensation," but expropriation nonetheless? To address this question, we turn our attention to two groups more often ignored by the revisionist literature: the cottagers and squatters.

*Of the cottager,* the Hammonds tell us in a classic phrase: "[B]efore enclosure he was a labourer with land, after enclosure he was a labourer without land" (Hammond and Hammond 1970:76). Many of their rights to common were not recognized or compensated. Where they were recognized, the granting of a small plot (in which case they faced the same problems as more substantial smallholders) could not fully compensate for the grazing and other rights that had been lost. *Squatters* were in an even more precarious position than cottagers because they had encroached upon the waste and were not established residents of the village with customary rights. If they could show that their encroachments were of long standing, they would be treated as cottagers; if not, they would lose entirely (ibid.:78, 79). For both types, the greatest loss was of the commons, which the Hammonds saw as the "patrimony of the poor" (ibid.:79).

There was an important difference between those with and those without legally recognized rights of access to common. For those with legally recognized rights, compensation was made in the form of land. Kerridge writes of "generous" awards of hedged closes reserved for cottagers' use as cow pasture: his examples list awards of 1½ acres per cottage in one, 19 acres for 9 cottages in another, 65 acres for 12 cottages in another (Kerridge 1969: 108). Elsewhere cottagers could receive individual allotments, although, as Chambers and Mingay admit,

> [U]nfortunately, the allotment of land given in exchange for common rights was often too small to be of much practical use, being generally far smaller than the three acres or so required to keep a cow. It might also be inconveniently distant from the cottage, and the cost of fencing. . . might be too high to be worthwhile. Probably many cottagers sold such plots to the neighbouring farmers rather than go to the expense of fencing them, and thus peasant ownership at the lowest level declined. (Chambers and Mingay 1966:97)

At Wigston Magna in Leicestershire, fifty of the ninety-seven farms created by the enclosure held fewer than ten acres; twenty-eight held fewer than five. The fifty farms accounted for some 8.3 percent of the land alloted. These were the cottagers, some of them descendants of once-prosperous peasants (Hoskins 1957:253, 256).

Many cottagers, however, had no legally recognized rights to commons, because they were squatters on the waste, or because they were tenants in their cottages. The owners of the cottages held the common rights; the tenant might have enjoyed them in the past but had no right to compensation when they were dissolved. Indeed, tenants, not only of cottages but also of small farms, were the great losers of the enclosure awards. Legal rights rested with owners, and owners were consolidating farms. The Hammonds' complaint that cottagers were "labourers with land" who had become "labourers without land" is perfectly appropriate (Kerridge 1969:108; Chambers and Mingay 1966:96–98).

It might be thought that the loss of common rights was not a major one. Population increase had placed increasing pressure on resources; commons were stinted (that is, individuals were limited in the number of animals they could pasture on the common), and with pressure, the quality of the resources was diminishing. Certainly the commons were inefficient in terms of economic productivity. Enclosure facilitated agricultural improvement that simultaneously made it possible to grow more grain and graze more cattle or sheep. But we must not allow the improvers to provide our evaluation. Their argument was victorious politically and economically, but there was another argument that did not reduce the commons to a place to keep a pig or a few geese. This was important, but the very statement tends to underestimate the extent of the loss. We need to listen to those sensitive historians who have tried to reconstruct the economy of the peasant smallholder and the rural laborer and the place of the commons within that economy. Joan Thirsk, for example, has explored the multiple strategies used to provide a livelihood in Lincolnshire marshlands and fens before the sixteenth-to-eighteenth-century drainages, showing how a landscape that improvers regarded as waste could provide for a relatively dense population (Thirsk 1957: chaps. 1 and 5). Likewise, W. G. Hoskins provides a good description of the diversified use of various resources in the Wigston commons (Hoskins 1957:190–194, 267–269). Both authors' evocation of peasant strategies reinforces a conclusion suggested for the sixteenth century as well. The legal rights of those who enjoyed recognized rights were scrupulously guarded in the enclosure agreements; those who possessed no recognized rights were displaced but not wronged, in a *legal* sense. The smallest farmers in the first group and the second group as a whole, however, were stripped of a variety of means of livelihood. Here indeed was a "plain enough case of class robbery, played according to fair rules of property and law laid down by a Parliament of property-owners and lawyers."

## CONCLUSION

I have examined the debates regarding the impact of enclosure on small farmers and squatters because one must make some judgment regarding the relative merits of the two extreme sides if one is to make any sense at all of the period. Furthermore, our approach to the debate can illuminate a number of other issues. This paper has taken a sympathetic view of the literature that stresses the transforming and proletarianizing effects of enclosure. It must be emphasized, however, that each version of the history of rural folk captures one side of a complex process; by stressing the one side to the exclusion of the other, it presents a distorted image. The "peasant expropriation" and proletarianization side, in its extreme versions, is vulnerable on a number of grounds. First, it concentrates on a few counties to the exclusion of the rest of the country. Second, its stress on expropriation can lead to a view that seriously underestimates the existence and relative stability of a peasantry and thus ignores a fundamental aspect of the process of proletarianization itself. The "peasant stability" side of the debate, again in its extreme version, restores an important aspect of the process, but by means of hocus-pocus statistics it attempts to deny that proletarianization happened.

One reason that it is difficult to evaluate the enclosure debates is that both sides are right, as far as they go. The enclosure movement, broadly conceived, simultaneously produced a peasantry and a proletariat in early modern England. This was clear in our discussion of the long sixteenth century. The movement continued in the eighteenth century with two important differences. Except for the early depopulating enclosures, the sixteenth-century movement occurred during a period when the peasantry was in a relatively strong position. They were protected, if inefficiently, by a state that saw them as a social and fiscal pillar of the political edifice. And they had emerged from a long crisis during which they had been able to improve the conditions of their tenure into a period of agricultural growth from which the more privileged of their number were able to benefit. The eighteenth-century movement, however, occurred after a crisis in which the peasantry had not fared well and had been reduced in numbers. Although their legal rights were protected in enclosure awards, they were no longer seen as pillars of the state. Their fate was not a problem for state policy, except as they came to be identified as "the poor."

In pointing to the creation of a peasantry and proletariat, I use the term "peasant" in a limited sense. Of course there was a peasantry in feudalism. I have reference, however, to the identification of peasantry with family farming, the presumed congruence of the household as a unit of production and consumption, and the conceptualization of peasants in terms of "family economy" and "domestic mode of production." My argument is that the breakup of the common fields, the decline of the community as mediator in production decisions, and the development of bourgeois property rights in early modern England destroyed the "hidden economy" in which peasant households had been enmeshed. To revert to my initial metaphor, these movements created the context in which the peasantry could *become* a sack of potatoes. They liberated and stabilized a family economy in the English countryside. Far from representing an anticapitalist principle, however, this family economy was the very expression of bourgeois individualism as it appeared in the countryside.

In arguing this point for the sixteenth century, I suggested that the family economy was created both for peasants and for cottage laborers (and, of course, for that large group who mixed farming with by-employments, the "peasant laborers"). In the eighteenth century, however, the break was more decisive. With peasantization and proletarianization being simultaneous, a family economy was being liberated in one sector and undermined in another. Cottage industry flourished, but a whole group of laborers was developing in industrializing cities, towns, and the countryside for which the image of family economy would be inappropriate. The family economy was being stabilized under unstable conditions; the peasantry was appearing in order to disappear.

Such statements must be made with care and must take into account regional differentiation. It has been suggested, for example, that the seventeenth-century tilt toward large farms did not characterize pastoral regions, where peasant farmers thrived (Thirsk 1970). And in certain counties—for example, parts of Lincolnshire and especially the northern counties of Cumberland and Westmoreland (Thirsk 1957; Beckett 1982)— peasant farming was widespread long after its disappearance in the Midlands and southeast. In the north, the serious decline among peasants accompanied the erosion of by-employments after 1815 (Beckett 1982). Furthermore, if we take into account the political incorporation of Ireland, we might make a case for the simultaneity of proletarianization at the center and peasantization at the periphery of the British social formation. Yet concern for regional differentiation should not draw our attention from the more fundamental disappearance of the peasantry *as a class* in England.

This disappearance was noted at the time and has spawned a large literature comparing the fate of English and Continental, or more commonly English and French, peasantries. This literature, especially that produced by recent theorists from Barrington Moore (1966) to Robert Brenner (1976, 1982), has concentrated on the different class and state structures that pressed upon peasants in England and France. These differences were indeed crucial, and any comparison must pay attention to strikingly different relations with the state, with landlords, and with merchant capital in the two instances. Yet a notable feature of such comparisons is the extent to which they take the peasantry itself for granted in examining their relations with superordinate classes and institutions. Peasants are seen as a class formed in a feudal past that experienced different fates in early modern England and France.

If this attempt to view the historical creation of a family economy in the early modern period has any validity, we must integrate these intravillage and intrahousehold transformations, especially as they link with larger class and state forces, in our comparisons of European experiences. I conclude, then, with a brief indication of what such an interpretation might look like for early modern England.

Much of the destruction of the family economy in England did not come from superordinate classes but from within rural villages, as a result of differentiation and class formation during the long sixteenth century. Yeomen were able to rise because they too were enclosers and engrossers. Differentiation occurred among rural laborers as well, with a small portion able to adopt a mixed strategy of by-employments and husbandry and a majority increasingly dependent upon by-employments and wage labor. Although most analyses of larger class forces and the state concentrate on the sixteenth through eighteenth centuries, with the Civil War as turning point, an analysis of the consequences of village transformations must look to an earlier period. The readjustments of the late feudal period liberated a family economy from one set of constraints. By means of migration as well as commutation, individual households were able to improve the terms of their tenancies. Village communities continued as important institutions, primarily by means of regulation of open fields and common, but they no longer served as loci of contention and struggle with a manorial system that was significantly altered. The locus of contention was shifted downward toward the individual and household, which simultaneously made possible and problematic class forms of organization. The immediate result of that shift in the context of an expanding commercial economy was that *differentiation* within village communities, always a characteristic of the feudal village, could become *class formation* within villages. The community was increasingly a shell that was finally cast off with enclosure. The circumstances surrounding the liberation of a family economy in late feudal and early modern England also made possible the destruction of such an economy.

Close examination of the process by which particular family economies emerge within distinct fields of power can therefore illuminate certain aspects of their later development or demise. As we turn to other cases, it may be that the differential fate of peasantries will have as much to do with the circumstances surrounding the dissolution of their hidden economy as it has to do with the larger constellation of class forces. An analysis that does not take family economy for granted but subjects it to historical scrutiny will be in a better position to inform us about these differences.

## NOTES

1. I am currently engaged in a comparative historical project that examines older peasantries in Europe and Latin America and explores the changing structure of the household, of relations between household and community, and of relations between peasant households and representatives of superordinate classes and states, in the context of the creation of the modern world. This essay summarizes part of the argument for early modern England.

It should be stressed that I am not a specialist in European history or ethnography. I come to this project as a Latin Americanist attempting to apply some of the questions and perspectives I learned in the "periphery" to the historical experience of a part of the "core."

2. Because the literature on early modern transformations is vast, and I am dependent upon secondary materials, the present essay concentrates on an assessment of broadly conceived structural changes and consequences. The larger project on which the essay is based pursues the structural argument but is also grounded in more detailed literature from three regions: East Anglia (especially Norfolk), the Midlands (especially Leicestershire), and the south (especially Sussex). The regions are not to be presented as case studies but as checks against simplistic generalizations. Moreover, by looking at different regional processes, I will explore different tracks *toward* household economy, each of which is embedded in different structures of power which, in turn, impart different logics upon the household economies that emerge. Agrarian history in these regions was markedly different (for example,

although Norfolk had open fields, they were of a different character than the open fields of the Midlands, allowing more room for individual maneuver and imposing less of a community structure on peasant households; see Campbell 1980, 1981). Here, however, such regional differences are deemphasized, and the picture that emerges will have a distinct Midlands tone. The structural consequences of rural changes in early modern England are still subjects of intense debate. An attempt to assess such consequences must therefore pay attention to the debates. This paper is concerned with enclosures and must consider the often vitriolic disagreements about the impact of enclosure on small farmers. The resolution I suggest goes beyond the question of expropriation or security of tenure and presents certain observations regarding the emergence of family economy.

3. On the web of use rights that emerged in such open-field situations, see E. P. Thompson (1976); and, for an ethnographic description, Behar (1986).

4. This line of argument depends on Tawney's classic article "The Rise of the Gentry" (1941). In support of his argument, Tawney listed two principal pieces of evidence: (1) the acceleration in market transactions for land in the late sixteenth and early seventeenth centuries, a market made much larger by confiscation of monastic estates and sale of Crown lands; and (2) the redistribution of land as a result of these transactions from relatively large to medium-sized landowners.

In considering the latter point, Tawney engaged in a disputed procedure: he counted manors. Taking the number of manors in seven counties, he counted how many changed hands during the course of the period. He also counted how many belonged to owners of several manors and how many belonged to owners of only a few; how many belonged to old peers and how many belonged to nonaristocrats or new peers. Tawney's article has been subjected to numerous critiques, and it is now common to dismiss his argument as a "vintage idea." The best known early critique was that by H. R. Trevor-Roper, who attacked the method, pointing out that manors differed dramatically in size and therefore could not be taken as a useful unit. Among a variety of other points, he made two that should be considered here. In the first place, he argued that the gentry did not derive their wealth from land but from positions at court. Gentry who depended solely on land were in fact poor and often fallen gentry. The agricultural revolution, and the rise of an agricultural gentry, were eighteenth- rather than sixteenth-century phenomena. Second, he argued that the distinction between aristocracy and gentry is too rigid, that there were many peers who were agricultural improvers and innovators in industry. In place of the aristocracy/gentry distinction, he offered a distinction between court and country that would crosscut the former (Trevor-Roper 1953; cf. Tawney 1954).

The first point, while raising the importance of the court as a source of wealth, actively ignores what all the evidence indicates was happening in the countryside. It need not concern us here. The second point has had a more lasting impact. In an examination of the aristocracy in this period that is at once critical and supportive of Tawney, Lawrence Stone has considered the very real evidence of crisis: incomes tied to low rents that lords are unable or unwilling to change (adopting instead the tactic of raising fines when leases were up for renewal), extravagance of consumption, lineage crises provoked by the failure of an heir, and so on. He also provides a more refined method for counting manors that demonstrates the remarkable land market in the late sixteenth and early seventeenth centuries. His detailed examination provides

important support for Trevor-Roper's contention that some aristocrats were economic entrepreneurs: they were the largest sheepmasters, the most important innovators in mining and manufacture, leasing out sections of their lands and sharing in the
profits. In pursuing this analysis, Stone also employs a distinction between court and
country: court peers adopting an aristocratic life-style and disdain for questions of
gain and loss; country peers joining the rush to improvement (Stone 1965).

5. Too often, our attention is narrowly focused on the enclosure itself and its
immediate effects. We ignore the whole body of changes that might be termed the
"prehistory" of enclosure. Even in those villages that remained open, significant
changes were occurring. Individuals were exchanging strips, consolidating farms,
turning former arable to ley pastures within the open fields in order to practice convertible husbandry, and so on (Kerridge 1968; Hoskins 1950, 1951). In his study of
Wigston Magna, a Leicestershire village that was not enclosed until 1766, Hoskins
stresses the disruptive character of the enclosure, terming it a revolution. But he also
traces the changes that had occurred over the previous period, beginning in the sixteenth century, that had laid the groundwork for that revolution. In the late sixteenth
and early seventeenth centuries, both manors were sold to the former tenants. Thus, a
village that had long held a significant percentage of free tenants became a village in
which all those who held land were freeholders. Some were quite well-to-do, others
relatively poor. With the passing of generations, some were able to accumulate more
holdings, and others of the wealthy freeholders lost their lands and prominence. The
point is that even with the open fields, individual landholders had more room for
maneuver, though not as much as they would have with enclosure. Although the
village still exercised some control over large landholders with bylaws that required
them to grant access to their lands after the harvest for gleaning and pasture, the
village community was decreasing in importance (Hoskins 1957).

6. In Wigston Magna, for example, where enclosure was accomplished in 1766
upon petition from a group dominated by nonresident owners, the revisionist analysis
is at first glance correct. The rights of smallholders were protected, although all owners received less land than they had previously held because of the commutation of
the tithe. Obviously, this affected small owners more seriously than large. Similarly, if
costs were lower than earlier estimates suggested, they were not inconsiderable. And
they were disproportionately large for smallholders, whose hedging costs per acre
were larger. Hoskins suggests that they were therefore forced to mortgage their land,
drawing them irrevocably into the market economy and subjecting them to the cycles
that could favor them during the Napoleonic Wars but could work against them
during a slump such as that which followed the Wars. The effects of enclosure were
not immediate. Within twenty years, smallholders still held about the same percentage of land, but the average farm size had increased as the number of farmers
decreased. By 1831, when the smallholders and their mortgaged farms had been
through a depression, the situation had changed more dramatically.

> If, finally, we survey the fifty years between 1781 and 1831, we can see the full
> measure of the change. The number of landowners fell from 96 to 64, and the
> occupying-owners from 49 to 29. The amount of owner-occupied land in 1831
> was still 37 percent—higher than it had been in 1781 and as high perhaps as
> before enclosure. If we had regard to this figure alone we should have said that

the enclosure had not had significant effect upon landownership. But the owner-occupier was a bigger man altogether. . . . The five largest men in this class had 56 percent of the owner-occupied land. A few small peasant families clung on . . . but many more . . . had lost everything, and others . . . were left with only a cottage. By 1831 the ranks of the peasant landowners, which had hardly been breached fifty years earlier, had been reduced to a mere handful of survivors. The three largest landowners between them owned 35 percent of the land; seven of them owned more than half the parish between them. (Hoskins 1957:265, 266)

Although Wigston represents a single example, and a rather special case at that, it demonstrates the kinds of questions that should be asked of macro-level statistics.

# TWO

# Reimagining the *Oikos*: Austrian Cameralism in Its Social Formation

### Hermann Rebel

*DeMan's second psychological objection goes: Marxism does not take into account the power of tradition! Again, one wonders how he can say that. What is Otto Bauer's "petrified history" but an ideology from earlier epochs reaching across to grasp new social relationships.*

—*PAUL LAZARSFELD, 1983 [1927]*

*There are histories that Reality does not allow to happen, because Reality would be too exposed in them. And so, these histories have to be told. In doing so one might force Reality to confess: yes, I am that.*

—*MARTIN WALSER, 1964*

Exploring the relationship between ideas and the historical social worlds in which they live and speak has long been and remains one of the most difficult areas of social scientific work. The infinitely mutual reflexivity of texts and contexts, of lived projections and introjections, of unending aliena- tions and (mis)appropriations, of disclosures and erasures all threaten, per- petually, to subvert and defeat in advance any search for a controlling analyt- ical formula. A significant illustration of this difficulty may be found in one recent attempt at outlining the basic tenets of a "rational choice" Marxism according to which Marx's discussion of the base/superstructure relationship appears "trivially true. . . [but] is falsifiable and indeed false." That author, to make his point, leads us through an inconclusive discussion about aspects of "scientific" validity in our observing of the functional and dysfunctional roles ideas play in purely economic and technical contexts, and he ends with proposing a research project about a "theory of ideology" that remains un- specified except for a methodology involving a relativistic and individually focused cognitive psychology of so-called "belief formation and preference formation" (Elster 1986:112–116, 199). Having substituted his own search for an unambiguous and scientifically and empirically "true" understanding of texts and their contexts for one he deems inferior (22–24, 190–193), he admits, however, to a prior defeat in the corollary areas (such as, of course, exploitation!) where combined realistic and nominalistic analysis proves too complicated to be grasped by empirical-quantifiable means. For him such researches have to be abandoned or, if kept, demoted to mere description or heuristics (80–81, 195–196).

It is significant that Elster's "methodological individualism" (1986:194) appears to be grounded in the Leibnizian solution to the problem of grasping an infinity of relative determinations: any final understanding of the purported richness of individual experience, of an individual ideation, will always elude allegedly impoverished theory and will be experienced only by a metaphysical divinity outside of and yet central to that impenetrable harmony of determinations (Hamacher 1986:106–108; Bloch 1968:73–81; Kondylis 1987:13–16). This view enforces a self-censoring social science whose most important goal is to formulate "properly modified and restricted" forms of individual "self-realization" in order to safeguard "the exploitation of economics of scale" (Elster 1986:195). The revival in the 1980s of Leibniz's notions about the individual and totality and about texts and contexts—that were originally formulated, in part, for the sake of gaining a career as a culture-bureaucrat at the Habsburg court—is intriguing not only because it points to an interesting, historically specific contextual problem in itself but also because it replays here and now what William Johnston has astutely identified as ancien-régime Austria's most characteristic cultural move—namely, positing a revolutionary cultural critique that seeks to disclose the deep structures of self-contained, individual "systems" while at the same time refusing to subject one's own system(s) to such scrutiny on the pretext of a primary epistemological responsibility for cultural "custodianship" (Johnston 1981). One has to agree with Johnston that we are a long way from a satisfying history of such split enterprises, but what follows will perhaps bring us in closer range by exploring the possibility of an alternative route which this particular early modern "methodological individualism" took toward our own century's social debates. After an initial, necessary conceptual excursion, we will consider, in their social formational contexts, several constitutive texts of cameralism, which was both the Austrian ancien régime's theoretical-practical keystone and an early social science whose concepts and words continue to echo into the present.

## TRANSFERENCE AND COUNTERTRANSFERENCE IN SOCIAL-HISTORICAL TIME

Rather than divide the analysis of social and ideational interplay into high and low tasks—so defined by what we presumably can and cannot know "scientifically"—we might think about another approach altogether and begin by dismantling (or "deconstructing") the apparent fittedness of texts and contexts, by holding the sources, multiple authorships, and mutual constructions of texts both apart from and against the articulating social formations in and around which they find expression. The objective of such an apparent avoidance of making a definitive and positive statement of causal and contextual connectedness is not finally to end with a mere analysis of different juxtapositions but to continue to reproblematize separately certain "obviously" (temporally) related texts and contexts with an eye toward determining and rendering their relationships more intelligible in terms of historical *experience* which at all times surrounds the intense one-dimensionality of here-and-now experience with a less easily grasped but ever-present sense of multiple temporality.

The vitality of phenomenology is that it appears to cleave closely to the problem of experience. It does so, however, only to sublate experiences in essences that in their turn offer nothing helpful to understanding the essential historicity of all experience. One of the reasons the phenomenological approach to the nature and apprehension of experience has proven so powerful in the social sciences and in psychology and criticism lies in its rediscovery and philosophical formulation of something that inquisitors, trial jurists, and readers of detective fiction have known for a long time; that is, to grasp "what happened" it is necessary to obtain and reconstruct repeated retellings of what happened, of what was experienced and continues to be experienced. The necessity of fiction at the heart of Husserl's notion of "reduction" (understood in a culinary sense) sanctions replacing our traditional search for historical truth with what may instead be called "narrative truth" (Spence 1982). To discover where the stories differ and falter for corrections, insertions, or deletions, for lapses or recovery of memory, for recognized contradictions, imputations, and so on is not to discover, finally, the truth in the sense of a fantasized universal-historical conclusion about what happened (as phenomenology would finally demand, thereby abandoning discarded "used-up" stories of experiences and their experiencing selves)[1] but to apprehend what was, is, and can be experienced from historical moment to moment as it is remembered, forgotten, reimagined, and reconstructed. The study of historical experience is to discover how experiences appear in, step out of, and reenter both parallel and divergent historical narratives about processes unfolding along different temporal strata and at different rates of flow.

It is with a view of historical experience as a problem of experiencing multiple temporalities that we leave behind late-Scholastic "methodological individualism" and its view of the individual as a closed and more or less successful, self-reproducing "system" of events and relationships (Luhmann 1986: an autopoietic system) whose career—conceived in Augustinian-Petrarchan terms as a conflicted but resolved narrative of sin and conversion—and whose encounters with other "systems" all require "an idealized, narrative time" (Freccero 1986:17–21; Luhmann 1986:321–322). Chronicling, fixing the dates of events, of actions, and of the production of ideas—in short, understanding the timing, the before and after of the phenomena that appear along a continuous and homogeneous flow of "physical" time—will not become obsolete but merely a secondary, technical task once we refocus on the multiple times of remembrance and abandon the imperious bourgeois subject that requires (and enforces) such historical labors to produce that historical time in which it can embed the beginning, progress, and end of careers.

Siegfried Kracauer's reflections on Proust's experiences with time and memory make part of our point by maintaining that "what does exist is a discontinuous, non-causal succession of situations, of worlds, or periods which, in Proust's own case must be thought of as projections or counterparts of the selves into which his being—but are we justified in assuming an identical being underneath?—successively transforms itself." For Kracauer, Proust's failure to do more than establish "temporal continuity in retrospect" is not merely the final epistemological aporia of the bourgeois biographical self (as one could argue) but is the aporia of all historical experience, which apparently "hinges on . . . retreat into the dimensions of art" while knowing at the same time that history has "[n]either an end nor is it amenable to esthetic redemption" (1966:76–77). This dissection of Proust's impasse has several useful results. It posits, first, a clear critique of the phenomenologists' monadological conception of the self ("an identical being underneath?"), and with that Kracauer has a privileged last word in his disputation of Horkheimer's exclusively high-cultural and personally autonomous estheticization of historical experience (Jay 1988); second, and closer to the present essay's attempt at a different approach to the historical text and context problem is that Kracauer urges on us, presumably as a way "to face up to the last things before the last" (1966:78), the practical recognition that historical periods (and social formations, for that matter) produce and shape "times" of their own that, because of their apparent internal cohesion but also because of their occasional coalescing and intersection with other temporalities, give off illusions that are strong to the point of claiming the "reality," necessity, and primacy of a homogeneous historical time (Kracauer 1966:72–74). His sense of an exploded unity of historical time to match an exploded unity of the self also explodes any "naturalized" temporal juxtaposition between texts and contexts (cf. also Rose 1984:3; LaCapra 1985: 105). This leaves a general analytical problem that has, for historians, the special twist of calling in question all presumptions about a natural *historical* convergence of apparently temporally simultaneous phenomena.

It is a historian's prerogative to demand "a clear awareness of the plurality of social time [as] indispensable to a common methodology of the social sciences" (Braudel 1972). At the same time, there persists a sense that it is the special burden of historians not to give up "the single white light that [we] must have," that to historians falls the special burden to do the impossible, which is to accept that "[e]ach social reality . . . secretes its own time" but that out of these times there has to be woven a "world-time" in the form of a master narrative (Braudel 1972:36–38). The step that has to be taken (and it is not really all that big a step) is to give up the need for a *certain* master narrative and to learn to live with a provisional (Kracauer 1966:78) but always morally serious (because we have to promise and act [Rose 1984:210–212]) narrative construction whose intent it is to help us remember and sublate the recurrent social-cultural deadlocks of thoroughly hegemonized historical experience, those moments, to which our historical sense continues to be irresistibly drawn, where we succumb to culturally permitted but unpredictably costly and always questionable victimizations. To conclude Braudel's vision of a historical social science's special responsibility, one might say that it is meant to achieve and then defend an overriding sense of the *provisional* character of all master narratives against "culturally compelled" histories of the moment that demand to become necessary practice (Rebel 1989).

To help stifle our present, historically produced, and therefore itself relative desire for an absolute master narrative with alternatively satisfying provisional master narratives, historians require no radically new approaches or techniques but need perhaps to learn some different ways of combining already invented moves. To dismantle the existing master narratives by breaking up the consensual unity and structure of historical time we need not only to learn to bring together different combinations of longer, shorter, and even mythic durations and to pay more attention to the narrative potential of "conjunctural" aspects (Rosenberg 1967; Wolf 1982:303–305, 311–313, passim), but need also to begin to experiment with tearing apart accepted and apparently "natural" simultaneities and other such conventional temporal connections around which almost all of our explanations of historical experience are constructed.

One of the first steps in this direction is to accept the necessarily psychological, memory-dependent dimensions of experience and to historicize the unconscious and repressed aspects that necessarily move in a timescape different from but not unrelated to what is consciously acknowledged. The psychological language by which these related differences may be grasped analytically focuses on the notions of compulsively repeated transference and countertransference, by which we recognize, first, how moments in both past and present become intertwined in the historians' own projective relations to their objects of study—that is, how the problems that preoccupy our "time" find their "displaced analogues" (LaCapra 1985:123, also 72–73) in our purportedly objective yet always somehow desired historical master narratives. It is also how the construction of historical texts by historical subjects is itself grounded in *imagined* contexts that permeate the creation, interpretation, and implementation of their texts and may span and conflate several temporalities in creative interpolations of the "present" and the "historical"—and is therefore not just a directed, consciously selective and controlled project but also operates unconsciously, projectively, transferentially, transtemporally. This second sense of historical transference is of special significance because it opens a way to close the transferential exchange across temporal boundaries with that countertransference by which historical subjects have an illusory, imagined relationship with their desired historians, with their own sense of historical place.

To restrict oneself to transference without countertransference is to gain a false appreciation of the difficulties involved in this kind of analysis and to fall into the trap of seeing the historical recurrence of projectively "erased" phenomena, acts, and texts as having in itself a naturally "recuperative" and transformative power for a "carnivalized" dissolution of transferential blockages in a process that makes the passage (in a homogeneous metatime) of "history" itself and not the analytical and reflective dimensions of temporally mixed historical experience the overriding source of human "therapy" in the broadest sense (LaCapra 1985:106–108). It is not only not enough for historians to achieve and impart a conscious sense of transferential processes across multiple historical times; they also have to be aware that there have been essentially two schools of transference analysis and that only one of these—the one that gives countertransference its due—can serve toward a deeper restructuring of the historical text/context problem.

When we turn to the counsel of those who formulated and have working experience with the transferential, we find that at the root of it lie the infantile and other traumas of separation, the shatterings of illusions of unity that remain an unassimilable, temporally suspended "reality" in our subsequently compulsive, desire-driven, and forever dissatisfying social relations, where we hope to recapture (transfer to a new object) an ideal lost unity (Lacan 1981:53–56). Far from being by itself a way of "working through," transference occurs as the strongest source of denial and resistance to change in social encounters and relationships—including the relationship with the analyst. By diminishing the degree and importance of "suffering" (cf. Lacan 1981:55–56) in the analytical relationship, by assuming that the repetition-avoidance of the trauma is less severe there than in the relationships outside it, neo-Freudian ego psychologists from Anna Freud through Franz Alexander to Leo Stone and Heinz Kohut have sought to focus on making therapeutic gains in strictly epistemological terms by which the analysand learns to recognize, to "bring into the realm of consciousness" in a "corrective emotional experience," the transference (seen merely as "the repetition of interpersonal attitudes") in order to "grapple again with unresolved childhood events and emotions" but now at a time when "his adult strength helps him solve the emotional difficulties that as a child he found insurmountable" (Alexander and Selesnick 1966:199, 322–323). One finds oneself agreeing with those practitioners who argue that by thus conventionalizing the analytical relationship and what finds expression there, one not only helps repress what it might be possible for the analysand (the historical subject) to say "unconventionally" (Malcolm 1982:75–78 and passim) but also sees, from a historian's perspective, that this is to impose a conventionally homogeneous historical time on the transferential process itself. By bracketing the analytical occasion as a factitiously benign and itself ahistorical encounter, the analyst (countertransferentially) keeps alive a reassuring sense of cumulative wholeness in "adult strength." The latter appears as a myth of intersubjective unity ascribed to the phenomenological-existential sense of a "therapeutic encounter" where transference allegedly finally breaks and recognizes itself against the "rationality" (another myth of unity) of the analyst (Alexander and Selesnick 1966:323–324, 369). Such an analytical process can only come to an in itself repetitious recognition of the trauma and ends by confusing such learned recognition and its subsequent "integration" with historical remembering.

When Lacan reminds us that even the appearance of the unveiled trauma may be a part of transferential denial (1981:55)—and how many compulsively repeated viewings of by now essentially familiar Holocaust documentaries will it take before we realize we are still not "remembering" any holocausts?—he makes the clear point that the dominant phenomenological-epistemological approach, satisfied with such an appearance, forestalls what should be the payoff of the analysis—namely, that the subject (and the analyst as well) stop acting out and start remembering. Only an analytical relationship in which the severity and complexity of the trauma's simultaneous revelation-concealment is not downplayed, a relationship in which it is primarily the *analyst's* recognition of and struggle with transference and countertransference, creates the possibility of breaking the cycles of endless repetitions; only in such practice can analysis claim its proper place as the only opportunity for "working through" (Malcolm 1982:100–103, 116). It is the always incomplete (and for the analyst genuinely tragic) termination of analysis in a painful memory-recognition breakthrough directed not merely toward the absent "original" trauma but toward its many historical/present incarnations that offers, at its most ideal, an opportunity not just for psychological "learning" to enhance the unifying-controlling ego function but for creating a new capability for change. This means abandoning a negative, because recognizably futile, but narcissistically pleasurable search for lost unity and exercising a broader range of cultural-historical capacities from a special vantage point, one that is of great importance to historians because it is "where . . . *continuity* is giving place to *contiguity*" (Winnicott 1982:101; emphasis in original).

For the historian who wants to (has to?) approach historical experience in terms of the language of transference, this second approach points toward constructing provisional histories that redeem (Rose 1984:89) that negative desire which is eternally compelled into play and authorized by commonly held and ostensibly positive master narratives of historical achievement. Such alternative "negative" narratives are not recoverable by analyses of historical events and texts brought together and kept apart by homogeneously continuous time; they can only be approached according to the ways they appear contiguously (i.e., adjacently, "tropically"), along varying trajectories of social time. As a postscript to this argument, I have to say that such a vision of historical work should not be confused with that merely natural "fragmenting" of historical time and its subsequent narrative-aesthetic redemption which has been advocated by the followers of current "postmodern" fashions (cf. the critique by Polier and Roseberry 1989; also Kracauer 1966 and Epstein 1990 are suggestive here). Instead, what I have in mind means to put pressure on resistant master narratives and requires not only breaking apart their apparently "natural" and factitious historical continuities and contemporaneities (as I will try in the following) but also bringing together and reconstituting any contemporaneity that has not been acknowledged before; which is to say that a denial of or failure to recognize an obvious contemporaneity between texts and contexts is as analytically (transferentially) significant as insisting on factitious historical-temporal conjunctures (Taylor and Rebel 1981; Rebel 1988).

## CAMERALISM IN ITS SOCIAL FORMATION: CANONICAL INCONGRUITIES

Cameralism, in the standard economic and political histories, is the common name given to that genre of prescriptive doctrines that appeared in Central Europe between the 1650s and the 1760s in the form of pamphlets, books of advice, scholarly theses, and so on, all focusing on the best management of a royal or other aristocratic dynasty's treasury properties, the so-called *Kammergut*. These writings were initially grounded in the late-Renaissance revival of a classical tradition of personal manuals of rulership and of household management (housefather literature), often modeled on Xenophon's *Cyropaedia* and *Oeconomia* respectively, and evolved to become the basis for academic subjects that were prerequisites in the training of both high- and lowborn, "public" and "private" administrators. The social formations with which cameralism is conventionally associated are German Central Europe's early modern, more or less absolutist, militarist, and economically and socially interventionist states headed by dynasties of variously titled and endowed autocrats who stood at the peaks of politically organized tribute-collecting pyramids consisting of territorial corporations of clergy, nobility, towns, and peasants. In this context, cameralism is generally perceived as a practical theory for better managing the production and distribution of goods within these institutional constraints in such a way that they continued to generate and even increase the predictable upward flow of tribute necessary for defense and for the just and orderly distribution of status and political power in the state.

Discussions about cameralism no longer focus only on the historical relationships between an economic doctrine and the economic fate of the Central European absolutist states in their shared epoch. There is recognition by historians that the language and concepts of cameralism were pervasive and turned up in the founding doctrines of social and other institutions not immediately connected to the economic and tribute-collecting formations of the state (Stekl 1978:62). The historical *place* of cameralism in the larger master narrative of the West has been expanded in the specialist literature to include certain key elements of social and psychological history as well, and this has fixed even more closely the relationship between cameralist texts and the absolutist context. The pivotal work in this regard was the series of essays published by Gerhard Oestreich between 1953 and 1967 (in English, 1982) on the theme of a deeper ideology and a practice of absolutism that were grounded in the so-called "Netherlands movement" associated with Hugo Grotius and with the Belgian humanist and classical historian Justus Lipsius (1547–1606), whose *politique* career was founded not on concepts of religious toleration but on obedience and who ended his days as a secure academic reconciled with Counter-Reformation Catholicism. Lipsius's recovery of Roman Stoicism's emphasis on self-discipline for state service, his modification of it in terms of what was needed for "persevering" through a state's crises and civil wars, the two-century-long reissuing of editions of his works, and the echoes of Lipsius's ideas among other humanists, especially in France and Austria, all indicate, for Oestreich, that he was the major figure who caught the true spirit of the forward-looking aspects of the early modern states as they sought to overcome decades of confessional turmoil and war. He sees Lipsius's "de-theologization" of public life leading not toward toleration but toward a "strong state" grounded in a civil service and army whose members are themselves highly disciplined and enforce in turn the broader social discipline required for civil order. In this conception it is discipline, subordination, and obedience that end religious civil war and are, by that token, "modern." In this statist definition of modernity (and who cannot detect here an "origin" of that compulsively repeated Western fiction that places the state outside of society?) it is the new disciplinary demands of "[b]ureaucracy, militarism and mercantilism . . . in [their] particular spheres" that are behind the shift "from corporative, regionally secured liberty to the modern political order" (1982:267–268; passim). By emphasizing a perception of the historically unique conjuncture of cameralism with its contextual state formation at that precise historical point where Europe, in order to recover its progressive development, needed to recover "unity" after extremes of conflict and by perceiving this moment of state formation and its ideology as making an identical contribution (discipline) to a master narrative of evolving modernity, Oestreich commits himself to an exclusive welding together of text and context in what we may agree is an example of "over-contextualization. . . [which] occurs when one so immerses a text in the particularities of its own time and place that one impedes responsive understanding and excessively restricts the interaction between past and present" (LaCapra 1985:132). Ironically, such factitious accounts are often logically mistaken—revealing thereby their countertransferential, wishful relationship to their historical subject—and Oestreich's is no exception.

Here cameralism is not only conflated with mercantilism and it is not only seen as serving the state as the entry for notions of administrative and economic discipline into the top levels of state administration, but it is also alleged to have been an effective means to harness and direct (and in that sense "modernize") the dangerous and disorderly forces unleashed by industrialization. Although Oestreich's account, in its emphasis on texts about discipline, appears to be an idealist one, we can see that it conceals at its heart a rather crude and arguably unconscious base/superstructure analysis. Even if we leave aside the whole problem of seeing the early modern "strong state" exclusively as restorer of order and agree thereby to suppress questions about an ecological fallacy that would require investigations into the same state's role in creating and perpetuating disorder (cf. Naujoks 1958), we can see that Oestreich's argument depends on a primarily contextual motive force and that he does not theorize or analyze that context very well. In that regard his argument falls flat and undermines and confuses the general master narrative linking cameralism and absolutism to each other and to contextual modernity.

Two brief illustrations will suffice. First, Oestreich determines that one of the impulses for a theoretically innovative and disciplining regime came from the plight of sixteenth-century German cities with their developing economies' allegedly increased demand for labor which they satisfied by drawing people from the countryside into an urban life for which these new workers had to be disciplined (1982:156–157). If we look, however, at what research reveals about the German cities' "modernization" in this period, a rather different picture emerges. From research on Augsburg and on the only initially impressive growth of its textile industry in the sixteenth century, it has become apparent that the real growth sector in the Augsburg economy was the patricians' newly acquired rural estates whose managers, in order to optimize their labor accounts in relation to the wider market in grains, depopulated and repopulated their rural labor forces as the market indicated. The city, very much under the patricians' control, served as a kind of labor bank for these rural enterprises, with the guild-organized (and tamed) textile industry serving not as a new industrial growth sector but as an increasingly

underfunded and poorly marketed industrial make-work program whose
primary purpose it was to absorb or give off labor to maintain the profitability of conservatively managed agricultural enterprises (Paas 1981). This is
not a narrative about disciplining for modernization; rather, it is a narrative
about disciplining for rural-urban dislocation and for labor exploitation in
yet another case of archaic latifundia agriculture. While it may be argued
that Oestreich could not have known about the Augsburg work by Paas and
others, the facts are nevertheless that it makes his sustained argument about
cameralism as a necessary modernizing discipline for ordering processes of
industrialization and economic expansion extremely doubtful (Oestreich
1982:196; cf. Pribram 1983:95–96).

Second, his model fails when he argues for a transition from feudalism,
which he associates with an ethos of status and loyalty, toward "the contractual thinking of modern times" in which "[r]elations based on command and
obedience, conceived as deriving from contractual agreement, created clear
functions of superiority and subordination, but . . . also presupposed a degree
of discipline" (1982:266). To his own admission that the contractual contained significant elements of status, which we may see as incommensurable
with "feudal" status, we can add that the feudal contained similarly incommensurable aspects of contractual discipline. A master narrative conceptualized in these terms misses completely, moreover, that the disciplining associated with texts on the early modern German state was conceived at least as
part of the disciplining of traditionally rebellious aristocrats to regulate their
families and dynastic properties better for the improved order and morality
of the state (particularly to curb aristocratic borrowing for conspicuous consumption) and, not to be trivialized, to furnish unpaid service in the
bureaucracy and at court (Kraemer 1974:41, 74–75; Bruckmüller 1984:82–
83; Fischer and Lundgreen 1975:518–519). These were forms of discipline
that were both closer to feudal ethics and far from serving explicitly "modernizing" ends.

The confusions we see in Oestreich are echoed in the literature where
Oestreich's argument has come to serve as a social-psychological capstone to
a preceding story about cameralism's primarily economic and political role
in modernization. The long-standing textbook and broad interpretive agreement that Austrian cameralism sought "to work out and implement a coherent economic policy of economic growth" (Wangermann 1973:24) and that
its chief representatives were early natural-law liberals who had a possibly
privately conflicted but publicly harmonious relationship with autocrats for
reasons of a middle-class struggle against the nobility (Krieger 1972:72–76;
cf. Rosenberg 1966:171–173 and passim) has now been strengthened by
placing additional "psychological consequences alongside the economic
ones" (Vierhaus 1988:28–30, 108), by perceiving a disciplining economic
psychology to furnish the "values of a dynamic and enterprising culture"

where the ability to obey was equated with reason (Raeff 1983:5, 27, 87 and passim; cf. Vierhaus 1988:114). In this neoclassical version of a lagging transition to modernity, the rate of German-Austrian modernization was so far behind that of the rest of Europe because of the alleged cost and diminishing returns of the large modernizing bureaucracy's inevitable inefficiencies (Raeff 1983:5, 173–174 and passim; Bernard 1979:27) and not, as one has to argue, because of the immeasurable costs of "disciplined," sacrificial self-exploitation under a tribute-taking command economy. The former is a vision that tries to forge links from cameralism to the liberal currents of European development, seeing, for example, the Austrian cameralist Justi, to whom we shall turn at length in a moment, as a thwarted Smithian (Kann 1960:175; Walker 1971:164, 167; cf. Vierhaus 1988:81–83) without recognizing the curious fact that the German "Smithians" who eventually replaced the cameralists in their university chairs did not develop as economic liberals in the English sense but remained fully immersed in the language and methods of cameralism (Epstein 1966:180–182; Pribram 1983:200–203).

The tendency, moreover, of this view to conflate cameralism with mercantilism places cameralism on what is perceived as the modernizing trajectory of mercantilism, even to the point where cameralism is perceived as going through a shift from treasury-focused fiscalism to trade-political "imperial mercantilism" (Bog 1969) which is presumed to be analogous to a change in the English "version" from fiscalism to a balance-of-trade concept. There is no question that German cameralists became more interested in trade after their observation of the Dutch and English models (Kraemer 1974:70–71), but they never broke through to an import policy that considered the profitability of reexports. Moreover, cameralism remained wedded to a backward-looking, neo-Stoic "housefather" tradition with its insistence on spending within tributary means and its refusal to service a public debt, whereas in England there evolved a different attitude toward the management of a growing public debt, of "indebtedness without insolvency," underwritten by both tribute and trade expansion (Braun 1975:295–296). That these two clearly antagonistic visions and conditions of political economy can still, in Braun's view, be classified as merely "two very contrasting stages of modernity" attests really both to the ideological strength of modernity as the master narrative and to the unresolvable (erased) incongruities it contains.

Whether even English mercantilism in its "later" stage was itself a part of a process of modernization is far from clear and is not really at issue here, but it is interesting to point out that it appears as "modern" from the point of view of a German liberal historical tradition that equates that stage with the aftermath of the Glorious Revolution (Hintze 1975:442–443), whereas it seems evident now that the change in English mercantilism comes much earlier and occurred probably in some connection with the business cycle (Frank 1978:78–81). While it is possible to argue that English mercantilism was the first European economic philosophy capable of responding to the market with a rational choice and was therefore "modern," we need also to remember that mercantilist England was corporatively organized and was the most regressively and highest taxing tribute-collecting empire of the European world (Mathias and O'Brien 1976). More to the point is that the notion of a disciplining cameralist-absolutist collaboration as a key stage in the progressive unfolding of modernity seems to lead to distorted histories in which cameralism bowed to "reality," concentrated on domestic trade because there was no foreign trade to be had, and (impossibly!) diverted "ample public funds to the individual peasant economy" (Bog 1969:168–169, 175). Others fantasize histories in which "seventeenth century ordinances presaged physiocratic attitudes" and led toward "the development of proto-industrial society" (Raeff 1983:93, 119), while in Prussia "mercantilist-cameralist" policies prepared the "transition to industrialization" (Vierhaus 1988:30). To anyone who has worked with the everyday phenomena on the social-historical end of these policies, such claims as well as those of Oestreich appear as cumulatively compounded errors that not only falsify the pedigrees of concepts and institutions but create forced connectednesses and temporal continuities that do not go far into or explore the historical range of either texts or contexts.

To begin to explode the "modernization" master narrative's allegedly natural contemporaneities with all its errors of misnaming and false continuities, we may take a stratagem from the storytellers' art and invent a different ending (cf. Celati 1986). One of the advantages of adopting a technique of "narrative" over "historical" truth is that we can argue that "historical" endings are never certain and are always multiple. In other words, distinct from a still dominant but clearly unworkable master narrative of cameralism and absolutism ending in modernity there appear other possible endings calling on misunderstood or hidden parts of the story that may not be as comforting but that have an effect contrary to the false congruities of the canonical story. We may find that, for the moment at least, it is easier to write unhappy endings to what claim to be happy master narratives. To bring to bear, in addition, the previous thoughts about the transferential aspects of the construction of histories on the question of an alternative ending to the history of cameralism in its social formation we can point to the most visible and yet most compulsively reneged memory of traumatized life in "modern" Central Europe, namely, the Holocaust. To read this last into its temporal contiguities, into related historical experiences, into those other moments in Central Europe's history when the veil was lifted from texts and social formations that promised unity and shelteredness but authorized annihilation, is to open a radically different perspective on the possibility of remembering not only the Holocaust but also a related early modern history for which historians may no longer have to misrepresent deliberate policies of economic stagnation as economic growth, disorder as order, or madness as harmony (incongruities already noticed by Walker 1971:151).

## REIMAGINING THE *OIKOS*

Replacing modernity with the Holocaust as a provisional ending to a new master narrative urges on us a new reading, particularly of those elements of the narrative that were previously suppressed because they did not fit into the tight web of overcontextualized contemporaneity that characterized the (antimodernists') "modernist" narrative about cameralist texts and social formational contexts. Immediately we recognize that what has been missing from the latter was a clear grasp of the theorized and practiced fundamental social unit. While there is a shared sense that "the family" and "household" were somehow at the heart of social relations, there appears a tacit agreement among historians—one clearly derived from the cameralist literature itself and therefore a case of countertransferential collaboration with the analysands' own transferential denial—not to examine the inner workings of the family. Once we had Otto Brunner's antimodern recollection of the neo-classical recollection of the *oikos*, the classical "good economy of the 'whole house,'" as the lowest unit of social and political authority, then what took place inside that entity ceased to be a matter for investigation (Brunner 1968; cf. Nicholas 1970). Historians have been able to follow this lead, in effect taking the view of the early modern bureaucrats, and reduce their discussions of the family to "life-style" questions, one where the state abandons the "wild" realm of the family to its own devices but interferes to curb appetites, moralize behavior, and eliminate perpetually troublesome "natural" conflicts over inheritance—in short, simply to rationalize and humanize a disorderly area of human affairs so that it could play its part in the state (Raeff 1983:85, 72–73, 76–77).

The alternative approach we take here to the fate of the *oikos* conception both in its early modern cameralist and modern historical inventions is that it demonstrates a clear case of a (re)invention of a tradition and that such a process cannot simply be discussed in a positivistic and functionalistic way by which invented traditions serve only consciously to install or resist hegemonies. Although good work has recently been done toward recovering the complexity of such instances of tradition-fabricating (Hobsbawm and Ranger 1983, especially the essays by Cohn and Ranger; Sider 1986; for a neo-classical view of the historicity of "tradition" see Raeff 1983:103), it is still work in which the anachronistic elements of the "invented" tradition and the positing of an authentic original tradition all point toward a homogeneously conceptualized historical time ending in modernity. It is a conception in which the temporally "contiguous" and the transferential aspects of such histories of tradition (found in both their past and present historical reinventions) cannot come into play (cf. Roseberry and O'Brien's Introduction to this book).

In the case of the reinvented *oikos* it is clear that both the early modern conceptualizers and their modern historians were and are engaged in transferential readings of a conception of the family household that was already in its Greek classical "origins" a contentious and transferentially invented tradition (Humphreys 1983:162–163, 179, and passim). The attribution of a single "whole house"/*oikos* concept that we find in modern neoclassicism represses, places under erasure, if one wills, that concept's Greek history. There were compelled repetitions and reinventions passing from a Homeric-aristocratic household entourage through Hesiod's more closed and competitive version suitable to the limited smallholder, learning to exclude even kin to secure the *oikos*, to, finally, Xenophon's decadent urban-conservative reformulation making the slave-managing farm the rural "private" antidote to urban "public" decay (Humphreys 1983:82–83, 133, 162–163). By investigating the *oikos* in terms of its posited and "erased" qualities as these appear particularly in its cameralist form, we can begin to lift it out of its overcontextualized neoclassical historical reading and recover its transtemporal qualities, its "traumas" of slave labor and of failed promises of justice that were held in abeyance but were also present and experienced at each of its contextual recollections. Within a Holocaust master narrative it becomes possible to argue that the saving fiction of a family "wholeness" that was somehow outside the market and below the historical process authorized historically specific traumas of social disconnection and physical annihilation.

The social formation in which cameralism appeared is the military tribute-collecting absolute state of early modern Central Europe. This state appears in the historical literature largely in its own terms. Just as the family and household economy is undertheorized as the fundamental social unit of this state so the latter is also, in its larger construction, sociologically underanalyzed. Part of the problem has been that in the predominantly neoclassical approaches to the subject there is a dearth, partly a result of the transferential nature of those approaches, of social analytical concepts. Similarly, we see the romanticized exclusions of the family's "natural" economy from the vital processes of history by historians on the left, going from Engels through Luxemburg and Chayanov to Horkheimer and E. P. Thompson (cf. the critical essay by Roseberry 1988). A break with this tradition was made by French post-Althusserian anthropologists who explored various reformulations of the "mode of production" concept in terms of the family economy (Bloch 1975; Kahn 1981; for another approach cf. Rebel 1983: chap. 5) with the result that the characteristics and processes of social relations of the family may be construed in terms of what Eric Wolf calls the "kin-ordered" mode of production (1982:88–100, 401, and passim) with all the analytical features (primary accumulation, surplus production, class, etc.) associated with a Marxist approach to social formation. Even readers on the left have found it difficult to follow Wolf's bold step of maintaining that his three modes of production (kin, tributary, and capitalist) are not "types" of society or cultural "stages" but social-historical conceptual "constructs" for imaginative analytical formulations of "certain strategic relationships" (100), including those within the family. Some of Wolf's friendliest critics find it difficult to let go of ideas of "autonomous" spheres (Worsley 1984a:174), and others assert that kinship links existed "prior to their function in [production]" and continue thereby to posit a prior "real presence" that forces analysis back into a single homogeneous flow of historical time ("the same story") between an absolutely separated past and present (Asad 1987:601–602). Moreover, in this critical view there is an insistence on a purity and completeness of modes of production that remains stuck in the far less useful language of transitions from one mode to another and that cannot see how Wolf's reconceptualization accounts for the existence of, say, a strong tributary component to modern "capitalist" societies (Asad 1987:598). However, Wolf's entire story throughout deals with the historical *articulations* of modes and demonstrates that pure modes of production without relations of dominance and dependence vis-à-vis other modes cannot be perceived historically and that it is the historical experience of these articulations that poses the key questions for social cultural analysis. In this sense, Wolf's rewriting of the analysis of social formation as focusing on the hegemonic-subaltern articulations among modes of production, each with cultural themes that are not merely epiphenomenal and superstructural but consist of linguistic and other formulations shared within and between modes and are designed to grasp the ambivalent ways in which social relations simultaneously reveal and conceal themselves, also helps break the hold of a homogeneously conceived historical time. It is with the articulation of modal themes in the historical convergence and dissolution of social formations with different social temporalities and different articulations of imagined histories and of invented traditions that we can theorize a contextual analysis appropriate to a transferential analysis of texts.

The remainder of this essay must be seen as only a tentative attempt to open up the particular convergence of cameralism and absolutism by retheorizing them in the ways just outlined. Seen from the perspective of an articulation of kin and tributary relations, the early modern Austrian reformulation of the *oikos* can be explored on the basis of the similarities to and differences from the classical model it recalls. In what follows we will see agents of the Austrian state reimaging the *oikos* for a purported policy science of social order, but we will also see them do so in a framework of family and treasury practice in which the social strategies of the royal and aristocratic families mobilize for their own dynastic (i.e., kin-ordered) maintenance and occasional capitalist enterprises the tribute-producing capacities of peasants and workers in such a way that the latter find it difficult, and even impossible, to form and live in families of their own—but are yet held accountable to a family project whose formalized appearance is not portrayed as aristocratic-dynastic but as universally "natural." Rather than appearing as a rationalizing agent, cameralism's disciplining now can appear as the "solecism" it was (Walker 1971:151), as an attempt to force an order where that could only be done with traumatic social costs experienced as disorder under a terrorist judicial state. Rather than yielding a history of modernity, this counter-canonical reading yields a history of a progressive loss of rational treasury and public welfare objectives giving way to the authorities' progressive imposition of personally fantasized and increasingly inapposite objectives—of which perhaps none could be more indicative of far greater insanities yet to come than the emperor Joseph II's cathected psychological involvement in the paternity cases of domestic servants (Bernard 1979:30–35, 41–42, 62–63).

## THE AUSTRIAN CONTEXT: ARTICULATIONS OF KIN AND TRIBUTE

By the late fifteenth century certain strategically placed aristocracies and princes in German-speaking Central Europe had to decide what to do with their growing peasant working class in the face of opportunities from an expanding market that included rural industries financed, supplied, and serviced both by domestic and, primarily, by external centers of mercantile investment and exchange. In the German-Czech provinces of the Habsburgs, aristocratic and ecclesiastical landowners had been experimenting with various combinations of incomes from direct production, services, dues, and rents since the fourteenth century. Between 1500 and 1600 they followed two fundamental directions: a few of them had already, by 1500, gone far toward becoming rentier landlords, letting their peasants inherit, subdivide, and alienate their leaseholds freely (Zauner 1971; cf. Sabean 1972). Most, however, took a less risky and socially conservative course and merely expanded, through purchases, their claims to taxes, rents, tithes, and services and sought to reduce all of these to tribute payments in cash (Grüll 1955). They converted tithes in kind to fixed cash payments, they terminated other dues and services with release fees and so on, and they burdened their peasants' houses and communes with administrative duties and labor services that could also be subject to release fees. This majority of landlords and estate managers did not favor a transition to collecting rents from increasingly parcelized and commercialized farms supported by a growing cottage industry but opted for the more certain incomes from larger, impartible, bureaucratically controlled and tribute-producing leaseholds engaged in agriculture with some industrial diversification. In the reign of Maximilian I of Habsburg (1493–1519), the royal adminstration of finance (*Hofkammer*) took a new course toward management of its estates and farms that favored the majority's course of development. One of the results was that the rural industrialization that occurred in these areas was severely limited by the curtailment of farm subdivision, of cottage construction, and of partible inheritance, and it lagged far behind rural industrialization in neighboring areas (Rebel 1983; Braun 1960; Schremmer 1972; Kellenbenz 1965).

Maximilian I waged a costly war against Bayezed II, drove the Turks out of Styria in the 1490s, and involved his resources in the Burgundian-French wars, all with the result that under pressure from his creditors he had to reorganize the administration of the royal treasury. As a significant part of this reorganization he halted the erosion of those royal properties administered by the crown's aristocratic creditors, pursued the active upgrading of his estates and incomes—following the methods already being pursued by most of the secular and ecclesiastical nobilities—and began a policy of pawning royal property (*Kammergut*) on short-term (ca. seven-year) contracts to his creditors, thereby setting a course of public finance by public debt secured in great part by treasury property that Austria would follow for the next two centuries. Not only did Maximilian I's restructuring of his treasury incomes lay the foundation for a state system of public finance that never managed to free itself completely from the private grasp of the royal house, but it also released a chain of far-reaching alterations in rural economic and social life.

What had begun as a restructuring of royal estates and finances dovetailed with, overtook, and by 1600 dictated the widespread adoption of the more conservative of the two courses of aristocratic investment and estate management. At first, the aristocratic officials of the royal household brought their own estates' administrations in line with the royal model; then the creditors of the Crown, rather than have two kinds of estates to administer (i.e., their own and the treasury's), followed suit and restructured their own holdings according to treasury guidelines. Finally, the Habsburgs mandated across-the-board changes for all estate owners to follow in the governance of the subject peasants' leasehold and tenure arrangements. This created uniformly heritable and impartible leaseholds that functioned both as units of tribute collection and as units of family and community administration within the bureaucratic framework of public and private estates guided by royal mandate. The peasant houses' kin-organized production and administrative functions were connected to the royal and aristocratic tribute-taking state in the sense that a family's accession to and retention of tenure were subject to the head's performance in maintaining his holding's tribute-rendering capacity.

The measure for this performance is of great importance for our story. At the death of a tenant or of his or her spouse, a state-regulated inventory of the farm was taken by bailiffs and other agents of the estate owner; and if the liens against the holding exceeded or came near to exceeding the value of its assets, then the administration of the holding could be declared bankrupt and the deceased tenant's family removed to make room for a new incumbent's administration (Rebel 1983). If we consider that these changes made the Austrian peasant house the primary unit of accounting in both the rural economy and in the system of public finance, then we see a sharp divergence in the Austrian social organization of production from such not-too-distant neighbors as the Zurich *Oberland* or from parts of Bavaria, where an early modern cottage-based system of mercantile textile production and distribution evolved during the eighteenth century. If we follow Rudolf Braun's and others' interpretation of the eventual direct and indirect emergence of factory production from early modern cottage industry not only as a more efficiently centralized organization of the means of production but as merchant capital's answer to the inefficiencies of input-output accounting controls in the dispersed cottage industry, then we see a special problem for Austria's economic development in the persistent historical presence of house industries confined to a limited number of peasant or town houses whose primary purpose, in accounting terms, was to remain solvent as tribute-rendering units. Looking ahead for a moment, it is significant with regard to accounting that cameralist social science, for all its interests in census-taking and in measuring and comparing economic and social indicators, took no interest whatsoever in the composition of rural households and in the measurement of actual input and output at the level of primary units of production. Indicative in this regard is that the first general Austrian census of people whose occupation was employment in *Hausindustrie* was not taken until 1902 (Sombart 1923:191–193).

The changes initiated by Maximilian I's fiscal reforms were solidly entrenched by 1650. While the foreground of the historical stage was seething with violent assassinations, mass murders, international religious and territorial wars, aristocratic *frondes*, peasant uprisings, millennial revolts, and the like, the Habsburgs's emerging absolute state had, behind the scenes, steadily competed with and slowly displaced rural industry as a focus for aristocratic investment and labor calculations. Throughout the Danubian states a new estate economy spread with this victory of state tribute over merchant capital which, we must add, did not represent a "feudal" victory over a "premature" transition to capitalism. Merchant industrial investments in Central Europe still functioned wholly within a number of competing tributary systems. Although the state's policies with regard to tenure had in effect frozen the aristocracies' traditional rent and labor-service incomes, the state encouraged the conversion of labor services to regular fees, legislated a number of new transaction fees (entry fees, death duties, etc.), and imposed a state tax system (the *Kontribution*) as well as *ad hoc* military subsidies (*Rüstgeld*, *Garnisonsgeld*, etc.), all of which passed through the estates' accounts and gave the estate owners annual cash flows and profits with which to participate in the European agricultural commodity trade and in the political and social life in the capital (Rebel 1983:126–137).

The state's successful competition for the wealth of the aristocracy committed the aristocrats' economy in a self-contradictory direction. Ironically, the estate owners and lien administrators were the only "capitalists" in this system, with cash flow from converted labor services allowing them to purchase labor directly for agricultural and industrial production. This was, however, a capitalism that was severely limited by its dependence on the flow of state-organized tribute and by the dominant form of labor appropriation (supported by state regulation after the 1590s) in which the heads of peasant households, acting as kin or pseudokin, administered their housecommunities' productive capacities. The second limitation on estate management meant that such rural industries as now evolved in Austria were contained by and accounted for within the relatively limited number of peasant houses. Although the aristocratic estates were thus limited in their capitalism, they invested in such enterprises as grain merchandising, viticulture, truck farming, brewing, and fishpond management (and in Bohemia, in textile production), all of which in time not only made Austrian rural estate management the most innovative sector in the Austrian economy until well into the nineteenth century but also supported a historically significant (and internally conflicted) aristocratic opposition to the expansion of the tribute-taking and bureaucratic power of the state in the century between 1750 and 1850 (Blum 1948).

At the bottom of this system was the peasant "house" conceived of both as a tribute-rendering and order-maintaining firm, as the lowest rung on the administrative ladder. The incumbent tenant heads of houses administered, in effect, what amounted to a monopoly on the disposition not only of private labor and resources but, more importantly, of welfare and of civic and social attachment. Their positions, governed by the supervision of impartible tenure by means of postmortem inventories, forced them to redirect, again with the help of state regulations, the economic and social production of their kin, fictive kin (godparents, in-laws), and pseudokin (wards, orphans) to help meet the terms of tenure. In this context, the economic diversification of the peasant house through rural industry only served to maintain the tenure of the incumbent tenant and of his designated heir, this especially in periods of wildly fluctuating secular swings of the economy, and it did not amount to an "industrialization" of the countryside (Rebel 1983).

From the perspective of social practice, there were at least two especially noteworthy aspects of the historical emergence of this house- and estate-based tributary state. Such profits as the heads of houses produced were only in part reinvested to make their tenure more secure. The rest, a for now indeterminate amount, went in the form of loans to the owners and managers of estates or to other more highly placed subjects in return for the holding in lien of such rights and privileges as the latter could grant through the estates' judicial and economic institutions. The heads of houses, in other words, were not primarily interested in the economic improvement of "their" farms but rather in making a personal career that aimed at stepping up into the lower ranks of the estate and possibly state bureaucracies, a career in which they were judged by their ability to manage a house in such a way that they could meet their tribute obligations and, in addition, buy into the pawn and lien administration arrangements that were the other mainstay of this tribute-taking system (Rebel 1983:200–207, 249–257).

The second socially significant result of these new institutions took place at the opposite pole of the family. The rigidly enforced impartibility of the deliberately limited number of tenant farms produced a vast class of effectually dispossessed children who were perpetually downwardly mobile, who served as the labor force that sustained the careers of the tenured who, in turn, were often not even members of the family but outsiders brought in to become "housefathers" exploiting legally defined pseudofamilies. Given the limited economic means and social objectives of tenant houses, their absorptive capacity for additional labor was also severely limited. It is when these limits were reached—in historical conjunctures of the structural features and the secular swings of the economy—that the system as a whole came under severe strain.

The Austrian state, in particular the tribute-collecting and -accounting royal treasury, lay concealed within the private household enterprises that were required to enroll in its service. This process began with the royal treasury's disinvestment in the actual management (but not regulation) of its own estates and the assumption of the costs and benefits of that management by private investors. These in turn developed a limited estate-capitalism and sought to connect their family treasuries to capitalist investment by capturing portions of the bureaucratically mandated and adjudicated increases in tribute, only parts of which they funneled to the state from the kin-ordered productive units at the bottom of the system. While research into Austria's later economic underdevelopment has generally been concerned with the supply-side aspects of this limited capitalist mode embedded in a tributary mode of production, a study of the encounter and inherent conflicts between and within early modern Austria's tributary and kin-ordered modes of production also holds much promise. In virtually all cases the requirements of the tributary mode took precedence over the requirements of "kinship," and it is in the articulations between these n.odes as they encountered each other in the social relations of the Austrian peasant house that apparently insoluble conflicts arose, conflicts whose socially and psychologically painful burdens were shifted to the lowest laboring class, rural workers, servants, and children. Here we want to explore the conceptual apparatus that sought to grasp this system and to understand why the state's intellectuals, the cameralists, acting as both academic philosophers and bureaucrats, remained essentially speechless about this "context," about the obvious conflicts within these structured social relations and articulations.

## THE HISTORICAL CONSTRUCTION OF CAMERALIST TEXTS

The modernizing, rationalistic-economic character that has been ascribed to cameralism seems confirmed by the cameralists' view of themselves. Even if we cannot see them as "scientists," they consciously saw themselves as such, challenging the rule of theological faculties (Fischer and Lundgreen 1975:546). "We raise systems, to raise the well-being of men," claimed the Halle professor of cameralism Johann Förster in 1782 (cited in Walker 1971:162). One might deny that this kind of self-conscious system-building had anything to do with "science" on the grounds that cameralism knew no scientific accumulation and communication of knowledge and "no such procedure . . . as a conscious resort to any fundamental theoretical code of principles which is conceived of as the basis of the whole movement" (Sommer 1930:160). This would seem to be too narrow a view, especially because it diminishes and distorts the importance of the cameralists in favor of the physiocrats as originators (Sommer [1930] cites Quesnay's *Tableau économique*) of modern policy and social sciences. If, for example, we look at both the intent and the attempted practice of J. H. G. von Justi's "police science," we see that he was ambitious about scientific communication, that his intent was to found university departments to carry on research and teach the new science. The preface to the second (1758) edition of his *Staatswirthschaft*, published when Justi was professor of cameralism at Vienna's *Theresianum*, is filled with references to a new scientific education for state planners and bureaucrats, as well as for members of other professions, notably the legal.

The objectives for these scientific researches were intended to transcend their immediate context because they were to be nothing less than a disclosure and implementing of the laws governing the relationships and interactions of all elements of the economic, social, and political life of states. Justi wanted to educate a new kind of man, whom he called the "Universalcameralist," who would avoid the limitations of the previous, contextually determined kind of cameralist, called the "Particularcameralist," who had worked strictly within and for the limited interests of specific departments of specific states. "This latter individual will believe that he has made significant improvements in one part of the government [but] will in the end realize that he thereby caused another part of the state's great household a greater amount of harm because he did not have insight into the coherence of this great economy and into the influence that the concerns of common welfare have on each other" (Justi 1758:xxi). The source of Justi's sense of a cost-benefit-balancing, scientific univeralism has been ascribed to another sometime cameralist in the service of Hanover, Gottfried Wilhelm Leibniz (Pribram 1983:95; Glockner 1968), and we will in a moment have occasion to come back to the significance of his influence. To give it its full due, we must first recognize that at the basis of Austrian cameralism and reaching a kind of apotheosis in Justi's writings was not an economic theory but a metaphysics for a new psychology that had several important historical sources. Tracing this textual construction of cameralism reveals a rather different perspective on raising "the well-being of men."

The same Maximilian I who initiated the momentous fiscal reforms described above was also hailed in his own time as "Germany's last knight." Married to a daughter of the House of Capet, he created an outpost of the Burgundian spirit in Vienna where, as common language for the courtly rites that were played out among his favorites, advisers, and scholars, the ideas of heroism found in the Arthurian legends were revived and reworked in a significant way. Now the enemies proper to the Estate of nobility were no longer giants, wizards, or other knights, but rather accident, envy, hatred. The new battlegrounds for the courtier were in his inner moral spaces where, with the help of *intelligentia*, *sensus*, and *ratio*, his will and desire battled against the random disorders of fortune. The *virtus* of the Christian knight was to be measured now by the degree to which he was capable of inner conquest in order to do all that was necessary for justice in political morality on behalf of social (i.e., racial) inferiors who were incapable of sublime action (Müller 1982:232–233; cf. Huizinga 1934:323–324; Brunner 1949:142–166). In the course of the sixteenth and seventeenth centuries there evolved among both professional and lay scholars in Central Europe generally and in Austria particularly an elaboration of these ideas which eventually amounted to a new official social psychology; that is, the new courtly heroism evolved to become a reconceptualization and empirical study of the individual's capacity for work, learning, and social participation, all grounded in self-discipline.

By the mid-seventeenth century and particularly in the context of the Habsburg monarchy, there evolved a critique directed against restricting this new understanding only to the instruction manuals for princes and nobility. It is in this "democratization" that we find *politique* reformers like Lipsius advocating studied applications of these new measures of man to representatives of the state generally, to domestic magistrates, and to the lower classes. Their investigations led them to the conclusion that the lower one went into society, the less capable people were of self-discipline. Consequently the new cameralist sciences for estate managers, state employees, and peasants that these intellectuals urged on princes and aristocratic patrons by the end of the seventeenth century focused on the need for a psychological reeducation of the lower orders to assure the "just functioning" (and not the "growth") of the state's economy (Oestreich 1982:93–94, 269–270). It is in their texts that we recover cameralist versions of the *oikos*, the good economy of the "whole house."

Toward the end of the seventeenth century there appeared in Austria within three years of each other two works concerned with separate but related spheres of social and economic philosophy: Philipp Wilhelm von Hörnigk's *Österreich über alles, wann es nur will* (Austria above all, if only it will) ([1684]; I use a modern edition, 1964) and Wolf Helmhard von Hohberg's *Georgica Curiosa Aucta* ([1687]; I use the 5th edition of 1715). Both books were widely read and distributed and epitomized the degree of sophistication that the neo-Stoic social ideal had reached as a source for cameralist social planning. They are, significantly, two vastly different works by two radically different kinds of authors; the *Georgica* was a guide for household management by a humanist country squire and military entrepreneur from Lower Austria (Brunner 1949), and the Hörnigk book was a macroeconomic tract by an intellectual careerist, petty entrepreneur, diplomat, and historian. What they had in common was a conception of the importance of the management of the rural house economy and of manipulating human psychology in the ordering of both the household and of the larger economy and society.

Hohberg saw as his audience both aristocratic and lesser heads of rural households, whom he termed "housefathers," and he sought to address himself to the interrelations of the many parts of the *oikos*, the house economy, and to the responsibilities these relationships imposed on the head of a house. What makes his book special in the genre is that embedded in the advice about when to prune the vines and how best to churn butter are such other matters as how to manage inheritance, how to discipline servants, and how to meet welfare obligations—and all perceived in the context of a larger system that was not only the tribute-taking state as such. This greater governing concept was that of custodianship, of not owning one's house but simply of managing it as part of God's "Oeconomia" that has been entrusted to one's care. It is easy to see how such prescriptions could align themselves with the existing practices of lien administration and peasant tenure. The responsibilities of the housefathers included not only informing themselves about the resources at their disposal and learning how to balance the accounts among these resources but also bringing their production processes into harmony with the needs and character of the dynastic overlords, of the larger society's and the state's needs for security (1715:10). What is not so easy to see is how this *oikos* worked for itself and with what results. In order to accomplish the subordination of the good economy of their house to the good economy of the state, Hohberg argued that housefathers were justified in subordinating the needs of their entire housecommunity, and especially of their children, laborers, and servants, to the needs of the head of the house. To this end he encouraged them to direct and supervise (by means of interrogation, spying, and physical punishments if necessary) the moral character of the servant population; this included punishing them "when necessary and just," by the withholding of wages (1715:234–235). Hohberg was reinventing the *oikos* to discipline it for the head's service career in the state.

The house that was managed best was one where work, justice, and love were properly distributed. In his preface, Hohberg invokes the classical history of the *oikos* and imagines Plutarch at dinner with the seven Greek sages to ask them what constituted a well-managed house. Of particular interest for us is the answer he puts in the mouth of Pittacus of Lesbos: it was a place where nothing necessary was lacking and where nothing unnecessary or superfluous was desired. This places the effectiveness of social practice not only on a minimal production of goods but also on the management of desire. It is on the basis of this particular rationale that Hohberg brings together the classic formulation of the good house economy with the courtly psychology of self-discipline. The economy of the *oikos* was reimagined in terms of a psychology of needs that could now be portrayed as a matter of discernment and of management and as measurable against and adjustable to the changing necessities of state. The classical notion of *oikos*, positively recalled and posited as a relevant model for both peasant and aristocratic household management, now contained concealed innovations with a logic of their own, one not entirely derived from their ostensibly kin-ordered modal character.

In the broader context of Hörnigk's more macroeconomic cameralism, Hohberg's management of needs and desires in the house reappears to take on a more ominous quality. What particularly distinguished Hörnigk's (and later, to some extent, Justi's) cameralism from West European mercantilism was that it sought to establish a favorable balance of trade not by an increase in combined exports and reexports but strictly by a curtailment of imports. If all branches of the domestic economy were developed for self-sufficiency, Hörnigk argued, then Austria's dominance in foreign affairs was assured—if "only it will" (cf. Pribram 1983:92). The operative word in Hörnigk's title was, of course, Austria's "will," which he perceived as statewide compulsions that had to be exercised to achieve the necessary austerity. Hörnigk was aware that for a primarily agricultural state to supply its own needs in all things would impose hardships but also that these hardships would be an occasion to strengthen the hands of all authorities in the state so that they could begin to exert the kinds of discipline that were necessary not only to bring the lower classes fully into the state's economy as the instruments of state policies but also to raise their moral quality. He theorized that the hardships of the new economic course were to be displaced downward for greater social integration (discipline) and the ultimate benefit of the whole. The image Hörnigk used to describe the new state was this: "One has to imagine the state as a rich man who keeps his wealth in many pockets. If he takes some out of one and puts them in another he doesn't become poorer. . . . He is master of both" (1964:141, cf. 177). Mastery and not growth was the key to this cameralism that aimed at deliberately creating a zero-sum economy in which certain social groups were singled out to bear the costs of disinvestment in the mercantile sectors (1964:132) while others in the agricultural and manufacturing sectors were to carry the costs of diminishing expectations and increased work discipline.

Where Hohberg's vision of the good economy of the peasant house sought in some ways to stay close to classical conceptions of *oikos*, Hörnigk's reworking of the place of the household economy in the whole economy altered the imagined classical idyll subtly and significantly. He built on what was already in the classical Greek perception of the moral economy of the house a significant flaw. The term *oikos* designated the state's organization of family units consisting of people who ate together, and it postulated that all, servants included, had to be fed. When this was not possible, when the state's population exceeded what the *oikoi* could feed, the state designated the hierarchy of those who would have to be abandoned and stricken off the rolls (Lacey 1968:73; cf. Lloyd-Jones 1983:177–183; Humphreys 1983). To this awkward moment the Austrian cameralists added new institutional and psychological twists. To them these negative aspects of a state economy based on house administration were not merely invoked in times of emergency and shortage but became a permanent necessity in a state that deliberately chose a path of curtailed imports, self-sufficiency, shortage, and domestic disinvestments. Moreover, also unlike the Greek model, responsibility for the hardships suffered in this system would not be assumed by the state; such measures were to be distributed in the private sector by heads of houses. While the classical *oikos* had theoretically required a (concealed) designation of victims for moments of failure, Austrian cameralism's updated version required it for the state's ongoing success. The Austrian *oikos* simultaneously, traumatically, had to produce and to deny that it produced victims.

Justi's more advanced cameralism, developed a half-century later, sought to transcend the purely system-rational perspective of the earlier theoreticians but did not abandon their notions of social psychology and of the moral economy of the house; if anything, he gave to the latter transcendent legitimation by welding to them the universalism of Leibnizian metaphysics. While it may be argued that Leibniz's concept of the ego in a sense prefigured Hegelian dialectics (Röd 1974:23–24), there can be no question that his thought as a whole was antidialectical. In support of the Ptolemaic view of the world, Leibniz had developed a metaphysics of relativity in which bodies were neither at rest nor in motion, all depending on the infinite possibilities of points of view. The philosophical ground for this early attempt at formulating a theory of cognitive relativity was his synthesis of certain of the classic and neoclassic philosophers in which there was no negative, only more or less of the positive. Emptiness was merely minimal fullness. In this formulation there were no costs, only more or fewer benefits, and on the basis of such a theory of the universal distribution of the positive, Leibniz's cameralist disciple Justi could kill off, in his theoretical social economy, any vestiges of attempts at an economic-rational accounting for costs against benefits.

Hörnigk had had a sense of cost-benefit analysis for at least specific details of the economy—holding Louis XIV's costs of maintaining streetlights in Paris against savings in crime or calculating the relative costs and benefits to the state of maintaining a beggar and a soldier (1964:126–127, 199–201). For Justi such costs as existed were seen only on what we would call the supply side of the economy; that is, he saw deficits and debts as temporary necessary costs that would be erased by future profit. When he focused on the still-central household economy, he was capable of the pettiest calculations in this regard, noting for example that the servant population's tendency to steal and cheat with regard to their weekly food rations (which he carefully, pathetically, spelled out) was a matter of great cost to householders, one that required increased strictness and controls (1758:I, 546–547). For Justi too it was a zero-sum economy, and anyone who was in the system at all was benefiting from it; the only loss anyone could incur was to be required to accept a smaller share—but if this led to the salvation or improvement of the system as a whole, then even this smaller share was a long-term benefit. It was in this denial of costs and in complicated calculations for a "just" distribution of often infinitely minute and interrelated benefits that Justi grounded both the moral and "scientific" claims for his policy science.

The social science capable of calculating the interrelations and welfare of the whole that Justi envisioned was to be a matter of precisely mathematical aggregate accounting. We must not forget here that he was working in a system where the greatest part of such accounting was concealed in the inner unaccounted-for workings of household enterprises. The input-output calculations of a Quesnay, pointing at the neoclassical econometrics of Pareto, Walras, and Leontief, were not only impossible in but above all not significant to Justi's vision of just distribution. He placed the state's efficient collection of tribute (*Abgaben*) above everything subjects must bear; and he postulated special rewards for the subject who could best fulfill what was demanded of him by the state "according to the main characteristics of his public person" (1758: I, 108, 377–380; II, 22–24, 35–38, 53, 312). Justi's police science was not economic-quantitative but social-psychological: it was the science of testing and placing individuals according to their capacities to exercise the "will" and to subordinate and adjust their private lives to the demands of the state. Obtaining a just measure of material rewards in the system was the by-product of prior measurements of one's rank which theoretically indicated one's capacity for such self-management. In Justi's conceptualization, servants were incapable of such selflessness, peasant and urban householders had the opportunity to learn it to varying degrees, and the higher ranks, administering and serving the state, naturally embodied it. His was an infinitely complicated system of psychologically difficult commanding and obeying in which everyone had to participate both by acting and being acted upon. For example, Justi saw as the duty of the housefathers the encouragement of all talents of all the children in the house; the psychologically difficult obverse, however, was that the housefather also had to choose the talents that best placed the house in the service of the state and, in corollary acts, actively suppress all others. The ability to suppress and contain the psychological agony of such "choices" became the measure of a person's worth.

Real costs were beginning to accumulate in this system, visibly and unavoidably, right about the time Hohberg and Hörnigk published their treatises. By the mid-eighteenth century, when Justi flourished, the Austrian state faced its first serious social crisis since the early seventeenth century. Committed to a social science concerned with allocating deliberately limited benefits and incapable of calculating costs as these accumulated in the "good economy" of the house, the Austrian policymakers of the later eighteenth century still failed to alter their thinking or their system-building in any significant way. The actual experience of costs continued to be displaced into realms outside the accepted calculation of justice—that is, into the family and into the psyche. The Austrian reinvention of the *oikos* and of its tough, "erased" logic about inclusion and expulsion, made the virtue by which one was measured and rewarded—unchanged since the emergence of the system out of the wars of Reformation and Counter-Reformation—the extent to which one could absorb and endure privately the publicly inadmissible contradictions and costs that allowed the system to work (Rebel 1983:264–269; cf. Dreitzel 1968).

## THE AUSTRIAN POLICE STATE: MASTERING IRRECONCILABLES WITH DISCIPLINE

The early sixteenth century's economic and social revolution, arising from the rural population's assumption of the partibility and free disposability of their holdings and their greater control over their communities, was halted in the seventeenth century by the violently enforced reorganization of royal and state finances and was not resumed until the second half of the nineteenth century. The so-called "unburdening of the land" that followed the turmoil of 1848 led finally, by 1868, to the state's granting of permission to the peasants to break up their holdings for inheritance and sale. The intervening three hundred years had, however, altered the circumstances of peasant liberation to the point that were one to say that the "emancipation" after 1848 was too late, one would miss the point entirely. Put most simply, the long interval had seen the unchanging, grinding operations of a tribute-producing social machine, one of whose necessary by-products was a steadily growing, downwardly mobile class of dispossessed children and of their children's children. The reimagined *oikos* had denied their historical existence (and experience) and by the time nineteenth-century peasant "emancipation" scrapped the old machine for a newer model, the social system of Austria had reached the point at which it could no longer cope with its dispossessed.

When we compare the increase in the means for employment and subsistence in Austria between the sixteenth and eighteenth centuries with the changes in the population during the same period, it is immediately noticeable that very little changed in the former to adjust to a steady growth in the latter. Using information from the province of Upper Austria we can point, for example, to the differences between the taxable hearth (i.e., house) censuses of 1526/27 and 1750 and note about a 30 percent growth in the number of new houses, going from 39,940 to 57,294 (Grüll 1957:317). This is a rough measure and does not address the question of improvements in census authority and practice (cf. Hoffmann 1952:243). Knowledge about population growth in this same period is also uncertain not only because the necessary aggregate work in Austrian historical demographics remains to be done but also because the detailed and interpretive work on specific parishes and villages that has been done by Michael Mitterauer and his colleagues at the University of Vienna's Institut für Wirtschafts und Sozialgeschichte shows a complicated regional and social distribution of demographic differences (cf. Mitterauer 1982). Nevertheless, on the basis of an estimated Upper Austrian population of 300,000 in 1600 we can note a 40 percent increase to the approximately 420,000 souls counted by Maria Theresa's censuses between 1754 and 1776 (Hoffmann 1952:243, 260). The rate of population growth was probably considerably greater than the official censuses show when we consider that it is unlikely that the house-based population figures for the eighteenth century included the beggars who lived in the interstices of this society. Thus, for example, Charles VI's special investigating commission of 1727 into the "beggar question" had turned up almost 26,000 destitute and homeless persons in Upper Austria alone—5,742 men, 11,117 women, 7,247 children, and 1,238 cashiered veterans (Hoffmann 1952:248)—and if we add only this number to the later-eighteenth-century census figure, we get a population growth of about 48 percent.

If we consider that the Austrian house in this period was more than a dwelling but was also the primary unit of production, employment, and welfare, then from the divergence between the increases in population and in houses we get a crude sense of some interplay between cameralist prescriptions for curtailed growth and what was happening. The authorities' restrictions on house construcion and on the expansion of cottage-based industries not only followed the spirit of Hörnigk's recommendations for a limited, deliberately closed system but also signified an increasing downward displacement of the social and psychological pressures accumulating in the system. The number of people declared sufficiently competent to run a house was proportionately on the decrease. This was a double-bound system both in theory and in social fact: on the one hand the state pursued population growth as the highest of all social goods, while on the other hand it not only failed to assist in the expansion of places of employment but actively curtailed the foreign exchanges and trading that would have expanded the home-based forms of mercantile and industrial investment and would have created more opportunities for employment in the limited number of houses as well as a potential increase in tribute income. It is in this context that we have to understand the paradoxes the royal and estates' administrations faced when they had to deal on the one hand with complaints concerning apparent labor shortages and on the other with a surplus population of beggars making the public thoroughfares insecure (Hoffmann 1952:93–94, 246–249). There is some reason to suspect that the physical deprivations and psychological pressures of working and living in the Austrian peasant house were so bad for the lowest class of dispossessed children and laborers that these often preferred begging to working (Hoffmann 1952:246; Rebel 1983:143–145). There is also a sense that many seasonally unemployed, or those unemployed because of short-term secular swings in the market, were also among this socially borderline and growing mass of homeless beggars (Hoffmann 1952:246). At the same time the strategies for self-improvement open to the heads of peasant houses were severely limited even for the majority of those whose house economies were diversified and included some limited industrial production (Rebel 1983:107–113, 204–205). Their labor and employment calculations, including calculations about the relative costs and productivities of child and adult labor, were on such a marginal scale that they had to make constant decisions about the number and nature of the people employed in and living from their enterprises, decisions about whom to keep and whom to let go—and about how to reward and maintain those who remained (Berkner 1972; Rebel 1983). In a society where, during the course of the seventeenth and eighteenth centuries, there was a sizable population increase with a much smaller increase in the means of production, and where strong evidence suggests that there was a conjuncturally determined tendency for heads of houses to fail in managing their tenures adequately (Rebel 1983:241), we cannot be surprised to find the paradox of a highly uncertain labor market and of cyclically and geographically distributed labor shortages borne on a steadily swelling current of personally (historically) experienced social catastrophe taking the forms of chronic unemployment and begging.

The measures taken by the state authorities reflect the cameralist vision of and prescriptions for the problem. The cameralists saw population growth primarily in terms of feeding the population and asserted that no problem would ever exist on that score (Justi 1758:I, 160–162). By concentrating on the relationship between population and food they evaded the social-psychological aspect of population growth that remains the major problem of the owners of "capital" to this day—namely, offering people something worthwhile to do. It is significant that the cameralists' reaction to unemployment, vagrancy, and begging was not to consider these problems in terms of the number of people involved; paradoxically, their answers to these questions reveal the predominantly social-psychological cast of their thought. One has only to listen to the language. Thus Justi: "All young strong beggars . . . must be immediately arrested and incarcerated in workhouses where they are to be exhorted (*anhalten*) to work. The old, infirm, and poor, in contrast, are to be cared for in hospitals and poor houses. . . . If the strong beggars and vagrants know they will be incarcerated and made to work, then they will either leave altogether [!] or they will choose work and feed themselves honestly: because freedom is precious to everyone." This is a psychology that holds that only *in extremis* will people work at the jobs that are available and that the means to make them take these jobs is to put them into an extreme situation. He concludes: "They have to be released from the workhouse when one senses diligence and honesty in them and when they can find someone who will sponsor them and vouch for their resolve not to return to begging" (Justi 1758:I, 323–324). It was, in other words, a policy for building workhouses and state-run factories which were designed not for general economic relief but to serve as places of temporary employment in a forced-labor regime designed to reintegrate laborers into the household economy of housefathers who volunteered to take on the responsibility for the psychological resolve to participate socially of the persons thus assigned to them.

By the 1750s the earlier draconian measures of the seventeenth and the early eighteenth centuries (Hoffmann 1952:248–249), by which the single were forbidden to marry or have offspring, illegitimate children were forcibly legitimated and assigned to families, forced-labor measures were carried through, and so on, had already failed and may be behind the hysterical language about the "extermination" (*Ausrottung*) of beggars that we find both in Justi's writings and in Maria Theresa's decrees (Hoffmann 1952:499; Justi 1758:I, 324). During the later eighteenth century, under Josef II, there was some response to the obvious contradictions in this system, and attempts were made to expand the opportunities for employment, to allow the number of small houses and cottages to increase, and to expand investment in the industrial sector; but these measures proved insufficient to alter the divergent paths of rapid population growth and the deliberately much slower increase in opportunities for employment (Hoffmann 1952:499; Mitterauer, n.d.). The Austrian state continued to be trapped by its contradictions that forced it to continue to put its faith in the psychological notion that the individuals who acceded to the headship of a house or other office in the state did so by demonstrating their capacity to absorb and neutralize the growing conflicts within and among the domestic social relations, enterprises, and labor accounts of the *oikoi* in their care. Those who were dispossessed, expelled, and destitute and therefore defined as congenitally incapable of any such self-discipline were automatically, "traditionally," branded as unfit to participate and were marked for life as victims, as coerced and "naturally" expendable objects for the police apparatus. Their experience remains to be recognized historically.

The historical denouement of a system that had consciously and necessarily *avoided* economic growth and had displaced its costs downward for over three centuries, without ever acknowledging theoretically or practically that there even were costs, was on display in *fin de siècle* Vienna, a city that attracted most of Austria's displaced, dispossessed, and unemployed rural population. While there are abundant elegant and insightful works on this Viennese preview of "the last days of mankind" as perceived by such bourgeois critics as Kraus, Schnitzler, Freud, and others (Janik and Toulmin 1977; Schorske 1980), these only tell us about bourgeois experience, which is significant and interesting but finally bears only indirectly on the experience of the dispossessed. William A. Jenks (1976) has briefly described that other side of early-twentieth-century Vienna with a sharp eye for detail. He shows us a city where workhouses, charitable shelters, flophouses, "warming rooms," public parks, soup kitchens, hospitals, and asylums were barely able to cope with the growing flood of people that continued to pour from the country into the city, increasing even during the "upswing" years of the early twentieth century. It is here that we find details that recall and stand as the final acts arising from the hiatus between cameralist texts and social-formational contexts, between historical experience and transferential denial in ancien-régime Austria. Rules about floor-space allocation per "tenant" of a public flophouse or the precisely measured and pitiful food rations all replicate the kinds of details one finds in cameralist writings, most notably in the "universal cameralism" of Justi, about the just allocation of economic and social goods. Most revealing are the pretensions of order and normalcy to be found even in the most debased and pathogenic circumstances. Furnishing perhaps the most telling example were those who organized accommodations for the down-and-out in the city's sewers, the final *oikoi* in this tradition. They styled themselves as "housemasters" (Jenks 1976:36), denying their social position with a psychological trick of language one could only find in a state where access to and control of a house had long been the coveted but, in any case, treacherous and illusory avenue toward social membership and power. Need one add that it is here that we finally find, drifting through, learning to speak the language and absorbing the bureaucratized "traditions" of the Viennese transients' daily grind of scavenging, enforced idleness, bargaining for minimum shelter and delousing, the young Adolf Hitler, a failed heir who had squandered most of his and the rest of his family's inheritance and for whose social imagination the still "disciplined" behavioral sink of *fin de siècle* Vienna provided the central institutional forms and rationales for what he would later identify, in yet another myth of lost unity, as the Final Solution? His historical experience works well in a provisional master narrative where an "original" trauma of dispossession, of exclusion from the "whole house" and of "expulsion from shelteredness" (Adorno), both reappears and disappears in compulsively transferential acts of revenge and annihilation whose historical recycling through dispossessing texts and social formations remains, to this day, far from broken.

## NOTE

1. Here we can take further the notion of phenomenology as a "bourgeois" philosophy (cf. Thomas 1987). The philosopher-capitalist simultaneously appropriates and denies the fictionalizing intellectual labor of others and claims the "higher" and authentically creative acts of reduction for himself.

# THREE

# Re-creating Peasant Economy in Southern Peru*

*Michael Painter*

## INTRODUCTION: RECIPROCITY AND COMMUNITY IN SOUTHERN PERU

The social relations of peasant production have frequently been characterized in terms of reciprocity, within a context of responsibility to the
community.[1] Aymara peasants on the north shore of Lake Titicaca, for example, generally recognize five types of nominally reciprocal obligations.
These include *ayni, p''ayna, mink'a, uraqipur turkasiña, wak''i*. The vitality of
these exchange relations and the continual references by peasants regarding
the need to maintain community solidarity invite an interpretation that exchanges such as those described here compose part of a "traditional" system,
which stands in opposition to capitalism. However, the organization of production in the region has undergone repeated and fundamental changes, so
that to speak of anything as being "traditional" without placing that tradition in a specific historical context is a serious misrepresentation. Many of
the terms employed do have their origins in colonial and pre-Hispanic institutions. Ideologically this plays an important role in justifying the relations described. However, the social, economic, and political contexts in
which the exchange relations presently occur are so transformed that the
linkage to this distant past is largely linguistic.

*Ayni* is the balanced exchange of labor or goods between nuclear family
units. Its most important role is in the exchange of labor power during
periods of peak agricultural activity, and it is the most frequently used
mechanism for assembling work parties for this task. Although the labor

*The author thanks Henry Bernstein, Jane Collins, Jay O'Brien, and William Roseberry for
reading and commenting upon previous drafts of this manuscript. Responsibility for errors of
fact or interpretation, however, is that of the author.

exchanges theoretically balance over time, so that all families participating in the web of *ayni* relationships give and receive the same amount of labor, inequalities in land distribution are such that families with more land consistently receive more days of labor from their relatives and neighbors than they give. When discussed in the abstract, the ideology of balance in *ayni* exchanges tends to be emphasized by peasants participating in the exchanges, although they do recognize this to reflect an ideal more closely than it does actual behavior. However, willingness to participate in *ayni* exchanges is regarded as an important indicator of who is *jaqi*, that is, people or humans, within the social hierarchy defined by the rural, Aymara-speaking population. As a result wealthy merchants of rural origin who find it in their interest to maintain their ties to the countryside often engage in token or symbolic *ayni* exchanges as a sign of solidarity with the people of their home community.

*Mink'a* refers to the exchange of labor power for cash as part of a continuing exchange of goods and services. The actual payment varies from case to case, but is normally lower than the prevailing daily wage rate. This is because, in addition to the cash, the party providing the labor power also earns the right to call upon the person for whom work is being performed for services in the future. The use of *mink'a* is most commonly associated with town-dwelling families who are the remnants of the former elite classes and professionals such as schoolteachers. The expression of a preference for *mink'a* exchange by a rural family seeking to secure labor services is often regarded as a sign of breaking solidarity with one's fellows, although between social equals a person whose labor is being sought has the right to indicate a preference for a *mink'a* or *ayni* exchange.

*Uraqipur turkasiña* literally means "to exchange land," and, indeed, it is an exchange of land for land. Theoretically members of two families might decide to exchange land for any one of a number of reasons, such as the desire to gain access to a new production zone and expand the diversity of crops that one can cultivate. In practice, however, land exchanges acquire their greatest significance in the current context as a response to the labor scarcity for agricultural activities arising from the growing dependence on income earned off the farm. In all of the cases of land exchanges observed or discussed in the course of fieldwork, the motivation for exchange was to give up access to a distant field and acquire one close to home in order to reduce the labor requirements of agriculture. Exchange of lands offers important advantages for some rural dwellers over actually buying and selling land. The major one is that it frees individuals from using scarce cash resources to conduct land transactions. It also facilitates land transactions involving members of officially recognized peasant communities, because, since recognized communities are by definition corporate landholding units, land transactions by individuals are illegal.

*Wak''i* is an exchange of labor for land-use rights. It normally involves what are locally defined as social equals, although its existence as a category of exchange appears to assume inequality in land distribution. In *wak"i* exchanges, one party provides the land and the other provides the labor to cultivate it. Inputs such as seed and fertilizer are provided according to mutual agreement. Theoretically, the harvest is divided equally between the landowner and the worker. However, this is in practice shaped by who provides the bulk of the inputs and by the larger context of exchange relations in which the two parties are involved with each other. *Wak"i* may be used in association with land exchange, so that the respective parties are able to maintain access to products from the area in which they gave up land.

*P"ayna* is the mechanism whereby community members contribute labor to activities supposed to be for the common good, such as the construction or repair of infrastructural facilities. Sometimes families have the choice of actually working on an activity or making a financial contribution. Consistently opting to pay cash rather than work may be regarded as indicating a lack of solidarity with one's neighbors by some. However, the labor demands imposed by the need to work off-farm mean that large number of families may opt for this rather than taking someone away from a cash-earning activity. Community leaders frequently claimed that it was becoming harder to assemble sufficient numbers of people to carry out important tasks such as road maintenance or the cleaning and repair of irrigation ditches, and attributed this to the growing importance of work off the farm.

The prevalence of exchange relations in the current context in no way signifies production relations that are outside of capitalism or standing in some sort of resistance to it. Rather, they are a response to the widespread rural poverty that is the product of a particular form of capitalist expansion, which seek to minimize the cash expenditure required to maintain an agricultural production regimen that subsidizes participation in other activities. The vitality of community and reciprocity as institutions may be the most telling indicators of the region's subjugation as reservoir of part-time and reserve labor power for the capitalist economy. Community and reciprocity have less to do with southern Peru's pre-Hispanic and colonial past than they do with the interaction of international capitalist expansion and national agricultural policies over the last forty years.

## RE-CREATING PEASANT ECONOMY

*Changing Social Relations in the Colonial and Early Republican Periods*
The incorporation of the Andean region into the colonial dominions of the emergent state of Spain signified incorporation as well into an expanding global economic system. Over time, the demands that the system would make upon the Andean people, and their responses to it, would radically and repeatedly transform social relations of production in different parts of the region. A detailed recounting of what this meant for southern Peru is beyond

the scope of the present work. It is sufficient to recall a few of the major forces that have shaped and reshaped productive relations in southern Peru in order to underline the importance of specificity with respect to time and place when attempting to link conditions observed in the present with the Andean past.

The social transformation resulting from the incorporation of the former Andean states into the Spanish dominions was intensified by a number of factors. Some of these were general to the Andean region as a whole, while others were more specific to what was to become southern Peru and Bolivia. Among the general factors was the population decline resulting from the diseases introduced by the Europeans (Newsome 1985). The southern Peruvian highlands were not depopulated to the extent of some of the coastal valley areas, where population declines on the order of 90 percent were reported. Nonetheless, depopulation was substantial and its effects on social organization were profound. Sánchez Albornoz (1978:34), for example, estimates a population drop on the altiplano of approximately 60 percent between the eve of the Spanish conquest and 1693. The population decline increased the social disorganization caused by the sudden decapitation of the Inca state, wiping out large numbers of local and regional authorities upon whom political and administrative responsibility might have otherwise fallen, and intensifying the shift of responsibility for the maintenance of vertically defined trade relations from the state to communities and kin groups.

Disease also exacerbated the impacts of Spanish labor demands, forcing the conquerors to draw upon ever-widening areas to satisfy their needs. In the Lake Titicaca area, these needs centered around the forced recruitment of labor for silver mining at Potosí. Discovered in 1545, the yields from Potosí increased steadily for several decades, peaking in the period 1590–1599 (*Klein 1982:298*). During this period, forced recruitment for mine labor drained off large numbers of people from the area around Lake Titicaca. Entire families would move to the mine when they were called upon to work, and they would take with them their livestock and stored foodstuffs, as workers were responsible for their own maintenance during the period of service (Toledo 1975:355–356).

The forced labor contributed to a general social reorganization in several ways. First, because people could be exempted from tribute obligations by establishing residence outside of their home provinces and becoming officially classified as *forasteros*, many people took advantage of the land that became available as a result of the population die-off and moved to other areas. Sánchez Albornoz (1978:60) reports that, in 1684, nearly half of the population of the sixteen provinces subject to recruitment to work in Potosí had achieved *forastero* status. Church death records from the parish of San Pedro de Moho, on the north side of Lake Titicaca, show that fully one third of the deaths registered during an epidemic in 1720 were of people classified as *forasteros*.

In addition, labor tribute to the Crown contributed to a continuing competition involving the state and local and regional authorities for the labor power of the peasantry. For example, in 1573, several *kuraka* from the northern side of Lake Titicaca met with representatives of the Crown and persuaded them to permit the populations in their jurisdiction to pay their tribute obligations to the state in foodstuffs and gold from the relatively nearby valleys of Carabaya, rather than forcing them to continue paying labor tribute at Potosí (Relaciones Geográficas de Indias 1965:68–71). This would allow the peasants to combine production for their own consumption with production of tribute for the Crown, and, not incidentally, make them more available for rendering services to the local lords. In order to limit the authority of local lords to impose tribute obligations on populations in their jurisdictions that might conflict with the requirements of the state, and forestall the establishment of a New World nobility capable of challenging the Crown, the viceregal authorities commuted miscellaneous and variable in-kind tribute payments into fixed amounts of cash and goods that were a matter of public knowledge. They were sufficiently successful that by the end of the sixteenth century the institution of *encomienda* had ceased to expand, and by the end of the seventeenth century it had disappeared altogether (Parry 1963:231). The direct control over tribute-paying peasants was replaced by the control of land as the basis of wealth for rural elites.

The state also sought to impose its authority through important changes in the land-tenure system. In 1571, the reforms of Viceroy Toledo required the peasantry to congregate in villages established by the Spanish. In the altiplano, these were founded at regular intervals around Lake Titicaca, and most of the current district capitals date from this period. Partly in response to the population decline due to disease, the congregation of the peasantry in towns sought to make it easier for the central government to keep track of the tribute in labor and goods it was supposed to receive, and to make it more difficult for local elites to withhold tribute from the Crown by underrepresenting the subject population.[2]

In spite of such efforts, the imposition of state authority in areas such as the collection of tribute payments was a continuing problem. Between 1683 and 1688, for example, the Crown conducted a census of the entire Viceroyalty, a particular goal of which was to gather information necessary to reorganize the labor tribute for the Potosí Mines. Unenthusiastic implementation of the census by local officials prevented the collection of much of the information the Crown had hoped to obtain on topics such as migration patterns and population composition. When tributary reforms were subsequently attempted, the Crown found itself forced to abandon them in order to avoid rebellion (Cole 1984).

One of the ways in which the Crown attempted to limit the powers of local elites was through the recognition of the *ayllu* as a legal entity with inalienable rights to land, in the early decades of the eighteenth century.[3] Prior to the conquest, the *ayllu* had been extended kin groups with no direct relationship to an area of land, although *ayllu* membership did largely determine an individual's access to land. With the social disorganization following the conquest, the *ayllu* became associated with areas of land, an association that was formalized in the early eighteenth century. This placed a limit on the ability of local elites to expand their landholdings as a means of tying the peasantry to them; and it created an institutional framework in which much of the responsibility for the distribution of tribute obligations, the assigning of quotas for payment of taxes, and the allocation of financial responsibility for religious festivals was assumed by the peasantry itself.

Struggle between the central government and regional elites over control of the peasantry as a basis for political power and the accumulation of wealth remained an important theme after Peru became independent, in 1821. Following the liberal reforms of Bolivar, the legal basis of the inalienability of *ayllu* lands changed several times, as did the legal powers of local elites to demand tribute in labor and goods. While the changes in the law did not, apparently, make much difference in the ways in which peasants and regional elites interacted, they did reflect the struggle between different factions of the dominant classes for control of the state machinery.

Capitalist expansion into new areas of the regional economy changed relations between the elites of southern Peru and the peasantry during the nineteenth century. The vehicles for this expansion were the growth of the wool export economy, which intensified competition between landlords and peasants over grazing lands and animals in herding areas, and the urban growth resulting in part from the economic expansion associated with the wool industry, and in larger measure from the improved commercial linkages associated with the construction of the Southern Peruvian Railway, which increased the demand for food and intensified competition over agricultural land.[4]

This struggle came to a violent head in 1867, when Juan Bustamante, himself a member of the regional elite, led a rebellion against regional authorities over the severity of their tribute demands. Although Bustamante received widespread support from peasants around Lake Titicaca, the rebellion was quickly and bloodily repressed by the subprefect of Azángaro, Andrés Recharte, who, without authorization from Lima, requested and received military assistance from Bolivian dictator Mariano Melgarejo, in the form of five hundred infantry, three hundred horses, and two artillery pieces. The rebellion and the manner of its repression was a clear indicator of the weakness of the state in relation to regional elites (Anonymous 1876; Vásquez 1976).

### The Aborted Transformation to Capitalist Farming

At the turn of the century, one would have noted the first signs of the economic growth that was to shape the course of change in southern Peru in the coming decades. The railroad linking the city of Puno to the coastal port of Mollendo via Arequipa had been completed twenty-six years previously, in 1876, opening the area up to an unprecedented flow of imported manufactured goods. With the joining of the Puno rail terminus with that of Bolivia, in Guaqui, by a steamship connection across Lake Titicaca, the departmental capital had become an important collection point for agricultural exports from the Peruvian and Bolivian areas of the Lake Titicaca basin. The rail connection linking Puno and Juliaca to the major bulking center for the wool export industry, Sicuani, had been completed just three years before.

The changes in the transport network made themselves felt in both the urban and rural areas of the region. Puno's position as the departmental capital was enhanced by rapid population growth. In 1876, Puno's population was 2,729 people, only 166 more than the second city in the department at that time, Ayaviri. By the turn of the century, Puno was growing steadily, so that by 1940, with a population of 13,786, it was over twice as large as the new second city of the department, Juliaca. Juliaca, in 1876, had not even ranked among the dozen largest towns of the department, with a population of 516. However, it contained over 3,000 people by 1919, and by 1940 it had supplanted Ayaviri as the second-largest town in the department, with 6,034 inhabitants.

In the rural areas of the department, competition for grazing land between peasant communities and large estates intensified (Orlove 1978). This was manifested in part in the growth in the number of estates in the altiplano from 696, in 1876, to 3,375, in 1915 (Appleby 1978:43). In spite of this expansion, independent peasant communities remained strong in Puno, both as wool producers and in agricultural areas. The combination of generally increasing wool prices and urban demand for food raised incomes in the countryside, allowing the rural population to begin to constitute a market for a growing range of manufactured goods. This provided the basis for a strong regional commercial activity, with the lacustrine ports serving as important centers. Items such as imported Scotch whisky were reported to be in more plentiful supply in towns around Lake Titicaca than in many of the major cities.

The collapse of international wool prices following World War I accelerated processes of economic differentiation and intensified land conflicts in herding areas. Estates sought to counter falling prices by increasing production so that gross revenues might remain relatively stable, even as per-unit earnings dropped. They expelled resident peasants, who had their own herds of animals and grazing rights on the estates, and attempted to expand onto the lands of peasant communities (Orlove 1977). The displacement of estate peasants and the search for ways to make up for revenue shortfalls by peasants in independent communities accelerated the process of urbanization that was already taking place. As rural dwellers moved to the towns in search of employment, the already growing urban demand for food in-

creased, initiating fundamental changes in the social relations surrounding
the marketing of agriculural products and intensifying competition in the
countryside for access to the best agricultural land (Appleby 1980:43–44).

Renewed efforts to displace peasants in the herding areas and heightened
competition over land in agricultural areas combined with changes at the
level of peasant production itself, and led to violence in many parts of the
region by the 1920s. By 1923, the peasantry of the Lake Titicaca Basin had
established linkages with a number of institutions and interest groups outside
the region who were sympathetic to their situation and willing to be supportive to some extent of their struggle against the regional elites. One of the
institutions that built strong ties to the peasantry was the Seventh-Day
Adventist church, which had undertaken missionary activity in the region
around 1912. The Adventists combined preaching the gospel with heavy
emphasis on the value of education and the importance of economic self-
improvement. As a result, they were violently repressed by the regional
elites and warmly welcomed by the peasantry.[5]

The peasants of the Lake Titicaca Basin also established ties with the
Tawantinsuyo Society, a Lima-based organization of intellectuals, students,
and political activists. Influenced by the writings of Castro Pozo, Haya de la
Torre, and Mariátegui, the organization was dedicated to improving the
material conditions of Peru's Native American population, as part of an overall strategy to organize the peasantry and forge an alliance between it and
organized labor as a basis for political action (see Chevalier 1970; Hazen
1974).

The national government also appeared to favor the interests of the
peasants over those of the regional elites. At the turn of the century, the state
was in the hands of the plantation elite of the northern coast, which through
the Civilista political party controlled the government in what was known as
the República Aristocrática. With their interests tied to a healthy export
economy, the north coast planters sought to cement ties with the markets for sugar in industrialized countries by developing Peru as a market
for the manufactured goods these developed countries had to sell. The
high labor demands of sugarcane production also predisposed the coastal
planters to have an interest in increasing peasants' freedom to move about
the country and sell their labor power on their own behalf, rather than
having to work through members of the highland elite acting as brokers.

The president of Peru during much of this period was Augusto Leguía,
who was the first national leader to establish the dominance of the state over
regional elites in many areas of the highlands.[6] As part of this effort, he would
frequently ally the national government with interests attempting to undermine the authority of regional oligarchs in a position to oppose him (e.g.,
Taylor n.d.). As a result, peasant communities frequently sent delegations to
Lima while Leguía was in office. One such delegation was from Huancané

province. They journeyed to Lima to protest the abuses peasants suffered at the hands of regional elites as they tried to establish schools in order to learn Spanish and other skills (Gallegos n.d.).

The uprisings of peasants in the early 1920s around issues related to access to schools and markets were repressed almost as quickly as they began by the regional elites with the assistance of the Peruvian army. While President Leguía was willing to support the peasantry in undermining the authority of the elites with respect to the national government, he was not willing to let peasants assume power in their own right.[7] Afterward, the elites conducted a series of violent reprisals against communities and individuals who had participated in the uprising.

The decades that followed were to witness frequent violence between regional elites and peasants. Changes in the position of southern Peru in the international economy were to continue to threaten the dominance of the elites, and provide opportunities for some peasants to move into new areas of economic activity providing the basis for a new entrepreneurial class. One important factor was continuing instability in international wool prices in the wake of their post–World War I collapse. In an effort to protect profits, the wool export houses entered directly into wool production. They bought out a number of estate owners unable or unwilling to continue producing in the newly unfavorable situation, and those estates that were not sold suffered, as this action exacerbated their difficulties in finding a market for their wool (Appleby 1978:50–51).

Changes in the regional transportation network also unsettled regional social relations, as truck transport began to replace steamships around Lake Titicaca, and to compete with the railroad for passengers along some sections of its route. By the early 1940s, regularly scheduled steamship service to most of the ports on Lake Titicaca had ceased, with only the link between Puno and the Bolivian rail terminus of Guaqui remaining. While the possibilities for investment in the railroad and steamship transport had been limited, it was relatively easy to acquire a truck and compete for passengers and cargo, and, in fact, large numbers of people who were not members of the regional elite did so. In addition to broadening participation in transport and marketing, the expansion of truck transport caused some towns strategically located along roads to grow, while some of the lacustrine ports suffered from economic decline.

Instability in the wool economy was a major contributor to continuing urban population growth, as increasing numbers of rural people sought employment opportunities or, failing that, joined the ranks of the petty traders purveying manufactured goods in the countryside and bulking small amounts of rural produce. The growing aggregate demand for food combined with the increasing competition among the ever-more-numerous urban-based merchants for access to food facilitated the establishment of new rural markets, improving rural-urban terms of trade on behalf of the peasants. This sharpened competition for agricultural land, and wealthy peasants bought out poorer neighbors, heightening inequalities in access to land, particularly in the best agricultural areas.

As a result of continuing repression and violent reprisals against the peasantry by the elites, and the growing number of families who did not own enough land to support themselves, seasonal and long-term migration out of the region grew in importance. Wage labor on the coast, in the emerging commercial agricultural enterprises and the maritime fishing industry, became more important. In 1937, fifty people from the district of Conima established a settlement near what had been the Spanish gold-mining town of San Juan del Oro, in the Tambopata Valley, on the eastern Andean slopes, some thirteen hundred meters above sea level. The migrants established coffee production in the region, an undertaking that was successful enough to attract the attention of the national government in the mid-1940s. The government established an Indian Migration Office in 1944 and, in 1946, decreed a process whereby migrants could claim formal title to the lands they had possessed. It also provided supplies to permit the completion of a road constructed with voluntary contributions of peasant labor to the provincial capital of Sandia, in 1945. As a result of improved access to the area and a more secure tenure situation for migrants claiming land, the rate of migration to the Tambopata Valley increased sharply in the mid-1940s. It continued to increase into the early 1980s before beginning to show signs of slowing (Collins 1988).

As a result of these changes, the situation in southern Peru at mid-century was highly conflictive (Bourricaud 1967:148–155). The elite classes demanded displays of ritual servitude from the peasantry whenever they could enforce it (e.g. Tschopik, 1951:159). At the same time, while observers were unclear as to the origins of this "caste-structured" (ibid.) social system or the reasons for its intensity, the signs of its dissolution were unmistakable. Bourricaud (1967) observed changes in Puno between visits to the area in 1952 and 1958. He noted in particular the peasantry's increased entrepreneurial activity and participation in wage labor, and discussed the phenomenon in terms of the emergence of a new social class, with its roots in, but distinct from, the traditional peasant society of the region (pp. 24–25, 221–227). Based upon observations made during the 1940s (Kuczynski-Godard 1945) and in the early 1960s (Martinez 1969), researchers felt that the seasonal migration between the altiplano and the Tambopata Valley's other regions was becoming a permanent population movement, which was symptomatic of the increasing landlessness of the highland peasantry. The continuing establishment of rural marketplaces and the emergence of an integrated regional market system in response to growing urban food demand meant improved conditions of sale for farmers and increasingly efficient purveyance of manufactured goods in rural areas (Appleby 1976).

Indeed, there was considerable evidence to suggest that southern Peru was undergoing a transformation of relations of production in agriculture. The rural population was becoming increasingly polarized into a class of capitalist landowners and rural proletarians. The landowners were clearly divided into two groups. On the one hand were the proprietors of the herding enterprises, whose interests were directly tied to the condition of the international wool market, and who were experiencing an intense land-consolidation process as the instability of that market forced the weaker enterprises out of business. On the other were agriculturalists, whose interests were tied to the growing urban demand for food within the region. The proletariat was divided into those who were hired as wage laborers on the agricultural and herding enterprises, and those who were being forced to seek work outside of the area as wage laborers or coffee producers. The region was also home to a growing group of merchants, which was predominantly urban-based and involved in the gathering of wool and foodstuffs from the countryside and the purveyance of manufactured goods imported into the region through the major urban centers. The merchants were internally class-stratified according to three closely interrelated factors: access to transportation facilities, the quantities and types of goods they handled, and the physical location of their base in the regional urban hierarchy.

### Re-creating a Peasant Economy

At the same time, however, several factors were combining to abort this transformation, and these would ultimately re-create a peasant economy in southern Peru. This reconstituted peasant economy would bear little relation to the peasant economy that existed in the region prior to the onset of the changes described above. However, it would be characterized by production relations that are not traditionally associated with capitalism, and by community-based institutions operating under an ideology of reciprocity and redistribution. Thus, in many respects, this "new" peasant economy would resemble the "traditional" one that occupies such a prominent position in the anthropological literature.

The major factor underlying the re-creation of peasant economy in southern Peru was national agricultural policy, which through the course of the twentieth century became increasingly oriented toward using agriculture to promote rapid industrial development. Since before the turn of the century, the country had pursued an agricultural policy that promoted the production of industrial crops, such as sugar, for export. The state also sought to promote rapid industrial development, again with a heavy export orientation. However, until the middle of the century, the weakness of the state precluded systematic pursuit of this development model in the highlands.

With the establishment of the Ministry of Agriculture, in 1943, agricultural policy was directed in two major directions: (1) the maintenance of low food prices for urban consumers, as part of an effort to keep Peru's labor force cheap and attractive to potential foreign investors, and (2) the promotion of continued development of export agriculture (Alvarez 1980, 1983; Caballero 1981, 1984; Painter 1983). The maintenance of low food prices was attempted through various measures, including a growing reliance on the subsidized importation and sale of wheat and wheat products and milk solids, and retail price controls. The state also allowed a market structure to develop which was oligopsonistic in relation to farmers and oligopolistic in relation to consumers (Esculies Larrabure et al. 1977; Figueroa 1979). The market structure exacerbated the effects of state policies in depressing producer prices, and did not pass low prices paid producers on to consumers. Smallholding farmers throughout the country responded by allowing agricultural production to decline, and placing greater emphasis on off-farm activities to earn an income. As domestic food production declined, the state placed even greater emphasis on food imports, making conditions even more unfavorable for domestic production.

Unassisted, this dynamic would have proven disastrous for the processes of growth and accumulation that were emerging. The impact on southern Peru, however, was accelerated by other events. Principal among these was the drought of 1956–1958, which was reported to have destroyed 80 percent of the crops and 30 percent of the livestock in the region in the first year alone (Dew 1969:89).[8] Occurring over three agricultural cycles, the drought caused rural families to exhaust their stored supplies of food and seed, and massive numbers of people left their homes in the countryside. Many went to the regional urban centers in search of work, and, from there, many who did not find it went to Arequipa and Lima. Schaedel (1967:109), for example, estimates that in 1958 alone, over 27,000 people left Puno and migrated to the cities of Arequipa, Cuzco, Lima, Tacna, and Moquegua. Competition for jobs in the mines and on the commercial agricultural enterprises of the coast intensified greatly. Migration to the Tambopata Valley to claim land and enter into coffee production also increased sharply (Collins 1984:425–427). The impact of the drought on the region was exacerbated by a drop in international wool prices at the end of the Korean War (Appleby 1978:67, 79, 91). This proved fatal to a number of the enterprises that had survived the previous decline in prices and market instability, and contributed to the migration of rural dwellers into the cities.

The rapid expansion of the regional urban population as a result of these circumstances increased the demand for food at the same time that local production was effectively eliminated by the drought. This demand was met to a large degree by the imported foodstuffs that had already become staples in the diet of the urban working class. Once they had been displaced from the regional markets, the economic conditions created by national agricultural policy prevented regional agriculture from regaining its former position as a major supplier of foodstuffs in southern Peru. Between growing cash require-

ments and the difficulties in earning a living through agriculture, peasants
continued to turn away from farming as a source of cash revenue in favor of
off-farm activities. However, the revenues offered by wage labor, coffee production, and petty trade, which were the major off-farm activities, were sufficiently low that it was necessary to continue food production for familial
consumption in order to subsidize the work done off-farm (Painter 1986).[9]

Ironically, major aspects of the massive relief and development effort
undertaken in southern Peru in response to the drought, which were intended to reestablish regional agricultural production, accelerated the re-
creation of the peasant economy that was under way. For example, development efforts such as the Puno-Tambopata Project sought to provide families
with an alternative to migration to the cities, but simply accelerated migration to the petty commodity production regime that was developing around
coffee cultivation. As a result, it broadened participation in a pattern of seasonal migration between the highland and valley areas that arises from people not being able to cover consumption requirements in either place, and
which stresses family labor resources in such a way as to promote environmentally destructive production practices in both areas. Similarly, the influx
of imported foodstuffs through the retail market system, disaster relief activities, and rural development projects utilizing a food-for-work approach pur-
veyed vast quantities of food into all areas of the region at prices that did not
reflect production and transport costs. Although responding to the need to
supply the region with food during the period when there was little local
production, these foodstuffs facilitated the replacement of local production in
the markets of the region, and their continued purveyance as part of development activities after the drought had ended was an additional obstacle to
reestablishing the position of local production in the markets.

The urban population of the region soared in the wake of the drought and
the subsequent relief and development efforts. In the case of Juliaca, for example, the population increased from 6,034, in 1940, to 9,248, by 1950. By
1960, the city was home to 20,403 inhabitants (Torres Juarez 1962), and, in
1972, the population was 38,475. The city of Puno increased from 13,786
people in 1940 to 44,166 in 1972. The distribution of the urban population
also changed substantially, with Puno and Juliaca increasing their primacy
over other urban centers in the region. In 1940, two out of five urban dwellers
lived in one of these two cities; by the early 1970s, almost half did. In addition, this urban growth occurred in a period during which the department of
Puno as a whole lost population. The Plan Regional de Desarrollo del Sur del
Perú (PRSDP) estimated the department of Puno's population to be 812,000
people in 1958, while the population recorded by the 1972 census was
779,594 (Appleby 1978:148).

The rate of growth of rural markets also increased sharply after 1960 (Appleby 1978:188). This reflected the intensified competition among petty mer-

chants to gather foodstuffs from the countryside and to purvey manufactured goods, as their ranks were swelled by the large numbers of migrants to the cities unable to find formal employment. Here too, however, opportunities were quite limited. In Juliaca in the mid-1970s for example, 9.5 percent of the businesses controlled over 60 percent of legal sales, then estimated to amount to approximately five hundred thousand dollars per month. At the same time, 22 percent of the businesses in the city controlled 67 percent of the total working capital (Velásquez Rodríguez 1978:50, 76–77). In these circumstances, the only option for migrants–cum–petty merchants was to try to compete with others in the same situation in the countryside. This involved not calculating a value on their own labor power in the transport of goods, and, as in the case of wage laborers and coffee growers, a continuing reliance upon familial agricultural production to subsidize their participation in petty trade and transport. The ability of petty merchants not to attach a cost for their own labor power enabled larger areas to be incorporated into the urban hinterlands, leading to the establishment of the additional rural markets.

The agrarian reform undertaken between 1969 and 1975 by the reformist military government of General Juan Velasco Alvarado marked another phase in the re-creation of the regional peasant economy. The large livestock estates were expropriated and reorganized into state cooperatives[10] worked by the peasants residing on them. The state also encouraged independent peasant communities to seek recognition as corporate landholding units in order to protect their access to land and receive support from the state in improving agricultural production and revenues. The reform removed the last vestiges of the landlord class from the countryside, but it did not provide the means for the rural institutions it created or supported to accumulate capital. Patterns of state investment continued as they had prior to the reform, placing priority on the rapid industrialization of coastal urban centers and developing new agricultural areas through the irrigation of the coastal desert. Thus, the coastal departments of Lima-Callao, Arequipa, Piura, and Ancash received 55 percent of all public investment under the Velasco government (Wilson and Wise 1986). The state also continued its commitment to keep urban food prices down, and it increased its reliance on subsidizing food imports to do so. The Velasco government also relied heavily upon retail price controls. Furthermore, conditions on the international wool market did not improve. As a result, neither the peasant communities nor the cooperative enterprises in the southern highlands were able to become competitive with enterprises producing similar goods on the coast or outside of Peru (Rénique 1987).

Thus, by the late 1970s and early 1980s, the highlands of much of southern Peru had become a labor reserve. Agricultural products had been replaced by labor power as the principal export of the rural communities of the region (Figueroa 1982, 1984). On the north side of Lake Titicaca, for example, virtually all of the rural population derived its cash income from off-farm activity in one of these areas. Only negligible quantities of food were sent to the urban centers of the region. The role of local markets was to redistribute products among producers of different production zones. However, agriculture remained central to the regional economy because the cost of replacing the food they grow with comparable foodstuffs purchased on the retail market would by far have exceeded the cash earnings of most peasants (Painter 1986).

The creation of this labor reserve benefited important sectors of the Peruvian economy. The wage laborers played an important role in the mining, fishing, and commercial agricultural industries. The small-scale coffee growers of Tambopata produced an export commodity under conditions that would be impossible for an enterprise that had to remunerate labor at a level consistent with its subsistence and reproduction costs. Similarly, petty traders allowed the rural population to constitute a market for manufactured goods that would be prohibitively expensive if their retail price included a component reflecting the labor expended by the person purveying them. This was possible because peasant agriculture satisfied a significant portion of the population's subsistence and reproduction requirements. Reciprocal exchange relations grew in importance in response to the need to maintain agricultural production as a family subsistence activity. Poor remuneration associated with off-farm activities meant that families' reliance on agricultural production for their own consumption grew together with their dependence on off-farm income.

## ANTHROPOLOGICAL DISCUSSIONS OF ANDEAN PEASANTS

The focus of social science research in the Andes has been on the continuity of present cultural forms with the colonial and pre-Hispanic past of the region.[11] This is not to suggest that elements of "indigenous culture," arising from the pre-Hispanic or colonial past, are not a vital force in the lives of modern Andean peasantries. Indeed, notions of indigenous culture help to shape the political behavior of both dominated and dominant social classes. Rather, while cultural forms have survived through the centuries, radical and repeated changes in the context in which they occur have fundamentally altered their significance. In resorting to explanations and interpretations that have their basis in presumed continuities with the distant past whose linkages to the present are left largely implicit rather than defined and examined, social scientists have re-created a past for modern Andean people that is more mythical than historical.

While it is difficult to assess the motivations underlying this tendency, the methods whereby the past is mythologized are readily visible, as are many of the consequences. The methodological approach is clearly exemplified in three widespread practices in Andean social science: (1) the treatment of abstract conceptual categories (e.g., verticality) as if they were real things; (2) the treatment of modern peasants as if they constituted a homogenous population, despite the considerable and widely recognized class differentiation that exists within the Andean peasantry; and (3) the coupling of the mythic images of the distant past with an anemic sense of how more recent history has decisively shaped the position of those we study in the larger social and political order of which they form a part. The result of these practices is to produce an almost uniformly conservative interpretation of social and political events, which proffers a myth of "original poverty" (see Platt 1982:28) in lieu of an explanation of current misery and oppression.

### Conceptual Categories and Empirical Phenomena

Few themes in Andean social science exemplify the tendency to confound conceptual categories and empirical phenomena as well as does verticality. In Murra's (1972) original formulation, verticality refers to the social relations that regulated people's access to different productive resources at different altitudes. The regulation of these relations was a central task of state policy in pre-Hispanic times, while their management devolved to the level of kin groups with the dissolution of the pre-Hispanic states (see Saignes 1978). Unfortunately, in some social science literature, the notion of verticality has been largely reduced to a question of adaptation to the particularities of the Andean environment. Rather than focusing upon how the relevant social relations are established and maintained, and on the mechanisms whereby they regulate access to productive resources, social scientists have largely turned their attention to the relationship between people and their physical environment.

The way anthropologists have viewed this relationship between Andean people and their environment is also revealing. Because we have evidence that controlling access to resources in different ecological zones was important in precolonial times, and because we observe that modern peasants continue to go to considerable lengths to maintain access to different ecological zones, when verticality is discussed historically it is in terms of the supposed continuity between past and present. It becomes a timeless construct, the essential characteristics of which can be identified in radically different eras and places. Radical changes in social relations between people are reduced to little more than a backdrop for discussions occupying center stage that have to do with the primordial nature of the need to maintain access to different ecological zones. How the pressures to maintain that access have changed over the years, and the different mechanisms by which access is achieved, have received scant attention, as have more difficult and interesting questions of how need and access were related to class position in the past and how they are today.

Constructed in this context, the peasants portrayed in the anthropological literature are either passive, "wresting an existence from the land much as their ancestors have," or they are consummate traditionalists, going to great and—according to some—heroic lengths to resist external threats to their heritage. When references are made to the position of peasants within states and the international economy, they are usually limited to the observation that neither the colonial Spanish state, the national Peruvian state, nor international development agencies understand the subtleties of vertically organized production in the Andes (Browman 1987).

This point of view is at once true and irrelevant. Most representatives of states, international development agencies, and other dominant institutions do not understand the importance of maintaining access to different ecological zones to the continuing viability of Andean agricultural production. However, this is hardly remarkable if one accepts that the concern of dominant institutions has, over the years, focused on the extraction of labor power, natural resources, and other commodities for the benefit of populations physically and socially quite distant from Andean peasants. In general, how peasants have maintained themselves while providing these things has been their own affair. The maintenance of economically and environmentally viable agricultural production units under the control of peasants has been an issue only to the degree that the ability of the peasantry to reproduce itself has been threatened.

By focusing on the lack of understanding shown by dominant interests rather than on what they have been trying to accomplish in their relations with the peasantry, we define our own role as that of educators of those interests. Our work directly with peasants is directed toward assisting them to maintain continuity with the past. The stage is set for a melodrama in which the villains are the harsh environment and insensitive or evil agents of change, and the hero the peasantry with its traditional practices and lifeways. The real culprits—systemic inequality and oppression—remain offstage.

### The Homogenized Peasantry

A second common practice in the anthropological literature on the Andes is the treatment of peasants as a homogenous population, despite the considerable evidence to the contrary, and despite a countertradition of criticism of this approach (e.g., Brass 1983, 1985; Sánchez 1982). The practice emerges most clearly in our discussions of the institutions that shape Andean life. As in the broader anthropological literature on peasants, Andean communities have been characterized as contexts within which peasants relate to one another in terms of reciprocal exchanges and redistribution of wealth. According to the dominant interpretation, it is through these institutions that peasants maintain a measure of autonomy in running local affairs and resist the changes thrust upon them from the outside. The community itself, and reciprocity and redistribution within it, are seen as mechanisms that limit the accumulation of wealth by individuals and, in the process, promote internal solidarity. The existence of ostensibly reciprocal exchanges of goods and services in the heart of highly commoditized economies is taken as evidence of the success of these institutions in their assigned tasks. Skar (1984:83) makes the point thus: "cultural norms largely expressed through the quality of work relationships effectively protect the subsistence sector of the economy from market intrusion."

Social scientists have looked to Wolf's (1955, 1957) discussions of the closed corporate community as justification of this view. Indeed, the existence of mechanisms of reciprocity and redistribution within the context of a community responsible for managing its internal affairs does form an element of his discussion. However, Wolf also talks about the circumstances under which such arrangements have been established in areas not suited for the production of commodities in demand by the larger economy. Furthermore, while the communities may be closed in the sense of running their internal affairs, they are firmly linked to the larger economy as labor reserves for mines, plantations, and other pursuits. Wolf also notes that, over time, communities that were once closed may become more open and vice versa, as the role they play in the larger economy changes.

Alberti and Mayer (1974), Orlove (1977), and Sánchez (1982) have pointed out that, while there is an ideology of reciprocity and redistribution within the southern Peruvian peasantry, its major function may be to mask the inequalities that exist. Some people consistently receive more days of labor through reciprocal exchanges than they provide, and are successful in avoiding the financial burdens implied by civil and religious duties. Golte and de la Cadena (1983) describe how poor farmers receive labor related to their cultivation of low-value crops for family consumption, while they tend to provide labor to wealthier farmers producing high-value crops for market. These observations echo that of Harris (1964:25–41) that, while some internal wealth redistribution may occur in peasant communities, this pales in significance when compared with the wealth extracted by the institutions forming the overall social complex in which peasant communities are embedded.

The homogenization of a differentiated peasantry is a tradition with a long history among researchers. The Zemstvo agricultural production data collected throughout Russia during the late nineteenth and early twentieth centuries were unsurpassed for their detail and comprehensiveness. The hypotheses that shaped their collection and colored their analysis were a product of the populist tradition in Russian agricultural economics. Culminating in the contributions of Chayanov, the economists of this tradition were among the first to study the social relations that organized peasant production, and they have offered much to our understanding of rural smallholders today. However, the approach was predicated upon assumptions of the homogeneity of the peasantry with regard to access to land, draft animals, and other productive resources (Harrison 1977, 1979).[12] The methods used reflected the assumptions of homogeneity and reinforced them. For example, census data were aggregated into community-level totals, so that subsequent analysis relied heavily on gross per capita figures regarding the distribution of income and productive resources.

Despite the critiques of Lenin (1974)[13] and subsequent generations of scholars (e.g., Brass 1983, 1985; Deere and de Janvry 1981), assumptions of homogeneity within the ranks of those we call peasants continue to hinder our understanding of rural social change. Where inequality and differentiation are clearly visible, anthropologists have frequently discussed them as phenomena of recent origin. Internal solidarity and relatively balanced reciprocal relations are generally assumed to be the norm, with inequality and differentiation treated as emergent issues symptomatic of the breakdown of traditional lifeways in the face of an expanding market economy. The methods used to collect and aggregate data continue to mask the depth of differentiation that marks rural smallholding populations. And as social scientists of an empiricist tradition, we often allow ourselves to be trapped by homogeneity that is an artifact of the data collection methods used. It is certainly easier to base our analysis on what "the data tell us" than it is to assess critically how and why we gather such data.

### *Ahistorical Analysis*

The problems described above have their roots in an anemic sense of history, which assumes change to be gradual and social life to be relatively constant over long periods of time. Social anthropologists have asked few questions about the origins of the social forms they observe in the ethnographic present, largely accepting the community as a basic unit of Andean social organization and a "natural"unit of analysis. They have tended in a remarkable way to "telescope" the 450 years between the fall of the Inca state and the present. Hickman and Stuart (1977:55), for example, state:

> We are fortunate to have relatively detailed information on Aymara social structuring during the 16th century and for the 1940s to the present. What happened in the intervening time may be inferred from these end points by referring to known processes of social evolution.

Arguing from a different perspective, Platt (1986:229) nonetheless makes a similar assertion:

The continuities here argued for between the sixteenth century and today should not worry historians unduly. Domestic production has been a nucleus of both pre-Columbian peasant farming and of today's petty commodity producer; accordingly, it is from this nucleus that a wealth of ideological elaborations emerge.

While the current reproduction of the Andean peasantry may have its roots in images of past production relations, historians and anthropologists alike need to be wary of facile assertions of continuity with the past based upon positivist assumptions regarding the nature of social change. As Murra and Wachtel (1986:2) note,

> there is no way of projecting seriously from present-day practice to institutions four centuries earlier. Even when these monographs provide interesting information, it is hard to use it to understand the Andean world: There is no way of knowing how these "communities" came to be heirs of the large polities we know to have been prevalent in the Andes before and after the Inca.

How much more dubious and ahistorical, then, is an approach that takes reconstructed images of the past as an explanation of the material conditions of life in the present?

It is not surprising then, that carrying such assumptions into the field with them, anthropologists frequently seem to arrive on the scene in the wake of an outbreak of change that has followed a long period of social dormancy. Hickman (1963:14) was explicit on the point when he said:

> It is only in the past twenty years that the Aymara have begun to take advantage of what opportunities there are for mobility and a richer experience in the non-Indian world.

Similarly, Lewellen (1987) describes "the traditional Aymara system as it has existed since conquest time" (p. 31), and then explains that "the boundaries of this system were struck hard and suddenly," in an ethnographic present beginning just prior to his arrival in the field (p. 32). As observers, we may applaud the changes that progress is bringing to our subjects, or we may mourn the demise of the traditional lifeways we have imagined for them, or we may be moved by the resilience of peasants and their institutions. However, because we do not look at these changes in a historical context, it is rare that we identify and document how they came about or what are their implications for the future.


THE IMPLICATIONS AND MOTIVATIONS OF IMAGINED HISTORY

The struggle for control of productive resources in southern Peru has been sufficiently eventful that assumptions about the continuity of observations in the ethnographic present with social, economic, or political arrangements in the past need to be examined very critically. The peasantry of southern Peru is not and never has been in any sense isolated from changes at the national and international levels. Rather, its form at any time was fundamentally shaped by continuing processes of change, and on occasion, the peasantry has played a decisive role in affecting the course of those changes. The fact that this is so apparent, on the basis of readily available materials, should cause us to reflect on the adequacy of the assumptions that underlie much of the ethnographic analysis that has been conducted on the region. Little has been said here that most anthropological students of southern Peru do not already know. The question we must try to answer is why so little of this historical context informs our analyses of the present.

Anthropologists working in the contemporary Andean highlands who have included historical discussions of the late pre-Hispanic and early colonial periods in order to help interpret what they observed at the time of their research have tended to use historical material in one of two ways. One has been to idealize the Native American states, and particularly the Inca state that immediately preceded the arrival of the Spanish, as representing a "golden age" during which the populations were relatively free of disease, hunger, and basic material wants. The other has been to focus on the tributary nature of the pre-Hispanic and colonial states and dismiss the significance of the conquest through assertions to the effect that for most of the rural peasantry the event boiled down to a change of masters.

These themes are more relevant to the present than to the past. Discussions building uncritically on the theme of how life was better for most people under the Native American states communicate two highly charged messages: (1) that the Spaniards who conquered Peru some 450 years ago bear major responsibility for the country's current underdevelopment; and (2) that ethnicity—either divorced from or assumed to be coterminous with class—constitutes an independent variable for explaining social structure. At the same time, those who treat the conquest as reducible to a change of overlords without a substantial number of caveats convey a distinct, but equally powerful, message: that exploitation can be satisfactorily studied and analyzed independently of time and place, and without reference to specific processes, mechanisms, and agents responsible for it.

The messages attributed here to these respective approaches are not, of course, set in stone, but have themselves changed considerably over time and according to context. For example, the idealization of the indigenous heritage originally arose in connection with progressive political movements seeking to overcome the limitations imposed by racism and regionalism on participation in Peruvian political life. Some of these represented petty-bourgeois interests as they made early bids for national political power (cf. Haya 1935), while others sought union between the proletariat of the cities and coastal plantations and the peasantry of the rural highlands as a prelude to a socialist transformation of Peruvian society (Castro Pozo 1924, 1936; Mariátegui 1928). Unfortunately, time and incorporation into functionalist interpretations by social scientists have imbued the point of view with new meanings that shift attention away from contemporary political struggles. Interestingly, this tendency remains constant, regardless of whether we look at the anthropology of the 1950s and 1960s, which portrayed peasants as struggling to overcome the past in order to embrace progress (e.g., Doughty 1968), or the anthropology of the 1970s and 1980s, which portrayed the same people as struggling to maintain the integrity of traditional lifeways in the face of capitalist expansion (e.g., Bradby 1975, 1982; Isbell 1978; Painter 1981; Taussig 1978, 1980).

Given our difficulty in overcoming this tendency to describe change in terms of a departure from a largely imaginary traditional social order, despite the considerable evidence that we ourselves have provided to demonstrate the inadequacy of this approach, it is well that we begin to reflect upon the reasons for the difficulty. Rosaldo (1989) describes the perspective as "imperialist nostalgia," and emphasizes that it is a historically produced cultural form:

> Such forms of longing appear closely related to secular notions of progress. We valorize innovation, and then yearn for more stable worlds, whether these reside in our own past, in other cultures, or in the conflation of the two. Imperialist nostalgia, more particularly, occurs alongside a peculiar sense of mission, the White Man's Burden, where civilized nations stand duty-bound to uplift savage ones. In this ideologically constructed world of ongoing progressive change, putatively static savage societies become a stable reference point for defining the civilized identity. Thus, when the so-called civilizing process destabilizes the savage forms of life, the agents of change experience their own transformation of the other as if they were personal losses.

Notions of community and reciprocity are particularly tempting as themes to be discussed from this nostalgic perspective because they have to do with qualitatively rich and multistranded relationships that are absent from a capitalist economy organized on the basis of the exchange of wages for labor power. By creating a fictional chronicle that laments the passing of such relationships, we deny our role as beneficiaries and agents of change, and recast ourselves as observers experiencing feelings of solidarity with those we observe. In our role as storytellers, we blur the struggles in which our subjects are locked with one another, and with faceless processes beyond their control. Thus we spare ourselves from having to answer to which of our subjects our solidarity extends.

However, the questions raised by our treatment of Andean peasants go beyond the methodological blinders that constrain many of our analyses to the epistemological bases of anthropological inquiry. One example should suffice to indicate the problem. In 1983, when peasants involved in a struggle between the Peruvian police and military and the guerrillas of *Sendero Lumino-so* killed eight journalists, the furor that resulted was sufficient that the government of President Fernando Belaúnde Terry named a special commission to gather evidence and explain how the violent acts came to pass. President Belaúnde appointed Mario Vargas Llosa, one of the most talented novelists of our time, to head the commission.

Vargas subsequently summarized the findings of the commission in an article in the *New York Times Magazine* (Vargas Llosa 1983). In it, he drew heavily upon the images of Andean social life that anthropologists have provided, and portrayed the killings as the result of the physical, economic, and cultural isolation of the peasants involved. Wrapped for centuries in their own small world, the boundaries of which were set by their poverty, the peasants suddenly found themselves caught up in a struggle that they neither controlled nor understood:

> He [a reporter] did not know he was headed for an encounter with another time, a gap of centuries mere language could not bridge. (P. 17)

> Of all the people in the department of Ayacucho, the Iquichanos are among the most destitute. Living on the inhospitable lands that have been theirs since pre-Hispanic times, without roads, medical care or technology, without water or electricity, they have only known the exploitation of the landowner, the demands of the tax collector and the violence of civil war. Although Catholicism is deeply rooted among them, it has not displaced old beliefs like the worship of the *Apus*, or god-mountains. (P. 33) . . . In the villages of Uchuraccay and Huaychao, life has not changed in almost 200 years. (P. 36)

> At the start of the hearing, instructed by the anthropologists who were the advisers to the commission, I spilled some *aguardiente* on the ground and drank in homage to the tutelary god-mountain Rasuwilca. I distributed coca leaves. Through an interpreter, I tried to explain to the dozens and dozens of Iquichanos gathered around us that the laws of Peru prohibit murder; that we have judges to try cases and sentence the guilty; that we have police to make sure that everyone obeys the law. And while I was saying these things and looking at their faces, I felt as absurd and unreal as if I were indoctrinating them in the authentic revolutionary philosophy of Comrade Mao betrayed by that counter-revolutionary dog Deng Xiaoping. (P. 49)

> The massacre had magical and religious overtones, as well as political and social implications. The hideous wounds on the corpses were ritualistic. The eight bodies were buried in pairs, face down, the form of burial used for people the Iquichanos consider "devils"—people like the dancers of the *tijeras*, a folk dance, who are believed to make pacts with the Devil. They were buried outside the community limits to emphasize that they were strangers. (In the Andes, the Devil merges with the image of the stranger.) The bodies were especially mutilated around the mouth and eyes, in the belief that the victim should be deprived of his sight, so he cannot recognize his killers, and of his

tongue, so he cannot denounce them. Their ankles were broken, so they could not come back for revenge. The villagers stripped the bodies; they washed the clothes and burned them in a purification ceremony known as *pichja*.

Knowing the circumstances does not excuse the crime, but it makes what happened more comprehensible. The violence stuns us because it is an anomaly in our ordinary lives. For the Iquichanos, that violence is the atmosphere they live in from the time they are born until the time they die. (P. 50)

Reading Vargas's narrative, one is struck by how these descriptions of an isolated traditional society are juxtaposed with information about the long-standing rivalry between the upland people referred to in the passages above with valley dwellers—a rivalry that has on different occasions been marked by violence; about how the geographic boundaries of this rivalry correspond closely to the boundaries dividing those areas tending to oppose and support the guerrillas; about the exploitation of the peasantry; about how the armed forces had visited the area on various occasions prior to the slaying of the reporters; about how the incident that drew the reporters to the area in the first place was one in which a group of peasants had killed members of a guerrilla patrol; and about how the village visited by Vargas and the other members of the commission was subjected to a reprisal attack by the guerrillas soon after their departure. Here too, assertions about tradition and isolation must be interpreted with care when placed in a broader context.

Few would argue with Vargas's observation (p. 56) that the peasants who murdered the reporters and others like them are the principal victims of violence in the countryside. And one must evaluate his remarks in light of the desire that an assessment of responsibility for the incident avoid providing a pretext for their further victimization. However, recognizing the victimization of the peasantry should not imply denying its agency in the processes of change occurring. To do so trivializes the political implications of the violence in which they participate, and that trivialization can do little but perpetuate it.

The lack of roads, education, and other basic facilities to which Vargas refers is an inescapable fact of rural life, and these lacks go hand in hand with the sorts of violence about which he writes, or which have been discussed here as part of the history of Puno. However, they are not a product of isolation from the social and economic system that surrounds them. Rather, they are a product of being very much a part of that system. The processes that create anthropologists and novelists also create the peasants of Puno and Ayacucho, as well as the market where we sell our observations about their problems and lifeways. Similarly, the culture of an anthropologist or novelist is clearly distinct from that of an Andean peasant. However, that does not necessarily imply that they are not connected. Each tries to make sense of a reality that affects them in different ways, and the metaphors used to describe one's experience with that reality are also necessarily different. Yet, in the end, the dramatic violence of a massacre or the more insidious violence of people losing their grasp on resources upon which they depend for their survival continually bring novelist and anthropologist together with the peasant, at times to conduct an inquest and at times to conduct a study of rural social change. When this happens, our choices are to examine the linkages that draw us together with our subjects or to objectify features of their existence as evidence of the distance between us. Clearly, it is more comfortable to do the latter, and this is the path that we as anthropologists have tended to choose.

## NOTES

1. This description of social relations of peasant production is based upon field research conducted in southern Peru in 1977 and 1979/80, sponsored by the University of Florida Foundation, an Inter-American Foundation Learning Fellowship for Social Change, and a Fulbright-Hays Fellowship for Doctoral Research (Painter 1981). Terms from the Aymara language are written according to the Yapita phonemic alphabet (Yapita 1981).

2. See Klein (1982:41–42) for a discussion of the actions taken by Toledo to establish state authority over the mine operation at Potosí itself. Larson (1988) describes Crown efforts to mediate competition over the labor power of the rural population between the mines and agricultural enterprises in the valleys of present-day Cochabamba departments.

3. In many parts of the Andes, the peasantry has maintained the records pertaining to this period. The people of the *ayllu* Pomaoca, in the district of Moho, for example, possess the original document defining their land rights, which was signed in 1721.

4. For a discussion of the impact of the growth of the wool industry on the regional economy, see Orlove (1977). Appleby (1976, 1978, 1980) discusses the significance of urban growth in southern Peru and its relationship to the wool export economy.

5. For accounts of the activities of the Adventist church in the region during this period, see Hazen (1974) and Lewellen (1978).

6. Leguía emerged from the planter ranks, but his relations with many members of his class were strained because of his courting of the support of the emergent workers' movement and his portrayal of himself as a populist (Gonzales 1985:173).

7. For a description of the 1923 uprising and a discussion of its significance in terms of regional class formation, see Collins (1988).

8. Droughts are endemic in the region, and localized droughts are a frequent occurrence. At irregular intervals, however, the entire region is afflicted by major drought that lasts through more than a single growing season. For example, a drought similar in severity, although less dramatic in its social and economic impacts, struck southern Peru in 1940. More recently, the altiplano was hit by a severe regionwide drought during the 1982/83 and 1983/84 growing seasons.

9. Collins (1984) discusses the process whereby possibilities for coffee production in the Tambopata Valley serving as a basis for capital accumulation were cut off (see especially pp. 430–431).

10. A number of different state cooperative organizations were created under the agrarian reform, with administrative structures varying according to the role they were envisioned as playing in the economy. Most of the coastal plantations, for example, were organized as Cooperativas Agrarias de Producción. The estates in highland southern Peru became Sociedades Agricolas de Interés Social (Martinez 1980).

11. For comprehensive and critical reviews discussing many of the issues raised here see Salomon (1982) and Stein (1984).

12. As Harrison points out in his critique, Chayanov did recognize inequality deriving from population increase, and from changes in the ratio of producers and consumers over the life cycle of a household. He did not, however, address the social inequalities that were the basis of class differentiation of the peasantry as described by Lenin (1974). For a discussion of the implications of the two approaches to inequality applied to a Peruvian case, see Deere and de Janvry (1981).

13. Anthropologists may find Lenin's critique of Zemstvo statistics for Novorossia (1974:71–86) of particular interest. Here he notes that much is made in analyses of agricultural data of the practice of "yoking" oxen, whereby smallholders share their animals in order to plow their land. Cited in the literature of the period as an example of peasant cooperation, Lenin notes that the cooperation arises from the unequal distribution of oxen so that middle and poor peasant families, on average, do not own sufficient animals to form a team. Thus the cooperation is a forced one, and the lines of cooperation tend to be poorer families exchanging their labor on the fields of richer ones for the loan of their oxen.

# FOUR

# Custom and Wage Conflict: Problems of Periodization and Chronology in Northern Nigerian Labor History

*Louise D. Lennihan*

## INTRODUCTION

In contemporary Hausaland, there are three basic agricultural wage contracts. They have replaced two nonwage institutions for mobilizing extra-household labor, one ideally redistributive and the other reciprocal. Examination of these wage contracts reveals a continuum along which capital increasingly replaces nonmonetary rights and obligations of employers and laborers. While capital is the basis of all three contracts, along this continuum employer-worker relations become increasingly objectified as social ties are reduced to cash exchange. The progression of objectification is not, however, a simple unilinear one through time. For one thing, all three contracts exist simultaneously. The most highly objectified contract has emerged as an option, not a replacement to earlier contract forms with their ensnaring social rights and obligations. I shall argue that these contracts are distinct cultural forms, constituting significant ideological and material changes in the social relations of production. Yet they do not displace one another, nor do they correspond to a discrete historical moment. In no way incompatible with capitalism, they demonstrate the complexities and contradictions of "actually existing capitalism" in northern Nigeria today.[1]

This fact raises methodological problems that go beyond the problems associated with oppositional models. There is no doubt that an oppositional treatment of, say, earlier reciprocal or redistributive institutions for mobilizing labor and wage contracts in the present would have negative consequences. It would miss the complex processes of capitalization and proletarianization. It would miss the struggle that takes place in the complex negotiations between employers and workers given these contemporaneous contract forms. Finally, it would miss the contention between employers and workers over the meaning of these contracts, over the social obligations each involves, ultimately over the ideological power of these contract forms to legitimate inequality in the rural social order. Instead I shall focus on two problems of historiography that emerge when oppositional models are set aside. These are the problems of periodization and the confusion of cultural difference with historical sequence, or chronology, a particularly dangerous confusion in the study of the development of capitalism where the notion of directional change is so strong.

## OPPOSITIONAL MODELS AND HISTORICAL INVENTION IN NORTHERN NIGERIA

Before demonstrating my own perspective, I should point out that my approach does not mean that oppositional models are absent in historical analyses of northern Nigeria. The neopopulist argument that rural differentiation is insignificant rests on at least two oppositions. One is the urban-rural dichotomy which underlies the claim that "[t]he sources of major inequalities in Nigerian society and the most significant forms of exploitation cannot be identified within rural villages but must be sought in the predatory activities of an urban-based bourgeoisie" (Williams 1988:386).[2] A second neopopulist opposition is that of smallholders and rural proletarians.[3] This opposition allows for the simultaneous discounting of differentiation among rural smallholders and the reification of the household as the unit of production. The standard argument brought to bear on any evidence to the contrary, one that draws on an ideal-type rural "proletariat," is that "[t]here is no large class of landless labourers" and that "[t]here is no evidence of a secular trend toward greater inequality in access to land among peasant farmers" (Williams 1988:385).

Similarly, my approach does not mean that the political manipulation of history, another central theme of this volume, is absent from the literature on northern Nigeria. Far from it. The implicit political implications of the neopopulist presentation of the agrarian past (and present) are well known (see Kitching 1982; Byres 1979; Solomon 1975). A second more explicit example is the early British colonial state's blatant invention of a "traditional," precolonial land-tenure system in which individuals did not hold proprietary rights in land and where land was not bought or sold. The purpose of this invention was to justify the nationalization of all land (and tax revenue) in the name of the colonial state and to eliminate any prospect of the development of a landlord class, considered to be deleterious to trade and political stability. There are several accounts of the ideological and material concerns that lay behind this invention, a classic example in which the British High Commissioner (1906) manipulated ethnographic data provided by his own political Residents when they undermined his position, cited utterly inapplicable sections of Baden-Powell's *Land Systems of British India,* and invoked the ghost of the American utopian socialist Henry George. It was quite a performance (see Watts 1983:158–161; Lennihan 1982:124–132; esp. Shenton 1986: chap. 3).[4]

## OTHER PROBLEMS OF HISTORIOGRAPHY: PERIODIZATION AND CHRONOLOGY

There is no question that historical invention and the use of oppositional models figure prominently in the political and historical discourse and analysis of northern Nigeria. But it turns out that once the blight of oppositional models is lifted, the anthropologist is left with other rather basic problems of historiography.

One such methodological problem is periodization and the related task of determining appropriate historical baselines. No matter how one approaches the historical project, no matter how it is defined or what its goals, the historian must decide how to block off time into periods that advance the process of historical construction. Whether one is concerned with the process and practices of a specific past, or with the construction of discourses about the "past," periodization is implicit to the historical project. A common strategy, of course, is to resort to such misleading ideal-type, temporal brackets discussed in the Introduction to this volume—precapitalist/capitalist, premodern/modern, natural economy/market economy, and so forth. But once these and other oppositions are dropped, an alternative periodization must be devised.

The second related methodological problem is the tendency to confuse cultural difference with historical sequence. This is particularly dangerous in the analysis of the development of capitalism where the notion of directional change is so strong. Discarding conventional periodization based on oppositions confounds this problem. Take the case of analyzing the development of capitalism. When the poles of precapitalist and capitalist are dropped as baseline and endpoint, one substitute is a treatment of time in which it is blocked off chronologically using a series of different cultural forms. But the sticking point is that their temporal sequence is ordered by their distance from the very same oppositional poles that have been discarded. Nowhere is this problem more apparent than in the historical analysis of "custom" or "tradition." This volume and others underline the fact that the definition of custom is a locus of contention and struggle (Hobsbawn and Ranger 1983; Scott 1972, 1985; Thompson 1974). In this struggle "ancient traditions" in fact may be recent invention or reinvention, while certain past customs of real significance may be forgotten or actively rejected. Nevertheless, there is the temptation to interpret cultural differences, or different cultural forms that are tied to such customs or traditions, as indicators of a particular historical sequence or chronology.

## BACKGROUND

At the empirical level, the use of capital to mobilize extra-family labor in northern Nigeria must be discussed in the context of several facts concerning labor in relation to land and technology. During my fieldwork in 1977–1979 and 1985, while the odd tractor was seen in the countryside, the hand plow and hoe were ubiquitous. Similarly, most rural producers had not been separated from the land.[5] While there were landless laborers, both local villagers and wandering men, a large landless proletariat laboring for the landed rich had not emerged. The household production unit (*gandu*, pl. *gandaye*) was the primary unit of agricultural production. Of varied composition, it included any combination of a senior male, along with his married and unmarried sons and brothers, their sons, and clients. Prior to the end of slavery, it also might have included slaves, and before the spread of wife seclusion, women of the household (Smith 1954). It was this production unit that recruited extra-household agricultural labor through wage contracts.

To understand fully the nature of these contracts it is useful to consider two nonwage institutions for recruiting extra-family labor which wage contracts have replaced. One is the now defunct institution of *sarkin noma* (lit. "the chief of farming"). A *sarkin noma* was a wealthy large farmer who was expected to help his neighbors in times of hardship. Should a village be struck by famine or a poor harvest, the customary expectation was that the *sarkin noma* would respond. First, he was expected to open his grain stores to the villagers to ward off starvation. Second, in lesser calamities, such as harvest shortfalls, he might pay the tax or tithe of individual farmers or even of the entire village. Third, he might make gifts or loans to individuals faced with the expense of their own marriage, the birth or the marriage of a child, the funeral of a relative, or one of the major Islamic holidays. Repayment of these "gifts" or incidental loans made in times of personal and community crisis might not be subject to a market calculus, but repayment in the form of labor service was customary. Confronted by a maize harvest threatened by rains, a *sarkin noma* could and did call on the labor of fellow villagers. As such the institution of *sarkin noma* was a system of redistribution where extra-household labor was provided to large farmers facing production crises in exchange for assistance to small farmers facing crises of simple reproduction. As in all such institutions, rights and obligations flowed two ways. But as others have pointed out, the actual symmetry of the exchange cannot be taken for granted (Painter, this volume; Scott 1972:101; 1985; Thompson 1974). If asymmetry did characterize this exchange, it appears not to be in the current material or ideological interests of either the rich or the poor to recall this fact. The accounts of the institution of *sarkin noma* are markedly uniform regardless of the economic position of the person providing the account.

In addition to there being little information on the precolonial origins of this institution, informants disagree as to the date of the death of the last *sarkin noma*. The problem, however, is not simply a chronological one of determining who died when. Rather it involves the politically and economically contentious dating of the demise of a system of economic redistribution, as well as an ideology of mutual assistance which legitimated marked inequality in the rural social order. At the time of my research, a big farmer was still called a *sarkin noma*, but the term referred to the size of his harvest, not his generosity.

A second, nearly extinct noncapitalist institution for extra-family labor mobilization is a *gayya*, a communal work-bee based on reciprocal labor exchange. Big and small farmers alike called a *gayya*. Similarly a village chief also called a *gayya* for a public works project like clearing a road or working on his own farms, in which case participation of the villagers was compulsory. Sometimes a few men might constitute a *gayya* to assist a poor or ill friend. The goal of a *gayya*, however, was to assemble a large team of men to render communal assistance for the completion of a farming task. Both poor and rich men theoretically participated, although a rich man sent a son or client in his place. There were other differences in a *gayya* of the rich and poor. A rich man might hire praise singers to announce his *gayya* and to encourage participants by praising the attributes of the hardest workers. To add to the festive atmosphere, the wealthy farmer also hired drummers and *yan hoto*. The drummers provided a tempo to make the work go quickly, while the *yan hoto*, entertainers who hurled heavy hoes high into the air while dancing to drums, provided additional festivity. At two in the afternoon work stopped. The host provided a drink called *kunu*, a gruel made with sorghum or millet flour, flavored with tamarind juice, honey, or sugar. Work resumed and continued until six P.M. when a meal was served. The rich served chicken and other luxury foods. Despite the expense, a rich man might call a *gayya* that lasted four days.

The *gayya* of the less well-off were more modest. Without entertainers, the event was less festive and attracted fewer participants. Food, however, was essential, both in the afternoon and evening. Not to feed workers was unthinkable, even if the meal was a simple one. Given the cost of food for even a few workers, the *gayya* of a poor man was usually just a one-day affair.

As in the case of *sarkin noma*, it is difficult to chronicle the origins and decline of *gayya*. Based on research conducted in 1966–1969, Hill refers to *gayya* as "[n]owadays an elusive word" and of "declining importance" (1972:251). She notes that "[f]ormerly common, and at times compulsory, *gayya* is nowadays unimportant in relation to *kwadago* [wage labor] and always voluntary" (ibid.). At the time of my research, *gayya* was rare and in most places nonexistent.[6]

## AGRICULTURAL WAGE CONTRACTS IN NORTHERN NIGERIA

In contemporary rural Hausaland, there are basically three agricultural wage contracts.[7] The first is *jinga*. The people where I worked agree that it was the oldest wage contract, although they cannot date its origin. Instead they speak in terms of when it was rare—at the outset of the colonial period—and how it became increasingly common as the colonial period progressed. By the late 1970s, a *jinga* contract worked as follows: An employer negotiated with one or more men[8] a sum of money, a piece-wage, to be paid for the completion of a set task—for example, weeding a designated field of maize.[9] While the employer was concerned with the timely completion of the job, the number of days the laborer worked did not determine the sum paid. Often local men in need of cash, but with their own or their father's farm to attend, *jinga* laborers worked to their own timetable. Normally they worked without supervision. *Jinga* workers expected to receive numerous small payments as the job progressed. These were made at the discretion of the employer. Requests for these payments and the employer's response often constituted a source of far greater contention than the initial wage negotiation. If an employer responded positively to each request he could soon find himself having paid the entire wage for the job long before the job was completed. One could argue that each payment reduced his leverage over workers when it came to ensuring their completion of the job. The worker's perspective on these payments was obviously different. One way he would attempt to shape his employer's response was to refer to the payment not as a wage due for work completed but rather as *kudin abinci*, literally "money for food."

The use of food as a metaphor in this strategy is probably best understood in light of past rights and obligations that might tie employers and *jinga* workers. Employers and workers alike mentioned the following: In the past, particularly in times of famine, payment for a *jinga* contract might take the form of food rather than cash. Employers also sent a noonday meal to *jinga* workers. By the time of my research, these two practices were defunct, but the place of food in both of them is noteworthy. Certainly their previous existence, as well as the subsequent practice of phrasing requests for small cash payments in terms of "money for food," invokes the centrality of the food provided to workers by a *sarkin noma* or a farmer holding a *gayya*.

If payments and fringe benefits in food associated with *jinga* contracts gave way to a direct cash calculus, other social rights and obligations did not. As in the past, a loyal worker who guaranteed the availability of his services to an employer, who could be trusted to work carefully and to complete the job in a timely fashion, expected to be rewarded for more than delivering his labor power. Requests for loans of food or money were common. Employers wishing to ensure loyalty had to entertain such requests. They also were expected to provide generous gifts on religious holidays, marriages, deaths, naming ceremonies, and so forth. In some instances, long-term patron-client relationships grew to the point where an employer assisted his laborer in obtaining land, a wife, even setting him up with a secondary trade. Recipients of such assistance of course took on varied obligations typical of clientage relationships (see Scott 1972, 1985). As in the case of the discretionary cash payments associated with a *jinga* contract, the social and economic calculus of these other rights and obligations involved never-ending contention between worker and employer.

A second wage form that emerged later than *jinga* involved contracts based on a time-wage. There have been several time-wage contracts that vary according to the length of the working day. The first was *wuni-wuni* (in other locales called *uni*).[10] Informants in my research locale hold that *wuni-wuni* arose about five years prior to the famine known as *Yar Gusau*, in 1942/43. *Wuni-wuni* involved a payment for a day's work, starting at about seven in the morning and ending with the afternoon prayer at five in the afternoon. A noonday meal was carried to workers in the fields. Payments did not vary with the nature of the task involved.[11] The actual wage, however, varied seasonally, rising during labor bottlenecks and dipping when labor demand dropped.

While Marx points out that "wages by piece are nothing else than a converted form of wages by time, just as the wages by time are a converted form of the value or price of labor power" (1967:551), it is nevertheless important to note the relative advantages and disadvantages to employer and laborer that time- and piece-wage rates bring. There is general agreement that the onset of *wuni-wuni*, for example, resulted from an increase in the number of strangers seeking farm work. While a *jinga* contract allowed a worker to request a small advance, it is said that strangers wanted to be paid at day's end so they could leave town when they wanted. Employers obliged because with the advent of an increased number of strangers—many of them laid-off workers from the nearby Jos tin fields—*jinga* became a less secure contract. Strangers were far more likely than fellow townsmen to take a daily advance and then run away without completing the job. It is reported that local laborers also liked *wuni-wuni* because they could earn quick cash before the big religious holidays.

At some point, *wuni-wuni* was joined by a second time-wage, *sha biu*. The date of this is not clear. Previously, on market or mosque day, workers employed to work *wuni-wuni* only worked until *sha biu*, which literally means twelve, or noon in this case. In time, *sha biu* became the predominant time-related labor contract. On the one hand, it is possible to view this as a shortening of the working day from ending at five to ending at twelve noon. On the other, the introduction of *sha biu* allowed for a second shift of afternoon time-rated work, *yammaci* (lit. to eat the west, e.g., the direction of the setting sun). *Yammaci* workers labored from about two until five in the afternoon. Originally, *sha biu* workers, like *wuni-wuni* workers, received a meal while laboring. Hill reports this was still so where she worked. In my research locale, as in the case of a *jinga* contract, a noonday meal no longer figured. Laborers worked for money, not food.

The most recent innovation in labor contracts is *farashi*, a third contract form that has not reached many areas of Hausaland. Hill does not mention it (1972:105). Watts confirms its absence in northern Katsina during his research in 1977 (personal communication). Ross did not find it in the Kano area during his research in 1975/76 (personal communication). Tukur Ingawa (personal communication), who conducted research in southern Katsina in 1980/81, does note its occurrence. There it is called *aikin kuyya* (lit. "the work of ridges"). *Farashi*, like *jinga*, is a contract based on a piece-wage. The difference is that while *jinga* contracts are negotiated for a set task—such as weeding a field—*farashi* is negotiated by the ridge. The employer specifies both the task (ridging, weeding, etc.) and the length of the ridge. He and the laborer argue until they determine a rate per ridge. Once the rate is determined, a worker completes as many pieces, or ridges, as he chooses. The number of workers on a job varies throughout the day. Often employers do not know how many men were involved, let alone their names. Not surprisingly, such customary fringes as a noonday meal, a kola nut, or a cigarette do not figure. Even more to the liking of the employer, their impersonal relationship to *farashi* workers means that customary expectations drop away. Few see their employers as sources of loans and gifts, or as patrons.

My informants provided conflicting accounts of the origins of *farashi*, saying it originated anywhere from five to fifteen years earlier and still was not practiced in many outlying villages. The position that tends to be associated with those who engage in wage laboring is that laborers initiated the demand for *farashi*, wanting to have the option to work hard and to be paid a sum that would immediately reflect their output. Others claim employers pushed for *farashi* because they increasingly found that *sha biu* workers required careful supervision, or they slacked off during the day.

Whatever its origins, *farashi* is popular with employers because no advances are involved, which removes the risk associated with the disappearance of *jinga* workers, but like *jinga*, as a piece-wage it guarantees the relation between output and wage payment. *Sha biu* as a time-wage subjects the employer to the variation in employees' work speed, especially if they are unsupervised. With *farashi* the burden of this variation is shifted back onto the laborer. It must be said that *farashi* is also the preferred form of contract among certain laborers: itinerants, others in need of instant cash, the young and strapping. The old and tired do not do well with this new wage form. Nor do employers who are particularly concerned with the quality or specifications of the work done by hasty *farashi* workers.

## CONTEMPORANEOUS CONTRACTS, THE WORK PROCESS, AND ABSOLUTE SURPLUS VALUE

In the above discussion, I presented *jinga*, *sha biu*, and *farashi* in the temporal sequence in which they are said to have emerged. Clearly these three contracts constitute a continuum along which capital increasingly replaces non-monetary rights and obligations of employers and laborers. But this is only half the story. To understand fully how these new contracts rearrange bonds of economic interdependence between employer and worker, if not between agrarian classes, one must take into account that each new wage form has emerged as an option, not a replacement to earlier contract forms. While the sequence of their emergence may suggest a progression toward increased objectification, they are contemporaneous. Various conditions favor the use of different contract forms. (This will be taken up later.) To understand the coexistence of these institutions, one must consider some of the larger historical specificities that characterize capital, the work process, and the realization of surplus value in northern Nigeria.

During the period over which these contracts have evolved, there have been virtually no technological changes resulting in greater labor productivity. Without technological change, the organic composition of capital is unchanged. The proportion of living labor remains extremely high as compared to the labor embodied in tools and machines. Following Marx's distinction (1976:1019–1028), the subsumption of the labor process by capital in rural northern Nigeria is formal, not real. This is to say that the employer has not revolutionized the actual process of production. Rather he attends to the intensity, quality, and duration of work under the existing production process. For example, work may be more intensive under a *farashi* contract, or its duration extended, possibly exhibited by the breakdown of *wuni-wuni* into morning and afternoon shifts. These changes, however, have not affected the character of the actual labor process, the actual mode of production. Following Thompson's (1967) discussion of time and work discipline prior to industrial capitalism in England, there are not new machines or new production techniques to impose severe labor discipline. The degree of work synchronization remains slight. The characteristic irregularity of labor patterns remains. So do mixed occupations. In all of these ways, capital's subsumption of labor remains formal, not real.

All three wage contracts reveal that employers have not taken *direct* control of the production process. Workers continue to experience independence in the workplace. Employers have not resorted to severe supervision or tightened labor discipline in an attempt to maximize output per unit of time. Rather, employers do their best to ensure the standard of work quality and intensity adhered to by their employees. Unable to realize relative surplus, employers concentrate on those features of the work process or organization of work—such as the quality, intensity, continuity of work, and the duration of the working day—which hold the potential for increasing absolute surplus value.

Needless to say, laborers are similarly concerned but for the opposite reason. Negotiations over contract form and wages are the ground on which the rich and poor, the employer and the worker, defend their opposing material and ideological interests. I would suggest that the coexistence of these contract types reflects the particular topography of the ground which I have just outlined. This is not to say that the progression toward increased objectification does not indicate the ultimate nature of the battle to be waged between capital and labor. But in the meantime skirmishes are taking place, their range increased by these three contemporaneous contract types.

The realities of the work process on the ground often create antagonistic interests on the part of both employer and laborer that lead to different contractual arrangements and preferences. The pure commoditization of labor is not in every instance in the best interest of the employer, nor are the rights and obligations of clientage always most attractive to the laborer. While history may be favoring the objectification of employer-worker relations, the agents of history, in this case those negotiating the terms on which labor is bought and sold, act differently.

## THE WORK PROCESS, CONTRACT PREFERENCES, AND LABOR ANTAGONISMS

### The Agricultural Cycle and Changing Labor Demand

When examining factors of work organization that lead to choice of one contract form over another, one of the most important to employer and laborer alike is the changing demand for labor over the course of the agricultural season, which runs from May to December. Between planting and the harvest, the terms of employment shift dramatically, favoring the laborer and the employer alternately. This affects attempts by both parties to control the continuity and intensity of labor, key factors in determining the rate of the generation of absolute surplus value. For example, labor bottlenecks occur during May and June when new ridging and planting take place, favoring the worker (Lennihan 1983:236). Because late planting can drastically reduce yields, employers go to great lengths to ensure that they will not be caught short of labor during this crucial period (Lennihan 1983:236).

As might be expected, many enter into *farashi* contracts. For one thing, it ensures the work will be done quickly by men wishing to maximize output because they are being paid a piece-rate. In this way the employer attempts to increase the intensity of the work process. Another good thing about *farashi* is that because it is contracted by the ridge rather than by the whole job, an employer can increase his total labor supply with miscellaneous laborers interested in brief employment.

From the laborer's point of view, brief employment, for example, in the afternoon on the way home from his own farm, may have appeal given the urgency of getting his own crops into the ground. But *farashi* has its disadvantages for the laborer. It is at this time that the grain reserves of the poor have often run out. As a result many prefer a *jinga* contract with all its ensnaring social obligations because it allows them to request cash advances and loans of food. Given the competition for labor, some employers may enter into *jinga* contracts. They understand that acts of patronage on top of a wage can help to secure labor from men in need of credit, housing, food, and so forth.

Often the subsequent willingness of the laborer to complete a *jinga* contract quickly and the acts of patronage forthcoming become the source of contract disputes. Arguments, both loud and muted, over the actual meaning of a *jinga* contract and its attendant social obligations result in labor antagonisms. It is not uncommon for an employer to insist he owes a worker nothing at the end of the job, that cash advances and loans have wiped out the wage. A laborer may walk off the job before it is done, sometimes because his employer has not been adequately generous, sometimes because he knows he has already received the full wage in advances.

There are, however, also times when labor demand drops, favoring the employer. One such time is August and September, when it rains almost every day, almost all day, making it hard to work. Also by this time crops are maturing, requiring less attention. At this time, one might expect *farashi* to predominate, being the least ensnaring contract from the employer's point of view. It is true that many employers do employ workers *farashi*. *Jinga* contracts, however, are common. After all, a wise employer tempers his labor arrangements knowing that shortly there will be a gradual upsurge in labor demand as different crops become ready for the main harvest from October to December. He also has next year's planting season to keep in mind. Another fact which enters his calculation, however, is that by this time early-planted crops have been harvested. With the worst part of the "hungry season" over, it is easier for him to sidestep requests for loans of food or cash advances to purchase food. At this time of the year, the reply is *ba kudi*, or "there is no money," given that the main harvest has not occurred and crops have not been marketed. It is hard to know whether disgruntled laborers accept this reply because they consider it a legitimate excuse or because they know labor supply exceeds demand. Contract negotiations as well as the nature of labor antagonisms reflect labor supply and demand at the specific moment a contract is negotiated. They also, however, are influenced by the employer's concern for ensuring labor continuity in the work process, just as they are influenced by the worker's knowledge that today's bottleneck will inevitably be followed by a labor glut.

*Skill*

The laborer's skill is obviously important in determining the rate of absolute surplus. Not all workers possess the skill required for certain crops and tasks. Strangers from the far north, where soils are sandy and ridging is uncommon, may lack the skill for this task, demand for which constitutes the major labor bottleneck of the season. Those from other northern areas where there is ridging, but with a different sort of hand plow, often are unskilled in handling the local tool. An employer's approach to such men is tricky. While they may be slow or awkward at ridging, there is no problem with their weeding skills. In fact, when it comes to weeding, they are known to be extremely hard workers. They claim this is because of shorter rains in the north. They extend cultivation time by working longer days than are commonly worked locally. True or not, because of their speed and endurance they prefer piecework. They also prefer *farashi* over *jinga*. For one thing, they have no intention of settling. Many have farms in the north and only seek brief employment, because of harvest shortfalls or because the rains come later in the north. As a result, the patronage associated with *jinga* has no appeal, although many employers would love to have first call on these hard workers.

Weeding upland rice is another operation some workers do not know how to do. Until recently in this area rice was a relatively uncommon luxury crop. Many laborers lack the experience to distinguish between blades of young rice and grass. Nevertheless, some seek to maximize their wage payment by negotiating a *farashi* contract, do a hasty job, and at best leave many weeds and at worst trample the rice. Great labor antagonisms grow out of such occurrences, particularly when the employer tries to recoup his losses by refusing to pay or by reducing the wage bill. An employer's attempt to maximize absolute surplus value in this situation clearly hinges on the skill of his labor force. Even if the weeding of rice comes during a labor bottleneck, he must keep in mind that only the most skilled worker should be entrusted to do this job *farashi*. The employer might well prefer to hire the inexperienced laborer *sha biu*. Of course he will find himself competing against employers luring workers with *farashi* and *jinga* contracts.

*Care*

Other factors that impinge on contract choice are the care and thoroughness required by different tasks and crops. Ridges can be prematurely inundated with weeds because grassy topsoil is not turned deeply. Obviously this concerns an employer, but how much will it affect the sort of contract he negotiates? It is true that *farashi* workers may do a sloppy job in an effort to increase their wage. And certainly there is labor antagonism over what the socially determined standard of adequate work quality is and whether the completed work meets this minimum standard. An employer might avoid this contention by entering into a *sha biu* contract, hoping a worker paid a time-rate might be more likely to work in a painstaking manner. So might a *jinga* client hoping for extra gifts and loans. Many employers nevertheless choose *farashi*, risk the possibility of sloppy work, and hope to come out on top of whatever contention follows. It is not just that *farashi* frees the employer from social obligations. In addition he knows that *farashi* workers have an incentive to work fast. This is very important when it comes to ridging, especially for early-planted grains that suffer dramatic yield declines from delayed planting, yield of course being a key determinant of the quantity of absolute surplus realized. The calculus is very different, however, when it comes to transplanting delicate seedlings, most of which are high-value luxury cash crops. How fast they are transplanted is less important to yield than their getting into the ground undamaged.

### The Stranger versus the Local Question

Another characteristic of labor that affects the work process, contract preference, and labor antagonisms is whether the worker is a stranger or a fellow townsman. There are advantages and disadvantages to hiring from both categories. What are some of the advantages of hiring strangers? First, unlike townsmen, strangers do not have local farms and therefore are a potential source of regular labor. Second, because employers may be seen as a source of patronage, there is another reason for hiring strangers. Many depart before religious holidays that require gift-giving. Similarly, because strangers traveling afar in search of work usually do not bring their families or are bachelors, their employers escape requests for large gifts and loans for the general maintenance of the worker's family or for ceremonial occasions.

There are disadvantages related to the transiency of strangers, however. Foremost is the fact that it diminishes their potential to provide a constant labor supply. For example, as mentioned earlier, there are men from the north where the rains arrive later or are inadequate who practice a brief southerly migration. With farms of their own, their stay is brief.

The most numerous category of laboring strangers is the *dan duniya*, (lit. "son of the world"). He is a man who disappears from his hometown under the cover of night, usually leaving his family and possessions behind. Some are running from the law or have been released from jail. A less derogatory term is *dan iska*, literally "son of the wind." Relations between such wandering men of the countryside and their employers naturally take account of the laborers' unknown past as well as their potential mobility. Typically, a *dan duniya* arrives in town and inquires about work. Nobody knows anything about him. He may arrive penniless. He requires lodging. Usually he does not have a hoe, so he must be lent one, which may disappear when he does. He may be a careless worker. He may vanish in the middle of the job, after taking an advance.

Nevertheless, many employers take a chance. When coming across a man who seems to be a good and reliable worker, employers may set out to develop ties of loyalty, seeking to win him over with offers of lodging and an evening meal. There develops the assumption that the employer has the first right to the man's labor service. In some instances this relationship may be institutionalized to the point where a *dan duniya* refers to his employer as his master (*mai gida*) and his employer speaks of him as his boy or client (*yaro*).

As for the hiring of a fellow townsman, there are advantages and disadvantages as well. The circumstances that force local men to take up wage laboring have been indicated elsewhere (Lennihan 1983; Shenton and Lennihan 1981)—bad harvests, inadequate grain reserves, the mortgaging of export and food crops at exorbitant interest rates, previous wage laboring and the neglect of one's own farm, rising bride prices, the inclusion of expensive European goods in religious ceremonies, and so forth. What remains is the question of why an employer might or might not choose to employ a villager as opposed to a stranger.

Foremost among the disadvantages of hiring a townsman is that his own farm competes for his time. Foremost among the advantages of hiring a local man, however, is the existence of a public reputation concerning both his character and work habits. Lazy, slow, or careless townsmen are well known and can be avoided. Similarly, townsmen have their own tools, which does away with the fear of loaned implements being stolen. Unlike strangers, locals do not require lodging. There is never the worry of where a townsman will take his evening meal. Finally, townsmen are less likely to vanish from town altogether.

This does not mean hiring a local man is risk-free. While less likely to be downright dishonest, many local men prove unreliable. In addition, employers incur another previously mentioned liability: fellow townsmen see them as a traditional source of advances, loans, and outright gifts, invoking the paternalism that figured when villagers worked for a rich farmer in the old social order.

## CHANGED SOCIAL RELATIONS UNDER WAGE LABOR AND THE DYNAMICS OF SOCIAL REPRODUCTION

To understand fully how these wage-labor contracts have rearranged bonds of economic and social interdependence between those mobilizing and those providing labor, one must take a step back from the fields and consider the larger issues of changed social relations and the dynamics of social reproduction. For example, are the employers of wage labor small capitalists? Or does wage labor merely serve—however differentially in terms of benefits—to redistribute labor? Is there somebody accumulating, even insecurely, on the basis of wage labor? If not, are any larger social relations reproduced via wage labor? How are these social relations the same or different from those reproduced wholly or in part through the past institutions of *sarkin noma* and *gayya*?

The question of whether employers are accumulating capitalists or whether wage labor merely redistributes labor is a difficult one. One might argue that if wage labor was merely a system of labor redistribution, wages would be a token of reciprocity and a day's wages would approximate the value of the product produced in a day. Similarly, there would not be a fight over the wage rate. One might conclude this if one looks just at the small farmer, some of whom buy labor for one task or at one point in the farming season, only to turn around and sell their own labor for a different task or at a different moment (Williams 1983:58). But if one considers the rich farmer, the picture is different. If wages were the same as or more than the value produced, it would not pay for the rich to hire labor to expand production. But rich farmers are small capitalists who at least attempt to push wages below the value a day's labor produces. Hence the struggle over wage determination.

But even if this were not the case, there is no question that the larger social relations reproduced via wage labor are qualitatively different from those reproduced wholly or in part through the earlier institutions of *sarkin noma* or *gayya*. The history of capitalism is about the massive material and social consequences that undermine previous understandings about work, equity, security, obligation, and rights.[12] In the past in northern Nigeria, the ideology of paternalism attempted to legitimate the social order that grew from these understandings. This rationalization was embedded in concrete material practices and produced such social contacts as *gayya* and *sarkin noma*. Rich farmers calling a *gayya* or a *sarkin noma* rationalized their social status, their property, and their privilege by emphasizing the benefits they provided the rest of the village. At least at the level of ideology, these contracts rested on a calculus of mutualism and redistribution or reciprocity. For example, the institution of *sarkin noma* was one in which "help" (labor) was exchanged for "help" (charity, gifts, relief). In practice these exchanges might not be symmetrical, and daily struggle might be expressed by an event as simple as a neighbor absenting himself. But the particular nature of the rewards a *sarkin noma* offered and the terms in which they were phrased and understood—"charity," "gifts," and "relief"—brought the rich farmer not only a mechanism of labor control but one that muted labor antagonisms.

When it came to the nature of the work process, the work performed for a *sarkin noma* or a *gayya* was task- rather than time-oriented with the result that social intercourse and work were intermingled. The working day lengthened or contracted according to the task, and there was no great conflict between labor and "passing the time of day" (see Thompson 1967:60). The "host" of a *gayya* provided food and entertainment, the emphasis being on making the task more pleasant, not shortening the time the job took.

Wage contracts signify the restructuring of work and the social relations between the mobilizers and providers of labor. *Jinga* may appear to be task-oriented work in which a worker negotiates with an employer to complete a certain task in due time. But despite appearances, *jinga* marks the shift from task-orientation to timed labor. Those who are employed under a *jinga* contract experience a distinction between their employer's time and their "own" time. The first element cited in the negotiation of a *jinga* wage is how long the job will take. Arguments about the fairness of the wage center on different estimates of this time by employer and worker.

*Sha biu* contracts introduce for the first time a time-wage, furthering the notion that time is money. Unlike a piece-rate, which guarantees a relationship between output and wage payment, *sha biu* subjects the employer to the variation in employees' work speed. The employer "must *use* the time of his labour, and see it is not wasted: not the task but the value of time when reduced to money is dominant. Time is currency: it is not passed it is spent" (Thompson 1967:61). *Sha biu* also heralds an increased number of strangers seeking employment. The presence of strangers does several things. It points to the existence of an incipient regional labor market, and advances the establishment of an ideology of economic rationality and a market calculus of "supply and demand." It allows employers not to acknowledge the breakdown of village-level mutualism, but instead to blame strangers for the increased insecurity and labor antagonisms experienced under *jinga* contracts, and hence the need for a time-wage. It helps to justify the withering of the paternalistic customs of old and the increasing impersonalization of the social relations of production. This would be far more difficult if the labor pool continued to be made up primarily of neighbors and kinsmen. With the introduction of *farashi*, the issue is greater time thrift among improving capitalist employers, and the furthering of the impersonalization introduced by *sha biu*.

Wages introduce a new mechanism for direct and immediate struggle and conflict—a quality of struggle absent in the muted struggles characteristic of *gayya* and *sarkin noma*. The wage is both a source and a symbol of this increased conflict and struggle. The ideology of paternalism rests on the notion of "mutual help," which is "voluntary" and certainly is not subject to direct negotiation. But in northern Nigeria the ideology of "help" has begun to give way to the ideology of the "wage," in which labor payments are increasingly determined by supply and demand in the labor market. The ideology of economic rationality in wage determination is obviously a radical departure from the ideology of mutual assistance.

In situations where there is at least the appearance of a true labor market, it is possible that the ideology of the "blind hand" fills the void left by the demise of the value of mutualism. But in the northern Nigerian countryside, and many other places like it, the regional market is imperfect, and the blind hand of the market is not firmly in place. What is left is the raw reality the wage form constitutes. The material interests of employers and workers are not a mutual interest, but opposed. Nowhere is this opposition and conflict more apparent than in negotiations over contract type and wage rate. As I said earlier, the wage is the source and the symbol of the conflicting material interests of employers and workers.

## CONCLUSION

Because the issues around the recruitment of extra-household labor are points of contention between contracting parties, separating historical sequence from self-interest is problematical. While the emergence of new institutions, increasingly more rational in terms of their relation to a "capitalist" order, may be traced historically, their coexistence argues that each has utility in a contemporary milieu. The different sorts of relations each labor contract implies cannot be mistaken.

The apparent order of the emergence of new forms of labor contract and the demise or decline of some (*sarkin noma* and *gayya*) fits well with a scheme that opposes precapitalist to capitalist. The sequence might be read as a transitional stage between these two poles. But the persistence of "archaic" customs alongside "modern" replacements confounds such a construction of history. To further demolish this model, there are ample strategic explanations for the use, under certain conditions, of one of these forms rather than another.

Each side mobilizes "custom" to support its position in the negotiation of a work relationship. At times, this will favor an "archaic" form, at others a "modern" form. These categories are actively employed by parties to these labor negotiations, who appeal to the notion of custom or tradition. But neither the order of the emergence of these institutions nor the deployment of these categories by participants in a social struggle should conceal from us that these institutions exist side by side in the present, not because some are survivals but because they function to the relative advantage of one or another party, at one time or another.

The danger of attributing a historical sequence to contemporaneous phenomena is that important dynamics of contemporary social relations may be obscured. This is not to say that the order of the emergence of social institutions or the representation or construction of such a sequence is not of great historical significance. Rather it is a warning that once they have emerged, the existence of these institutions and their relations to one another have their own contemporary significance in the "actually existing capitalism" of present-day northern Nigeria.

## ACKNOWLEDGMENTS

I thank Jane Schneider, Jay O'Brien, Bill Roseberry, and Henry Bernstein
for their helpful comments on earlier drafts of this paper. I also benefited
from discussion with Gus Carbonella and Jon Poor. Finally, I acknowledge
the generous support of a PSC-CUNY and SSRC postdoctoral fellowship I
held while conducting the field research upon which I base this paper.

## NOTES

1. Henry Bernstein (1990:78) coins the term "actually existing capitalism" to distinguish the myriad variety of on-ground manifestations of capitalism from an ideal type drawn from a Western European– and United States–inspired construct.

2. See Kitching (1982) and Byres (1979) for a critique of urban bias and neopopulism.

3. This opposition is also central to analysts operating in the neoclassical tradition (Hill 1972; Norman 1972).

4. If one doubts the ongoing significance of this invention of the early colonial days, one only need note that it was not until the Land Use Decree of 1978 that it became possible to hold agricultural land in fee simple, a fact not mentioned by neopopulists when discussing the absence of landless in northern Nigeria.

5. There are exceptions in the densely settled zones surrounding the cities of Kano and Sokoto, but others as well (see Hill 1977: chap. 3; Mortimore and Wilson 1965). How the 1978 Land Use Decree, which for the first time allows for the registration of private title to land outside the urban areas, will affect the question of landlessness is not yet certain.

6. I found two exceptions to this in the town where I conducted research. One involved a husband's collecting firewood to heat water for his wife for forty days following the birth of a child. When I was there, it was still typical for a *gayya* to be called for this task. A second instance of a *gayya* I encountered in 1978, involved two grown brothers and their sons. For two or three days, all four worked on one brother's farm, then for the next two or three days they moved to the other brother's. I would hardly call this typical, however, as I only encountered such a *gayya* once in my fieldwork. Paul Ross (personal communication) reported more frequent instances in his field locale of Kano. See also Hill (1972:208, 251–252).

7. I have dealt elsewhere with the historical factors affecting the increased importance of agricultural wage labor in the colonial period (Lennihan 1981: chap. 3; Shenton and Lennihan 1981), and also with the frequency and purposes of such labor transactions in a contemporary Hausa community (Lennihan 1988).

8. At the time of my fieldwork, only men participated in the labor contracts described below.

9. Hill's (1972:105) discussion of wage labor holds that *jinga* was a relatively unimportant system of contract labor. This is very surprising, for *jinga* was the most frequent form of labor payment where I worked. In the area of her research, the predominant labor contract involved a day wage. A laborer was paid a "standard" wage, which varied somewhat seasonally, for some five or six hours' work. While Hill

does not name it, in my research locale this contract is called *sha biu*. In Hill's area a man was still served "free porridge" ( *fura*) while at work (ibid.).

10. It is known as *uni* in Kano (Paul Ross, personal communication) and as *aikin rana-rana* in southern Katsina (Tukur Ingawa, personal communication).

11. Reddy (1984:63–64) and Hobsbawm (1964:8) draw attention to important differences between wages that are fixed by customary expectation and wages that involve bargaining in the context of some degree of market calculations.

12. See Scott 1985:345. I am indebted to him for the clarity of his analysis of the ideology of paternalism. The comparability of the northern Nigerian and Malaysian cases is uncanny. In the following section I borrow several of his concepts and terms.

# FIVE

# Toward a Reconstitution of Ethnicity: Capitalist Expansion and Cultural Dynamics in Sudan

*Jay O'Brien*

Discourse on ethnicity and related issues seems to be problematic, both for its anthropological guardians and especially for their cousins in neighboring academic and policy-making fields. While real advances in the understanding of ethnicity have been made in anthropology in recent years, fuzzy primordialist notions seem still prominent in other disciplines and predominant in popular conceptions. When I ask students in my introductory sociocultural anthropology classes how many are German, Irish, Chinese, French, and so on, there is always a show of hands, some of them raised more than once. If I go on to ask about the proportions of the mix among those responding more than once, knowing snickers always greet my suggestion of such fractions as thirds or fifths. It seems that everybody knows the arithmetic of biological reproduction—and also knows that it is the same arithmetic that gives you your ethnic identity.

Anthropologists are, of course, much more sophisticated, and few would now accept that ethnicities are immutable primordial identities. Many anthropologists have contributed to the development of an understanding of the mutability of ethnic identity, which includes notions of situational identification, ethnic assimilation, colonial construction of ethnic units, and ethnogenesis. Nevertheless, the primordialist notion remains strong outside the discipline, and sometimes even seems implicit in the concrete analyses of some anthropologists. It could be that this circumstance reflects an incompleteness in our rethinking of ethnicity. Indeed, two important books by Wolf (1982) and Worsley (1984b) offer strong criticisms of the units and modes of cultural analysis current in anthropology. Wolf characterizes contemporary anthropology as preoccupied with dividing its subject matter into distinctive cases, or societies, "each with its characteristic culture, conceived as an integrated and bounded system, set off against equally bounded systems" (1982:4), concluding that

[b]y endowing nations, societies, or cultures with the qualities of internally homogeneous and externally distinctive and bounded objects, we create a model of the world as a global pool hall in which the entities spin off each other like so many hard and round billiard balls. (Wolf 1982:6)

What is missing, according to Wolf, is an appreciation of the interconnectedness of social and cultural phenomena and the historical contingency of the units that present themselves for analysis. While these programmatic statements from the introduction to Wolf's book can justifiably be said to overdramatize things and to ignore the permeability of boundaries, for example, in a Barthian analysis, the more nuanced analysis in Wolf's later chapters should lead us to take seriously his general complaint about the overvaluation of units and the undervaluation of interconnections in anthropological analysis of cultural processes. Our concern with Galton's Problem would seem to be a case in point. Wobst (1978) has made a forceful case that ethnographic preoccupation with identification of units has hampered the ability of archaeology to develop methods and concepts appropriate to grasping the fluidity of organization of Paleolithic hunter-gatherers.

Part of the problem is illuminated by Worsley in his criticism of contemporary anthropology's situational understanding of ethnicity (1984*b*:246). This understanding, he argues, tends to assume a market model in which individuals make choices, such as which ethnic identity to embrace, without constraint in much the same way that American consumers select which make of car to buy. The result is that the role of inequality and power relations in restricting the field of choice, and ultimately in shaping the larger cultural constellation, is left out. In particular, such a model of ethnicity is incapable of grasping the nature of cultural dynamics within and between societies divided by class. Worsley also detects formalism in anthropological discourse on ethnicity, in which it is treated as qualitatively the same kind of phenomenon regardless of historical period, social context, or level of operation (1984*b*:246–249). Thus, the ethnicities of the contemporary San, the classical Roman, and the Welsh nationalist are viewed as functional equivalents. Similarly, for analysts such as Colson (1968; cf. Worsley 1984*b*:367), ethnicity expressed through "tribalism" is seen as qualitatively the same as ethnicity expressed through "nationalism," only on a smaller scale.

The common theme that seems to unite the concerns of Wolf and Worsley is that our present conceptual tools for analyzing cultural dynamics are insufficiently attuned to the role of social relations—particularly those characterized by inequality—within and between groups in shaping ethnic identities and, indeed, the variable principles by which ethnicity is defined in different circumstances. In the remainder of this chapter I take up this challenge in the specific field of the social relations of the agricultural labor force developed in Sudan under the impact of capitalist penetration in the twentieth century. This labor force came to be structured and expressed in ethnic terms on the basis of principles that I argue were fundamentally constituted in the context of capitalist incorporation (see O'Brien 1980, 1983, 1984; Ali and O'Brien 1984).

## THE FORMATION OF THE AGRICULTURAL LABOR FORCE IN SUDAN

The British opened the vast irrigated Gezira Scheme for cotton production in 1925. Considerations of security and social control led the British to establish smallholding tenancies as the Scheme's basic units rather than fostering the development of a large landless proletariat. There was nevertheless a need for large supplementary supplies of wage labor for peak-season operations that tenant families could not complete alone. In response to this need, the colonial regime enacted policies to mobilize a large, seasonally migrant wage-labor force composed of peasants and pastoralists who maintained their village plots and their herds in addition to working for wages for a few months of the year (see O'Brien 1983).

The form of involvement in wage labor, and in markets more generally, which the British authorities promoted had therefore to be one that was compatible with the maintenance of peasant and pastoral productive systems; indeed, it had to presuppose their continued functioning as a prerequisite to the successful operation of the export sector. This condition meant that participation in wage labor varied from group to group depending on their differing divisions of labor, conditions of social reproduction, techniques of production, and so forth. The policies implemented to stimulate the appropriate type of labor supply are familiar from other parts of the continent in the colonial era: taxation in cash, undermining of craft production (particularly textiles), and aggressive marketing of a few key consumption goods of broad appeal (tea, sugar, coffee, manufactured cloth). These and other policies engendered cash needs that could not be met within existing productive systems without basic alterations, yet did not necessitate full integration into labor markets for their fulfillment. Neither did the conditions of the labor market, attuned to peak seasonal labor demands, allow much scope for full proletarianization (see O'Brien 1984).

For some, seasonal migration for wage labor became a regular part of their annual work cycle. For many more, it became an irregular part of life, occasioned by crop failure, disadvantageous livestock process, or special expenses (such as for marriage), or was a temporary necessity for youthful households. The mosaic of patterns of incorporation into the agricultural wage-labor force mirrored differences between local and social groups which were generally conceived in terms of cultural differences among them. If one knew a person's ethnic identification, one could fairly reliably predict what form her or his incorporation would take, including type, pattern, and intensities of work. The result was a highly segmented labor force structured on a basis that was expressed in terms of ethnic identities. Groups whose internal division of labor involved women in agricultural production, or allowed it in principle, tended to migrate to Gezira in family groups and put all family members to work in activities such as cotton picking. Other groups, particularly those that practiced a strict seclusion of women, often preferred to intensify village production and to meet their cash needs through production of a cash crop demanded by the British, a preference that sometimes required relocation to more favorable areas. When members of such groups did engage in seasonal wage labor, it tended to be only adult men.

The situation was, however, not a simple matter of one-way cultural determination of social forms of production. Indeed, once incorporation had become widespread, the process seems more generally to have moved in the other direction, from social form to ethnic identity. The following two case studies are offered as illustrations of different ways in which this occurred.

### West African Immigrants

Owing to the relative sparseness of population in Sudan and the lack of developed wage-labor markets, the colonial regime encouraged immigration into Sudan of West African Muslims, especially poor Hausa peasants from the former Fulani sultanates (see Duffield 1979, 1981, 1983). In the early 1930s the government and the Gezira Scheme management organized an active coordinated program of settlement of such refugees in the scheme (see O'Brien 1980, 1983, 1984). As a virtually landless population they served as a stable pool of cheap wage labor year round. Other groups of West African immigrants were encouraged to settle in underpopulated areas outside the Scheme, particularly in the Rahad/Dinder region east of the Blue Nile from Gezira, where they cultivated their own rainland plots and could be drawn upon as seasonal wage laborers for Gezira.

The groups involved in this immigration showed considerable cultural diversity. The largest number of them were Hausa-speaking peasants who affirmed distinct, named ethnic identities among themselves. There were numerous other groups as well, including Fulani, Borgu, Bornu, and various Chadian peoples. All of them were Muslims and most of them spoke Hausa at least as a second language, but many different languages and cultural forms were represented among them.

Right from the beginning, resentments against these groups began to develop among the indigenous populations with whom their work brought them in contact. The Gezira authorities used them in two important ways to discipline tenants in the Scheme. If a tenant failed to carry out an agricultural operation on schedule, the Inspector hired settled labor to do the job at double the going wage and charged the expense against the tenant's account. Any tenant who failed to cultivate his plot to the satisfaction of the British

Inspectors or who absconded (as many did during early cotton blights and the depression) were replaced by immigrant settlers. More generally, the long experience that most of the immigrant groups had of disciplined agricultural work under conditions of exploitation predisposed them to adapt to the rigors of market relations efficiently and impersonally. They bargained hard, and collectively, over wage rates and then worked very hard to maximize returns to their labor time. In contrast, many of the local, mainly Arab, populations—many of whom were only part-time or recently settled cultivators—held agricultural work in low esteem, avoiding it when possible and working at it desultorily when it became necessary. Despite the dramatically higher labor productivity of West African settlers, tenants often tended to prefer hiring less hard-working locals with whom they could establish family-style patron/client relations and create long-term obligations to work.

The settlers came to be known generally in Sudan as "Fellata" (from the Kanuri word for Fulani). This term was applied indiscriminately to all "Westerners" and quickly took on basically pejorative connotations linked to stereotypes of these people as hard-working and slavish. In a context in which the contacts that local populations had with these diverse people were socially homogeneous, the cultural differences among them were glossed over and ignored.

The settlers responded to these conditions of hostility, discrimination, and confinement to the lowest rungs of the social ladder through a process of cultural realignment. Some material differences with the local populations were reinforced. Some of the settlers moved into previously vacant economic/ecological niches, such as riverbank vegetable cultivation and commercial fishing, which they had occupied in West Africa. In regions where cultivation had previously been mostly restricted to sandy ridges, they moved out on the heavy clay plain where their broad-bladed, short-handled hoe, destined to become known in central Sudan as a "Fellata" tool, was more suitable to weeding the muddy soil in the rainy season. In addition, they did make some changes in their material culture in adjusting to Sudanese conditions. The small-bladed, long-handled hoe used in dry weeding on sandy ridges by their Sudanese neighbors was added to their tool kit. Generally, they also adopted local styles of dress and house-type.

Along with these changes, they began to elaborate a number of key symbols to differentiate themselves from the culturally dominant Arabs in ways that served to legitimate the differences and endow them with dignity. In particular, they tended to adopt fundamentalist, ascetic Islamic practices and beliefs that served as a counterpoint to the "paganism" of the surrounding Arabs, who practiced spirit possession (*zar*), ecstatic trance, and veneration of saints, and drank alcoholic beverages. In rural areas at least, they practiced an increasingly strict seclusion of women within the household compound and confined participation in wage labor to adult men only. They articulated an ethic of hard work and moderate consumption. Gradually, the name "Takari" came into use among them as a term applied, regardless of ethnic origin, to all of the people otherwise called Fellata. The term derives from the respectful name applied in the Hejaz to any pilgrim from West Africa. As the adoption of this name indicates, there was a tendency toward the obliteration of the intergroup and subgroup differences under a specifically Sudanese identity of Takari.

Mark Duffield (1979, 1981) has argued that this process represents the formation of a new specifically Sudanese ethnic identity corresponding to a definite location in the colonial social system. Partly in defensive adaptation to circumstances of discrimination and lumping together by others, these diverse cultural groups have drawn on commonalities of their past heritage and contemporary circumstances to forge a more or less coherent ethnic identity. It is of course uneven, with small groups living in more remote rural areas showing less integration than others. I have encountered some villages of people who steadfastly affirm their separate identity, yet have met some of their relatives in more central areas who claim the Takari identity.

### The Joama' of Central Kordofan

The Joama' people are another group that has played an important role in the agricultural wage-labor force. From the beginning they have been prominent as regular suppliers of cotton-picking labor in family groups. They occupy the transitional zone of central Kordofan where the sandy ridges of northern Kordofan penetrate the heavy-clay plain of the rich central agricultural region. Settled cultivators identified as Joama' have been recorded as living in this area since at least the seventeenth century. They are Muslim Arabic-speakers and generally claim Arabian origins, claims much disputed by their neighbors and by Western scholars (most notably MacMichael 1912). Such evidence as exists suggests that this zone has been a scene of cultural blending for at least a couple of centuries. The area straddles the great east-west "highway" of the precolonial trade routes linking Sudan and the Ottoman Empire with the western Sudanic states, a route that was followed by thousands of African pilgrims to the Hejaz and along which the British laid an important railway line soon after conquest. This has long been an area of movement and mingling of diverse peoples. The name of the Joama' itself roughly translates as "gathered together," further reinforcing the impression of mixing. In villages across this zone one encounters considerably varied stories of the origins of the Joama' and how they came to occupy their present homes. The account current in a particular village or cluster of villages often sounds remarkably similar to the reputed origin of some nearby Arab group. For example, in some eastern Joama' villages, the favored account traces their origin to a little-known brother, Jumi' (the "in-gatherer"), or Jimi', the Arabian founding ancestor of the Jima' group that

lives immediately to the east of the Joama' and whose claims to Arabian
ancestry are respected. Other groups of Joama' claim to be recently settled
branches of the Baggara Arab tribes.

Whatever the cultural dynamics of the earlier history of these people, their
contemporary identity is clearly bound up with their modern position in the
wage-labor force. This position has been characterized by annual family-
group migration for cotton picking, initially in the Gezira Scheme, but latter-
ly more often in the pump-irrigated schemes along the Nile. Women and
children were centrally involved in both village agriculture and wage-earning
labor but, unlike the case with many Arab pastoralists and recently settled
former pastoralists, Joama' men generally appeared to work as hard and as
long (at least) as did the other members of their families.

The Joama' soon became famous in central Sudan as good, reliable cotton
pickers and were highly sought after. With the rapid expansion and differentiation of capitalist agriculture beginning in the 1950s, an elaborate recruitment system for seasonal labor evolved, and the Joama' belt became a
prime recruiting ground. Representatives of tenants or management would
travel to the region in advance of the picking season and negotiate with
prominent men to supply stipulated numbers of pickers at agreed rates. Recruiters would supply transportation to the scheme, cash advances and food
for each family while at work in addition to fixing piece rates for work performed. As this recruitment system became entrenched, newcomers to the
agricultural labor market—or people who sought to move into a different
sphere of it—increasingly found it necessary to be in the places recruiters
usually went to find such labor. It also helped to be identified to the recruiter
as a member of an ethnic group, such as the Joama', reputed to be good
workers at the particular sort of job being recruited for. In response to these
conditions, some of the thousands of immigrants and seasonal migrants from
further west who annually moved through the Joama' area began to settle on
the fringes of Joama' villages and insert themselves into the Joama' pattern of
seasonal migration.

Joama' villagers were quick to take advantage of the abundant labor float-
ing through their neighborhood. Many villagers cleared as much land as
possible and used their earnings from wage labor to hire labor to cultivate
larger fields. In a very short space of time all available land was privately
held by individuals and cultivated every year. There was thus no vacant land
for latecomers to cultivate for subsistence purposes during the long part of
the year when wage labor in capitalist agriculture was unavailable. Instead,
Joama' landowners began to offer migrant families small grants or loans of
land, take them on as sharecroppers, and in other ways give them access to
land for subsistence crops in exchange for their labor. Then, after the local
harvest both would migrate for the cotton-picking season to Gezira. Even-

tually, the more successful larger landowners were able to withdraw from wage labor altogether.

In research in a Joama' village in 1977, I found a number of families with known origins outside the village who appeared to be in different stages of assimilation to the group. Four families identified themselves to me as Joama' and were referred to by other villagers as Joama', but after some weeks in the village I learned from one older man that these families "used to be Fellata" (that is, West Africans). They had come to the village in their youth and been granted plots of land by the speaker's father. In this man's view, the "Fellata" families had proved their worth through hard work and cooperation and had become legitimate Joama'.

Another group of three brothers and their families had settled in the village more recently and occupied a somewhat different status. They had established a separate small hamlet with a number of relatives (Ballala, from Chad) about two hundred meters from the village and had been given very little land. Most of these families had rented or sharecropped land from the Joama', until all but the three remaining families had moved a few kilometers away to a new Ballala village a few weeks before I arrived. The families who remained behind had moved their houses into the main village and continued to cultivate small plots that had been given them by a large landowner. Villagers referred to these people as "good Ballala" who were "just like the Joama'."

The comparison between the situations of these two groups of families is suggestive of a process of ethnic assimilation in which each represents a different stage on the way to becoming Joama'. If so, it is a process of formation of an ethnic identity which corresponds to access to a specific location in the agricultural wage-labor force. Not all those assimilated to the ethnic identity of Joama' occupied the same position with respect to the labor force. Some were independent, landowning peasants, while others were virtually landless agricultural laborers both in the village and on the capitalist farms. But the ethnic identity that each affirmed was conditioned by a local social structure articulated to a regional and national social structure primarily through the participation of most villagers in wage labor according to a definite and distinct pattern identified as the Joama' pattern. There were also a few other individuals and families from different ethnic backgrounds who had settled in the village and become Joama', including one of the two richest merchant-moneylenders and an Islamic healer, each of whom received a grant of land and patronage from one of the village's leading families.

An indication that such a process of assimilation has been going on longer than the few decades reflected in the cases discussed is given by the division of the population of the village roughly in half between the two principal Sufi tariqas represented there. The Sammaniya tariqa was the sect most popular in rural areas of precolonial central Sudan and to which the Mahdi belonged, as did the bulk of his Joama' army. The Tijjaniya tariqa was brought to significance in Sudan by West African immigrants, the poor among whom were almost uniformly Tijjaniya. It could be that the Tijjaniya adherents in el 'Igayla are people of West African descent who did not feel the same sorts of pressures on their religious identifications as they experienced with respect to their ethnic identity. If so, it also suggests that not all West Africans participated in the formation of the Takari identity.

## ETHNIC PROCESSES AND THE LABOR FORCE

These are but two examples of a diverse set of ethnic processes that have characterized the formation of the agricultural labor force in twentieth-century Sudan. As these cases illustrate, there is not a single ethnic process at work, but many. The dynamics of each, as I have tried to suggest here, derive from the specific intersection of precolonial local characteristics and capitalist encroachment. In rural areas the social composition of a particular ethnic identity has tended to be more or less heterogeneous but to take its central character from a predominant form of market participation. In urban areas and some rural trading centers, a more narrowly occupational definition of ethnic identity—or ethnic definition of occupational identity—has occurred. In both sorts of conditions, access to certain locations in the labor force and markets has tended to become regulated by ethnic identity, often involving substantial cultural change. Whether through coalescence and synthesis of a new identity, assimilation and accommodation of individuals and small groups to shifting established identities, or through other means, people came to participate in labor migration circuits and other markets as "ethnics" of a particular sort.

The ethnic segmentation of the labor market and the ethnic processes that were associated with its development in Sudan corresponded to conditions of capitalist expansion on the basis of absolute surplus value—that is, by insertion into existing communities in ways that required people to work longer to maintain themselves at the same level (see Marx 1977 [1867]:643–672). By the mid-1970s capital had fully penetrated Sudanese society in the relevant sense and its further expansion had begun increasingly to bring it into direct competition with subsistence production for land and labor. Under these radically changing conditions, exacerbated by the impact on Sudan of international economic trends and internal political crisis, the dynamic of the labor force began to change dramatically. The needs of rural populations for cash in order to meet subsistence requirements expanded and deepened rapidly. Forest and pasture land disappeared, eliminating direct sources of building materials, fuel, and supplementary foods. Terms of trade shifted drastically to the disadvantage of small producers. People generally experienced increasing pressures on their labor time, leading to the adoption of ever-narrower calculations of returns to individual labor time as the sole criterion of work. A shift toward capitalist expansion on the basis of relative surplus value began to occur, based primarily not on direct technical improvements in labor productivity but on socially dictated intensification of work effort, spurred indirectly by technical changes in agricultural operations other than the main peak labor-demanding harvests.

The result of the combination of these forces has been a breakdown in the ethnic structure of the labor force (see O'Brien 1980, 1983; Ali and O'Brien 1984). Individuals who previously migrated with their families to pick cotton began to split up between different jobs in order to maximize income from the work they did. Thus, men, and women unencumbered by small children, began to work in the higher-paying sorghum harvest while children, old people, and women with children continued to pick cotton. As workers generally sought higher returns to labor time, increasing numbers eschewed payments in kind of transportation, food, and so on, in favor of higher piece rates. Employers in turn, faced with escalating recruitment costs attendant upon inflation in petroleum and other prices and a generally rising wage bill, sought to cut costs wherever they could, and began to cut back the long-distance recruitment effort. The structure of the labor force has consequently taken on increasingly direct social form, with people of all ethnic groups seeking the highest-paid work available to them at the lowest cost. Age and sex were becoming more reliable predictors of patterns of labor-force participation than ethnicity.

An important consequence of these recent trends has been a tendency for long-distance seasonal migration to decline in significance and for labor markets to become more localized within distinct regions. Increasingly, seasonal workers seek to minimize costs of job searches and to work as close to home as possible. Those who find no wage-earning opportunities close to home, such as many people of Darfur, resettle more or less permanently in areas closer to centers of employment, such as Gedaref District. Paralleling these developments in labor markets, the government began in the late 1970s a program of administrative decentralization based on regions created out of two or more provinces each (Rondinelli 1981). As employers and employees increasingly confronted each other on the basis of class, class struggles became regionalized. The new administrative framework provided a basis for capitalists operating on a regional scale to attempt to divert local class conflicts into interregional competition and opposition to the central government and the import/export interests that dominated it. If this strategy is successful, regionalism may come to replace ethnic rivalry and tribalism as a political strategy for small capital and the petty bourgeoisie. Such a development does not imply the disappearance of ethnicity as an important form of identification, but only a change in its structure and significance as class and regional identities take over some of its functions in organizing political and economic relations.

Crosscutting these emerging axes of conflict, however, is an increasingly important dimension of nationality. The rigidly restrictive Nationality Law denies citizenship rights to immigrants and most of their descendants born in Sudan. Such rights are indispensable to gaining secure access to independent farmland, higher-paying jobs, and other means of upward mobility. Takari groups are thus effectively frozen in the bottom layers of the unskilled cheap-labor force. Recently, thousands of Eritrean and Ethiopian refugees have been joining them through a resettlement program that has been moving them from refugee camps to labor-supplying villages around the major schemes. The social disabilities of these groups rest on their statutory position as legal foreigners deprived of the rights of Sudanese.

## TOWARD A RECONSTITUTION OF ETHNICITY

The chief intent of this analysis has been to indicate—through specific cases taken from Sudan—the way in which ethnicity as it has been encountered in the contemporary Third World, particularly by anthropologists, has been constituted by the same world-historical process that has produced modern capitalism, wage labor, and class structures. As historically constituted social identities, contemporary ethnicities have fundamental determinations that are as modern and capitalist as are those of the giant multinational corporations. They are not natural objects, slightly modernized traditional identities, relics, or billiard balls. This observation further implies that accounts of the impact of capitalist encroachment on Third World peoples which have taken ethnicity as an artifact of precolonial structures have been little more than pseudohistories, based implicitly on oppositional models of noncapitalist society. This is the case because the method of reconstituting the precapitalist past of these societies has often consisted of subtracting supposed capitalist effects on them and then analyzing the abstract effects of adding back in the subtracted elements. That is to say, the starting and ending points of analysis, regardless of theoretical stance, have tended to be identical; analysis itself is pseudohistorical, being based on imputed absences of capitalist characteristics in the past or in existing supposedly autonomous units. The results vary depending only on the oppositional models employed—for example, market/nonmarket, high technology/low technology, exchange value/use value, and so on. Many anthropologists and ethnohistorians have transcended the view of ethnic identities as relics of a traditional past, but to the extent that they continue to treat them as bounded objects they also tend implicitly to employ oppositional models of capitalist and noncapitalist forms in which ethnicity as an organizing principle remains undifferentiated and particularly characteristic of noncapitalist forms. Reading of their work by nonanthropologists almost automatically transposes the opposition back into the terms of modern and traditional. Wolf's project in *Europe and the People without History* (1982) represents an important step in challenging such oppositional models.

The limitations placed on our analyses by pseudohistorical construction upon a basis of oppositional models seem to me crippling. In the case of African studies, these limitations appear to account for the difficulties encountered and the tortured models developed in attempts to reconstruct precolonial states, class structures, and market systems that are known to have existed but whose bases are poorly understood. Thus we are given "peripheral" or "nonmarketplace" markets latent within "nonmarket societies" (Bohannon and Dalton 1962), an "African mode of production" in which exploitation takes place only between (classless) societies through trade (Coquery-Vidrovitch 1978), and "tributary" modes of production dominating social formations that comprised numerous distinct modes of production (Amin 1976). Capitalist penetration is thus reduced to market creation and/ or replacement of one external dominating structure by another, with qualitatively unchanged "traditional" local communities either quickly dissolving or persisting in stunted form.

Such impoverishment of theory leaves us incapable of contending with the complex dynamics of modern ethnic processes, and of finally transcending the apologetic tribal atavism thesis which ascribes contemporary political fragmentation in African countries to the effects of primordial ethnic loyalties. It also renders us unable to anticipate or adequately analyze fundamental transformations within the bounds of capitalist political economy as that which has been restructuring the agricultural labor force in Sudan over the past decade. Analytically, tribalism, regionalism, and class struggle come to appear as mutually indeterminate alternative forms of social conflict linked by an implicit evolutionist schema. Social forms such as the ethnic segmentation of the Sudanese labor force tend to be seen as the result of traditional resistance to change or simple colonialist manipulation, a fundamentally ethnocentric view that misses the most central determinant of the process. It obscures the fact that the extractive economy imposed by colonialism foreclosed complete market integration as an option for all but a very few Africans by developing a sharply seasonal demand for wage labor and maintaining a need for people to meet most of their consumption requirements outside markets, primarily through their own direct efforts. Under these circumstances ethnicity represents an organizing principle articulated by the Sudanese people through their creative struggles to respond to colonial encroachment, and thus also was not simply imposed on them by colonial divide-and-rule policies. Ethnicity was, of course, not invented by capitalists or people reacting to them. In the contemporary Third World, however, we can fully comprehend ethnic organization—and its historicity—only in relation to modern social struggles in the context of peripheral capitalist development. Such an understanding must avoid substituting a new formalism for the old, and therefore must be sensitive to the variable character of peripheral capitalism as well as to the specificities of central capitalism and socialism as they affect the principles of ethnicity.

## ACKNOWLEDGMENTS

This chapter originally appeared, in slightly different form, in *American Anthropologist* 88, no. 4 (1986). Research in Sudan was carried out between 1974 and 1979 with permission of the Anthropology Research Board of Sudan under a grant from the Economic and Social Research Council, Khartoum, and a Ford Foundation grant to the Manpower Research Project of the Faculty of Economic and Social Studies, University of Khartoum. Ellen Gruenbaum, George Saunders, Bill Roseberry, Ann Binder, and the editor and reviewers of the *American Anthropologist* provided helpful comments on early drafts.

# SIX

# The Orientalist Paradigm in the Historiography of the Late Precolonial Sudan

*Jay Spaulding and Lidwien Kapteijns*

This study is a critique of a set of outdated and in essence racist concepts that has dominated European historiography of one portion of the Sudan's precolonial past.[1] This historiographical tradition—exemplified by authors such as H. A. MacMichael, J. S. Trimingham, and P. M. Holt—has not only distorted an important period of Sudanese history but has also supplied an unfortunate conceptual framework for much modern Western thinking about the Sudan. Journalists, employees of the development industry, political decision-makers, and other nonspecialists are rarely in a position to critique the ready-made paradigm forged by the professionals and are therefore condemned to perpetuate its unworthy stereotypes. An infallible source of negative images is the Orientalists' assumption that all Sudanese people are to be evaluated against the standard of diverse texts couched in the Arabic language, a method of reasoning through which the Sudanese are inevitably predestined to emerge as biologically degraded (when measured against a largely mythical literature of noble genealogical trees), religiously degenerate (when measured against the canons of bookman's Islam), and culturally impoverished (when measured against the accumulated wealth of the good and the fair from all Islamic ages and lands). If such textualist Orientalist analysis is outrageously unjust to those Sudanese who do adhere to Arab identity and Islamic faith, it removes those who do not from the realm of humankind entirely and relegates them, in MacMichael's words, to a loathsome simian "Monkeydom of Nations" (Collins 1983:122). What follows is not merely a theoretical disagreement among historians of the late precolonial Sudan but also an open invitation to all to rethink the prevailing Western intellectual assumptions concerning causal factors in the conduct of Sudanese society past and present.

## THE ECLECTIC ORIGINS OF SUDAN STUDIES

Intellectual discourse concerning the Republic of the Sudan enjoys a long prehistory in the form of indigenous literatures both written and oral, the accounts of geographers and travelers over long centuries, and the works of antiquarians who viewed the land as an integral if admittedly peripheral part of the eastern Mediterranean cultural world. The modern academic study of the Sudan, however, may be said to have begun with the Anglo-Egyptian conquest at the turn of the present century. One important early forum for the integration of the Sudan into Western conceptual schemata of the twentieth century was the journal *Sudan Notes and Records*, first issued in 1918. Many contributors were government servants high and low, who used the pages of the journal to share anecdotes of their encounter with the unfamiliar in a new land. Others, however, were academics of current or future professional eminence, whose contributions laid the foundations for the disciplines within which subsequent formal study of the Sudan would be conducted; examples drawn from the social sciences would include G. A. Reisner, the Egyptologist and ancient historian; A. J. Arkell, the founding father of Sudanese prehistory; and E. E. Evans-Pritchard, the distinguished anthropologist.

Among these pioneering scholars' most durable accomplishments (though, alas, one of questionable intellectual merit) was the geochronological partition of the Sudan into discrete and bounded academic fiefs and, conspicuously, into a "north" composed of Orientals and a "south" inhabited by "people without a history" (Crawford 1948:8). For example, for half a century the south was to be "known" through the discipline of anthropology and the early north through prehistory and archaeology; it was as unthinkable to compose an ethnography of a northern community as it was to search for stone artifacts south of Malakal. The long-overdue tasks of intellectual self-criticism and interdisciplinary discussion began in the 1950s but are by no means yet complete.[2]

The present study concerns one geochronological segment of the Sudanese experience as delineated by European thinkers of the early twentieth century, namely, that of the northern half of the country after the disintegration of the medieval Nubian kingdoms (ca. A.D. 1300) and before the onset of colonial rule. In political terms this historical episode saw the formation of kingdoms based in the Nile valley (Sinnâr) and the western highlands (successive dynasties of Dâr Fûr). In cultural terms this interval has often been seen to be meaningful in a way that earlier segments of experience were not, in that significant continuities out of this age, through the colonial period, and into the present have been alleged to exist. In intellectual terms, academic discourse about this period has clung to otherwise-discredited pejorative stereotypes and has thus far evaded serious critical scrutiny. The burden of the present study is to help rectify this anomaly.

Scholarly treatment of the precolonial northern Sudan after 1300 has its own history. By a pact no less effective for being tacit, this region and period were declared a district closed to the disciplines of archaeology, anthropology, and history; slow to acquire a correspondingly influential disciplinary patron of its own, this closed district long remained the preserve of intellectually eclectic amateurs. As early as 1912 H. C. Jackson published the first English-language treatment of Sinnâr: *Tooth of Fire* was a small work of enchantment, brimming with enthusiastic affection and, in spite of its obvious imperfections, containing the germ of a potential tradition of historiography (Jackson 1912). Many contributors to *Sudan Notes and Records* over the decades to come, individuals too numerous to mention here, wrote with diverse passions on more limited topics; they generated both a significant corpus of empirical data and an exotic potpourri of interpretative ideas. Particularly significant in the latter regard was the polymath A. J. Arkell in his alternative capacity as amateur historian; he not only drafted a history of Dâr Fûr but also made a special vocation of erecting innovative structures of theory to lend meaning to the ever-swelling volume of facts. Being keenly aware of the provisional and contingent character of his interpretive architecture, Arkell himself was often the first to refurbish or demolish his own intellectual edifices in the light of new evidence or better ideas—a particularly endearing quality that always left room for improvement in an admittedly imperfect world.[3] In 1951, as the Sudan approached independence, O. G. S. Crawford offered a new reading of the later precolonial history of the Sudan (Crawford 1951). *The Fung Kingdom of Sennâr* was a much more somber book than *Tooth of Fire*, bearing the deformities of attitudinal influence from the rising school of historiographical orthodoxy to be introduced below. Nevertheless, Crawford marshaled the full body of evidence and interpretation assembled by the *Sudan Notes and Records* contributors and made considerable progress in disciplining this motley and recalcitrant melee toward coherence. Moreover, from hitherto unexplored quarters he introduced an impressive body of new source materials in the form of the records of Jesuit and Franciscan missions to Ethiopia that entered the Sudan at the close of the seventeenth century—though his lack of facility in German would seem to have crippled his appreciation for the longest and by far the richest of these records, the account of Theodoro Krump. Crawford's *Fung Kingdom* represented a worthy benchmark within the open-ended and eclectic tradition of historiography that gave it birth, yet it was not, and did not claim to be, a flawless synthesis; ample opportunities remained for future improvements by the author himself, Arkell the indefatigable revisionist, Jackson the romantic, or any number of other inquiring minds. The appearance in the late 1950s of a formally

recognized academic discipline of African history in Britain and the maintenance of cordial liaison between British academic life and the corresponding
institutions of the independent Sudan created what appeared to be a highly
propitious investigative environment. It was not to be.

## THE FIRST INCARNATION OF THE ORIENTALIST PARADIGM:
## GROSS RACISM AND REIFIED ISLAM

The flaw that doomed the cheerful and exuberant eclectic tradition was its
irrelevance to the dominant and entrenched paradigm of contemporary
European academic thought concerning Northeast Africa. Edward Said has
labeled this intellectual tradition "Orientalism," and delineated some of its
salient characteristics as an institutional phenomenon. "The history of
Islamic Orientalism," he noted, "is relatively free from skeptical currents
and almost entirely free from methodological self-questioning" (Said 1981:
128). Under ordinary circumstances there has prevailed "a sort of consensus:
certain things, certain types of statement, certain types of work have seemed
for the Orientalist correct. He has built his work and research upon them,
and they in turn have pressed hard upon new writers and scholars" (Said
1978:202). It is meaningful to speak of a "guild tradition of Islamic studies
. . . that has both protected and confirmed individual scholars in what they
did, regardless of the methodological perils and innovations challenging
scholars in most other humanistic fields" (Said 1981:129). The intellectual
content of the Orientalist paradigm as it was imposed upon the Sudan has
been definitively characterized by Wyatt MacGaffey as a mind-set composed
of "patterns which combined idealism, or the method of contrasting ideal
types, with pseudo-Darwinism, which sought the origins of political development in the interaction of differently endowed groups" (MacGaffey 1966:16).
A particular merit of MacGaffey's analytical perspective is its high level of
abstraction, from which vantage point one may perceive, as will be demonstrated below, that the same idealist and pseudo-Darwinist paradigm has
manifested itself at lower levels of abstraction not once but twice in succession in the study of late precolonial Sudanese history. In both cases the
skeleton of theory was fleshed out with what Said has aptly characterized as
"a series of representative fragments, fragments republished, explicated,
annotated, and surrounded with still more fragments . . . a canon of textual
objects passed on from one generation of students to the next" (Said 1978:
128–129).

During the years embracing the World Wars the late precolonial period
of northern Sudanese history found, in Islamic Orientalism, a dominant
academic disciplinary patronage.[4] Henceforth the laurels of intellectual respectability would go not to the humble scribblers of the eclectic tradition,
immersed in the mundane details of Sudanese reality, but to the scholar who

could first fabricate a reading that conformed to the fashionable idealist and pseudo-Darwinist Orientalist prejudices of the day. Through the cumulative weight of successive publications in 1912, 1922, 1934, and 1954, this distinction was achieved by the prominent Condominium official H. A. MacMichael (MacMichael 1912, 1922, 1934, 1954). The marriage of raw political clout to banal intellectual conformity proved irresistible, and the eclectic tradition was progressively muzzled and eclipsed. By the 1950s, while MacMichael's writings were being published in sumptuous format by Cambridge University Press, Crawford was obliged to issue his *Fung Kingdom* privately through an obscure provincial printer at his own expense.

At the hands of MacMichael the idealist Word was made Flesh in terms of racism, "the doctrine that a man's behavior is determined by stable inherited characteristics deriving from separate racial stocks having distinct attributes and usually considered to stand to one another in relations of superiority and inferiority" (Banton 1970:18). For MacMichael the precolonial Sudan was a land of "chaotic savagery" (MacMichael 1934:11) inhabited by a flotsam of "offscourings swept from east and west by prehistoric upheavals" (Mac-Michael 1934:19), a human detritus that had coagulated into collective racial entities defined by a promiscuous mixture of physical and cultural criteria. Thus the Beja were "a fine virile people, poor in worldly substance, Mohammedan by religion, but predominantly Hamitic in origin and speaking To-Bedawi or Tigré. They are as wild as hawks" (MacMichael 1934:15). The Baqqara were "a more or less homogeneous racial congeries" (MacMichael 1934:16) in contrast with the "black aboriginal Nuba, who are strangely heterogeneous in physical type and language" (MacMichael 1934:17), not to mention the "tall longshanked dolichocephalic Nilotes" (MacMichael 1934:18) and the "fetish-ridden tribes of Fertit" (MacMichael 1934:19). But MacMichael's special affection—if that is the right word—was reserved for the Arabs, "a feckless people, excitable, but kindly and honourable by instincts, following the rainfall in their perennial search for pasture" (Mac-Michael 1934:15). According to MacMichael the conduct of the Arabs could be inferred from ancient texts, for the political behavior of Arabic-speaking Sudanese people in the twentieth century was a racial trait inherited down the centuries from their putative pre-Islamic Arabian forebears: "The line of cleavage between the two great Arab groups of descendants of Qahtân on the one hand and of Ismâ'îl and 'Adnân on the other has not been obscured by the lapse of ages, nor by the tremendous unifying force of a common religion, nor by continuous intermarriage, nor by migration to distant lands" (Mac-Michael 1922:II, 3). Thus for the Arabs, as for the other races of the precolonial Sudan, biology was destiny, but in their case a comparatively happy one, given their "moral ascendancy over the more backward Sudanese" (Mac-Michael 1934:28), a superiority demonstrated through their adherence to Islam.

For MacMichael, the possibilities for attaining knowledge about the history of the precolonial Sudan seemed very limited, though he did concede that "in each of its component parts there survived garbled memories of racial wars and tribal quarrels, intrigues and jealousies of petty local tyrants" (MacMichael 1934:12), and he was willing, in passing, to acknowledge briefly the previous (albeit irrelevant) existence of Kush, Meroe, and Nubia. By far the most important event of precolonial history, however, was the coming of the Arabs, for it was this event, according to his conceptions, that established the interaction of opposed ideal types, Arab and non-Arab, that was to dominate subsequent Sudanese history. In MacMichael's view the historical process of interaction between these two idealized racial types had both a negative and a positive component, namely, murder and rape, usually in that order. In the restrained euphemisms of polite discourse "it is enough to say that the Christian Sudanese barrier... now finally crumbled and fell before the oncoming Arab hordes" (MacMichael 1934:29), who thereby "gained a moral and cultural ascendancy, intermarried with the local population, acquired lands, and in general prepared the way for their own eventual control" (MacMichael 1954:24), that is, "for the ultimate transfer of power to their own descendants" (MacMichael 1934:28).

In his major work, *A History of the Arabs in the Sudan*, MacMichael sought to augment the plausibility of this vision of historical process by repeating it, with endless permutations, in regard to every Arabic-speaking community of the Sudan. The gross paradigm brachiated into an intricate, florid tribal Arabesque whose spurious foundations were obscured by the weaving of an elaborate and erudite superstructure of cross-reference to literary works of the Islamic heartlands and their European commentators. The realities of ordinary time collapsed; what matter if a tribal genealogy written in the fifteenth century also reported the conquest of Kordofan by the Turks in 1820? It provided MacMichael with an opportunity to display his Orientalist virtuosity by citing "a canon of textual objects" that included the Qur'ân and Genesis, Abu'l-Fidâ and Ibn al-Athîr, Ibn Khaldûn and al-Mas'ûdî, al-Tabarî and Wad Dayf Allâh, al-Shiblî and Ibn Sa'îd, Yâqût and al-Dasûqî, Na'ûm Shuqayr and Hajji Khalifa, Wüstenfeld and de Slane, D'Arvieux and Sale, Huart and Palgrave, Wright and Sprenger, Van Dyck and de Meynard, Burckhardt and Burton, Sarkissian and Ludolf, de Herbelot and Menelik—not to mention abundant references to his own writings (MacMichael 1922:II, 181–212). To borrow the judgment of Said, MacMichael placed "overall intellectual incoherence" (Said 1981:144) at the service of "synchronic essentialism" (Said 1978:240), an essentialism of race, propelled by hatred and lust, through a strange history without time, to be justified morally by Islam.

MacMichael's published academic discourse sought to lend an air of scholarly finality if not historical inevitability to certain controversial policies he himself was in the act of designing and executing as a high official of the Anglo-Egyptian administration. In addressing his associates in government privately, MacMichael offered an image of Sudanese reality that violated every tenet of his own published paradigm. From the administrator's perspective, as opposed to the scholar's, the problem with the Sudan during the 1920s was not that it was inhabited by inherently incompatible groups of people but rather that politically and culturally self-assertive sentiments then current in the capital showed every sign of spreading throughout the length and breadth of the country. It seemed to MacMichael that this assertiveness had already reached a point at which the only protection against "the insidious political intrigue which must in the ordinary course of events increasingly beset our path in the North" lay in the forcible closure of the southern Sudan in order to erect a "solid barrier" by creating there "a series of self-contained racial units . . . with structure and organization based on the solid rock of indigenous tradition and belief" (Collins 1983:173). In both north and south, the sentiments that advocated unity should be squelched by creating a new indigenous elite to be supported by, and to dominate, various units designated "tribe." "Where such does exist," MacMichael ordered, "the aims of the Govnt is to foster and guide it along the right channels. Where it has ceased to exist it may still be possible to recreate it" (Collins 1983:58). In short, MacMichael's scholarly vision of the Sudan as a land divided into a "north" and a "south" on racial and religious grounds, and fragmented by the processes of history into numerous "tribes," was less a reflection of any social or historical reality than one colonial administrator's prescriptive utopia.

While MacMichael's primary focus was the distribution of political power in the Sudan through the interaction of the idealized racial entities of Arab and non-Arab, it was also possible to construct a reading of the same racist dynamic in terms of religion; this, through the medium of many writings, was the vocation of J. S. Trimingham. Trimingham's Sudan, like MacMichael's, consisted of an opposing pair of idealized racial entities whose history and culture, and most particularly their religion, were to be understood in terms of the mixing of blood:

> The population of the Sudan falls naturally into two great classes, a northern Muslim area and a southern pagan area, the so-called Arab and negroid areas. . . . The Muslim area embraces the peoples of the dry desert and steppe regions of the north who are Arabic-speaking and Islamic. In this region there has been some admixture of Arab blood with that of the original population. . . . The Southern Sudan . . . on the other hand, is totally different in race and culture, and includes all the heterogeneous dark-skinned pagan peoples of the south. . . . It is rare to find anything approaching a pure racial type among

any of the peoples of the Sudan, for this land has suffered from many events of racial dispersion. All its peoples are variations between the pure Caucasian and the pure Negro type." (Trimingham 1949:4–5)

Like MacMichael, Trimingham enveloped the unwholesome racist fantasy in as complex a net of erudition as his capabilities allowed, but his attention span was shorter and his reference library smaller, with the result that the idealist dynamic in his *oeuvre* lies but shallowly submerged under ripples of textual cross-reference, and numerous inconsistencies in concept and terminology between one Trimingham work and another are clearly visible. To choose an example of mature Trimingham analysis, one may single out his 1969 characterization of the religious life of pastoral people in the northern Sudan. The actors in the drama, of course, are two contrasting idealized racial types: the Hamites, a race to be distinguished by the fact that they herd livestock, and the Sudanese, introduced a few pages previously as "Negroes" but now seen to be the result of "an early blending of Negro and Hamite" subsequently debased by an additional "Negro admixture" (Trimingham 1969:19). The defining characteristic of this race is its inherited propensity to practice agriculture. For Trimingham, the religious practices of these peoples must inevitably reflect the underlying racial dichotomy: "One feature of what we may call Hamitic Islam as contrasted with Sudanese Islam has been that popular religion was based on Sufism in the form mediated by personal and family *tariqa-ta'ifas* and inseparable from the saint cult" (Trimingham 1969:24). It would be pointless to attempt to impose rational meaning upon what is so clearly gibberish, and even the urge to do so may perhaps be seen as confirmation in Said's maxim that "the intellectual regulation by Orientalists of discourse about distant and alien cultures positively and affirmatively encourages more of itself" (Said 1981:148). Salient is the fact that when harnessed to the idealist and pseudo-Darwinist paradigm, "Islam" too became a reified analytical entity—as Said put it, "a real object called Islam" (Said 1981:39).

The historical role assigned to this reified entity labeled "Islam" may be inferred from the controlling metaphor used by Trimingham, MacMichael, Holt, and others to describe its behavior (cf. Said 1978:311–314): "Islam" arises; it spreads; it enters; it penetrates, sometimes painfully, in a series of thrusts; it erupts; it fecundates; it fertilizes; it engenders; it rarely if ever withdraws. The other reified entity in this lubricious reading of racial and/or religious history is non-Arab and non-Islamic; she is inferior, vulnerable, open; she is probably passive or even receptive, but if she resists, she will be subdued and penetrated by force. She is fertile; her experience of intercourse with the reified racial and/or religious. Other of the idealist and pseudo-Darwinist historical paradigm may indeed result in offspring. At best, however, they will be a degenerate bastard breed of half-Hamites, given to Sufism, saint worship, and perhaps even agriculture.

## THE SECOND LIFE OF THE ORIENTALIST PARADIGM: THE MODERN ARAB SUDAN

At the close of the 1950s the emergence into political independence of many new nations occasioned some significant readjustments within the leadership of the guild of Orientalists; Old Masters sought new careers or early retirement as a refugee clan of phased-out former colonial officials from the Sudan and elsewhere sought secure academic niches from Christchurch to Calgary. One of the survivors in this academic scramble out of Africa was P. M. Holt, a librarian from Khartoum who by 1965 had been named Professor of Arab History in the University of London. In his inaugural lecture Holt defined his field of special competence as Modern (after 1500) Arab History. "One area, the Sudan," he concluded, "is in better case than some of the more central parts of the Arab lands: the last twenty years have seen the output of a number of important works" (Holt 1965:15). In explicitly minimizing the significance of works produced before 1945 (Holt 1965:14), Holt signaled his rejection of the eclectic tradition and his allegiance to the Orientalist paradigm. Through a series of contributions to the second edition of the *Encyclopaedia of Islam*, the *Cambridge History of Islam*, the *Cambridge History of Africa*, through *Studies in the History of the Near East* and the several successive editions of *A Modern History of the Sudan*, Holt firmly entrenched his interpretation of the late precolonial Sudan at the summit of the existing corpus of historical writing about that place and period (Holt 1965, 1970, 1973, 1975, 1979).

Holt's major contribution to the historiography of the precolonial Sudan was to recast MacMichael's and Trimingham's explicitly racist rendition of the idealist and pseudo-Darwinist paradigm in terms more palatable to the postcolonial age. Like his predecessors, Holt accepted the idealist premise that precolonial Sudanese history should be understood in terms of interaction between the now familiar opposing pairs of reified racial and/or religious entities. For example, in the most recent edition of his *Modern History* the "central theme" around which his discussion of the precolonial period is organized is the characterization of the "indigenous tradition" of the precolonial Sudan as "a product of the mingling of Arab Moslems and Africans," a natural consequence of "the penetration of the region by [Arab] tribes" and the ensuing "intermingling" through "intermarriage between Arab immigrants and the older Nubian population" (Holt 1979: flyleaf, 3–4, and 1988: cover, 3–4). However, Holt shrank somewhat from his predecessors' explicitly lurid vision of this historical process; he devised a new rubric under which the paired idealized entities of Arab and non-Arab, Muslim and non-

Muslim, could continue to carry on the conduct of precolonial Sudanese history precisely as before, but without evoking resonances of a low-budget Hollywood biblical epic. He achieved this effect by raising the two sets of interactions themselves to the level of reified, idealized analytical entities. Modern Arab History, according to Holt's new version of the Orientalist paradigm, should be understood in terms of "two processes, related but distinct: one of arabization, the other of islamization" (Holt 1965:6). The shift of primary focus from delineating and characterizing races to an emphasis upon historical process was certainly healthy, but by making idealized, a priori entities out of processes whose content was undefined and unknown, Holt begged the very question a historian might be expected to address: how and why does historical change come about? Under Holt's analytical paradigm the only possible answers to this question were "islamization" and "arabization," meaning nothing more or less than the respective processes of movement out of one idealized category called non-Muslim or non-Arab into a second called Muslim or Arab. Further, according to Holt's conceptions, these two processes always and inevitably moved in the same direction; his analytical schema contained no reified entities of process called "de-islamization" or "disarabization." In this may be discerned his preservation of the pseudo-Darwinist vision of hierarchy among idealized analytical entities, and the survival of implicit assumptions of superiority and inferiority concerning Arabs and non-Arabs, Muslims and non-Muslims. In short, nothing of significance had changed; both the idealist and the pseudo-Darwinist components of the old Orientalist paradigm stood unscathed, and concrete reality was one level of abstraction farther away than ever.

As Holt worked out the implications of his revised Orientalist paradigm in actual practice, he took two further steps that had an important and deleterious impact upon the development of the historiography of the precolonial Sudan. First, he excised from the realm of admissible historical evidence most of the fruits of the eclectic tradition, including not only the insights gathered in the field by the *Sudan Notes and Records* contributors and the synthesizing ventures of Jackson, Arkell, and Crawford but also the bulk of the relevant travel literature. Apparently it was asking too much to expect a "Professor of Arab History" to take seriously a literature of primary sources about the precolonial Sudan which, as fate would have it, happened to be couched in Latin, Portuguese, Italian, French, German, and English; on the rare occasion when Holt stooped to cite a non-Arabic source at all, it was often as a target for ill-considered ridicule. For example James Bruce, in his account of eighteenth-century Sinnâr, made explicit reference to institutional provisions for the judicial execution of unsatisfactory monarchs. Though abundantly verified by other travelers and typical of many comparable African courts, this feature of the Funj constitution did not conform to Holt's preconceived notions of what a "Modern Arab Sudan" should properly have been. Therefore he rejected Bruce's testimony as a "gratuitous generalization" (Holt 1965*a*:944) and added elsewhere the defensive and methodologically revealing apology "but the evidence in the Arabic sources for this practice is not clear" (Holt 1979:33). By "the Arabic sources" Holt clearly did not mean the living memories of Arabic-speaking folk of the northern Sudan, who to this day find no difficulty in recalling the institution in question in some considerable detail.[5] Through arbitrarily confining his source literature largely to materials written in Arabic, Holt ensured that his reading of the precolonial history of the Modern Arab Sudan would be fragmentary, superficial, and short (Holt 1966:219–221; Holt 1988:217–229).

Holt's second step in applying the revised Orientalist paradigm, which had the effect of further diminishing the authentic Sudanese voice in Sudanese historiography, has been the elaboration and refinement of a technique for inferring the significance of phenomena and events in the Sudan by derivation from texts produced long before and far away in remote districts of the Islamic heartlands—by a logic analogous to that of contemporary Americans who infer the meaning of the daily news from obscure passages in Leviticus under the guidance of fundamentalist Christian radio preachers. While the previous generation of Orientalists had contented themselves with mining the written texts of the Islamic heartlands for genealogical references (a natural preoccupation for those who assumed that history was transmitted biologically), Holt expanded the technique to include a wide range of cultural artifacts. Historical research now meant trait-chasing, and the ultimate goal of the exercise was to be able to impose upon the precolonial Sudan the whole inventory of cultural features that constituted "Islamic civilization" as embodied in the corpus of aged texts. For example, a recent Holt review of a book about the modern Sudan takes the reader as far afield as medieval Egypt and twelfth-century Iran, apparently to consider the possibility that the institutions of early-twentieth-century Dâr Masâlît were derived from, or are explained by, the various phenomena to be observed there (Holt 1986:565).[6] To the extent that Holt's revised Orientalist paradigm embodied anything more than the crude racism of its predecessor, this search for history-by-*qiyâs* (analogy) was expected to reveal its concrete content. The results, to take the enterprise on its own terms, have been disappointing; nothing even remotely approaching the erudite edifice of the racist genealogists has emerged.

## CONCLUSION

The Orientalist paradigm of history, as applied to the late precolonial Sudan, is idealist in that it reduces meaningful reality to two pairs of opposing reified entities which it labels "Arabs" or "Muslims" on the one hand and "non-Arabs" or "non-Muslims" on the other; it is pseudo-Darwinist in that it assumes the inherent superiority of the former. In the first incarnation of the Orientalist paradigm as gross racism, the "Arab Muslims" asserted this superiority in technicolor through murder and rape. In the present denatured version of the paradigm, historical interactions between the same and identically endowed opposing idealized entities are themselves reified as two idealized unidirectional entities of process termed "arabization" and "islamization." While these terms in themselves might perhaps be harmless descriptive metaphors in the hands of a historian prepared to disaggregate them into objectively meaningful components, in orthodox Orientalist discourse they serve as an all-purpose analytical phlogiston to be injected liberally among the interstices of empirical data whenever the question of causation may arise. At no time, however, has the vitality of the Orientalist paradigm depended upon its ability to convey historical truth; it has survived and flourished because it has served certain entrenched interests inside and outside the Sudan. It is detrimental to the Sudanese, because it defines the problems of the country in terms that cannot be solved.

A number of contemporary students of the Sudan, scholars whose professional expertise and benign intentions are beyond doubt, have nevertheless often chosen to express themselves in the idiom of the Orientalist paradigm, if only in a search for gripping metaphor or rhetorical flourish.[7] In several quarters there have been attempts to blunt the sting of the paradigm through the formulation of ingenious constructs that preserve its idealist binary opposition but sacrifice its pseudo-Darwinist component. While one may certainly respect the efforts of these reforming scholars to ameliorate the less-pleasant features of the orthodox Orientalist paradigm, it is difficult to avoid the conclusion that they have labored with inferior conceptual tools unworthy of their intent. Further, their subtlety is wasted upon the nonspecialist, who has no difficulty in retranslating their adjusted and refined concepts back into the more familiar long-standing stereotypes of "pagan Negroes" and "Muslim Arabs." The Sudan is ill served by those who derive meaning from the past and propose solutions to present problems in terms that are at best empty and irrelevant and at worst racist and divisive.

## NOTES

1. This essay addresses the historiography of the late precolonial Sudan from the final decline of the Nubian kingdoms in about 1300 until the imposition of foreign rule, a process that began as early as 1820 in the northern Nile Valley but was not consummated until World War I or even later in parts of the west and south. In previous writings we have developed at length original interpretations of late precolonial Sudanese history; here we seek to make explicit the critique of older paradigms contained therein. Specifically excluded from consideration are the comparatively

sophisticated historiographies of the nineteenth-century Turkish colonial period and of the Mahdist state; though by no means above criticism, they are not entirely reducible to Orientalist idealism and deserve more extended and subtle analysis.

2. A full discussion lies beyond the scope of the present study. Some important landmarks would certainly include the first major anthropological studies undertaken in the north (Cunnison 1966; Asad 1970), the first substantial treatment of southern archaeology and prehistory (Mack and Robertshaw 1982), a persuasive reading of the history of the northern Nile valley "as a continuous narrative of the cultural development of a single people" (Adams 1977:5), the opening of a sustained dialogue between anthropology and history in regard to the communities of the Ethiopian borderlands (Donham and James 1986), and the beginning of exploration, by anthropologists, of the relationships between colonial regimes and the academic disciplines that developed within them (Asad 1973).

3. This assessment is based primarily upon one author's personal correspondence with Dr. Arkell, the latter's contributions to *Sudan Notes and Records*, and his numerous unpublished manuscripts on deposit in the National Records Office in Khartoum and the library of the School of Oriental and African Studies, University of London. Arkell's *History of the Sudan from the Earliest Times to 1821* was too obviously written under the cold eye of H. A. MacMichael (see discussion, pp. 142–145), who provided a tone-setting prologue: "At the close of the last century the whole of the vast heterogeneous area of the Sudan was in a dark age of chaos. Security and justice were no more than names, savagery and barbarism were the only realities, and practically nothing was known about the country by the outside world" (Arkell 1961:v).

4. Statements about causalities lie beyond the scope of this essay, but they are hypothesized to lie implicitly embedded in the structure of power relationships among scholars within the institutional architecture of the British Empire and its neocolonial analogues.

5. For an introduction see Spaulding (1985:129–131); for evidence, in Arabic as well as other languages, see the sources cited therein.

6. Proponents of the history-by-*qiyâs* method tend to avoid direct statements on the model "X caused Y," apparently in order to preserve a Nixonian posture of "deniability" if directly challenged. Their implicit intent to assert causal relationships is usually obvious, however, and they should be held fully accountable.

7. Striking examples are Hall and Amin (1981:1–2) and Voll and Voll (1985).

# SEVEN

# Popular Memory and the Palestinian National Past

*Ted Swedenburg*

*There's a battle for and around history going on. . . . The intention is to reprogram, to stiflle . . . the "popular memory" and also to propose and impose on people a framework in which to interpret the present.*

—MICHEL FOUCAULT, "FILM AND POPULAR MEMORY"

It happened during the height of the great terror panic, just three days before a bomb would go off at a West Berlin disco, killing a U.S. serviceman, wounding thirty-five others, and providing the pretext for U.S. air raids on Libya. On 2 April 1986 an explosion on a TWA jet approaching Athens killed four U.S. citizens. A mysterious group—the "Ezzedine Qassam Unit" of the "Arab Revolutionary Cells"—claimed responsibility, saying it was in retaliation for the U.S. Navy's clash with Libya in the Gulf of Sidra.

The name "Ezzedine Qassam" was unknown in the country whose citizens were the targets of violence, and it was reduced to insignificance by the media barrage on the terrorist danger. The essential fact was that U.S. citizens had been murdered. Only brief items such as these appeared: Qassam was "a Palestinian who fought and was killed by the British during their occupation of Palestine in the 1930s" (*Washington Post*, 4 April 1986); he was "killed in 1948 in Jerusalem in Arab-Israeli fighting" (*New York Times*, 3 April 1986).

There is no such confusion among Palestinians in Israel and the Occupied Territories with whom I conducted fieldwork in 1984 and 1985. For them, the name Shaykh 'Izz al-Din al-Qassam carries rich historical significance. He is remembered as a hero of the Palestinian struggle for liberation and a symbol of patriotic sacrifice. By and large, Palestinians know that he was a Syrian, not a Palestinian, who took refuge in Palestine in the early 1920s after being sentenced to death by the French mandate authorities. He became a popular Islamic preacher in the city of Haifa, speaking out against British rule and Zionist colonization, and advocating spiritual renewal and political militancy as the means of fighting these dangers. In the late 1920s, having concluded that only armed revolt would end British rule, stop Zionist colonization, and bring national liberation, Qassam began secretly to organize guerrilla bands, recruiting his men from the urban lumpenproletariat and the peasantry of nearby villages. Only a few days after going up to the hills with a band of followers, Qassam and his men were discovered, and on 20 November 1935, some fifty years prior to the TWA operation, he and three followers were killed in a battle with the British mandate police forces, near the village of Ya'bad. Their martyrdom electrified the Palestinian populace. In a matter of months, owing in part to Qassam's example, a rebellion against the British mandate was launched. That unsuccessful revolt, lasting from 1936 to 1939, was the last great popular insurrection in Palestine before the *intifada* erupted in December 1987.

My field research in Israel and the West Bank concerned the revolt that Qassam helped trigger. I was interested in how elderly male Palestinian villagers, particularly veterans of the rebellion, remembered this significant event in their past, and in the place of that disparate memory in a national history. I chose to study this insurrection because of its symbolic importance as the first massive Palestinian mobilization on a national scale. Yet, despite its symbolic significance, published accounts marginalized the popular character of this national, anticolonial insurgency (cf. Swedenburg 1988). My aim was to contribute to the retrieval of a subaltern history of the revolt and at the same time to analyze the possibility for a popular memory of revolt under the difficult conditions of Israeli rule. In other words, I wished to understand the context governing the emergence of the statements I collected about the revolt during fieldwork.

Palestinian memory, I soon learned, cannot be understood on its own terms. Its "truth" does not rest solely in "the field." That memory is produced under conditions peculiar to the Third World, where, as Mary Layoun observes,

> [t]he problems and solutions of. . . culture are not only those that take place within a sacred national *interior*—the creative national mapmaking of the colonial powers made that clear. Instead, they take place in what is more like an international railway station than a national inner sanctum. (1988:57)

Because Palestinians have yet to win national independence and enter the postcolonial era, their difficulties are even worse. They produce their history in a space that resembles a bomb shelter under constant shelling more than a railway station. As they attempt to construct an "authentic" identity for themselves, they are constantly aware that this must be accomplished in a relation of subordination and antagonism to Israeli repressive and ideological apparatuses. They know too that those apparatuses, which impinge upon their production of history, are backed up by the West and the United States in particular. So in a real sense, how Palestinians remember their past also has everything to do with how they are "remembered" and imaged in the

West. My attempt to understand Palestinian memory, therefore, required thinking it in relation to the history of Jewish colonization in Palestine and its Imperialist support.

The "Ezzeddine Qassam Unit" that carried out the TWA bombing was attempting to draw such historical connections—between the Palestinian struggle of the 1930s against Zionist colonization and its British backers, and the battle against Israel and its imperial ally today. But the bombing only momentarily disrupted everyday life in the United States, while serving merely to reconfirm that Palestinians are savage terrorists. Because there is no ideological space for Palestinians in the West, the message was fated to misfire. The sheer force of the dominant Zionist narrative, Edward Said has observed, simply does not permit the emergence of any "socially acceptable narrative to absorb, sustain and circulate" counterfacts about Palestinians (1984:34). For instance, the fact that Palestinians were the victims of the Zionist venture and paid a high price for its successes cannot be placed meaningfully within, or against, official narratives. The story of the advance of Western civilization in the East, through its proxy Israel, pushes Palestinians to the margins. Lurking in the West's shadows, the "wild" Palestinian Other occasionally blasts his or her way into center stage with explosive charges and machine-gun bursts. These infiltrations of the Western narrative, lasting for a flicker of the television screen, are ultimately counterproductive, apprehended as irrational interruptions of an unfolding story of Western progress rather than as statements within a plausible counternarrative. Palestinian violence does not remind us of the crucial part the West plays in suppressing Palestinian rights; instead it serves as retrospective justification for everything "we" in the West do (Said 1984:37). The killing of U.S. citizens in the name of a Palestinian hero sparks no interest here in Palestinian history. That past remains murky, impenetrable, irrational, and violent.

Given the absence of any space for Palestinians to assert their narrative, U.S. support for Israeli suppression of the Palestinians can continue relatively unchallenged. This massive aid impinges upon Palestinian memory itself. Yet even acts like the TWA bombing in the name of Qassam, the unrecognized reminders of a historical repression (de Certeau 1986:4), should alert us to the suppressed or ignored interrelations between our own national history and that of others. It reminds us that "our" history is equally a story of our suppression of other histories, of the fact that our cultural identity appears to be produced within a sacred inner shrine only because of unmarked tombs in other places. "There is no document of civilization," Benjamin remarks, "which is not at the same time a document of barbarism" (1969:256). Palestinian attempts at historical self-representation must be understood as an effect of their narrative absence in the West.

## MEMORY IN THE WEST

Recent studies of popular memory, of history as a cultural construction, and of the "national past" (cf. Popular Memory Group 1982; Bommes and Wright 1982; Wright 1985) were crucial to how I conceived my research project. They show how Western historical writing, hiding behind a language of objectivity about "the past," obscures one of its key functions: the deployment of narratives that play an essential part in the construction of peoples' identities. In the contemporary era, history is preeminently a restaging of a *national* past. The nation is that totality according to whose ideological terms people are bound together, in the name of a "general interest" that conceals and displaces class differences (Hall 1979:321). As the "prevailing universe of discourse," nationalism is "a name for the general condition of the modern body politic, more like the climate of political and social thought than just another doctrine" (Nairn 1981:103, 94). The national past serves as one of the fundamental discursive producers of identity.

The rise of history as a specialized discipline was intimately connected to the emergence of the Western nation-state and modern capitalism. Coincident with these developments, there arose within civil society a network of institutions devoted to the codification of the past as official history, to the selection and collection of relevant traces of the past in archives, and to the professionalization of historical study. An expansive network of "historical apparatuses"—state rituals, publishing houses and mass-media organs, schools, museums, and historical sites—was established, whose job it was to address the official historical narratives to the people-citizens of the Western nation-state (Popular Memory Group 1982). The purpose of such institutions, Foucault observes, was not to show people "what they were, but what they must remember having been" (1989:92). These historical apparatuses produced a "memory" of a unified social body that was not fractured by class, regional, or religious difference. Official versions of history ensured that the official past was internalized as if it were a set of facts beyond change and independent of memory (Terdiman 1985:21). And as the past was "nationalized," the traditions of subordinate groups were variously appropriated, recast, or obliterated. The past became a national myth.

This dominant historical discourse was not simply imposed upon a passive people. For the rise of the modern nation-state in the West was connected to a new type of political-ideological form. Bourgeois democracy marked the entry of the lower classes into the political terrain and the narrative of history, the end of rule through discourses of stratification and "natural" hierarchy (Nairn 1981:41). Gramsci called this novel political form "hegemony," by which he meant the exercise of political control through a combination of persuasion and force, such that persuasion is the predominant feature. The hegemonic order inserts the masses into politics so that they believe they exercise ultimate self-determination within the social order (Anderson 1977:30); their consent is secured through this incorporation. Hegemony is not a fixed moment, therefore, but the result of the ruling bloc's mastery of the class struggle, of its gaining authority over the economic as well as the political and ideological levels (Hall 1980:332–333). In Gramsci's conception, universal suffrage, bourgeois hegemony, and national feeling are all parts of a package (Buci-Glucksman 1982:124).

The national past therefore never achieves its form automatically. Official discourse shapes subaltern memory both by establishing "acceptable" forms through which the people should contemplate and evaluate the past and by disqualifying alternative forms. The historical apparatuses are continuously at work, articulating subordinant memories with dominant principles and reducing their antagonistic character (Laclau 1977). In order to win popular consent, however, dominant history must always appeal to the people by including them in its narrative. The fact that the official past must be retold in the language of democracy means, potentially, that the popular classes can assert their own interests and recast official versions in different ways.

The past, in this conception, is a terrain of everyday struggle. "Popular memory," as Foucault terms subaltern historical consciousness, is one front in the battle over hegemony. The people's historical sensibility is formed out of the contradictory relation between the official representations of history and private remembrances, in the conflict between the agencies of public meaning and the subaltern invocations of the past. According to this conception, the popular classes, who live in a world of ideologically constituted systems, are not the bearers of an "authentic" historical knowledge. One cannot do "history from below" simply by going to the people to garner "facts" that disprove the dominant interpretations. Popular memory is the ever-mobile and unstable result of the people's relation of subordination to hegemonic historical agencies. The public past is one ideological form through which the masses live their condition of subalternity.

These recent studies of memory and the national past in the West, which show how dominant apparatuses reshape history so as to suppress the memory of class, gender, or racial antagonisms, provide useful conceptual tools for understanding the subaltern memory in Palestine. Their weakness, however, is that they too are blinded by the "prevailing discourse" of nationalism. They tend to proceed as if nationalism were the autobiography of the West and to ignore the different trajectories of nationalism in the colonial world. Moreover, caught up in the delusion of the national inner sanctum, they write as though colonialism were not constitutive of the capitalist West's very being.

It is therefore symptomatic that discussions of Gramsci generally overlook the fact that he considered modern imperialism one of the basic features of the "expansive hegemony" that developed in the West from the 1870s (Buci-Glucksman 1982:124). Put another way, the uneven development of capitalism was fundamental to the rise of the Western nation-state (cf. Nairn 1981). Capitalist industrialization did not diffuse evenly from Europe and North America over the rest of the globe but unevenly, under the aegis of colonialism. Rather than bringing equal access to industrialization to the colonies, colonialism fostered underdevelopment, perpetuating and often strengthening existing semifeudal economic forms. Colonialism also failed to extend to the colonies the democracy that was practiced at home. The form of rule prevalent in the colonies was not hegemony but what Gramsci termed "domination," where coercion significantly outweighed consent. "Domination" denied colonized peoples not only self-rule but history as well. As Cabral notes, colonialism is premised on "the permanent, organized repression of the cultural life of the colonized people" (1973:39).

The studies of popular memory in the West, therefore, are not easily applicable to studies of memory in the colonial world, where "domination" rather than "hegemony" prevailed. Colonialism, in general, does not incorporate the subaltern natives but coerces them—in part because, in order to rule, it must subdue precapitalist forms. In order to govern other peoples, colonialists must deny them the right to self-government. Such is the situation under which the roughly two million Palestinians ruled by Israel (1.4 million in the Occupied Territories, 600,000 citizens of Israel) live today. Zionism, an exclusivist and settler variant of colonialism, which aimed at the establishment of a strictly Jewish state, diverged from classical colonialism in that it aimed to exclude rather than to "civilize" the natives or exploit their labor power (Rodinson 1973). Unlike English colonialists in India, for example, who tried to turn middle- and upper-class Indians into Englishmen with brown skin (Sharpe 1987), Zionists were never interested in making Palestinian Arabs into imitation Jews. In its early stages, the Zionist movement denied or ignored the natives' presence. When Israel gained its independence, it expelled the indigenous inhabitants in as great a number as possible and rubbed out their traces. Not only was the tie between the Palestinians and their past violently severed when Israel was founded in 1948; "it is periodically and ritually resevered in [Israel's] sustained war upon [Palestinian] national peoplehood" (Said 1986:149).

Against an exclusivist and expansionist Zionist nationalism, Palestinians have attempted to construct a historical identity and to "authorize" their own past by elaborating what Maxine Rodinson (1973) terms a defensive nationalism. The effort to sustain the sentiment that all the Palestinian people share a national past is a significant part of their battle for an independent state. Palestinians conceive of themselves as having had a special relation to Zionism over the last hundred years. Their self-representation, formulated in opposition to Israel, is inversely specular. When Zionists claim that

Palestinians, unlike Israelis, have no special national identity because they are simply "Arabs" who can easily live anywhere in the Arab world, they ignore the fact that although nations typically claim to be distinct essences with timeless pasts, *all* nations are recent constructions (Anderson 1983:16). They also miss the irony that it is chiefly in their relation to Israeli actions that Palestinians have acquired their notion of a distinctive identity.

Palestinian popular memory therefore is a terrain worked on by two markedly different historical apparatuses with rival strategies of memory control: the "coercive" mode of a colonizing machine versus the "incorporative" mode of a movement aspiring for hegemony. The Israeli state attempts to dominate Palestinian memory by erasing its most visible traces and suppressing memories that might sustain a national identity. The Palestine Liberation Organization (PLO), the official representative of the Palestinian nation, attempts to forge a "national-popular" past by recalling memories of a unified national struggle. But since it does not control the state apparatuses, the Palestinian leadership must rely on the masses. The situation is fluid because the subaltern classes are not simply passive participants: having been invited to join the national struggle, they have an interest in democratizing it from within. This paper attempts to locate the space created for popular memory under these conditions.

## COLONIAL MEMORY

*Whoever has emerged victorious participates to this day in the triumphal procession in which the present rulers step over those who are lying prostrate. According to traditional practice, the spoils are carried along in the procession. They are called cultural treasures.*
—WALTER BENJAMIN, "THESES ON THE PHILOSOPHY OF HISTORY"

### Historicizing a Territory

After Shaykh 'Izz al-Din al-Qassam's death, an imposing tombstone was placed over his grave in the Haifa suburb of Balad al-Shaykh. It quickly became a site of popular pilgrimage. But after 1948 that suburb was emptied of Arabs and settled by Jews. Qassam's tomb has been vandalized, the graveyard permitted to go to ruin (Furani 1984). No historical marker commemorates his death at the site of the famous battle near the West Bank village of Ya'bad. Some villagers from the area were able to show me the spot where, legend has it, Qassam fell. Although several villagers asserted that a commemorative marker should be erected on that site, they also feared that if one were put up, the occupation authorities would knock it down and arrest those responsible.

The fate of Qassam's historical markers illustrates the means by which Israel simultaneously establishes its own identity upon the land and obstructs Palestinian memory. One of the major tasks of the modern state is to establish and fix the special relation between a people's history and its land. The construction of a unified national identity, writes Poulantzas, requires "the historicity of a territory and the territorialization of a history" (1980:114). For a colonial settler-state like Israel this is a violent task, since it entails the suppression of the past of the vanquished. "[T]he modern nation-state," says Poulantzas, "... involves the eradication of the traditions, histories, and memories of dominated nations involved in its process." But a "nation without a state of its own is in the course of losing [*est en perdition de*] its tradition and history" (1980:113).

The Zionists originally imagined *Eretz Israel* (the land of Israel) as uninscribed and empty ("a land without a people"). As they settled it, all disruptions of that fantasy, all previous Arab inscriptions, had to be effaced. In order for Zionists to implant an exclusive national identity in that space, they had to eliminate sites that memorialized the Palestinians' past and embodied their relation to this territory. Every parcel of land had to be plowed with Jewish history, for as Benedict Anderson observes, "In the modern conception, state sovereignty is fully, flatly, and evenly operative over each square centimetre of a legally demarcated territory" (1983:26). The territory was to be "worlded" as Jewish (Spivak 1985:133; Heidegger 1971:44–45).

"Zionism came fully into its own," Edward Said has observed, "by actively destroying as many Arab traces as it could" (1979:103). The most radical act of Zionist "worlding" occurred when Jewish military forces dispersed some 770,000 Palestinians from Israeli territory in 1948 (Flapan 1987:216). The new Israeli state then obliterated most of their historical vestiges, wiping some 374 Palestinian Arab towns and villages off the face of the earth. Those Arab traces were then variously plowed under by Israeli farmers, resettled and given new Hebrew names, or planted over with Jewish National Fund forests, thereby acquiring Jewish identities (Jiryis 1976:79). The conquest of land proceeded apace as well. In 1947, Jews made up 45 percent of the population of Palestine but possessed only 7 percent of the land. By 1983, they accounted for about 60 percent of the population of historic Palestine and held 85 percent of the land. Palestinian Arabs, 40 percent of the population, were left with less than 15 percent (Benvenisti 1984:19; Benjelloun-Olivier 1983:87). Today the expropriation of more property and the establishment and expansion of Jewish settlements in the Occupied Territories (numbering 135) proceed virtually unchecked. Palestinians are impeded from maintaining or restoring such Arab historical sites as remain in existence. A whole variety of activities like hiking, archaeological digs, tourism, environmental activism, and planting trees on Arbor Day (*Tu Bishvat*) have become part of the Zionist program, participating in the continuous process of "worlding" (Benvenisti 1986:19–20, 23–24, 27–28, 200), of investing the land with the conqueror's identity and normalizing the conquest and erasures.

Westerners also participate in this process as tourists. When we visit
Israel, the historical and touristic apparatuses ensure that we "see" there
both a vibrant Western nation built in "our" self-image and the monu-
ments of a Judaeo-Christian past which we share with Israelis. The touristic
institutions magically occult traces of the long Arab-Islamic historical inter-
lude separating the biblical era from contemporary Israel and the signs of
a modern Arab presence. Arab remains appear merely as the decayed debris
of an irrelevant interruption of the sacred narrative of the Jews' "return"
to "their" land. The present-day Arabs we see there seem, like the object
of the ethnographer, to live in some distant "allochronic" space: unlike us
and the Israelis, the natives do not inhabit the modern era (Fabian 1983).

### Cultural Repression
*Only images in the mind vitalize the will.*

—WALTER BENJAMIN, ONE WAY STREET

Because Israel also targets Palestinian cultural expression for repression,
it can even be dangerous for Palestinians to write about Shaykh 'Izz al-Din
al-Qassam. In 1983 the military authorities put West Bank writer Sami
Kilani on trial for publishing a volume of poetry dedicated to Qassam.
The charge sheet stated that invoking his name in verse constituted an act
of "incitement," a punishable offence (*al-Fajr*, 11 November 1983). After a
military court failed to convict Kilani of poetic incitement, the officials who
filed the charge punished him with sentences of town arrest and administrative detention that lasted nearly three years. (He has been held in detention
ever since the *intifada* began.) On each of the three occasions when soldiers
broke into the Kilani household in Ya'bad to take Sami away, they confiscated his entire library as well. Each time he was released from jail, Kilani
had to rebuild his book collection from scratch.

Qassam is one of the many figures of insurgency engraved in Palestinian
psyches, with the potential to inspire struggle against colonial domination.
Hoping to tame the will to fight, the colonialists continually attempt to erase
such pictorial inscriptions from native memory by hindering the circulation
of Palestinian national symbols and inhibiting the growth of civil society.
Since, as Benedict Anderson observes, nations accumulate memory through
the printed word (1983:77), it is not surprising that Israel seeks to deny
Palestinians access to recollection by heavily censoring their publications.
The authorities block the production and circulation of books on Palestinian
history and culture; the censor has banned some sixteen hundred titles (now
reduced to 750) on such subjects from the Occupied Territories. The censor's
primary concern, writes Meron Benvenisti, is "to eradicate expression that
could foster Palestinian nationalist feelings, or that suggests that Palestinians are a nation with a national heritage" (1983:1, 3, 130–131). Israeli

state apparatuses also ensure that the educational curriculum teaches Palestinian children little about their people's history (Graham-Brown 1984:37–81). Those Palestinian institutions which attempt to produce and accumulate memory—universities, research groups, newspapers—face constant harassment, and their heads are frequently arrested and even deported. Even private memory is not exempt. Many veterans of the 1936–1939 revolt kept personal papers, diaries, photographs, communiqués, and other memorabilia from the insurrection. All those I met had lost their personal archives, either when the mementos were seized in military searches or because these men destroyed the records themselves out of fear of incrimination if the security forces discovered them.

### Colonializing Historiography

Recent official Israeli histories brand the rebels of 1936–1939 as the original Palestinian "terrorists," forefathers of today's *fedayeen*. Shaykh Qassam's movement, according to Israeli historian Shai Lachman, was "the first Arab terrorist movement in Palestine" (1982:86). Current Western obsessions with terrorism make this act of naming a potent means of disqualifying Palestinian history.

Homi Bhabha has defined colonialism as "a form of governmentality in which the 'ideological' space functions in more openly collaborative ways with political and economic exigencies" (1986:171–172). Indeed, Israel's repressive agencies, which mutilate the Palestinian past in order to inhibit memory, work in tandem with the historical-ideological apparatuses which deface that past. But official histories of Palestine written by Israelis are not meant primarily to persuade or speak to Palestinians. Rather, they address an Israeli-Jewish audience, in order to consolidate its national identity by reaffirming its superiority to an inferior and hostile Other. Colonial-nationalist ideology unites its subjects by denigrating the Palestinian, building the victor's history atop the wreckage of the vanquished (Benjamin 1969: 256–257). Other versions of these histories, produced for a wider Western audience, help secure the commonality of interests of our "superior" cultures. In addition, they play on U.S. and European feelings of guilt regarding Nazi atrocities by keeping alive the notion that the warlike Arabs threaten Jews with a new holocaust. The versions tailored for foreign consumption abroad are more virulently anti-Arab than those produced in Israel, where more liberal accounts are tolerated. Recent examples of revisions of the Palestinian past include Joan Peters's *From Time Immemorial* and Leon Uris's *The Haj*. The former a "history," the latter a work of "historical fiction," both these 1984 U.S. best-sellers carried the same message. They deny that "the amalgam of peoples in Palestine" have a history or even the right to bear the name Palestinian. Instead they identify them as primitive tribals for whom terrorism, asserts Peters, has been a "tradition" for genera-

tions (1984:354). Such disfigurations of Palestinian history have rendered
Israel's denial of Palestinian rights virtually invisible in the U.S. and have
facilitated the escalating flow of U.S. military and financial assistance to
Washington's main "strategic asset" in the Middle East.

Israeli scholarly accounts also target the image of the 1936–1939 revolt for
disfiguration.[1] The official historical narrative can allow space for only one
authentic national liberation movement in Israel-Palestine: that which led to
the founding of Israel in 1948. Dominant accounts of the 1936–1939 revolt
therefore occlude its anti-British and anticolonial character by naming it as a
series of "riots" and "pogroms" directed specifically against Jews (for instance, Ginat 1982:30). According to the logic of Israel's autobiography, only
the Jewish movement deserves to be called national and anticolonial. It denies the essential role the British performed in facilitating Zionist colonization prior to 1947–1948 (cf. Rodinson 1973); it suppresses the fact of Jewish
assistance in the British army's counterinsurgency campaign during 1937–
1939. The official accounts thereby ascribe the revolt's failure not to massive
British repression but to self-disintegration. By shining the spotlight on
Palestinian self-destruction, Israeli histories cast the British military's superior firepower and its brutal methods into the shadows. The rebellion de-
generated, it is claimed, into a reign of terror against the so-called "moderate" internal opposition, an orgy of rebel plunder of wealthy Palestinians,
and internecine rivalry among revolt commanders. This deterioration was
inevitable, the argument runs, given the backward nature of Palestinian
society, where feudal landlords and a venal religious caste controlled an
ignorant, fanatical mass of peasants through demagogy and manipulation.
Arnon-Ohanna's judgment, that the armed rebel bands simply reflected
the backward conditions of the peasant society from which they emerged,
is typical:

> The absence of cooperation and mutual responsibility, the deep-seated di-
> visiveness of a society based on patriarchal lines and *hamulas* [patrilineages],
> the ancient inter-village and inter-*hamula* wrangles over stretches of land and
> water sources, over blood feuds, family honor and marital problems—these
> were simply transferred to the [guerrilla] bands movement. (1981: 24)

Moreover, in many official accounts, the insurgents of 1936–1939 appear as
mere bandits, gangsters, or mercenaries (Bauer 1966:56). The claim is often
made too that the revolt received funds from Germany and Italy and that it
was, therefore, "an arm of the international fascist movement" (Bauer
1966:23).[2]

Such official accounts retrospectively construct a Palestinian "essence"
that can be used to validate negative judgments regarding current Palestinian practices. They confirm Palestinian society's retrograde, fanatical, anti-
Semitic, violent, and terroristic nature. Such a society, it virtually goes with-

out saying, is the polar opposite of a progressive, forward-looking, peace-loving, and compassionate Israel. Elpeleg asserts, for instance, that in 1936 the Palestinian rebels of 1936–1939 often employed "horrifying means" of violence and were unable to distinguish between criminal and political actions. The Jews by contrast practiced self-restraint during the revolt: "one of the extraordinary manifestations of the Jewish spirit to be seen in Palestine" (1978:45). To accord any historical legitimacy to the Palestinian movement of 1936–1939 might lend credibility to the current Palestinian fight for an independent state. Official Israeli histories conclude, therefore, that the internal disintegration of the 1936–1939 insurrection signifies a lack of true national identity that disqualifies Palestinian claims to nationhood today. And according to this logic, the reduction to ruin of the physical traces of the Palestinian past and the censorship of living Palestinian memory are natural and necessary practices.

## THE TRACKS OF REPRESSION

*There is no popular memory to be retrieved in its virginity.*
—LES REVOLTES LOGIQUES, NO. 13

The effects of Israeli repression of memory were immediately apparent from the gaps, silences, and omissions in the accounts of the Palestinians I interviewed. Surviving rebel fighters in the revolt who remained in Palestine (many were made refugees after 1948 and were not present to be interviewed) were often reticent about the revolt, even though fifty years had elapsed. The successive experiences (for West Bankers) of Jordan's repressive rule and Israel's military occupation had etched fear and suspicion deep into many veterans' consciousnesses. Although I was always accompanied by a Palestinian colleague, several refused to talk about the rebellion at all. This was due in part to the U.S. government's unquestioned backing for Israeli policy, which made them distrust me, a U.S. citizen. But the atmosphere generated by the occupation means that people are even suspicious of local researchers. According to Sharif Kana'aneh, director of Bir Zeit University's Research and Documentation Center, researchers from the center who collected testimony from refugees about their former villages encountered difficulties similar to mine: "People are not frank. They show fear and do not want to speak. They also refused to speak on their tribal [sic] differences" (al-Ghazali 1986).

Such fears are not unfounded. Some villagers we met in Israel were questioned at length by military intelligence about their roles in the 1936–1939 revolt immediately after the 1948 war, and a few West Bank friends were similarly interrogated after the June 1967 war. Abu Sulayman,[3] a *qa'id fasil* ("band commander") in the Jenin district during the revolt, was reluctant to talk about his rebel past because, he said, he dreaded the return of his old enemies, the English, to Palestine. "After all," he said, "it's called *Great Britain*. And as they say, the sun never sets on the British Empire." Even my Palestinian friends in Jerusalem and Ramallah chuckled with disbelief when I told them about Abu Sulayman's farfetched fears. But later it became clear that his apprehensions about the English were a displacement of his concerns about the Israelis. A few months after the interview, Abu Sulayman's son Salim, who was under town arrest when we visited, was charged with membership in a "terrorist" organization and deported to Jordan—one of twenty-seven Palestinians to be expelled from the Occupied Territories in 1985.

Fortunately, because I was always accompanied by a Palestinian colleague, most revolt veterans ultimately agreed to speak about their experiences. But their reminiscences were punctuated by silences when we broached certain topics. One such subject was rebel attacks on Jewish colonies. According to published accounts, Jewish settlements were a secondary objective, while the British armed forces were the primary rebel target.[4] Yet old *mujahidin* were so reluctant to discuss these raids with me that one might imagine that they had hardly occurred at all.

Some men explained that their silence on this subject was due to their fears of retribution from Jewish colonists for their participation in such assaults. Abu 'Ali, one of the very few fighters willing to describe these attacks, always talked of them in the third person. Although it was clear from the details of his account that he was personally involved, Abu 'Ali always prefaced his tales with "so-and-so told me that . . ." But veterans' reticence on this subject was also a response to the Israeli work of ideological disfiguration: the claims that the Palestinian national movement was/is inherently anti-Semitic. The Zionist movement's successful tainting of Palestinian nationalism with Nazi associations makes Palestinians handle the subject of hostile action against Jews very cautiously. Wishing to undercut the claims they assumed I had heard, veterans emphasized by omission that the rebellion was against British colonialism and not the Jewish people. In revising the past in such a way, they contributed to a PLO self-portrait unblemished by anti-Semitism. This remembrance of the revolt as a purely anticolonial struggle untainted by anti-Jewish feeling might be interpreted as a sign of Palestinian desires to live peacefully, in the future, in their own state alongside Israel.[5] The silences and gaps, therefore, were not merely unfortunate lapses in memory, but effects of repression. More positively, they were counter-narratives to the official Israeli accounts of the revolt, as eloquent as any utterances.

Israeli repression pushed a handful of old veterans to adopt a defeatist version of the past. Such men had been understandably overwhelmed by Israel's long string of military successes and apparent cultural and technological superiority. In their judgment, the Palestinian movement had been incapable of mounting an effective riposte. For all its efforts, in their view, the national movement had reaped an endless harvest of defeats and disappointments. "It was a mistake to rebel against the British in 1936–1939," one former band commander told me, "because we were too weak to win. We should have compromised instead." His implication was that Palestinians were *still* too puny to defeat Israel, that they should stop struggling, cut their losses, and make any compromises necessary to get out of their horrible mess. Such defeatist sentiments were the effects of Israel's coercive power, of nearly twenty years of military rule in the Occupied Territories. Yet they did not signify that Israel had won Palestinian consent. These negative assessments of the Palestinian past bespoke not an endorsement of the Zionist position but passive acceptance of the powerful Zionist reality.

In any case, accommodationist views were held by only a tiny minority. Most veterans responded to Israeli propaganda by asserting counternarratives. My colleagues and I were sometimes even able to use official Israeli claims to incite reluctant men to speak. Occasionally, when we told someone, "Israeli and English books say that the rebels were merely bandits and terrorists who used the revolt as a pretext for robbery," he would explode angrily that these claims were wrong and that the rebels were mainly honorable and heroic nationalists (*wataniyyin*). He sometimes then went on to give a detailed account of the revolt. The fact that, despite fifty years of defeats and disappointments, Palestinians *do* adhere strongly to a nationalist interpretation of the revolt testifies to the PLO's success in molding consensus in the face of adversity. It shows how, contrary to Israel's aims, repression of all manifestations of Palestinian identity often incites a militantly nationalist memory.

## FORGING A NATIONAL MEMORY

*Forgetting represents a force, a form of robust health.*
—FRIEDRICH NIETZSCHE, ON THE GENEALOGY OF MORALS

Israel's chief antagonist in the battle over memory is the Palestinian national leadership, the PLO. Rather than effacing the people's recollections, the widely supported PLO incorporates their memories within a larger narrative. It attempts to articulate subaltern memories with its hegemonic principles to create an agreed-upon definition of what the "real" past was like (Mouffe 1981:173); it works to consolidate a vision of that history for the purpose of political mobilization. To confront Israel's overwhelming strength, the middle-class Palestinian leadership must depend upon and motivate the masses (Nairn 1981:100). It must incorporate their concerns and appeal to them in a language they can understand.

But because it is based outside of historic Palestine, the PLO leadership is hampered in its attempts to construct counterhegemony. Since 1967 it has managed to gain the support of the overwhelming majority of Palestinians inside Israel and the Occupied Territories. This backing was not won automatically: only after six years of ocupation, in 1973, did the masses in the West Bank begin to detach themselves from the "traditional" elites tied to the Jordanian monarchy and align themselves with the PLO.[6] The development of Palestinian national consciousness in the West Bank, suppressed during Jordanian rule, was sped up by the occupation (Gresh 1985:14, 63–64.)

Support for the PLO today is loosely organized and expressed through a variety of "national" institutions—universities, newspapers and journals, research institutes, trade unions, and women's groups—which emerged as a result of the national movement's sustained effort to build a Palestinian civil society in the face of the occupation. In recent years bodies devoted to the preservation, collection, and dissemination of memories of the past have come to play a crucial role in the Palestinian struggle to articulate a national identity (Khalili 1980; Ashrawi 1978). Although constrained by military rule, these institutions contribute to the leadership-in-exile's efforts to deepen its emergent hegemonic relation with Palestinians "inside" (those residing in historic Palestine).

The past that these institutions advance is basically nationalist, a history that binds in the interest of unity. Palestinian national identity is the dominant framework for memory, the optic through which historical events come into focus. That framework teaches Palestinians to remember their successes as a unified people and to be aware of the dangers of fragmentation. Official versions of the past are used to bolster unity under middle-class leadership. The nationalized past illuminates the present, the present scene reanimates and reinscribes the past. Official versions have used similarities between the present battles and earlier ones to awaken repressed memory material and to infuse it with new meanings (Freud 1967:121). This nationalist version of the past is both continuist and progressivist. The present leadership is seen as the heir to the earlier one. Yet a progression has occurred since the 1930s. If the 1936–1939 revolt is an important symbol of insurgency and unity for a Palestinian people that is essentially the same, the national movement today is even more mature. Today's leadership represents the fulfillment of the efforts of the past.

The revolt was the first time in which the peasant masses were significantly drawn into the national movement. Official Palestinian accounts[7] acknowledge the peasantry's critical role in the insurgency in part because the PLO needs to invoke popular mobilizations of the past in order to motivate the populace today. But dominant versions employ these images from the past in a manner that both evokes and tames subaltern traditions. The *fallahin*'s practices are subsumed within a coherent narrative that deemphasizes their ruptural force. Dominant histories incorporate peasants by exalting their heroism and sacrifice and at the same time reducing them to bit-players and sword-carriers. Official histories depict the rebellion as a common undertaking, in which the urban elite, the protagonists, coordinated its own actions against the British with those of its rural supporters. While "the masses" are said to have pushed the reluctant leadership to take more radical positions, these accounts depict them as militant but mute, without conscious agency (cf. 'Allush 1978:143, 147, 156). While local peasant leaders are anonymous, the names of elite leaders like Hajj Amin al-Husayni, authors of memoirs and subjects of biographies, function as metonyms for the whole movement. Differences between elite and subaltern are downplayed and popular initiative is minimized, while unity under the Arab Higher Committee[8] is stressed.

The official accounts attribute the revolt's shortcomings to internal discord, to the failure to follow the experienced leadership, or to the peasants' inherent deficiencies. Since the valiant and resolute *fallahin* were susceptible to manipulation and limited by their tribalism, localism, and inadequate political consciousness, they could not go it alone. A leadership from the ranks of the educated classes was required to compensate for these failings: it had to organize, coordinate and control the subaltern classes.[9] Although these accounts frequently criticize the urban leadership for its mistakes and timidity in prosecuting the revolt (cf. Kayyali 1978:231), they take it for granted that the peasantry could not have effectively filled in as leaders. In the end the revolt splintered because the urban leadership, most of which had been jailed or exiled, was absent. Once peasants took control, the movement was doomed to fail, owing to the *fallahin*'s shortcomings. These interpretations have a presentist orientation, for they imply that the masses today should continue to look to the leadership for guidance and orders. The implicit message of official accounts is that the people today must remain united under the current (middle-class) leadership.

At the same time, official interpreters handle the revolt gingerly. They depict it in reverential tones while keeping it at arm's length, never examining its details too closely. No official in-depth Palestinian studies of the revolt exist; nationalist discourse constantly evokes it as an inspirational symbol but rarely submits it to careful historical investigation. Thus troubling subjects like class fissures, acts of treachery, or peasant actions independent of party or elite control, can be presented as exceptional. Authoritative discourse smoothes over the past's jagged edges and evens out its irruptions, serving up a national conformism.

When the nation remains a vision, not a territorial-institutional reality, remembering a unified national past is an urgent task. The Palestinian conditions of disruption and disaster intensify the normal impulse of leading classes to construct a continuous story of the nation. The past is seen as a crucial battlefield in the war to safeguard the Palestinian present for the future. The inclination therefore is to freeze a certain memory of the past, rather than reconstellate it. Nationalists tend to regard tradition as something to be preserved in its pristine form rather than opened up for revolutionary uses. In such an atmophere, it is to be expected that local institutions concentrate on salvaging the past rather than elaborating historical narratives. The feeling that Palestinian history is threatened with extinction encourages preservationist work. Institutions like the Society for the Preservation of the Family at al-Bira, the Bir Zeit University's Research Center, the Research Center for Arab Heritage of al-Tayiba, and the Arab Studies Society in Jerusalem sponsor an array of projects designed to rescue the past: collecting testimony from refugees in order to document the histories of destroyed villages; gathering and publishing folklore and folktales; sponsoring folkloric dance and music troupes; and encouraging traditional crafts, particularly women's needlework.

But Israeli repression hampers the elaboration of a coherent vision of the Palestinian past. Censorship, book banning, and the pressures on local educational institutions, publishers, and booksellers severely limit scholarly and popular writing on Palestinian history. Such constraints channel nationalist efforts into symbolic evocations of history. These coded representations have served as the building blocks of a constructed national past. In part because of the need to evade the censor's blacking out, they evoke an essence through "mythicizing vagueness" (Wright 1985) rather than suggest coherent historical narratives.

One of the central signifiers of the national past to emerge is the multivocal figure of the *fallah* or peasant. The *fallah* has been made the symbolic representative of the cultural and historical continuity of the Palestinian people. His traditional life-style is seen to encapsulate the shared values deemed worthy of preservation. Owing to his crucial role in the 1936–1939 revolt, the *fallah* epitomizes the anticolonial struggle. The peasant additionally signifies a prolonged attachment and deep love for the land of Palestine in the face of land expropriations and population transfers. Her *sumud* ("steadfastness") is the model for confronting these dangers and maintaining a permanence of place (Shehadeh 1982). The olive trees which *fallahin* tend and the wild thyme (*za'atar*) they gather have been elevated, through constant invocation in poetry and song, to near-sacred symbols of the relation with the Palestinian soil. Through its imputed oneness with the peasant, the entire populace shares these bonds with the land of Palestine.[10]

Another reason for the symbolic centrality of the *fallah* and the rural way of life is that colonialism puts them in jeopardy. Objects of significance often take on the aura of heritage when their basic terms of existence are put into question (Wright 1985:95). The West Bank has witnessed massive land expropriation (about 55 percent has been seized by Israel) and a decline in the

economic importance of agriculture. Although by 1984 roughly 70 percent of
the West Bank population still lived in rural areas, the percentage of the
workforce employed in agriculture had declined from 47.5 to 28.4 since 1970
(Graham-Brown 1983:179; Benvenisti 1986:8). Approximately one-third of
the West Bank work force commutes to Israel daily for waged work. Roughly
77 percent of that work force is from rural areas (Tamari 1981:39). Palestinian villages are becoming simulacra of peasant communities.

Such transformations of the rural community make a romanticized
peasant centrally significant. Yet the peasant's representative power was acquired through an erasure of internal differences and a forgetting of social
antagonisms. As the *fallah* was fashioned into a signifier of *national* resistance,
he/she ceased to evoke conflicts with landlords, moneylenders, and state officials. When it made the peasant into a signifier, official discourse effaced
his/her regional specificity. It also generalized him as an independent small
farmer—never an oppressed sharecropper or a landless laborer. As the re-
pository of popular wisdom, the practitioner of a customary life-style, and the
keeper of a continuous tradition, the *fallah* now stands for a solidifying past
rather than a specifically subaltern history.

To confront the drastic ruptures and fragmentation of Palestinian society
caused by colonialism, the national movement has forged an ideology of
timeless rural tradition. Urban Palestinians participate in an imaginary
identification with a romantic and idealized rural past-present through
evocations of the peasant. Artists paint scenes of the picturesque village and
of pastoral simplicity, while folklore collectors discover an unbroken tradition of national resistance. Even left-wing folkloric troupes stage tableaux of
a pristine time before the colonial onslaught when villagers practiced "primitive communism." This is not to say that such constructions are merely
middle-class fabrications. Rosemarie Sayigh found that Palestinian refugees
in Beirut remembered their village past as "living in paradise" (1979:10),
and I encountered similar romanticizations of rural life among villagers "inside." Mainstream nationalism remolds such memories into a conformist
vision.

## THE KUFIYA

One of the most important images associated with the peasantry is the *kufiya*,
the Palestinian headdress. The story of its adoption as a national signifier
illustrates how national unity is created through the forgetting of difference.
In the 1930s, prior to the rebellion, the *kufiya* was worn strictly by rural
males, peasants and Bedouin. Held in place by a headcord (the *'uqqal*), its
function was to keep out winter cold and shield against the summer sun.
Symbolically, it marked the wearer as a man of lower status. The *kufiya* set
the peasant apart from the *effendi*—the educated man of the town and city,

who demonstrated his social preeminence by donning the maroon-colored *tarbush* or fez. While the *kufiya* signified social inferiority (and rural backwardness), the *tarbush* signaled superiority (and urbane sophistication).

Fighters in the revolt, drawn mainly from the ranks of the peasantry, wore the *kufiya* as a matter of course. During the insurgency's early years, *kufiya*-clad fighters who slipped into the towns were conspicuous and likely targets for arrest by the British army. In August 1938, at the height of the insurgency, the rebel leadership commanded all townsmen to discard the *tarbush* and don the *kufiya*. The order was issued to help the rebels blend in when they entered the cities, but it was also a move in the wider social struggle. As one educated Palestinian wrote privately in September 1938,

> The Igal [and *kufiya*] of the Arab today is surely a liberty cap but conceived in an original and native fashion. . . . By making Supreme Court judges, big Government officials, important merchants and the entire professional class and in fact everybody, wear an igal the rebels have made a grand sweep in the direction of democracy. . . . The fellahin do not conceal their delight at seeing their "uppers," the effendis, come down a peg and look like them in the matter of headdress; they feel proud of having raised themselves in the social scale. (Totah 1938)

And fighters occasionally had to force reluctant *effendis* to put on the new garb (Morton 1957:53). The order was not, therefore, merely a matter of military strategy; it was also an inversion, a reversal of the "natural" semiotic hierarchy of clothing. It entailed the taking-down of a superior-status marker and a violation of the symbols of power (see Guha 1983:61–63).

But even at the time, nationalist accounts claimed that urban Palestinians embraced the *kufiya* enthusiastically as a national symbol. Official colonial sources, which noted that the fashion spread with "lightning rapidity," saw this more as the result of a conspiracy than as a manifestation of the spirit of unity (*Palestine Post*, 2 September 1938). Once the rebellion ended, the *effendis* of the town reassumed the *tarbush*, owing in part to British pressure (Morton 1957:98–100).

In the mid-sixties the Palestinian *fedayeen* reanimated the *kufiya* as an emblem of national struggle and as an image of unity. The *kufiya* evoked as well as produced the memory of a moment when all Palestinians—rural and urban, Christian and Muslim—combined without distinction in collective action. The fact that an earlier generation of fighters had *imposed* this item of apparel, as the sign of the conjunctural hegemony of the rural over the urban and of the inversion of the social hierarchy, was largely forgotten in the course of its revival by the guerrillas.

Indeed, this was how people usually related this well-known story to me. Over and over, Palestinians young and old told me how townsmen donned the peasant *kufiya* during the revolt. Almost always, they recounted it as an allegory for national unity. Today, Palestinian elders of village origin continue to wear the *kufiya* on their heads, held in place by the *'uqqal*. Young Palestinian men and women—in town and village—also wear it, draped around their necks as a scarf rather than as a head cover, as a badge of national identity and activism. Its revival indexes the development of a more democratic nationalism that incorporates women to a greater degree than in the past. Yet this adoption of the sartorial mark of the peasant and his "traditional" mode of life as symbol of the people simultaneously writes the popular classes into national history and erases—in the name of unity—the memory of the struggles that prompted that rewriting.

These dynamics of memory and forgetting share the vision of horizontal comradeship with all varieties of nationalism (cf. Anderson 1983). National ideological apparatuses strive to produce a seamless historical narrative that retrospectively smoothes over disharmonies and dissolves social tensions in the name of a unified totality (Macherey 1978). Official nationalism rearticulates subaltern versions, incorporates them into its totalizing discourse, and neutralizes their potential for causing rupture. It should be stressed that unification of this sort *does* fulfill a positive function, since nationalist discourses and practices have effectively mitigated sectional divisions among the Palestinian people and enabled the liberation struggle. Given the requisites of the anticolonial battle, "active forgetting" is a positive force, without which there could be "no hope, no pride, no *present*" (Nietzsche 1969:58). Working much like secondary revision (Freud 1965:537), nationalist discourse screens out memories that disrupt its unifying logic in order to produce an ordered and intelligible past. For the purpose of common struggle, sectarian, regional, and class differences of the past are purged from memory. The roughing up of *effendis* who rejected the *kufiya* in 1938 is forgotten so that the *kufiya* can produce a harmonious past and present. The projection of a coherent national narrative for political purposes necessitates the forceful, "active forgetting" of past dissension. Nationalism purchases its coherence through "tendentious revision" (Freud 1965:537) and the obscuring of difference, in the interest of the Palestinian middle-class leadership.

## ENABLING MEMORY

Where the colonizers suppress the people's memory, the national movement enables it. Nationalist ideology provides individual remembrance with an authorizing vehicle (White 1981). It offers the narrator a collective identity within which to situate her stories meaningfully and holds out the prospect for a hopeful ending. By necessity populist, nationalism gives him the opportunity to construct a meaningful role for himself within a larger history. Without a national liberation movement, Palestinians' sense of identity and spirit of resistance would be much impoverished and they would have difficulty imagining a future. Many Palestinians might then evaluate the revolt as an event in a narrative of defeat, remembering it as just another meaningless step—like the losses of 1948, 1967, and 1982—along a never-ending trail of disasters and disappointments, rather than as a stellar moment in an epic of intrepid struggle for national independence.

By means of what Nietzsche calls a "positive faculty of repression" (1969:57), dominant Palestinian discourse also marks out areas of silence—but through integration rather than coercion. Omissions produced by official discourse concern activities that could blacken the revolt's national reputation. Because a Palestinian colleague and, in most instances, members of the family were present at all my interviews with ex-fighters, they put forward an account that appealed to a local public. And through me, they felt they were addressing a U.S. audience, which they recognize as a powerful determinant of their situation. They wished to present themselves to the U.S. as people deserving the status of a nation with its own state. Accordingly, and in line with official discourse, informants often practiced self-censorship, presenting an image of the revolt suitable for both national and foreign consumption.

They were less willing, therefore, to speak with me about the revolt's shortcomings than with my Palestinian colleagues. They hesitated, for instance, to discuss Arab sales of land to the Zionist movement, an issue of great concern to the national movement in the 1930s. Whereas Zionist land purchases from non-Palestinian sources predominated until 1928, thereafter purchases from Palestinians (both big landowners and *fallahin*) constituted the larger portion. By the middle of the 1930s, transactions with Palestinians were accounting for 89 percent of the total land purchases by Jews (Porath 1977:83–84). But rarely did anyone I spoke to state that Palestinians—whether big landowner, small farmer, or especially someone from their own village—had sold land. Villagers remembered such dealings chiefly by attributing all the responsibility to those famous cases involving absentee Lebanese and Syrian landowners, whose large estates in Palestine were purchased by Zionists. One slip-up in this representation occurred while we were interviewing two elderly men at al-Tayiba, a village near Tulkarm inside Israel. Two young men who were present told us about a prominent local family that sold land to Jews in the 1930s. My colleague told me later that when I left the room for a moment, the elders shouted at the youths for telling a foreigner negative things about the Palestinian national movement. It was not just the desire to maintain a pristine national image that motivated peoples' guarded approach to this subject. It also stemmed from the fact that covert land sales by Palestinians remains one way (although much less significant than outright expropriation) by which Arab land falls into Israeli hands.

Villagers also hesitated at relating any stories about assassinations, robberies, or clan feuds that occurred during the revolt or in its name. The fact that Israeli historiography presents such actions as typical of the whole revolt strengthens their understandable reluctance to air dirty linen in public and mitigates public self-criticism. Another virtually taboo area concerned the *khawan*, men who betrayed the revolt, and the *'umala'*, the Arabs who spied for the British. As in most peasant insurgencies, traitors (*khawan*) to the cause who were found out were punished and sometimes executed by the rebels. For the elderly, such instances of division and bloodshed that occurred during the revolt were often overdetermined by preexisting clan or family differences and therefore remained sore points. But more significantly, former rebels balked at recalling instances of local internal dissension during the revolt because they did not wish to tarnish the shine of this central national symbol and forerunner of today's liberation movement. To cast a shadow upon the memory of the revolt might also enshroud the image of the PLO. Through narrative lacunae, the elderly tried to project an unsullied national past and present.

Another gap appeared in accounts of the economic situation in the 1930s. Published accounts tell of a rural economy in crisis, with *fallahin* under tremendous pressure from growing landlessness, high indebtedness, rising taxes, and the cycles of global economic recession. The written sources stress that Palestinian landlords, moneylenders, and merchants played their part in reducing many peasants to misery.[11] Knowing these general "facts" about life in the thirties, I hoped to elicit memories of class oppression. But when I asked, "How were conditions back then?" old men routinely answered, "Life was good, we were very happy." Their remarks did not so much indicate a nostalgia for a lost past as critical judgments against a burdensome present. Life in the 1930s, they implied, was quite fine by comparison with conditions today. Outside the formal interview situation, the elderly complained constantly about current problems: the dispersal of families, the forward march of land expropriations, the absence of civil rights, fears that the repressive military occupation might never end. The bleak present functioned as a screen, filtering out dark memories and endowing the thirties with golden tones. The selective vision afforded by present conditions blocked out some harsh features of daily life under British colonial rule. To many old people, the 1930s seem an idyllic time compared to the earth-shattering disasters of 1948 and thereafter. This revision of the past was also consistent with efforts to reduce the memory of class antagonism.

When pressed further, old men filtered less and some averred that the 1930s did have their share of economic problems. But still they did not complain of exploitation by Palestinian merchants or capitalists. Instead, they recounted one ideologeme again and again—that in the thirties the British mandate government deliberately imported cheap agricultural products into Palestine as part of a conspiracy to wreck Arab agriculture and to facilitate the Zionist conquest. The dominant interpretation, in its popular form, accounts for past economic troubles by focusing on external causes and obscuring internal class difference.

Other veterans who made critical judgments about the revolt often explained away its shortcomings by displacement.[12] Even villagers who acknowledged that robberies, murders, or land sales occurred during the revolt usually did not provide details. Such things happened, they usually said, only in *other* places, never in *our* village or *our* district. While acknowledging the partial validity of claims regarding unprincipled rebel practices, they shifted responsibility away from their own locale. One old peasant from the Ramallah area, by contrast, criticized the rebels active in his district for committing robbery and extortion, but then claimed that the *thuwwar* (rebels) did not act in this fashion in the Jenin area. For him, the practices of insurrectionists in Jenin exemplified the revolt's true character. Remembrance through displacement and condensation preserved the rebel movement's good name, although within regionally circumscribed limits. Other revolt veterans faulted the enemy for all the unsavory acts usually ascribed to the rebels. Palestinians, they claimed, could not be blamed for internal divisions. Domestic turmoil was the result of conspiracies hatched by the British or Zionist intelligence services, who paid mercenaries to commit robberies or murders in the name of the revolt, to stir up disputes between rival commanders, and to exacerbate clan or family difference.[13] The not-too-hidden lesson for the present is that while no significant internal differences exist(ed) within Palestinian society, the people must be vigilant in maintaining unity, because the enemy did and will continue to exploit the slightest hint of weakness or vacillation. There was large agreeement, therefore, on the popular level, on the need to maintain a unified, nationalist memory of the past.

## SUBALTERN TRADITIONS

Given these conditions, in which Israeli repression heightens the tendency to put forward a nationalist memory, what were the possibilities for a popular memory of revolt? I found that subaltern historical consciousness has neither been eliminated by Israeli censorship nor given its entire shape by mainstream nationalism. The people I interviewed did not simply echo the dominant versions or submit to repression. Popular traditions lead a submerged existence in the everyday realm of private conversation rather than being expounded in the public arena. But there is no "pure" popular memory: it is caught up in the web of what Gramsci calls the subaltern "common sense." Unlike the relatively coherent and systematic discourses that issue from official sources, common sense is "ambiguous, contradictory . . . multiform" and "strangely composite" (Gramsci 1971:324, 423; 1985:189). As the historical result of an "infinity or traces," common sense bears the deposits of "Stone Age elements and principles of a more advanced science, prejudices from all past phases of history at the local level and intuitions of a future philosophy which will be that of a human race united the world over" (Gramsci 1971:324).

Common sense, moreover, is not a comprehensive knowledge shared by all the people but is divided into local and regional varieties (Foucault 1980:82).

Ironically, Israeli policies are partly responsible for subaltern traditions. The authorities' harassment of those institutions which sustain support for the PLO limit the national leadership's ability to channel common sense. They constrain the PLO's capacity to harness subaltern opinion to hegemonic principles and to produce or disseminate elaborated interpretations of Palestinian history. Mainstream nationalism, while enthusiastically embraced, has imprinted specific histories in people's minds only to a limited extent. Because official agencies have effectively disseminated only a *general* historical narrative, many local versions of the past remain relatively untouched as long as they do not directly contradict the official story.

This opening permits a certain circulation of local versions of history. Among these are "popular-democratic" interpretations of the revolt emphasizing local initiatives, which emanate from submerged peasant traditions of independence from state control, forged out of the experience of collective struggles. These traditions can be put to use to contradict or reinscribe official historical discourses (Hall et al. 1977:50). They resemble the "negative" class consciousness Gramsci described in rural Italy—the countryside's dislike of the town, the peasants' hatred of state officials—and which he named "subversivism" (1971:272–273). However, no red thread of class consciousness ties memory together; elderly villagers do not remember the revolt in a "pure" language of class. Popular memory is a complex web of popular-democratic, nationalist, religious, clan, and localist strands. Different groups and individuals combine elements of these discourses in various arrangements and articulations. Official Palestinian nationalism, the dominant discourse, tries to fit these elements into its system of meaning, to make them equivalents in a signifying chain, and to marginalize the dissonant strands. Popular-democratic memory-traces therefore rarely appeared full-blown, but interwoven with other, discontinuous expressions of subordinate memory. "Subversivist" recollection was expressed indirectly, in the interstices of a nationalist opinion, and in conjunction with "religious" or "regionalist" discourse.

Informants therefore couched popular-democratic statements in nationalist language, as divergent rather than oppositional versions of a national past. "Subversivist" accounts were not counterhegemonic but inflections, negotiations, and maneuvers within the dominant Palestinian code. For instance, ex-rebels often disputed the official versions' emphasis on the leading role and advanced political consciousness of the urban middle class. Some villagers asserted that the revolt was the work of the (urban and rural) poor and not the rich. "The revolt would have succeeded," claimed Abu Ahmad of Ya'bad, "if wealthy Palestinians had only sacrificed for it as much as poor people did." The impoverished classes who fought, gave their lives, and contributed generously to the rebels, he asserted, were the true nationalists. The rich, who gave only small contributions and never joined in the fighting, played an insignificant role. Other surviving *mujahidin* remembered the revolt's dynamics in terms of a rural-urban opposition: the *fallahin* and not city people, they said, really "made" (*'amalu*) the revolt. These fighters' accounts also focused on actions taken independently in the rural areas: peasants deciding on their own to form armed bands, rebels supplying themselves with weapons and food, local commanders planning when and where to hit the British forces, and so on. While not denying the importance of the national leadership, they stressed the significance of local initiatives taken without orders from on high. Some veterans even claimed that the *fallahin* were more nationalistic and revolutionary than the *effendi* leadership. Such glosses were often ambiguous, for men who expressed pride when recalling the rebels' independent actions nonetheless compared their level of military organization unfavorably with the PLO's fighting capacity today. "We were dedicated," they would assert, "but the overall situation was *fawda* (chaos)." Some elders, in contrast, claimed that in the thirties the movement was more nationalistic and militant than today, thereby deploying the past to criticize today's movement and leadership.

Some surviving *mujahidin* also employed the language of regionalism in their "subversivist" memory. Popular initiatives were often presented as strictly local phenomena, actions initiated by the men of a village (or villages) without orders or direction from the leadership. Informants often recounted rebel actions in their village or area with great pride. Although their language was localist, it unsettled the official version which claimed that the hand of the leadership guided effective action at all times and marginalized peasant activity. In addition, veterans maintained that local practices and knowledges were essential for the revolt. One such practice was the *faza'* or "alert," a traditional village practice of mobilizing in cases of outside aggression. This form of alarm was crucial to the rebels' abilities to get men into battle at a moment's notice. Informants also underscored the significance of their knowledge of local geography—the hiding places, the trails, the smuggling routes—for the prosecution of the rebellion. Such essential skills could only have been in peasant hands.

Democratic-popular positions were also articulated through religious discourse. Shaykh 'Izz al-Din al-Qassam, for example, was remembered first and foremost as a good Muslim, a man of religion. At the same time, villagers stressed that Qassam, by recruiting exclusively among peasants and the urban poor and by living among the poor of Haifa, was behaving in a "religious" fashion. They also pointed out that his association with the lower classes and his militant nationalism set him apart from the other religious leaders of that time. Such accounts of Qassam illustrate once again the disparate character of commonsense memory, its combination of religious, nationalist, and populist elements.

Many old rebels therefore gave the national past a subaltern inflection by recalling the revolt more as a peasant struggle than as a movement guided by educated city people. They remembered the revolt through the exemplary activities of local rebel commanders or of leaders like Qassam who organized among the subaltern, rather than through the names of official urban leaders. When asked about the revolt, they recalled the local heroes and martyrs with relatively unblemished reputations like Qassam as metonyms for a national movement that was popular, honorable, and lofty in its aims and actions (Swedenburg 1987:18–20). In the eyes of elderly villagers the *fallahin* were less the signifiers of the whole people than a *distinct part* of the people with its own local traditions of revolt. They recalled peasants as much in terms of their *difference* from the privileged classes as in terms of commonalities. Villagers who voiced heterogeneous opinions about the revolt, through popular-democratic inflections of mainstream nationalism or subversivist localism or Islam, articulated a more inclusive "national-popular" tradition (Gramsci 1971:130–133, 421) than official Palestinian historiography, which has tried to turn such polyphony into a conformism.

## MEMORIES OF REVOLT

*In every era the attempt must be made anew to wrest tradition away from a conformism that is about to overpower it.*
—WALTER BENJAMIN, "THESES ON THE PHILOSOPHY OF HISTORY"

The history of the Zionist colonization of Palestine is represented in the West as a heroic undertaking, as the establishment of an exemplary outpost of liberal and democratic values. Owing in large part to the hegemony of this version of the history of Palestine in the West, Israeli practices not only imperil the Palestinian present, they threaten the past as well. "*[E]ven the dead,*" Benjamin aptly remarked, "will not be safe from the enemy if he wins" (1969:255). Unlike popular memory in the West, Palestinian subaltern memory is threatened more by violent erasure than hegemonic recoding, menaced more by ruination than by incorporation into dominant discourse. Because the response to these dangers requires a unified front, popular memory has undergone secondary revision for the sake of the nation. Unity in struggle has required a strategy that might be called anti-imperialist nostalgia.

But despite their double jeopardy, Palestinian popular traditions of revolt remain alive, although hidden. Enmeshed within common sense are memories which progressive Palestinian political groups and intellectuals are trying to renovate and make "critical" (Gramsci 1971:330–331)—memory materials with which they carry on both the fight against colonialism and against the leadership's attempts to reduce the tradition to a nationalist conventionalism. For some intellectuals and elderly veterans, the 1936–1939 revolt is not a symbol whose meaning is fixed. Rather than an object of veneration to be held at a respectful distance, it is a signifier to actively renew. Even the *kufiya*, for instance, is not established for eternity as the symbol of national unanimity. Sami Kilani once told me a story he heard in prison from a septuagenarian *fallah* named Abu Muhammad, a fighter in the 1936–1939 rebellion who had subsequently been detained many times for his political activity. In the early 1980s he was in jail for giving military advice to guerrillas fighting against the occupation. Abu Muhammad used to spend hours recounting stories about the revolt to his prison comrades, men thirty or forty years his junior. One day, he recalled with laughter that many educated city-dwellers, when ordered to don the peasant *kufiya* in 1938, did not know the proper way to wear it. The *effendis* simply could not keep the symbol of national struggle from slipping off their heads.

It is through informal channels that anecdotes like these are recirculated, reinvoked, and rewritten. Counter-images are relayed through subaltern circuits, by means of tales told at home, smuggled books, privately recorded cassettes of nationalist songs, and banned poems. They are one means by which the popular classes and progressive groups simultaneously work to assert a Palestinian national identity in the face of cultural repression and to expand the space for equality and democracy within the unified national sphere—to keep nationalism from being a slogan, chanted in unison, authored by the middle classes.

## POSTSCRIPT

This paper was written prior to the outbreak of the *intifada* in the Occupied Territories in December 1987 and should be regarded as the product of the specific circumstances that prevailed there in 1984 and 1985. The *intifada* marks a real historic break regarding both the perceived image of Palestinians in the West and the role of the popular classes in the national struggle. Clearly, the U.S. public no longer sees Palestinians as simply terrorists. The national movement, moreover, is being pushed and prodded by popular initiatives from below. Fragmentary evidence suggests that this historic shift is also affecting memories of the 1936–1939 revolt and images of the peasant. That semantic shift in Palestinian culture, however, remains to be researched.

## ACKNOWLEDGMENTS

This paper is based in part on field research carried out in Israel and the West Bank in 1984–1985, with grants from the Social Science Research Council and the Graduate School, University of Texas at Austin. Thanks to James Brow, Robert Fernea, Jane Henrici, Paul Keyes, Smadar Lavie, Jay O'Brien, Forest Pyle, Jennifer Sharpe, and Mike Woost for their comments on various versions of this paper.

## NOTES

1. I base this reading on Arnon-Ohanna (1981), Bauer (1966), Elpeleg (1978), and Lachman (1982), representatives of dominant Israeli historiography. Yehoshuah Porath's invaluable two-volume history of the Palestinian Arab national movement during the mandate period (1974, 1977) is the best example of the minority liberal trend. Significantly, Israeli authorities prevented the Arab Studies Society in East Jerusalem from publishing an Arabic translation of Porath's work.

2. I uncovered no credible evidence that significant aid was given in the course of my research.

3. A pseudonym. All ex-fighters I refer to by name are designated by pseudonyms throughout.

4. British sources counted 1,779 Arab attacks on the police and army, 309 attacks on Jews, and 1,324 cases of firing on Jewish quarters and colonies between June 1936 and April 1939 (Sanbar 1984:52–53).

5. The quite different responses Karen Buckley turned up in her interviews with elderly Palestinian refugees at Damascus in 1986 are instructive. When she asked for accounts of the 1936–1939 revolt, several refugees responded spontaneously with tales of rebel attacks on Jewish colonies. The contrast between their open discussions of this subject and the reticence of elderly Palestinians in the West Bank and Israel supports my suggestion that Israeli repression enforces silence. It also intimates that Palestinians in Syria are less sensitive to charges of anti-Semitism.

6. The PLO, based *outside* the Occupied Territories, won this support through its efforts both through its uneven military achievements in Jordan and Lebanon and its more substantial gains in the diplomatic sphere.

7. For representative "official" Palestinian histories, see Zu'aytir (1955); Kayyali (1978); 'Allush (1978); Frangi (1983); Yasin (1975).

8. The official body that led the national movement in 1936–1939, chaired by Hajj Amin al-Husayni.

9. See Chatterjee (1986:153) regarding the Indian national leadership's views on the peasantry.

10. See Parmentier (1984) for a further discussion of these points.

11. For a review, see Swedenburg (1988:181–185).

12. Young people were more likely to "remember" the revolt critically than were the elderly. From my friend Nuhad I heard stories her father, a police officer under the British mandate, told his children about infighting and disorganization during the revolt. The tales were designed to leave his children with an unfavorable impression of the insurrection. When her father discovered that she had relayed these tales to me, he shouted, "How can you trust an American?! What do you think he might do with such stories?"

13. Archival evidence suggests the British and Zionists did employ such tactics. See Porath (1977:246, 249, 253).

# EIGHT

# The Production of Culture in Local Rebellion

*Gavin Smith*

In the introduction to this book, we learn that we debate among ourselves and that in the process the characteristics we apply to a traditional past or other are our terms of contention or our basic preoccupations of the present. We are not a homogeneous lot.[1] We differ—in our backgrounds, our present well-being, and our future concerns—and, because we are different, we find ourselves disagreeing: it seems obvious to me that "proper government" should not concern itself with what I do inside my home, amongst my family; it seems equally obvious to you that parents cannot be relied upon to behave properly to their children and hence any "proper government" must concern itself with these matters. I of course may or may not notice that your notions of "government" and "family" have different parameters from mine. Indeed in some sense it is important that we do not acknowledge too thoroughly the differences we give to such keywords in our society. There must be some common discursive ground between us. Just as the local shopkeeper cannot reject my dollar bills, on the grounds that they do not look as he would have them look, being too dirty, too clean, or too crumpled, so we must accept certain words as common currency. I think this is all perfectly conventional; it is important to the argument of this chapter that the reader accept these assumptions. In the case to be discussed here it is not crumpled dollar bills or "proper government" that is the relevant currency but the notion "community."

The people I lived with in Peru were engaged in a struggle over land which pitted them against the nearby haciendas (ranches), the army, the civil guard, and the government in Lima. Though not on the scale of Zapata's followers in Morelos, or Mao's in China, they were rebellious peasants. And among themselves they argued: the terms they applied to their traditional past and to the institutions and practices they saw as emergent from that traditional past were a function of their preoccupations of the present. But, even as they shared in this perpetually threatening and often terrifying struggle with others, they felt that there were differences among themselves in background, in well-being, and in concerns about the future, and so they argued. Perhaps that is too strong a word: they engaged in dialogue, they conversed. Yet "argument," "dialogue," and "conversation" are not quite the same. Philosophers engage in dialogue about the nature of being. They are paid to do so, and should the dialogue cease, so would their pay. What commitment they have is to maintain the dialogue. At dinner I converse with friends over the virtues of burgundy over claret. Since I can rarely afford either, the conversation is largely academic. There was nothing philosophical or academic about what these people in Peru disagreed over: their livelihoods depended on it. And so, yes: they *argued*.

Returning once more to the introduction, there we hear Eric Wolf noting that anthropologists endow other cultures with the qualities of internally homogeneous and externally distinctive and bounded objects, despite real heterogeneity *within* cultures and, at the very least, fuzzy boundaries between them. What this paper is about is how not just anthropologists and historians but the participants themselves are committed both to the importance of the differences among them and simultaneously to the ongoing production of an image of themselves as internally homogeneous and externally distinctive; as though, when the curtain rises for the audience of anthropologists and historians and, perhaps more especially, politicians, these actors must collude with their audience in this fiction, even as they belie it with their offstage discord.

If this is so—if rebellious peasants, even so small a group as this collection of no more than six hundred families, are shot through with differences among themselves and argue, not just about the use of the oxen today, but about institutions and practices the parameters of which are crucial for each person's future well-being, such as "the family," "the community," and "our way of life," and if, partly as a result of their internal discourse and partly as a result of their external struggle, each person's views of these notions changes—then what sense does this make of the terms of reference we anthropologists and historians in the audience use to describe what we see? Our conceptual apparatus for understanding both "peasant rebellion" and "peasant community" may need rethinking.

Convention suggests, for example, that certain strata of peasants are more prone to sustained rebellion than others or that peasants are attracted to a certain kind of charismatic nonpeasant leader or that they rebel to defend a past rather than create a future. But does any of this make sense if we envisage a collection of rebellious people, fearfully arguing among themselves and, as a result, modifying their position? If at the end of their argument the results are always the same—that this stratum of peasant ends up favoring rebellion and that stratum not, that they will follow that kind of leader and not this, and so on—then of course we may as well minimize the role of argumentation and the content of what is argued. But what if it is precisely the intensity of the arguments themselves that determines the relative participation of (and helps to define) one stratum or another, or goes toward the construction not just of notions of "leadership" but also of what is to be fought over and possibly killed for: community, land, and culture? Then surely the neat *tableau vivant* retrospectively constructed—possibly by analysts and participants alike—is misleading. It is a retrospective construction imagined for the purposes of our basic preoccupations of the present. And, as such, it may obscure precisely what those preoccupations were in the immediacy of the struggle—preoccupations that themselves contributed to the reconstitution of historically embedded institutions and practices whose "proper usage" relies on reference to their place in an (imagined) history of the past.

These embedded institutions and practices that were endlessly being negotiated were preeminently embraced under the rubric of "community." Since Wolf's seminal article (1955) anthropologists have moved a long way from the reified notion of "community" and "a community way of life" by placing peasant communities in historical context and showing how their boundedness and even their apparently internal leveling processes are outcomes of (differing) external economic and political forces of exploitation and domination. Nevertheless when peasants, confronted by the changing demands of a capitalist world, rebel, we are often tempted to slip back into stereotypical and decontextualized notions of the peasant community as one of tradition and homogeneous solidarity. Yet what we see in the case that follows is that heightened political struggle intensifies discourse within, bringing to the forefront of people's minds their most vital preoccupations, precisely because it tugs urgently at their sleeves, impelling them to articulate just what those preoccupations should be. Intensified discourse also has a less obvious consequence. In the push and pull of debate, history itself is reconstituted. Nor is this just the relative weight of one institution or another being weighed and rebalanced; the elements of society, apparently so embedded in an unchangeable past history, are actually reconstituted. Moreover, if we advance from the notion of culture as a fixed blueprint by which people act, toward a notion of culture as something produced and reproduced through history, then the evidence to be presented here suggests a further step. Cultural production does not occur with equal intensity from one day to the next. The productivity of culture (to stick, for the moment, with these rather labored economic concepts) increases at historical moments of heightened resistance and rebellion, because the valued components of culture are challenged, threatened from without, and so must be articulated within. And then, through this process, each participant constructs a means for identifying *with* or *against* each relevant component of culture.

A disturbance in the countryside means just that: peasants rebel and things are disturbed—not just in the routine world of the provincial capital where journalists write articles, policemen reports, and lawyers briefs, but among the peasants themselves. Here is the paradox: to explain a disturbance, something "must have happened." For something to have happened, there must be a beginning and an end—a subject and an object. And yet for disturbance to remain disturbance, it must resist these closures. From the peasants' point of view, the openness and incompleteness, the dialogic character of disturbance, provide their resistance with a vital element of its ongoing momentum.

This process can be seen sequentially in the local rebellion we are to look at, first in the open-endedness of the early account of rebellion given by the administrator of the remote Hacienda Tucle on 24 April 1964 and then in the more complete account in the local newspaper on the following day. The administrator's account is as follows:

> With great urgency I write to inform you of the following: The personnel of this hacienda, having already been considerably threatened, have now become aware of a veritable invasion by the community of Huasicancha. Invasions occur in the following places: Analanya, a large flock of sheep, cattle, and horses. In Picpish they are building huts and there is an alarming quantity of livestock in the community. In the zone of Anchi a large quantity consuming the best hacienda pasture—this confirms that by night they passed through the areas of Huachamachay, Arauca Pachca [etc.] with many animals. This movement of the *comuneros* of Huasicancha was still continuing at 1 P.M. and at Cabildo Pata there is a community authority (Ascensio A) who is giving orders to all who leave the village telling them where to go and with what flocks, all of them carrying staves and other movables in the direction of the *puna* of the hacienda.
>
> The matter must be dealt with urgently in order to avoid confrontations with the hacienda staff and the mixing of their animals with ours. Pedro P has already lost ten of his animals and we shall certainly lose more. I am sending this with the truck driver to make clear to you the gravity of the situation that faces us here at Tucle. (ARA)[2]

The disturbance in the highland pastures was first introduced to the townspeople of the provincial capital the next day in a more comprehensive version, however:

COMUNEROS BREAK PACT: INVASION AT TUCLE

Approximately a thousand peasants of the community of Huasicancha yesterday morning invaded the lands of the Tucle Livestock Co. in an area covering over ten kilometers.

Carrying flags, sticks, and banners with the phrase "Land or Death" on them, the peasants installed themselves—challengers—some three kilometers from the hacienda buildings.

The residence is guarded by forty employees.

As part of these acts of invasion the *comuneros* have taken with them 5,000 head of sheep and 1,500 cattle and have taken over the area, putting up their own shepherd's huts.

Manuel Duarte, the chief administrator of the hacienda, said he thought the invaders were being organized by foreign elements with communist inclinations.

The Tucle Livestock Co. is one of the most important of the region. It covers an area of 45,000 hectares and owns 20,000 Corriedale sheep and 2,000 Brown Swiss cattle. (*El Correo* [Huancayo], 25 April 1964)

The headline implies a decisive historical event. But the statement that *a pact had been broken* between landlord and rural dwellers in the high pastures suggests that this was simply the way in which the Huasicanchinos' centuries-old war of attrition against the haciendas was now being brought to the forefront of townspeople's awareness. Indeed, for the people of the provincial town, Huancayo, and, by extension, the people of Lima too, the Huasicanchino land-recuperation campaign was a clearly defined historical *event*: the people of Huasicancha "invaded" hacienda land in 1964, a struggle followed that reached its conclusion eight years later when the people of Huasicancha took possession of over a hundred thousand acres of land and the Hacienda Tucle was destroyed. Such is the imperative of closure in retrospective accounts of the past. And today, with a set of preoccupations quite different from then, it is one in which the Huasicanchinos themselves collude.

We do not need to deny these "facts," but we can cast them in a different light by trying to reproduce the process by which the heterogeneous preoccupations of the Huasicanchinos during that period gave rise to an intensive, ever-incomplete and ongoing constitution and reconstitution of key components in their culture: in its actual, local setting, their community.

During the mid-1960s the Peruvian Andes experienced widespread rural unrest. This was especially so in the central Andes, whence the following evidence is drawn. The term "peasant land invasions," popularly used in the press, is misleading, however, partly because it does not capture the wide variety of forms these popular initiatives took and partly because it reflects a hegemonic bias which many peasants themselves denied: the term "invasion" assumed that the land occupied by the peasantry did not belong to them. What was happening in the Andes was the attempt (by small farmers and rural poor) to realize—that is to say, to make manifest—a quite other interpretation. To this extent it is no corruption of the word or exaggeration of what was happening to say that this was extensive, relatively uncoordinated rebellion. One especially notorious instance provides the case we are about to discuss here.

Following the events described above, the Huasicanchinos conducted a war of attrition against the neighboring haciendas Tucle and Rio de la Virgen which lasted until a victorious settlement was formally recognized in the courts during my fieldwork in 1972–1973. Though the ups and downs and ins and outs of this campaign are very much a part of what concerns us here, the greater detail necessary for a respectable historical account must be left for elsewhere (Smith 1989). Here, suffice it to say that, far from the campaign I am about to discuss being something new, the Huasicanchinos' attempts to recover land from neighboring haciendas were long-standing. In the 1880s—during and after the war with Chile—they had expropriated and occupied all the local haciendas for a period. Again, during the 1930s they pressed their claims specifically against Hacienda Tucle. And in 1947–1948 they had undertaken a full-scale campaign against the hacienda, one that involved considerable bloodshed and yet led to disappointing results. It was followed by a period of savage repression (the Odria *Ochenio*), a period from which the people were emerging as the 1960s arrived. Resistance of one kind or another, then, was more the rule than the exception. And even during the more intensive eight years of resistance to be discussed here, moments of apparent victory and defeat came and went, as did participants in the campaign. Equally elusive to outsiders was what the Huasicanchinos' goals were from one moment to the next.

Huasicancha is a high-altitude community, lying to the south and west of the Mantaro Valley in the central Peruvian Andes. In the period that concerns us, pastoral farming was complemented by subsistence cultivation and some artisan and trading activities. Alongside Huasicancha were a number of vast livestock ranches (*haciendas*), of which the Hacienda Tucle, owned by Maria Luisa Chavez and her son Manuel Duarte, was the closest. A number of Huasicanchino families worked as shepherds for this hacienda, while still others perpetually grazed sheep by illicitly using hacienda-controlled land. All Hacienda Tucle's land as well as parts of the other haciendas in the area were claimed by the people of Huasicancha and other nearby communities. By the 1960s out-migration was such that 40 percent of the total communal membership[3] of three thousand people actually resided outside the community, while a further 25 percent migrated from the village for some part of the year.

The conflict between the Huasicanchino pastoralists and the surrounding haciendas has been so long-standing that it is a state of affairs taken for granted by all in the community. A common remark that slips from the lips of man and woman when reflecting on the matter is, "It goes back to the beginning of time." And indeed it certainly does go back to the beginning of written records. Hobsbawm (1974) has quite rightly argued that the Huasi-canchinos have been in conflict of one kind or another with landlords over the centuries. But the force of this conflict took on a cumulative momentum relatively recently.

From the end of the last century, conflict between the hacienda and the Huasicanchino pastoralists was a result of the irresistible force of an emerging capitalist livestock ranch coming up against the immovable block of erst-while pastoralists becoming involved in a commodity economy as rural and migrant petty-commodity producers. Driven by competition toward the rationalization of production, the hacienda was perpetually trying to sub-sistitute a wage system for a labor-rent system (in which pastoralists were allowed access to hacienda-controlled pasture in return for labor service) by enforcing absolute control over territory to the exclusion of local pastoralists. Increasingly during this century it became these same market-induced im-peratives for the reproduction of their enterprises which drove the Huasican-chinos to resist. And it was this long history of resistance which, in turn, put Hacienda Tucle in the "backward" state it found itself in by as late as 1964, when similar livestock companies nearby had at least partially succeeded in becoming capitalist firms.

The competition that drove the hacienda owners one way, drove the Huasicanchinos against them in another. But for the Huasicanchinos the process was not an even one, and these uneven imperatives provided an in-eluctable force underlying the production of culture during the Huasicanchi-nos' intensive political engagement. So let us turn for a moment to look at the differing forms of the Huasicanchinos' enterprises in the immediate context of the hacienda and in the more extended context of the overall Peruvian economy. In the mid-sixties Huasicanchinos were evenly distributed be-tween the highland village and a variety of work centers, among them Huan-cayo (the provincial capital), Lima, and La Oroya (site of the American-owned Cerro de Pasco Company's smelter). In all cases they made their livelihoods through the operation of domestic enterprises whose form varied from one Huasicanchino to another. In Lima, migrants were engaged in multi-occupational enterprises that included ambulant street-selling, trans-portation, market-stall operation, and a myriad of other petty activities. In Huancayo and La Oroya, some owned market stalls or shops, others had skills as electricians, mechanics, and builders, while still others had jobs as low-paid employees in government offices. And in the majority of cases the entire household membership produced various combinations of these. Again, in the village itself, though differences in wealth were not great (com-pared with the Mantaro Valley itself [see Long and Roberts 1978, 1984]), households varied in their commitment to arable as opposed to pastoral pro-duction, while still others offset their paucity of either by engaging in weav-ing, tile-making, or petty crafts and trades.

What is clear, then, is that the Huasicanchinos were a heterogeneous lot, and that is what matters for what we are about to examine. While it is important not to lose sight of the role of debate and negotiation in constituting this heterogeneity (as well as being produced by it), once this caveat is accepted, it will be helpful to the reader of what follows to draw up a much-simplified dramatis personae. We find among the Huasicanchinos migrants (notably in Lima and Huancayo) and village residents, most of whom have themselves had some experience of migration and a number of whom still do so seasonally.

Among the migrants we find established older figures who now have quite settled residences in Lima and some in Huancayo. Their visits to Huasicanacha were few in 1964 and virtually nonexistent by 1972. Other migrants with quite extensive experience in the city were part of what I call "confederations of households" (Smith 1984) that tied them into the workings of domestic enterprises in other work centers and the village itself. In the vast majority of cases these migrants had emerged from families with a long history of pastoral farming in the highlands. But beginning to establish themselves in the cities and perpetually attempting to constuct such confederations were a new group of migrants whose backgrounds had been less closely linked to pastoralism directly. Their livelihoods as petty traders, craftsmen, and small arable farmers had not given them so secure a network of reciprocal linkages as that of the ex-pastoralists, and so their confederations were often more shaky.

In the community itself we find households firmly tied in to the rural end of the household confederations. Likewise we find, too, smaller flock-owners who rely more heavily on craft skills and once-off jobs (many of which may require temporary migration) to get by. Like their city counterparts, they strive for interpersonal linkages that will offset their volatile lives, but face constant setbacks. And at the least fortunate end of this group of people are those whose poverty makes them uncomfortably reliant on the occasional work, exchange, or straight generosity of other Huasicanchinos. But increasingly during the period to be discussed, we find in Huasicancha a few independent farmers whose small numbers belie their growing influence in Huasicancha's politics and economy. These are farms headed by men returned from work in a local mine, whose proximity to Huasicancha made it possible for them simultaneously to engage in quite remunerative wage labor and operate enterprises on increasingly commercial lines. (For greater detail, see Smith 1989.)

Elsewhere I have shown that the heterogeneous domestic enterprises of the Huasicanchinos, both rural and urban, inclined them toward different developmental logics as they were reproduced through the generations (see Smith 1989). Here we need note just two factors. First, as different sectors of the national and regional economy experienced expansion and contraction over time, so enterprises inserted differentially into those sectors, developed in different ways. Second, for rural and especially urban enterprises, as even wider areas of social relations came to be expressed in commodified forms, so the imperatives of commodified relations of production began to take hold (see Marx 1976: chap. 23; Bernstein 1979; Friedmann 1980; Kahn 1980; Smith 1985; A. M. Scott 1986). The effects were contradictory. While the Huasicanchinos' heterogeneity was thereby increased, the volatility of the Peruvian economy as a whole (and even more so, of any one sector within it) had encouraged petty-commodity producers to share the desire for a foothold in farming. This was because not only was the future development of any one sector extremely unpredictable (especially so for the poorest and least-informed participants in it) but also inflation made accumulation in cash-based enterprises almost impossible. Hence the attraction of retaining a foothold in the farm, and, given the ecology of Huasicancha, this meant preeminently pastoral farming, with its need for pasture.

It is at this point that the role of praxis plays its part in the production of Huasicanchino culture. Because members of each enterprise were fighting for the maintenance (or expansion) of their "way of life" (simultaneously a gloss for "livelihood" and for "culture"), precisely what the *essential* elements of that way of life were came to the forefront of attention. Because different enterprises required different elements of that "way of life" for their repro-duction, what was essential and what was less so had to be negotiated. Be-cause these matters were sufficiently important to drive people to concerted resistance, the commitment to engage in these negotiations was very great. A "multiplicity of dispersed wills" were confronting external forces that threatened the future of their "way of life" by denying them access to the land upon which it depended. Against the overwhelming forces that denied the validity of this reality, the contrary assertion of these truths by the Huasi-canchinos meant intensive dialogue among themselves about what "own-ership" of land meant, how labor might be justly given over to others, or what it meant to identify oneself with (be a "member" of?) a community, and so on, as well as a multiplicity of relationships subsidiary to these. And such discourse meant the exchange of words whose meanings were both fixed and obvious and at the same time—and because of their very importance—ever-reconstituted and elusive.

With the end of the repressive years of the Odria *Ochenio*, open political debate returned, and in the Mantaro Valley an increasingly commercialized small, independent farming population began to seek political leverage through a multitude of *federaciones campesinas* (peasant leagues). From 1958 to the national elections of 1962 and again in 1963, migrants from Huasicancha, resident in the valley and in Lima, were influential in channeling much of Huasicancha's campaign for the restitution of land through these *federaciones campesinas*.

Among the migrants who were now well established in Lima and Huancayo there were a few people who had set up small shops or permanent *talleres* (workshops). At the same time, those who did not have some special skill, such as an electrician or mechanic, were shifting into investment in market stalls or (secondhand) pickups or vans. People such as these saw the *federacion campesina* as a channel through which the land-recuperation campaign might be steered, but they saw land recuperation as just one of a number of issues that Huasicanchinos should address to improve their lives. To this end in 1958, one of their number, Elias Tacunan, an electrician, APRA (*Alianza Popular Revoluciarario de America*) party organizer in the smelting town of La Oroya, and now almost a stranger in the village, ran for the position of *Personero*[4] in Huasicancha, together with similar figures drawn from the migrant Huasicanchinos in Lima and Huancayo.

Organizing a meeting at the small settlement of Vista Alegre, in the highlands near Huasicancha, Tacunan formed the first of his *federaciones campesinas*, the *Movimiento Comunal del Centro*, based on five municipal districts in the highlands. Although the recovery of "communal" lands was a major source of enthusiasm for the *Movimiento* among the highland villagers, Tacunan intended to spread the federation to include the more commercial migrants in the Mantaro Valley. Though strategically useful to refer to land claims in terms of customary usufruct, the fact was that these migrants' commercial enterprises relied as much on exclusive forms of property as did the haciendas in claiming pastureland. Sensitive to their concerns, therefore, Tacunan stressed the more vague platforms of better conditions in the villages and improved educational facilities, while not clarifying his position with respect to the payment of an indemnity to the hacendados for their expropriated lands.

But village records, two old diaries, and informants' accounts lead to the impression that most Huasicanchinos in the village itself, and indeed the bulk of the poorer migrants too, looked upon the activity of the federations with a certain bemusement, as though it were a conversation taking place on the other side of a partition, in an adjoining, crowded, and ill-lit room. Suspecting that Tacunan's ambivalence concealed a contractual notion of the exclusive ownership of the pastures, one older Huasicanchino was moved to clarify his own view thus:

> The well-being (*riquesa*) of the *gamonal* [the more traditional term for the hacienda owner] derives not from his vast herds (*rebaños inmensos*), nor from his pastures which by right belong to the Community of Huasicancha, but from the giving (*dotación*) of labor by our children and our forebears, who have lived for years and years in poverty while serving an unjust patron (*un patrón injusto*). (AC)

The Huasicanchinos' attitudes to the *Movimiento Comunal* were by no means unequivocal or unanimous, then. Many of those still in the village who had been involved in resistance campaigns earlier in the century were lukewarm toward the political initiatives spearheaded by commercial migrants personified by Tacunan.

The migrants' monopoly of the community's positions of authority was an especially visible expression of a process in which Huasicanchino social relations had become increasingly dominated by the dictates of nonfarm economic activities beyond the highlands. Changes in the fortunes of the various sectors in which enterprises were inserted had combined with the hacienda's move toward commercial rationalization to undercut the preeminence of the community as an institution. For on the one hand the hacienda's dominance in controlling pasture and on the other the tendency of increasingly commodified pastoralist households to pay rent to other villages for pasture combined to preempt the community itself from acting as the most significant conduit for access to pasturelands. And the instrumental use made of community office-holding by migrants like Tacunan served less to integrate the highland pastoralists into national and regional political institutions than to draw attention to the distinctiveness of the pastoralists' interests.

There was plenty of debate in the air, therefore—among Huasicanchino migrants, among villagers, and between migrants and villagers—when, from 1960 onward, spontaneous land occupations and other rural insurgency throughout Peru began to be reported with increasing frequency in the papers. Around the haciendas Tucle, Antapongo, and Laive there were signs that the daily cat-and-mouse hide-and-seek between hacienda foremen and *individual* herders who trespassed as part of the quotidian struggle for livelihood was being replaced by open confrontation between the community as a whole and the haciendas.

For, in fact, the word "trespass" is misleading. Huasicanchinos found by the administrator using hacienda-controlled pasture without a formal contract were referred to as *pasaderos*. There was an ongoing argument between community authorities and the hacienda administrator as to whether pasaderos were merely exercising their right to graze and, once caught, were prepared to pay a forfeit in labor (the community authorities' view), or whether they were illegal trespassers obliged to do labor service as a punishment (the administrator's view) (ARA, FHT, AC). As the administrator tried to increase the punishment to draconian extremes, in order to discourage repetition of the "offense," so the dispute grew and the daily round of finding pasture became inherently confrontational. The boundary therefore between the daily business of "trespassing" and the headline-grabbing "land invasion" was not a clear one. It reflected a specific tactic for gaining armed support on the part of the hacendado, on the one hand, and the increasing incentive of the community authorities to reestablish their position as the conduit through which *all* Huasicanchinos' access to pasture passed, including pasaderos'.

What we witness now, therefore, is an attempt by various factions of the peasantry in Huasicancha itself to reassert the *community's* control of the key areas for the social reproduction of enterprises. The specific form the campaign took—the massive invasion of hacienda-controlled land from April 1964 on—must be understood in terms of the community authorities attempting to maintain leadership over otherwise individually initiated "trespassing" by Huasicanchinos acting in small groups.

Because leadership was always questioned, it is misleading to see the unfolding campaign in terms of a succession of different leadership factions. Nevertheless we might pause for a moment here to help the reader through the complexities of what follows with a summary. As we have seen, the campaign began with the well-established migrants from Lima and Huancayo at the helm, with the occasional support of the large flock-owners in Huasicancha. This was followed by a group of small flock-owners from the village supported by the older "confederated households" (see below) in and beyond Huasicancha. Over the period, however, newly established migrants began to make their feelings heard, though never acquiring a vigorous role in directing the campaign. Finally a small group of independent farmers with flocks developed from earnings in the local mines were the figureheads who signed the settlement that concluded the campaign.

Let us return now, to the early days: through 1962 and 1963 the threat of hoof-and-mouth disease made hacienda staff especially diligent in preventing the unbathed animals of the villagers from straying onto hacienda land. Meanwhile among those caring for the smaller flocks, pressure to trespass grew: drought made pasture scarcer, encouraging greater movement of flocks; villagers hitherto working at the local mine were returning with cash which they invested in sheep; and the number of animals owned by migrants and held in village flocks on the basis of reciprocal arrangements between households were now steadily increasing. As a result the number of conflicts occurring between hacienda staff and villagers increased (ARA, AC, FHT).

There was a possibility that this would lead to a rift because the community authorities were the better-off migrants. In the community meetings throughout 1962, these people were urging discretion on the local front while the national political scene clarified itself (AC). And increasingly the community Personero, Elias Tacunan, fudged his position on land redistribution, the better to keep his hand free for bargaining with national political figures on behalf of his *federacion campesina*. A rift was postponed, however, because inter-household linkages (between villagers and migrants and between pastoralists and arable farmers) acted as a centripetal force crosscutting quantitative differences in wealth and qualitative differences in the sources of household incomes (see Smith 1979). Moveover, with confrontations increasing daily between poorer Huasicanchinos relying on "trespassing" and the hacienda personnel, the large flock-owners began to share with the bulk of migrants a renewed preoccupation with "the community." For migrants (as much community members as the village residents), community institutions were a means to keep *formal* control over the direction of events in Huasicancha, where they were now investing some of their resources; for the large flock-owners emphasis on the community and on that aspect of people's identity which derived from community membership was a means of keeping a handle on the poorer *comuneros*' movement on the scarce pasturelands.

Soon, however, pressure for the removal of Tacunan became manifest. It was initiated by those villagers caring for the smaller flocks, because the areas that were left to them to pasture were most easily accessible to hacienda staff. Many of these people had reciprocal ties with Huancayo and Lima migrants, whose animals constituted part of the flocks being pastured "illegally" on hacienda land. As temporary migration and off-farm incomes began to play an increasing role in household reproduction even for the village households, so these ties—expressed through the idiom of shared community identity—were essential to ever-larger numbers of Huasicanchinos.[5]

Assembly records for this period are replete with a myriad of uses of the term "community" (*comunidad*) covering a wide range of resonances, from the strictly legal constitution of Huasicancha as a *Comunidad Indigena* ("Indigenous Community") recognized by the national government and with formal title to local pastures, to the more affectual notion of the community of Huasicanchinos as neighbors with shared interests, to a notion of the Huasicanchino community as the embodiment of certain self-evident (hence never explicitly stated) principles for living a proper life. Meanwhile perhaps its most obvious meaning—as a place of common residence—was one accepted not just by residents but by migrants too—who often referred to their (empty and padlocked) houses as a sign of their community membership.[6]

The point here is not to try to demonstrate an ultramaterialist position by seeking to associate each utterance of the term with groups of people sharing similar "material" conditions. The possibility that certain Huasicanchinos held consistent notions of "community" each time they used the term and that these were always marginally different from notions of "community" held by others seems unlikely. What is clearly demonstrated in the records is that the term was used so frequently and became such a keyword as the struggle for land unfolded from one year to the next. In the process of this discourse "community" as an essential element of identity for Huasicanchinos became covertly reconstituted—a reconstitution, moreover, that was never completed so long as "community's" various resonances remained preeminently relevant to the social reproduction of the heterogeneous Huasicanchino enterprises, hence an ongoing discourse within and about the community.

On 11 April 1963 Tacunan was removed from office as Personero, accused of stealing money from community funds. This was the first of what became a series of attempts to remove the older migrants, more thoroughly incorporated into urban life. These incorporated migrants had established their domestic enterprises during the lean years in Huasicancha—from an earlier campaign in 1936 through the repressive years of the Odria regime in the early 1950s. While their attachment to Huasicancha was emotionally strong, therefore, the reproduction of their enterprises was more thoroughly tied to commitments in their place of migration than in the village.

The strongest element carrying out this "coup" were the migrants and villagers who were tied into reciprocal obligations with one another. There were also those few better-off, relatively independent flock-owners who had either remained in the village after 1948 or who had returned from migration and were beginning to invest in sheep. And to these were added a group of poorer migrants in Huancayo and Lima who had no strong inter-household links to Huasicancha to speak of but who relied for occasional favors on the better-off Huasicanchinos.

The new officeholders were small flock-owners who received the support of the older pastoralist families. Reliant as they were on funds raised from the migrants, the new authorities were unable to take a particular direction in the campaign without migrant support. So they decided to petition the president of the republic directly and get the migrants involved in the process (de la Cruz Diary, Huasicancha). And so, duly dressed in ponchos and felt hats sent from the village, Huasicanchino migrants presented themselves to the president as members of the traditional peasantry and delivered a petition linking their claims to their customs and practices that went back to time immemorial.[7] And on 30 November 1963 an agreement was signed with Hacienda Tucle stating that there would be no more trespassing until the government adjudicators had made some decision. The new officeholders now reminded villagers at every meeting that aggression would lose them the support of President Belaunde.

For the moment, then, community authorities committed themselves to legitimate channels for the recuperation of land. But things were to change in January of 1964 when, after an inspection by the civil judge of Huancayo, the feelings of the community as a whole vis-à-vis the hacienda reached boiling point.

Concluding that the judge had been bribed by the hacendado prior to the inspection, many villagers had their patience tested to the limit and now dispensed with the cautions of the authorities and began to invade land in small, independent groups, causing the hacienda administrator to believe that a full-scale invasion was occurring (ARA). Similar invasions continued throughout February, prompting the community authorities to call a meeting in March which placed them in charge of a land occupation to "reivindicar nuestros pastos legítimos" ("recover our legitimate pastures"). Three authorities who felt unable to support a policy of confrontation were per-

mitted to resign and were replaced by others.[8] On 16 March Demetrio de
la Cruz, now Personero of the community, went to Huancayo where he
appeared before a judge with the community's lawyer to denounce the violent acts of the hacendado. In the subsequent six weeks invasion tactics were
discussed, areas of the *puna* allotted to particular groups for invasion, and
attempts made to persuade hacienda employees to leave their posts. Then on
24 April the invasion was carried out, eliciting the responses of the hacienda
and the local press we have already seen.

The army was called in, creating a climate of fear in Huasicancha, for by
this time so-called "land invasions" were occurring throughout the central
highlands and confrontations with varying degrees of violence were reported
in the press almost daily (de la Cruz diary). Many people in the village felt
that the time for compromises had passed (ibid.), and when a ministerial
inspector was sent once more to survey the landmarks on 7 May, de la Cruz
had a violent argument with him and left. Returning from this inspection, he
and another community authority were caught by the civil guard, together
with three other elected authorities. All were accused of being communist
agitators and imprisoned without trial (JT; de la Cruz Diary).

The effect was to throw the Huasicanchinos into yet another period of
intense discussion. Soon after the arrests Belaunde announced that no land
being occupied by squatters would be considered for land reform. Throughout Peru many peasants therefore withdrew from land. From the point of
view of those migrants in Huancayo and Lima who were in touch with
national and regional developments this seemed to be a promising development favoring a conciliatory stance, and they wrote to the community authorities urging them to negotiate a compromise with Manuel Duarte, the
owner of Hacienda Tucle (AC). On the other hand the extent of rural mobilization in the central Andes was far greater than anybody had witnessed in
this century, and the preoccupation of the army in numerous separate areas
had given the Huasicanchinos actually "invading" the land more success
than they had anticipated. Responding to the migrants' letter in the general
assembly, they stressed that Hacienda Tucle was unable to contain their
activities. Alongside the migrants' reference to the contemporary political
currency of negotiation and compromise, they juxtaposed the history of
Huasicancha's past resistance campaigns, reminding the audience of the
period in the 1880s when Huasicanchino *guerrilleros* and their allies had expropriated all the neighboring haciendas.[9] Nevertheless one speaker was
severely chastised when he sought to ridicule the migrants by saying, "Noso-
tros, Huasicanchinos, no somos profesores; pero sí somos guerrilleros" ("We
Huasicanchinos aren't schoolteachers; we're guerrillas"). An older man re-
joined, "No somos profesores, ni guerrilleros. Como todo el mundo sabe, los
Huasicanchinos son 'Los Zorros'" ("We're neither schoolteachers nor guerrillas. As all the world knows, the Huasicanchinos are 'the Foxes'" [referring

to the popular nickname in the neighborhood for the Huasicanchinos])
(AC). So the pressing question of finding a new set of leaders provided the
opportunity for further debate along these lines.[10]

Increasingly we hear the voices of those migrants who, originally lacking a
significant base in livestock (and hence the networks associated with
livestock-rearing) were now beginning to establish themselves outside the
village with sufficient consistency for the process to have become institutionalized (see above, p. 185). And they were joined by a much smaller group
who were returning from work in a local mine to become "independent farmers" in Huasicancha.[11] The fact that livestock were being used as part of
the campaign (to "eat up the hacienda," in the words of informants) meant
that Huasicanchinos were reluctant to sell animals to raise cash for legal fees,
and it was therefore the migrants with access to cash and credit who took
most responsibility for paying legal fees.

But refusal to pay the *coto* (head tax) was assumed to mean renunciation of
*comunero* status and hence of any claim to pasture or to a voice in the community. This meant that so long as there was a significant body of Huasicanchinos determined to continue the campaign, those wishing to gain from the
eventual outcome had to keep up their participation. As a result, heated
discussion took place to influence the course of events, but threats to withdraw support were never especially effective. Moreover, the village residents
were aware of the fact that they had the whip hand, inasmuch as a steadily
increasing number of migrants from one year to the next were investing in
sheep. In the last analysis, as de la Cruz put it a few year later, "We had their
sheep."

There were few backsliders, therefore.[12] And the much vaunted solidarity
of the Huasicanchinos noted by the Huancayo observers of the time, or the
*unión* (unity) recalled by informants reflecting back today on those times,
must be seen within this context. Far from the singleness of purpose visible
from geographic or historical distance, the heat of discussion over different
perceptions of the key elements of what was being fought for gave momentum
to the struggle directed outward, just as the fearful commitment people had
to its outcome held them together like warring Siamese twins. Such is the
stuff of community:

> What is shared in community is not shared values or common understanding,
> so much as the fact that members of a community are engaged in the same
> argument, the same *raisonnement*, the same *Rede*, the same discourse, in which
> alternative strategies, misunderstandings, conflicting goals and values are
> threshed out. (Sabean 1984:29–30)

The need to find officials to replace those in prison now provided a forum
for further debate. While some—especially migrants engaged in volatile
petty-commodity production in the cities—relied on the *regularity* of livestock

sales, there were other Huasicanchinos who were not preoccupied by difficulties deriving from unsystematic husbandry such as irregular sales or care
during the lambing season. For them this was not a view of farming that
prevailed in their enterprises: they observed no special season for lambing.
These latter were not therefore seriously hindered in the running of their
enterprises by a long-drawn-out war of attrition. And this attitude toward
time was shared by the migrant households with whom they had reciprocal
arrangments and other villagers and migrants with few or no livestock whose
only possibility of such investment lay in the future.

Among and between these groups debate set in. From the forum of the
Sunday meetings in village or migrant club, to urban workplace and village
street-corner, to the confines of the household "patio," discussion was ani-
mated. As one informant put it,

> At meetings, did we talk about what to do? Of course we did. But we had
> already discussed it the day before. And the day before that. We talked of
> nothing else. What else mattered? After all, we are talking of a moment when it
> seemed as though everybody ruled in Huasicancha. Hah! And those with office
> did not rule ( *Y ellos con cargos no mandaban*). And so it was. (Field notes, Huan-
> cayo, February 1973)

"Everybody ruled" and "those with office did not rule": for with de la
Cruz and his colleagues in prison a new set of officeholders was decided upon
from among the old-established migrants resident in Lima and two of their
village relatives. Their ability to assert their own interests, however, was
proscribed by a generally held view that they were now only superficially
leaders for the purposes of dealing with outsiders and that others really
"ruled in the community." This form of realpolitik was sufficiently acknowledged among Huasicanchinos to have a name: *la cumbre oscura* ("the summit
hidden [by clouds]").

The informant's assessment is born out by a committee meeting called by
the Inter-Ministerial Commission in the village itself. Not surprisingly, these
new officers invited their figurehead, Elias Tacunan, to attend. The strength
of feeling that surfaced in the debate is captured by these outraged notes
made by a village resident and inserted into the community records:

> It was set up at the request of Manuel Duarte, who had bribed (*habia comprado*)
> the two delegates of the Ministries who came to Huasicancha. . . . The com-
> munity received them with a band, and then a general assembly was sum-
> moned by the guests, in which the two ministerial delegates took over entirely.
> The authorities of the community were not permitted to speak. Señor Elias
> Tacunan, who represented FEDECOJ as the general secretary, was, however,
> permitted to use his words, which he did entirely in favor of the *gamonal* and for
> expropriation by the agrarian reform and not by the demand that the commu-
> nity is making. From this date Tacunan has lost all prestige as a respresentative
> of the community. (AC)

It is to be noted that the reference to "the authorities of the community" is not to the newly appointed officers but rather to the old leaders who had been brought up from the prison in Huancayo especially for the occasion.

The next day the Huancayo newspaper carried the headline, "PROBLEM TUCLE-HUASICANCHA STILL AT PAGE ONE." But the hacienda administration had been impressed by the evident differences of opinion among the Huasicanchinos, and a few days later another headline appeared in the paper, "TUCLE: WE ACCEPT AGRARIAN REFORM," underneath which it was recorded that, aware of the fact that the villagers of Huasicancha only wanted the land in order to rent it out to those who were not residents of the village (the migrants?), the hacienda administration would accept a limited amount of expropriation on condition that the beneficiaries were to be found among all neighboring communities save Huasicancha.

Within a few days the hacienda appeared to achieve what it had been seeking. On 4 November the newspaper carried a large public announcement: "To PUBLIC OPINION: ACT OF AGREEMENT BETWEEN THE COMMUNITY OF HUASICANCHA AND THE TUCLE LIVESTOCK COMPANY." The Commission had arranged an agreement between the hacendado and the representative of Huasicancha, Santos C., Ramon M., Francisco Y., Hermino Z., and Cleto Y. The settlement was remarkably favorable to the hacienda and apparently an abject defeat for Huasicancha. But an immediate result was the release of the imprisoned authorities. By January 1965, following a now-familar pattern, the Huasicanchinos removed the officers who had signed this agreement and replaced them with their predecessors. The *comuneros* then rejected the settlement on the grounds that it had been signed by people who had never had the proper credentials from the community.

Throughout 1965 those in the remote area around Tucle and Huasicancha and those in the urban centers were strikingly at variance in the way they read prevailing conditions. In Lima, President Belaunde had declared that the Departments of Junin and Pasco would be the targets of land reform in that year. In the rural locales, however, the government's presence was not represented by these generous intentions but rather by the suspension of individual guarantees and the presence of U.S.-trained "rangers" in pursuit of the guerrilla fighters calling themselves the "Tupac Amaru" cell (Bejar 1970).

Increased guerrilla activity meant that government sympathy with those especially stubborn peasants who, suspicious of promises, refused to withdraw from land was now replaced by a campaign of fear. This substitution of a climate of fear for the previous government policy of negotiation effectively drew more sharply the line between "within," where discourse among participants proceeded apace, and "without," where dialogue between government representatives and *comuneros* had ceased altogether. The sense of confrontation was now very high, when two apparently unrelated occurrences gave rise to overt resistance. First the army contingent at the *fundo* was withdrawn, then the Huancayo court delivered a judgment in favor of Tucle in the civil case with Huasicancha. In the wake of these two superficially unrelated events, an apparently mysterious fire occurred at the hacienda. The growing hysteria in Huancayo vis-à-vis the peasantry is reflected in the local newspaper headline: "RED TERROR CONTINUES: HACIENDA BUILDING BURNT DOWN."

In fact, overall, the Huasicanchino campaign is not very well captured by the expression "red terror." By late 1967, when de la Cruz was replaced in office by that cohort of Huasicanchinos who had returned from the local mine over the past three years and were now setting up as independent farmers, strategy and tactics were well established. They were to deplete the basic resources of the hacienda: pasture and sheep. Simply by persistently trespassing onto hacienda land with livestock, villagers undermined the basis of the hacienda's land-use system. Normally flocks were circulated over extensive areas of pasture to allow one area to recuperate while another was being used. Perpetual trespassing on pasture being left to rest played havoc with this system. Trespassers' flocks were swollen too by rustling; nor was an opportunity ever lost to damage or kill hacienda animals when they could not be carried off.

Nevertheless this long war of attrition in the 1960s plus the century-old history of Huasicanchinos' resistance to the Chileans and subsequent insurgency through the 1880s (see Manrique 1981; Smith 1989) combined to give them a reputation in the central sierra as *guerrilleros* (lit. warriors[13]). The Huasicanchinos themselves were not unaffected by such a potent appellation. In Huasicancha, however, the term is used with great caution. For what distinguishes them—both in their own eyes and in the eyes of their neighbors—is the effectiveness of their fight, not the fight itself. Unsurprisingly, informants are not at all unaware that many peasants are prone to resistance, to picking a fight. It would be hard to live in the central sierras with any other view. Yet, important though their reputation as *guerrilleros* might be to them, it is, above all, the *effectiveness* of actions which selects those actions from experience to be reconstituted in memory, letting the rest fall away and hence producing a specific notion of resistance.

Tactics made army surveillance very difficult as it did too for the patrols by the hacienda *caporales* who were familiar with the hazardous mountain terrain. Small groups of invaders entered the hacienda land at widely dispersed points with their livestock. Hacienda staff, called upon to patrol over thirty thousand hectares of mountainous terrain, could not travel in sufficient numbers to take immediate action once invaders had been spotted. Forced back to base for reinforcements, more often than not they returned to find the invaders gone.

The civil guard and army were still less successful. The fact that rural unrest was widespread in central sierras meant that no large contingent could be kept in the area for any length of time. Instead a varying number of men (depending on the perceived state of affairs in the area) were quartered either at the hacienda buildings or in a location where they could keep an eye on the Huasicanchino bridgehead, whence invasions occurred. But the job was boring and morale low, exposing their Achilles' heel:

> On at least one occasion—it's hard to tell: it may have happened a lot more than once—a group of men arrived at the guard post near Huaculpuquio well stocked with *aguardiente* (cane alcohol). After some friendly banter and some joshing between themselves and the soldiers a bottle appeared and was passed round. Unhappy at how the soldiers' suspicions restrained their jollity, one or two men left the group, returning some time later with three or four young women and a couple of musical instruments. All with good effect. The following morning their *cabo* (corporal) found his men all but incapacitated while villagers had long since driven their flocks past the post into the high pasture. (The wonders of aguardiente. It seems one never gets a head for it.) (Field notes, Huasicancha, May 1972)

Then, when the frustration and impotence of being confined to the observation post drove more adventurous small contingents of soldiers to journey away from the hacienda in pursuit of trespassers, as likely as not they were led deep into the high mountains and there abandoned by trespassers turned decoys.

In effect it was a war of attrition in which one side was continually diverted from getting on with its business while the other side was pursuing its familiar daily struggle of livelihood: pasturing livestock whenever and wherever possible. As a result a gradual decline in the morale of both the hacienda administration and the civil guard set in from the latter part of 1966.

The relative conditions of the two disputing sides by the end of the following year is nicely captured by a subtle change that was taking place in the role of *Personero*: while he continued to control the invasion campaign by designating people to "enter" the hacienda in specific places, this no longer meant so much a cat-and-mouse game with the hacienda *caporales* as the actual allotment of *estancias* and surrounding pasture to specific families who began to settle in that area and protect it not only from hacienda personnel but also from fellow villagers. This reinstatement of the authorities of the community for the distribution of means of production cannot be overestimated, and the fact that these positions were now energetically sought—and successfully gained—by the new independent farmers who were systematically accumulating flocks had the effect of subtly reconstituting the various resonances of "community."

Meanwhile, for the owners of Hacienda Tucle the climate was changing. While there remained government sympathy toward reasonably efficient public stock companies like the Ganadero del Centro, which ran the neighboring Hacienda Laive, nationally famous for its cheese, this was not so for haciendas like Tucle. Hobsbawm (1974:140) has suggested that "Tucle, as its neighbouring estates were frequently forced to note, was somewhat deficient in diplomacy, legal acumen and good management." And this was undoubtedly true, though it cannot be isolated from a context in which *this* hacienda for over a century had been forced to deal with perpetual peasant resistance. I have shown elsewhere how, time and again, the ability of Hacienda Tucle to institute rational management practices was preempted by peasant resistance both of newsworthy moment and in a myriad of daily forms (Smith 1989). We have seen too what little success the administration had on the few occasions when it favored diplomacy over less-subtle means. Likewise for legal acumen, we should note the kind of opposition Tucle had in the Huasicanchinos. For the sake of the territorial survey made by the civil judge, children had been carefully trained in the misnaming of landmarks. On another occasion, determined to have the army removed from a spot where it could observe their use of one squatter site as a bridgehead for deep incursions into hacienda land, the Huasicanchinos acquired a number of army uniforms, dressed themselves as soldiers, and, with the help of a migrant who was an ambulant photographer in Huancayo, managed to produce photographs for the Huancayo district judge of "soldiers" molesting village women. (The army was instructed to withdraw from the area.)

So it was that by the time the military government of Juan Velasco replaced President Belaunde at the end of the sixties, the positions of the two sides were reversing: as Hacienda Tucle became increasingly decrepit and incapable of carrying out the changes necessary to make it into a capitalist enterprise, the leadership of the Huasicanchino campaign was falling into the hands of independent farmers the rationality of whose enterprises was ever more capitalistic.

Much of the Huasicanchinos' reconstruction of their experience of struggle has the ongoing effect of constituting "the rebellious peasant" that they are so very conscious of being seen as by "outsiders." Yet it is at the moment when the Huasicanchinos' accounts refer to the *effectiveness* of their dealings with opposition that the narrative imperative toward plot and closure is resisted. This is not just because, in their eyes, the story is as yet unfinished. It is also because what is being *accounted for* is not a global history of well-marshaled forces and decisive battles in a distant past, nor socioeconomic trends of *longue duree*, but the *effectiveness* of piecemeal victories when a major loss is turned into a minor gain, or the tight band of urgency is loosened for a week or a month, through sleight of hand or slip of tongue. So what identity the Huasicanchino feels as a rebellious peasant is not captured so much in the notion *"guerrillero"* (as we saw earlier in an interchange in the general assembly) as in the *apodo* (nickname) *"Los Zorros"* ("The Foxes"),[14] and many are the stories in which a person *vivo* and with *astucia* is juxtaposed against others' *ánimo* and with *educación* (the words lose much in translation: a quick or sharp person possessed with cunning juxtaposed against those with formal training and those with just guts: *ánimo* in its sense of *valor* [see Smith 1975, 1977]).

## CONCLUSIONS

A relatively successful rebellion by a peasant community in the face of a large ranch pressing forward toward capitalist rationalization would appear to be a perfect case for imagining an idealized peasant culture characterized by its uniformly shared implicit critique of capitalist culture (see, for example, Taussig 1980), or for accepting the notion of community in terms of a homogeneous body of people deriving their solidarity from their uniformly shared perception of the world in terms of custom and tradition. In fact, of course, we now have a well-established body of literature on the peasantry which addresses both the importance of socioeconomic differentiation among them and the way in which different kinds of peasant communities have arisen through history as a result of their resistance and incorporation into modern nation-states. The evidence here adds a somewhat different angle to this literature.

In the opening of this chapter I called attention to Eric Wolf's observation that anthropologists tend to endow other cultures with unwarranted homogeneity; yet more recently, a number of writers have written some elegant prose describing the phenomenology of a particular peasant group's culture (Marcus and Cushman 1982), often remarking on precisely the dialogical open-endedness I have stressed here. Their emphasis on the notion "discourse," however, has led them either to limit the dialogical element to discourse alone or to expand the notion of discourse to embrace virtually all forms of social interaction. Far from their understanding discourse to be about struggle, in the example I have presented they would see the struggle to be over—and only over—discourse itself. Yet such a conclusion can only be patronizing of the people studied, making them appear like dogs fighting over a useless scrap of bone.

Nothing could be further from the case here. Huasicanchino discourse can only be understood to the extent to which it was *not* an academic discussion about the Immaculate Conception or the allusions in T. S. Eliot's verse, but about what the participants saw to be *the* most immediate elements of their livelihoods: the community, the extent of reciprocated aid, ways of possessing land, and so on. I have tried here to begin an inquiry into the ways in which the constitution of the meaning of an institution is constructed through intensive negotiation during and within usage—a negotiation inseparably embedded in the praxis of daily life, itself embedded in very real material constraints and imperatives. The construction of meaning cannot therefore be understood merely by the analysis of discourse alone, even if the term is expanded to include social intercourse more generally.

But I am suggesting something more. I am suggesting that it is not just the known importance of certain institutions and practices to social reproduction that so thoroughly commits people to negotiating over the meanings of these institutions. It occurs also when, during political struggle, negotiation takes places in the face of present threats to that ongoing reproduction. Because of the intensity of discourse during resistance, experience of these times has the power to engrave lasting images into the channels of participants' minds. One has only to talk to people about past moments of collective rebellion and resistance to discover the heightened imagery engendered at those moments of intensive cultural production.

But because the authors of so many phenomenological studies of the production of peasant culture remove it from the far broader sociological forces of which it is a part, disparaging the plow to focus on the pulpit, dismissing the sword to idolize the word, they are more than a little coy about the political agenda implied by their writings. Yet it would certainly not be through verbal statements that Huasicanchinos would expect to have revealed to them the realities of the state. Ninety-nine times out of a hundred a speech given in Huancayo by a junior minister, a general, or a campaigning politician would have to be sifted through very carefully indeed to find anything of immediate relevance to Huasicanchinos. Nor would Huasicanchinos assume that the state took their verbal expressions seriously. And this reality reaches back into the recordable past. It is within this context that political consciousness must be assessed. In effect it is this that defines the space within which people whose entire lives are spent in such a situation put together a social world. It is a space in which hegemonic definitions of the world are simultaneously loaded with the symbols and actuality of terror that derive from massive power differentials and yet at the same time are articulated in fragmented and discontinuous form. Under such circumstances the role of local dialogue in negotiating the interpretation of these fragments in order to assess their immediate or long-term relevance to the peasantry becomes an important dimension in the formation of political consciousness. Without such a dimension, "consciousness" loses any significant creative dynamism.

Aware of the limitations of such a one-dimensional view of consciousness, social and cultural anthropologists have preferred the notion of culture, but they have not thereby found greater precision. Studies of culture tend to be bereft of the critical features of class relations which cannot be neglected in *any* contemporary social formation. The failure to integrate cultural studies within class analysis has meant that anthropologists have found great difficulty in relating the local cultural distinctiveness of a group being studied within a larger social formation to the particular class configuration of that social formation. As a result we are deprived of the possibility of seeing cultural production *specifically* in terms of simultaneous interdependence and opposition *at the level of the social formation* (not just at the level of the local field-site).

This locating of the production of culture within the context of larger societal forces, both for integration and for autonomy, can be seen by condensing the evidence presented above. Local initiatives in the countryside gave rise to policy responses on the part of the state. Specifically, the Huasicanchinos' immediate and daily grievances stemming from relationships with Hacienda Tucle in the early 1960s were met by official statements that a thoroughgoing land reform was about to go into effect. This gave rise to intense discussion among Huasicanchinos during which a wide range of possible interpretations of the prevailing situation were exercised. Eventually the Huasicanchinos made what might be called a very forceful political statement: they occupied stretches of disputed land. Promises of reform if they removed themselves then gave rise to further interpretations of reality, various manifestations of which we saw in the case material. Eventually, however, they chose to stick with their own "land reform" in preference to promises of one state-run, at some time in the indefinite future. This led to arrests, imprisonment, violence, and very real fear on their part: feelings no doubt as emotionally pregnant as a circumcision, face-scarring, or other manifestations of "cultural specificity." And these were feelings quite familiar to Huasicanchinos, as no doubt they are for peasants the world over.

Most of the Huasicanchinos' political expression then should not be seen out of the context of these conditions. Their political action and *what specific identity they derive from engagement in that action* arises precisely from these conditions. Whichever way you look at it, therefore, whether as a political analyst seeking out the coefficients of political mobilization or as an anthropologist concerned with the production of culture, the very *specificity* of this situation matters. The production and reproduction of culture, moreover, in this light, is an intensely political affair.

I have tried to get at this particular process by showing how insertion into different sectors of the economy reproduced and even increased the preexisting heterogeneity of Huasicanchino enterprises—enterprises, moreover, absorbed increasingly into the bottom end of a highly volatile commodity economy and hence drawn together by a common need for the security deriving from access to pasture. While at one level it was taken for granted that customs and practices served agreed-upon goals, at another the heterogeneity of enterprises meant that there was in fact a plasticity in meaning. So one reason why Huasicanchino political expression took the form it did was that key institutions remained in place while transformations in their meaning and practice occurred at first as a result of articulation with more dominant systems and then as a function of internal heterogeneity. It is tempting to propose that shifts from one meaing—for example, of "community"—to another correlated perfectly with the sway held by one or another group when it came to prominence in the leadership of the campaign. No such correlation exists, and this at least for two reasons: one, "leadership" was never hegemonic; and two, meanings arose not just from the material interests of one or another group but from engagement in the debate itself.

The question is how we are to fit this kind of everyday and essentially *local* contentiousness into the bigger stuff of rebellion and revolution. James Scott's (1985, 1986) name is most commonly associated with the expression "everyday forms of resistance," and yet he is less concerned to understand the ways in which local resistance might be more broadly organized than to suggest simply that daily resistance matters and is too often overlooked. Eric Hobsbawm, in contrast, has pointed out that "[a] movement which only claims to 'recuperate' communal lands illegally alienated may be as revolutionary in practice as it is legalist in theory. Nor is the line between legalist and revolutionary an easy one to draw" (Hobsbawm 1973:12–13). Yet both Hobsbawm and Wolf see the kind of rebellion I am talking about as "self-limiting and, hence, anachronistic" (Wolf 1987:373). The very elements that give them what potency they possess militate against broader alliances. But, while the structural constraints built into local forms of resistance are undeniable, this should not obscure the role that experience in concerted resistance itself plays in the historical accumulation of a people's consciousness. Seen in this light, the local focus of political activity and the particularistic character of cultural identity itself need not be a hindrance to the development of class consciousness, but an essential contributing factor.[15]

Contentiousness has a momentum of its own. Among some people it even becomes inseparable from the daily coin of common discourse, as is the case for the Huasicanchinos. (For France, see Tilly 1986.) Hence it is inseparable from the production of culture. The Huasicanchinos were not *de facto* a homogeneous mass sharing common interests. And so, although the historical act of the land-recuperation campaign required performance by "collective man" (Gramsci 1975:348), this acting in unity not only *presupposed* "the attainment of a cultural-social unity through which a multiplicity of dispersed wills, with heterogeneous aims, are welded together with a single aim" (ibid.), it required a *continuous process* of the intense negotiation of meanings—a process, moreover, in which the attainment of a cultural unity was never complete but was always unfinished business throughout the intense periods of resistance. Among the Huasicanchinos themselves, this meant the intense constitution and reconstitution of key institutions. In the process, the words used to refer to them therefore undergo "changes which are masked by a nominal continuity so that words which seem to have been there for centuries, with continuous general meanings, have come in fact to express radically different or radically variable, yet sometimes hardly noticed, meanings and implications of meaning" (Williams 1976:15).

What I am proposing is that words referring to key relationships have a rich set of reasonances. When (heterogeneous) people get together to resist or rebel, they become energetically committed to negotiating over those resonances. In this sense contentiousness (to return to Tilly's useful word) is both an internal and an external matter. It is this kind of engagement, moreover, that gave to the Huasicanchino resistance a momentum of its own—dare I say, beyond the perceived interests of the group and beyong interests emergent from the long- or short-term economic goals of one or another participant, until eventually we arrive right up against the existential issues about identity and existence which are the constitutive components of culture itself.

But stressing the importance of this kind of political praxis in the production of culture does not mean that political engagement can be artificially separated from the daily imperatives of social relations of production. In the case of Huasicancha, political mobilization has brought into play existing institutions to serve the purposes of the political struggle, as the land-recuperation campaign demonstrates. The institution of "the community," for example, as well as a myriad of subordinate institutions contained within that notion, was essential both for the daily reproduction of Huasicanchino enterprises and for political resistance. The same goes for reciprocal ties between households and for a variety of other relationships. The use of such institutions, in times of political struggle, itself modified the institutions, but it also gave a political dimension to the preservation of those institutions in subsequent periods of quiescence. Community institutions not only served a daily livelihood function; they also became inseparable from the political identity and survival of the participants. Then the campaign was articulated through this ongoing interaction at the level of the expressive meaning of institutions bound up with the "community." As a result, political engagement had the effect of modifying the idiom of community and at the same time investing it with contemporary relevance and vitality. Participants had not only negotiated among themselves over the essential meaning and value of key institutions; they had simultaneously asserted themselves against outsiders intent upon denying their meaning and value by blowing them into oblivion.

## NOTES

1. This article has been presented in various forms in various settings, and I am grateful to participants on those occasions for the comments. I am especially grateful to the editors of this volume for their comments and to Jane Schneider and Gadi Algazi for their useful advice.

2. ARA refers to the archives of the Agrarian Reform of the Ministry of Agriculture; AC refers to Huasicancha's community archives; FHT to documents found at the *fundo* of Hacienda Tucle; and JT to documents in the Juzgado de Tierra, Huancayo.

3. Membership in the community had legally recognized status. All household members whose head was a *comunero(a)* were themselves members of the community. In 1972 there were only eight households without community membership. This contrasts sharply with the settlements in the nearby Mantaro Valley (see Long and Roberts 1978, 1984).

4. The *Personero* was the senior authority in the officially recognized *Comunidad Indigena*.

5. Elsewhere (Smith 1984) I have discussed the particular characteristics of these reciprocal linkages, referring to them as "confederations of households."

6. The interest migrants had in retaining a foothold in the community and the interest residents had in allowing them to do so is best understood in terms of the complex intertwining of their enterprises most visible in the "confederations of enterprises" (see n. 5) and the dispersal of migrants' animals throughout the flocks of village residents. Government attempts to discourage cityward migration by insisting that full-time residence be a prerequisite for community membership were interpreted by villagers as an effort to "chop the head off the chicken" rather than as a means for reducing local demand on land.

7. The fact is that Huasicanchinos, some of them electricians and junior government clerks, presented themselves to the president in this traditional gear. I am not concerned to interpret how the president might have read this or how the migrants intended for him to read it, but simply to stress that such acts inevitably affect the ongoing reconstitution of tradition. The complexity of the issue can be illustrated by the last term—"time immemorial"—which appears to be a clear reference to tradition but which in Peru at the time had a clear legal resonance, since all land claims using the term "time immemorial" referred to the registration of Community properties that began in 1919.

8. This "minor incident"—entirely absent from oral accounts—is significant for our understanding of "solidarity." A number of migrants from Huasicancha, now permanent residents of the jungle colony of Satipo, date their departure from this period.

9. Although General Caceres, who led the resistance against Chile, initiated this campaign by referring to it as "una guerra en pequeña o de guerrillas" (Caceres 1973), the highland fighters were in fact more generally known as *montoneras* than as *guerrilleros*.

10. The arrest of the elected authorities caught the Huasicanchinos by surprise and made them extraordinarily suspicious of any outsiders arriving from the direction of Huancayo. All adult males were afraid of being taken for "undesirable elements" and thus hid in nearby caves and other retreats when outsiders approached. This explains the headline that appeared in Huancayo's newspaper at the time: "INCOMPREHENSIBLE COMMUNITY OF HUASICANCHA: LED BY WOMEN."

11. I use the term "independent farmers" because these enterprises contrasted with others among Huasianchinos in which reciprocal linkages were quite extensive (see Smith 1984, 1989).

12. But see n. 8.

13. There is of course no harm in glossing the Spanish word *guerrillero* by the English word "guerrilla" (as I have done earlier). But from the word's entry into English during the Peninsula Wars, it has connoted a rather special kind of fighter.

This connotation is present too in its Peruvian usage, but I wish here to draw attention to its proximity in Spanish to the word "war" (*guerra*) and to the notion that such a person's life is perpetually embedded in that practice and its associated behaviors (as for "warriors").

14. "How is the fox? Above all he is alone. He comes. He does his work. And he disappears. Then he is cunning (*tiene astucia*) and he is quick (*vivo*)."

"And the vixen?" ("*Y¿ la hembra?*")

". . . worse." (". . . *mas mala*") Field notes, Huasicancha, August 1972.

15. The evidence presented in this very microscopic study of a local rebellion has implications too for what Wolf (1969) and Hobsbawm (1973) have to say about the role of leadership, and the role of tradition, in peasant rebellion. This evidence doesn't so much contradict their conclusions—for example, about the role of outside leadership—as it casts these observations in a different light. For example, referring to the role of tradition for a (middle) peasantry faced with a commercializing society, Wolf (1987:371) remarks "[h]is is a balancing act." And much of what we have seen here has to do with negotiating a balancing act, the effect of which is a continuous, dynamic, and ever-incomplete constitution and reconstitution of that package of concepts embraced by the notion "tradition."

# NINE

# House and History at the Margins of Life: Domination, Domesticity, Ethnicity, and the Construction of Ethnohistories in "The Land God Gave to Cain"[1]

*Gerald M. Sider*

> *So the 20 of apirl [1920] I was 18 years old and the 21 of apirl we got married we where married at a dubble wedding to cupels stood the one time the grendfield mission nurse made our wedding cakes we had quite a lot of people and we serves a supper for everyone and we dance untill 3 oclock in the morning My husband brother played the viloin his right arm was cut up about 6 inces belo his elbo they tied the bo on to the stump of his arm and he played for our wedding dance he had a T.B. arm and he had to have it cut of he could play the violin well so we stayed to his Home for to weeks and we moved to our own house we bought a house from my father it was a log cabbon with to Bed rooms and cithen so 2 weeks after we were married we walked 18 miles to get to our home so we setled down in a plase called Sobasquasho were my Grate Grand father setteled down when he first came to Labrador he was a french Canadian he came from 3 rivers Canada when I got married I did not have much money of my own I saved a nough to bye my self a warsh board I worked for 2 dollars a mounth from the local people and from the grenfield missom 4 dollars a month*
>
> —ELIZABETH GOUDIE, AUTOBIOGRAPHY, 1963

## I

From the northernmost point of the northern arm of the island of Newfoundland it is 18 miles across the Strait of Belle Isle to the southern end of the Atlantic Labrador coast. Going 250 miles north from there, about a fourth of the way up (or as local people say, down) the hard-rock, dangerous coast— along which no roads yet run—the land splits, and the sea runs 150 miles into the interior, mixing, as the tides drive inward to the end, with such an immense volume of river water rushing southeast to the sea from the height of land in northern Quebec that one can drink the mix well before the river mouths are met. The easternmost part of the opening to the Atlantic is now called Grosswater Bay, formerly Eskimo Bay; its western, inland end passes through the narrow channel of Hamilton Inlet, past the Hudson's Bay Company trading center at Rigolet, widening again, 30 miles wide, to become

Lake Melville, nearly an inland sea. At the far inland end Lake Melville splits; the northern arm is called Grand Lake, running a further 40 miles northwest, inland; the southern arm is Goose Bay, where during World War II an airfield and an attached town were planted, now much grown and still of prime military and commercial use.

The tiny hamlet of North West River sits, very lightly, at the meeting point of Lake Melville and Grand Lake. Forty miles down into Grand Lake are a fan of rivers—the Naskaupi, the Beaver, the Red Wine, the Susan. South of Grand Lake, through a channel to Lake Melville with the settlements of Happy Valley and Goose Bay on one side, and Mud Lake on the other, is the opening to Goose Bay. Into the far interior of Goose Bay flow two massive rivers, fueled by the immense snowpack of the central Labrador plateau: the Goose River and the Grand. Where the Grand River (now renamed the Churchill in homage to the country whose capital would sponsor its transformation and defilement) drops off the pre-Cambrian granite shield that forms the core of Labrador's interior plateau, down to the tilted and carved coastal plain, Newfoundland built, in the 1960s and 1970s, one of the largest hydroelectric projects in the world.

The rich profusion of marine life from the seacoast through the interior bays, the large numbers of fur-bearing animals, and the life-sustaining deer around the shores first brought Inuit and Innu ("Eskimos" and "Indians") here, and then a substantial proportion of the few early European settlers who came to "the Labrador," trading and trapping, from the late 1700s on. Two English men wintered along Lake Melville in 1777, marooned and suffering. In 1785 a Canadian spent the winter here on purpose, sponsored by the merchants of Quebec. The first English winterers, as the early settlers were called, along with some early Moravian missionaries, were attacked— occasionally fatally—by Inuit. It was only after 1800 that several "Canadienne" families, most founded by a European-born father and an Inuit mother, were established here and persevered.[2]

Lydia Campbell was born in 1817 to one of these first families, the daughter of an orphaned Inuit mother and an English settler. In 1893, when she was seventy-five years old, she wrote down the story of her life in copybooks supplied by a summer-visiting missionary. Beginning in 1963, Lydia Campbell's sister's great-granddaughter, Elizabeth Goudie, then sixty-one years old, inspired by her great-grandaunt, began to write down the story of her life.

Both women lived their lives along the waterways from Eskimo Bay through Hamilton Inlet and Lake Melville to Goose Bay. Both women were married to men who trapped furs in the winter to sell, or to trade for supplies, at a Hudson's Bay Company outpost, and who fished and hunted in the summer for trade and for subsistence. As the fur-bearing animals came to be found in sufficient numbers further and further in the interior during the late nineteenth and twentieth centuries, Elizabeth Goudie spent far more time alone, or with just her children, than did her great-grandaunt Lydia Campbell. Elizabeth Goudie lived six months or so each winter in a cabin at the western end of the bay, while her husband was trapping far inland. Lydia Campbell (whose Inuit mother taught her own husband how to trap) wintered in the same area but set traps with her husband, who worked in the vicinity of their winter house.

Together their autobiographies span almost the entire history of Euro-Canadian settlement in Labrador, starting before the Hudson's Bay Company (also referred to as "the Company" or H.B.C.) consolidated its monopoly control over the Labrador fur trade, its servants, and the settlers. Their histories extend through the nineteenth century, when the H.B.C. acted as the state and the church, as well as dominated the economy, through the advent of mission churches and doctors, and the increasing presence of state institutions, which along with the air base, mining, lumbering and hydroelectric projects gave predominance to wage labor and brought almost all the Euro-Canadians, most of the surviving Innu, and a substantial portion of the remaining Inuit into the new towns.

These two autobiographical ethnohistories, the focus of this essay, show us the transformations of gender, domesticity, and ethnicity occurring in the context of the intensification of merchant capital and the emergence and consolidation of state institutions and capitalist forms of productive relations and property. In the midst of all these transformations we will also see subtle but fundamental changes in how history is understood—given voice or silenced, becoming both rooted in and distanced from the material and social realities of peoples' lives.

While the long coastline of Labrador is rocky and fjord-riven its whole length, the interior is dramatically different from north to south. The northern portions are tree-barren, characterized by lichen, moss, and the barren-ground caribou; the southern portion is often swampy and becomes heavily forested—coniferous woods mostly, with spruce predominant. The forest lands contain most of the commercially valuable fur-bearing animals; seals range the entire coast.

From 1785 to 1835, when the Hudson's Bay Company began its period of near total control over the forest fur trade, there were a small number of independent trading posts scattered along the major rivers and lake shores. Hudson's Bay brought in servants along with the Company's trade goods; it was often these servants, recruited from the hungry outskirts of the British Isles—from places such as the Orkneys; from people who had the least protection when the naval press-gangs caught up with them—who became settlers. Well into the nineteenth century there were only a few European settlers along the shores of Lake Melville, although this was one of the major settlement areas and a focus of the Labrador fur trade.

W. H. A. Davies, an employee of the Hudson's Bay Company, writing in 1841, estimated the population around Hamilton Inlet and its inland lakes and bays as 15–20 H.B.C. "servants," 45 "planters" [settlers]—8 white and 37 "half-breed esquimaux"—plus 34 Esquimaux, and 48 Montaignais-Naskapi Indians (Zimmerly 1975:68). Briefly and powerfully he describes the planters' life and their general situation:

> They most commonly winter on the immediate shores of the Bay if possible, for the convenience of hunting ducks in the spring, for the subsistence of their families.... [T]heir annual migrations to and from their summer residence...are performed in open whale boats, in which they will often make voyages of a month's duration, the women managing the boats as well as the men, and pulling an equally good oar. Even in summer, some of them are continually changing their quarters; passing the first part of the summer fishing salmon, in the neighborhood of Rigolet, and then going to the entrance of the Bay, to pursue the cod fishery, until it is time to return to their winter quarters. The life these people lead is one of great hardship and fatigue, from their constant exposure to the weather and the necessity of using the most strenuous exertions to subsist their families, for the provisions they are enabled to purchase from the traders are never sufficient to support them the long winter. (Davies 1843, Zimmerly 1975:67–68)

As hard as the settlers' life was in the early nineteenth century, it became even harder before the century ended. Population rose substantially in the last half of the nineteenth century, and the number of fur-bearing animals in the vicinity of the coastal bays declined sharply. By the 1890s men could no longer trap with their wives in the vicinity of their winter cabins. At the end of summer, shortly after the families moved to the interior of the bays to be near firewood and to seek shelter from the coastal storms, men left their wives and children to go a hundred miles or more into the interior to work their long and almost completely isolated traplines, at first making one three-month trip, and later two trips, coming back out briefly in late December or early January to carry out their first catch, to rest, and to see their families. Women and children in their winter cabins were also often isolated, both by the substantial distance between houses and the difficulty of travel—which was mostly by snowshoe, for the forest snowpack is often too soft for dogsleds, not having the crust of open tundra snow.

Once the men no longer trapped in the vicinity of their winter houses, families could cluster their winter homes in small settlements, but these clusters seem to have developed slowly and remained small—two or three houses in most, ten houses or so in a few places—through the first two decades of the twentieth century, with a substantial portion of the houses remaining isolated, perhaps owing to the need for fuel, perhaps because of the women's winter hunting needs, as they provisioned their families with game.

These winter houses, clustered or separate, were also isolated from even the minimal amenities to which poor rural people in England or central

Canada had access: the first churches in this area of Labrador came very late in the nineteenth century, as did the first doctors. Schools, mail service, minimal hospital facilities, and minimal welfare provisions are twentieth century developments. Before, whatever people got came from the Hudson's Bay Company agent, who married people, dispensed medicines, provided minimal credit in advance of the fur, salmon, or cod harvest—if not enough to keep people alive and well, enough, as we shall see, to keep them terrified of the potential consequences of selling a portion of their harvests to an independent trading schooner, even when they were half-starved.

The absence of effective governmental institutions and the isolation of individuals and of the small settlements molded social relations in central Labrador through the first two decades of the twentieth century. The family within a household was ordinarily the only available and reliable source of aid and sustenance, good times or bad times. In 1919 the "Spanish Flu" pandemic devastated Labrador. It

> had struck the place like a cyclone, two days after the mail-boat had left. . . . Whole households lay inanimate all over their kitchen floors, unable to even feed themselves or look after the fire . . . the entire settlement [at Cartwright, just south of Hamilton Inlet] was down. It suggested most forcefully a tropical typhoon. . . . A feeling of intense resentment at the callousness of the authorities, who sent us the disease by the mailboat, and then left us to sink or swim, filled one's heart almost to the exclusion of all else. . . . The one and only doctor on the coast . . . was one hundred and eighty miles away, and might have been ten thousand for what chance we could have of getting his assistance to us. . . . Shortage [of firewood] is the most serious menace we face. The weather is getting bitterly cold. [A traveler came through Indian Harbour, at the Atlantic edge of Grosswater Bay:] . . . out of twenty-one people he found ten dead, two or three next door to death, and the rest too sick or dismayed to do a thing. Some of the people had died at the beginning of the month, and were still lying as they died. . . . In one house four out of five were dead. (Gordon 1974 [1920]:163–164, 167)

Henry Gordon, the Anglican minister at Cartwright, made it clear that many of the people died not simply from the flu but from lack of anyone to care for or help them.

Being physically isolated from the government and government services was not an obstacle to developing intensely antagonistic relations to the government. These were, however, a complex set of antagonisms, rather different from those that emerge, for example, in the work process and in daily life among factory workers, who are directly supervised, manipulated, and dominated; whose experience of working is often simultaneously an experience both of their own skills and abilities and of an insistent, hectoring, exploitative domination continually calling forth resistances, evasions, collusions, and accommodations; who usually experience daily life as a domain where work experiences can be discussed, defined, played with, denied, adjusted, elaborated, and transformed—all in and among multiple and connected networks of kith and kin.

Although the Labrador settlers' lives were very hard—a lot of pain and suffering, with little recompense—and although much of the hardship was imposed both by the unfavorable terms of trade and by government policy, there was very little recognizable "class consciousness." Several factors may have contributed to this: people were not directly dominated and supervised in their work processes; government agencies and services were not present in the landscape, so that the hardships this brought seemed to the people more a matter of omission than of active policy; people were quite isolated, one family from another, so that the social relations that might have formed a basis for the development of an outspoken and effective oppositional orientation were not well developed.

In the context of changing relations within the household, the changing presence and well-being of different peoples (Innu, Inuit, and settlers), and changing ways of earning a living, people formed concepts about what we would call "gender," "ethnicity," and a separate "domestic" sphere of social life, and they embedded these concepts in ethnohistories: their visions of interwoven pasts, presents, and impending futures. These concepts, and the ethnohistories as well, became frameworks for talking about mixtures of antagonisms, intimacies, and distances—a broader and more diffuse set of antagonisms and intimacies than those usually associated with class consciousness.

Gender, ethnicity, and domestic relations were used as frameworks for judgments and critiques of domination: when Elizabeth Goudie, for example, critically judged the government's "modernization" program, she did so most forcefully in terms of how it treated her husband's and sons' histories. The fate of the Inuit was also, if more complexly, a source of judgment. Gender, ethnicity, and domesticity are emergent concepts whose range of applicability came to extend well beyond the specific social relations from which they emerged.

The question that I find the most haunting about Newfoundland and Labrador is the comparative absence of a politically assertive and deeply critical "traditional" folk culture. The "ordinary" (as it were) people of Newfoundland and Labrador are, and have been, extremely poor—along with the people of Prince Edward Island, the poorest in Canada. Their situation, in some major material respects, is reminiscent of that of people in South and Central America, Africa, the Caribbean, and Blacks and Indians in the United States—all peoples among whom there has been substantial, and at times vigorous, folk-based challenges, taking a variety of forms, to the political domination and economic exploitation that they face. Central to each of such challenges is a folk culture that is *not* simply derived from current and ongoing social relations but takes some distance from the material and social realities of people's lives and uses this distance as part of a perspective—to examine, to judge, to criticize, and to make claims. At issue here is thus the basic question: how do people distance themselves from domination? The two women's autobiographies will lead us to look for the wellsprings of this distance not in physical space nor simply in the domain of ideas and values—"culture"—but in the historically perceived connections and disconnections between the social relations of daily life and work and the social relations of production.

## II

In 1893 Lydia Campbell was asked by the Reverend A. C. Waghorne, a missionary who had spent the past three summers in Labrador, to write down her life story. He sent her copybooks and published her writings in serial form in the St. John's (Newfoundland) *Evening Herald*, 3 December 1894–6 February 1895. He corrected spelling, added punctuation, and left a few sentences out. The typescript of her writing is thirty-six double-spaced pages and includes her own headings.

It is impossible to determine the extent to which Lydia Campbell shaped the story of her life in writing for a specific audience. In his introduction to the newspaper serials, Waghorne writes:

> The last few years I have been in the habit of exchanging clothing for the interesting skin and bead work, &c., so ingeniously made by the Labrador women. About two years ago, in forwarding my parcel of clothing and literature, I sent also to an old Labrador woman of Grosswater Bay, of whom I had some knowledge, an exercise book, and begged her to be kind enough to write to me some account of Labrador life and ways.

In the early pages of her text, Lydia Campbell adds a few phrases of the sort that would please a missionary pastor: "So, you see, ups and downs has been my life all through, and now I am what I am. Praise the Lord"; ". . . the Good Lord has safely brought me through." After a few descriptive entries about her sister and her daily work, she pauses in the narration and writes:

> Well, as I said, I can't write much at a time now, for I am getting blind and some mist rises up before me if I sew, read or write a little while. In that way I can't tell you as I could if it was a while back. I had my life wrote down and gave it to the Rev. A. A. Hadam, but he lost it.

With that, the "praise the Lord"s decline markedly. Just after mentioning her lost life story she writes, "*We are told* whoever trust in the Lord shall want no manner of good" (emphasis added); and for the remainder of the text, despite an appeal to the reader to take pity on her and her husband and send some material for clothes, she seems very much to be telling her own story on her own terms.

She starts by asking to be excused for her writing and spelling, for she had never been to school (but was taught to read by her father—from the Bible— long before she taught herself to write). She describes herself as "a native of the country," "old Lydia Campbell, formerly Lydia Brooks, then Blake, after Blake now Campbell." Then she turns to describe her work:

> I has a lot to do with 3 little motherless granddaughters to work for, besides their poor father and a big son, going off hunting and wood chopping, and the weather so cold as to need all the warm clothing possible. . . . The weather 30 below zero often, and myself off to my rabbit snares, about 4 miles going and coming, over ice and snow, with snow shoes and axe and game bag. Some days I has 3 rabbits . . . for I has about 24 snares, made myself [and] set them up, and I gets pretty tired some days. Often the snow is deep and soft; just now about 3 feet deep in the woods; but it can't be expected otherwise with me to get tired, for I am now the last birthday 75 years old.

She then describes her family:

> I have been bereaved of my first husband and 4 of his children. One is left to me, Thomas Blake. It is his little children that I has to look to now. The present husband that I has now is nearly as old as me. We has 3 children left by him out of 8—2 boys and a girl.

Along with many other Labrador settlers at this time, they have two dwelling places—one along the ocean shore, for summer fishing, and one up the bay, inland, near wood for winter fuel and the trapping grounds. Her description of coming home to her winter house contains the basic themes of her text: a history of family, the rigors of work, sorrow at the death of loved ones, who often died young in this cold and isolated land, the closeness of families, the beauty of the land, and their substantial—but far from complete—self-sufficiency.

> My eldest son, Thos. Blake, my first husband's son, and his motherless children, is near us, next door—none near us but them and our dear children's graves. We can see their headstones at a distance, over on the cranberry banks, so pretty it looks in the fall when we come home from our summer quarters, above 70 miles from here. When we are sailing up in our large boat, to see the ducks in our bay when we are nearing the river, and when we get ashore to the pretty river banks and walking up the path under our large trees, some 50, and some 60 or more feet high, we often meet with a flock of partridges flying up to the trees. Before we get to the house, so pretty, then is the scramble among the young ones who will see the first turnips and potatoes, and sure enough, all around the house is green with turnip tops, and between them and the wall of

the house is hanging red with moss-berries, some falls, and then we get home to our winter house for 10 months or more.

She talks of learning to hunt, in large part from her elder sister, of her and her now-deceased daughter hunting deer, and how they surprised the men of their family by feeding them deer they killed, and then she writes at length of her elder sister and her disabled, housebound husband:

Now this is the 13 or 14 of January . . . we are all scattered today, my husband, Dan Campbell, is not yet home from Labacatto, he went up there to see our brother-in-law Mensie Meshlin, a Canadian about 70 years old, not able to work now, but his wife Hannah, my old sister, she is over 80 years old, yet she can take her gun and axe and game bag and shoots a white partridge or two, now and then. I have known the old woman fighting with a wolverine, a strong animal of the size of a good sized dog, she had neither gun nor axe but a little trout stick, yet she killed it after a long battle, it was very wicked. I wish there were more Hannahs in the world for braveness. She brought up her first family of little children when their father died, teached them all to read and write only in the long winter nights, and hunt with them in the day, got about a dozen foxes and as many martins, take the little ones on the sled, haul them on over snow and ice to a large river, chop ice, about 3 feet thick ice, catch about 2 or 3 hundred trout, large ones, and haul them and the children home . . . and then the men of the Hudson Bay Company's servants used to get her to make a lot of things, that is clothing, such as pants, shirts, flannel slips, draws, sealskin boots, deer skin shoes for the winter, socks, leggings, dickies, mits made of duffel and deer skins, coats, caps washing starching ironing and what not. She had all the care of the children while a widow; in that way a Canadian got married to her, for she had everything to his hand such as we used in this country. My husband is [now] come home from the Labacatto, and he found them not very well in health. My poor old sister have not been able to go to her rabbit snares for two weeks; she is failing fast now; she tried to sing hymns morning and evening, with prayers, and she can't go on now, poor good old saint—may the good God be with her to the end.

Later, Lydia Campbell describes her natal family. Her father came out from England, around 1790, as a "'prentice boy," after his father and guardian both died. He stayed in Labrador to avoid the British naval press-gangs, marrying a woman of the country.

Her mother was an orphan, regarded, as Lydia Campbell says Eskimo[3] regard all orphans, as a "witch"—who was regularly cut to draw blood to cure ill people. Her mother ran away one fall, with only a little food, no axe, no fire, and no blanket, having to ford rivers and to sleep under trees. She was taken up by French trappers, recaptured the next spring by the Eskimo, and then joined and married an English trapper, from which marriage Lydia was born in 1818.

Lydia then writes a long passage about how drink and tobacco and debts are killing the Eskimo, destroying them as a people—a passage both with much detail about specific families and with a clear sense of general trends and causes. She describes senseless death upon senseless death, and the impact on the survivors.

She describes herself, matter-of-factly, as a "half-breed," noting that Eskimo women were hard workers and brought crucial skills into their marriages with European trappers. She also notes that the Eskimo were afraid of the Indians, and were sometimes killed by them. Though knowing this history, she shows no animosity to Indians, telling several stories of getting and giving food between her family and Indian families. Indeed, one of the most poignant stories she tells is of an old Englishman, married to an Indian wife, who, realizing that he is near to death, has a dream—a dream that he tells Lydia.

In this dream he was "going to cross a large river, in company with a lot of Indians, and they [the Indians] crossed on foot, [walking] over the water . . . and he began to cry and wisht that he could cross over to the pretty country." He then walked across the water, managed to climb the riverbank, and "there was a point of pretty shining woods and he saw the Indians passing that point of woods. And when he saw them going he wisht that he was among them." An Indian woman and a boy gave him something to drink, and he felt light and full of joy. He dreamt he went home and told his [Indian] wife and his people, and they told him it was Jesus and his mother.

The lines and the ties between the somewhat diverse cultures—Innu, Inuit, and Euro-Canadian—are complexly drawn and interwoven, and far from sharp. Here the Innu, to whom the Euro-Canadian settler is attached in more ways than his marriage, are described as holding up the image of Jesus to the Canadian. Lydia Campbell writes of Eskimo and Indian beliefs and ways as "superstition," starting with the brutalization of her orphan mother, but then describes her own belief in christening to keep souls from being lost as a "silliness." In a passage she heads "My silliness in my younger days" she writes:

> I remember as having no better thought that when a little child died, that his or her soul would be lost, as many are thinking yet, unless they are christened. So one day as I was getting myself and children—2 little uns—one three weeks old and the other 5 years old, to see my rabbit snares, I put my little baby in on the bed. It rolled on to the floor and stund itself for a little while. I got a fright because she was not christened. So I took the book and baptized it with my dickie [a parka of Eskimo design] and out-door clothing on, and my Sarah, 5 years old girl, standing by. The father and grandfather, and Aunt Sarah and Uncle George was off hunting. I alone reading to it. When she could suck I thought she was all right, and I took it out on my back, and lead the other by the hand with my axe, through the snow, to my rabbit snares, and got a few rabbits—not for want or hunger—but for custom.

Custom—the traditions and skills of work and of daily life—for Lydia Campbell takes place equally within and outside the home. The house as a separate sphere is primarily for people, either men or women, whose disabilities keep them homebound.

When Lydia was eleven, three or four years after her mother died, her father took her to live with John Whittle, an elderly English trapper, and Sarah, his blind and crippled Inuit wife. This part of her autobiography tells an extraordinary tale. Sarah had been married, decades earlier, to one of the very first English trappers to come to the Labrador, and her half-brothers killed him. She remarried, to John Whittle, and when she went blind, Lydia's father had to threaten John Whittle with beatings to keep him from starving to death both Sarah and her son by her first marriage. Soon after Lydia arrived to live there,

> [o]ld John Whittle and father, Ambrose Brooks was his name, they said one day that they had a lot of oooko and veoto to make, and that little Lydia was too young to make them for the winter, that they would have to look for a woman somewhere to keep [help, teach] me. I was glad to think I was going to have a chum with me. Off they went and was gone for a day or two; I was left alone with that poor little lame woman. . . . So they came home and brought a paralytic woman, and when the poor thing tried to show me how to do and cut out the things I had to make, she was worse than me, for she jumpt and trembled so, did poor native Betsy, that she would give it up, and then the blind Sarah would slide along the bench, for she could not walk, and put her fingers on it, she would run over it and tell me what way to do it. I was then about 11—no wonder I found it hard in that times. Well, I would laugh at them sometimes, when they had rum. . . . They would be jealous of each other—the blind woman and the paralytic woman—while the licker lasted—one speaking in Esquimaux language, the other in broken English; then they would laugh sometime, and the old John Whittle would call out at them so rough that they had to be quiet. Well, that was strange to me. . . . In the winter I was left alone with the lame woman, Sarah by name, and the weather was so cold that father and John Whittle could not get home for the cold and drifting for about a week. . . . Poor little woman with her native dress and a dicky and breeches on and little seal skin boots on her feet on a little stool plaiting deer sinew for to sew on boots tops.

And it was this old blind woman who realized, early one morning, that the house she and Lydia were alone in was completely snowed under—Lydia thought it was still night. Sarah got her to stand on a chair on the porch and chop a hole in the snow to get air.

Lydia Campbell's text ends with a moving description of her life with her husband and her current family, and with her family in the past:

> Well we grows our own potatoes and turnips for the winter (and we gets plenty of trout for the winter, fresh trout caught through the ice, and we gets plenty of

partridges, white and spruce ones, and rabbits with other provisions we brings in the summer time, but we has no milk, we gets cranberries, as much as we wants for the winter, we gets a fox now and then, and a Marten and others. Their skins is valuable, and Seals in the spring on ice. [And] we never stops work unless we are eating or sleeping in the night or singing or reading and prayers, until Sundays. . . . My old man and me builded a boat this spring, and we builded one last Spring. . . .

In my father's house. . . no other house near to ours than about 30 miles distant, but we would enjoy ourselves pretty well for there was my sister Hannah to be talking and reading with me, Father and Mother and an old English man by the name of Robert Best, my best friends I thought was all that was all living together. . . . Hannah and me we would go and slide on the Mountaineer [Innu] sleds, what father would buy from them, and we were thought a great deal of, by the Mountaineers they would bring some pretty snow-shoes to us two sisters, and some pretty deer skin shoes to wear out or in, they all painted so pretty. It was and is our custom to give anyone dark or white something to eat, while they are at our house, and bedding, so the Indians kind was always good to us. Poor despised Inalans. The traders selling them rum and the foolish people buying all they could, and they getting lost, falling overboard, losing their souls and bodies, but that is changed now.

### III

In 1963, following the death of her husband, Elizabeth Goudie began, at age sixty-one, to write the story of her life. She was living—since 1942—in the new town of Happy Valley, near the Goose Bay air base. Her first forty years were spent living in cabins out in the country, from which her husband went winter-trapping five or six months a year. The following texts come directly from her handwritten notebooks, which number over two hundred pages. She starts her story, and begins her manuscript, in 1914:[4]

> I was the eldest of the family of Joseph and Sarah Blake the first I remember so well my father expected me to start getting out of bed at 5 o'clock in the morning and having my mothers Breakfast on the table by 6 o'clock in the morning to me it seemed to be a very hard task but I made a try at it this was the beginning of a hard working life for me and this was expected of the average Labrador girl at that time

This introduces one central theme of her text: the hardship of her work. There is also, from the outset, an emphasis on expectations and rules, and a certain impersonal distance from her own experiences, which become treated as sociological or historical abstractions ("this was expected of the average Labrador girl"). But it is usually not a critical distance.

Her father, like Lydia's, was an orphan, at fifteen, and thus "had to learn to be a trapper" to support her four sisters. Her mother was motherless at two; at fourteen she went as a servant to the Hudson's Bay Company manager's sister, where she stayed until she married. When Elizabeth was born, her father was a logger for a lumber company that soon went bankrupt.

Elizabeth left home at fifteen. She had gone to school for two winters, two and a half months each.

> 1917 I went to work for the Grenfell Mission [which had a cottage hospital in central Labrador since 1912, providing the first regularly "available" medical care] and I got 4 dollars a month there and 10 dollars a summer of used clothing this was what the mission gave their girls at that time I served as an aid on the womans ward we were out of bed 5 in the morning and on our feet until seven in the evenings we got one afternoon off a week and we were let off to go to church on sunday this was where I met my first boy friend

In 1918 her "boy friend" joined the army, and went to St. John's, in Newfoundland, for training.

> but later that year the war ended and he did not get over seas the war was ended 11 of november and my boy friend [and another discharged soldier] was brought to Battle Harbour by the mail steamer and they traveled all the way up the coast by foot or dog team when they could hire one so it was not until february they got back to their own home village at North West River . . . when these 2 young men returned in february was the first time we knew the war was over . . . So we got engaged in feb when he was going in the country in 1920 [to trap] and when he came out the first of april we set the date for our marriage the 21 of april so I learned when he came out of the country he almost lost his life it was a bad rapid in the river open water . . . he drove [was dragged] down the rapid about a half mile in 30 below zero so the other man got him out after a while he had to walk about a half mile [to his trapping cabin] . . .
>
> so he stayed that night [with me] for a rest the second of april he had to travel 40 miles on snowshoe and Haul his load before he got to north W[est] river [to sell his furs] and then he had to walk 25 Miles more up the Gross Water Bay to the Hamilton River to get my father and mother consent before we could get married I was to the head of Grand Lake so he Hired a dog team and send up for me . . .

This commitment to culturally appropriate behavior—her husband asking for her hand—in conjunction with her menial wage labor provides an important cultural context for understanding the developing "loneliness" of Elizabeth Goudie's life as a trapper's wife: more than lonely, she is increasingly isolated within an encroaching dominant culture.

> so I had 2 years before I started a family so in them two years I enjoyed myself with Jim that was his name we used to go hunting and fishing I learned to shoot with the gun we enjoyed our selves out in the quiet country I used to be left alone when he was a way in the country the most dreadful thing being a trap-

pers wife as you would not hear from them from the time they would go away until they would return again there where no way to get mail the trappers would not come in from the trapping grounds until a period of 3 months we used to stand on the shore and watch them leave in their canoes only about 6 inches above the water . . . [When] the ice completed froze over I went to catch trout for my winter I walked about 4 miles and carried my food for a week and I catched trout I catched about 5 Hundred . . .

the custom for trappers wifes are to have something cooked for them when they come home we use to have pie and cake and then they would rest up for a week so we went to North West River to sell his furs after he had a rest so I put on my snowshoes and went too so we had 2 or 3 days there and then we went back home he rested up for a month and went back in the country again . . .

his wife would spend a more lonely time she was always at Home . . . it is a life not full of people or what people could offer . . . but every day had something to make you happy we were satisfied . . .

This is loneliness: her isolation is related to this, but differs in crucial ways. As with loneliness, isolation is partly rooted in the physical distance between people; unlike loneliness, isolation was intensified by the increasing presence in Labrador of the government and an externally based elite. The most profound forms of isolation are inescapable, for they are inextricably interwoven both with domination and with evading domination:

I had my first son he was 8 lbs 1/2 he was just like his Dady he was dark complected and I was proud of him when he was 17 days olld I had to take him to the Doctor he had sore eyes and the Doctor ask me his name and I dident have a name then so the Doctor looked at him and he was Hairy about the shoulders and neck so he said he would call him Esau so His name is in the Hospital Book at North West River as Esau but later I named him Horace

Having been raised with the Bible read daily in her home she knew who Esau was and what the name meant: Esau the hairy, the hunter, the birthright-dispossessed, the loser. And she is here being forced to realize that it is not her "values" that she shares with a wider world (as the anthropological concept of culture and the naive notion of "subcultures" would have it) but some common symbols which, as here, can be used to confront her with just how distant she and her values both are, and are not, from the people who have the power to inscribe her family's names and their isolation upon the record books of the state. Her isolation is, precisely, a form of belonging to a larger society.[5]

Elizabeth Goudie grew from childhood to middle age in a period often marked by extreme hardship for trappers. World War I brought a severe rise in the prices for staple commodities; commercial fur-bearing animals continued to decline in the vicinity of the coast, and the depression brought a collapse of the market for furs. Only the wage labor related to military construction during World War II brought substantial relief.

it was the begining of the first world war well the cost of living went up awful high I remember my father coming home with his winter supplies [from trade with H.B.C.] and he told mother the flour were 26 dollars a barrel that was one Hundred and ninetyeight lbs so I can remember him telling mother we were only to have one slice of bread between meals so that meant we had to eat as much meat and fish as we possibly could so that meant that the children that were big enough had to fish and Hunt Rabbits

To a far greater extent than in the nineteenth century, what and how much a family ate depended upon the skills and situation of the husband:

I had an aunt that could not nurse her babies and she had to get a bottle for them and what she used for food was flour she took the dry flour and packed it in a white cloth and boiled it for 4 hours and then she would take it from the cloth and it would be like a piece of chalk you use for the Black Board in school only it weighed about a lb. in size and then she would take a piece and grate it up and make a pap . . . she would boil it again and add sugar and a little butter and a little salt and she raised 8 children like that until they were 10 months old and then she gave them meat gravies and fish some of them growed up to be old men and women so when we were put to the test we could always manage . . . this aunt I am speaking of she was always half starving and poorly clothed her husband didn't have a very good trapping place and he didn't know how to manage trapping very well so it was not until her sons grew up big enough to go up the Hamilton River to make a trapping place she had better times then but she did not live many years after that when she was about 40 years old she took T.B.

The price inflation that began with World War I continued through much of the 1920s, bringing extreme hardship to the settlers, whatever their skills:

it is 1925 and I am expecting my third child the winter is not very good so far the furs are not very plentiful My Husband is quite worried because there are nothing in sight for the summer . . . so Jim came out of the country from his traps and still he didend have many furs I was in the 4 month with child he went to Davis Inlet to the Hudson Bay [Company] and sold the few furs he did have so he brought home some food it really was not enough for the spring . . . he went out near the coast line and got a few seals and I cleaned the skins and sold them . . . about 4 dollars a piece and that bought a little more food so we managed until open water [when the ice went out] so later on in early summer he got a cod fishing place . . . but the fish was not plentiful . . . we had to take out food on credit from the H. B. Company for the summer . . . we were well out to the coast line to a place called Tikkle . . . and while we were there a trader [a trading schooner] came through the Tikkle with food supplies and we went aboard and had a look around but we could not buy any food because we had no money we had some fish and [the trader] he would have bought it and would have given us a better price than the company but we had to keep our fish to put against our Credit Bill [for] the food we took out for the summer . . . my stomach just longed to taste that food I was in the 8 month with my child

The terror of being cut off from further food supplies by Hudson's Bay Company, if caught trading away a portion of their catch, is keeping Elizabeth Goudie hungry and hurting. With the increasing difficulty of earning a living, as the balance of prices and costs shifts against them, the Goudies' increasing long-term dependence upon the Hudson's Bay Company is increasingly separating and distancing her from her immediate and pressing physical needs.

Elizabeth Goudie was more distanced than Lydia Campbell from the native people of Labrador, Innu, and Inuit—a distance that was historical, physical, and cultural, though still bridged by occasional, transient contact at times of need or extreme loneliness.

so the Hamilton Inlet [was] populated by the white People that came out hear from scotland, England & canada so we were told they married in the Eskimo and Indian according to my Parents this happened about 2 hundred years ago . . .

After a summer fishing trip with her husband,

so everyone went to their winter homes and started preparing for winter so we started up the bay and so on the way . . . we went on Eskmou Island my mother told me all the Eskmoues died some years before that of a epidemic that they got off a ship wreck that went on the rocks out the mouth of the Hamilton Inlet . . . they had no help from any [one] and they all died out and no body didn't know any thing about it until they went out in the spring they found all the graves and food and material so we wanted to know if their was still any signs of it so we stayed there over night and explored the Island and we found about a Hundred grave some of them . . . was still on top of the ground they were leg bones and back bones lying on top of the ground under rocks still not decayed we dug some beads out of the ground and pieces of clothes so we started back for our winter place

A year or two later:

Jim and Charlie were away on their trapping lines there were no settlers in that bay so the closest people were [at] Hope Dale and that was 40 miles so sometime late that fall 2 Eskmoes families moved in that bay to it was about Christmas time we found out and they were 3 miles from us so when Jim and Charlie came out from their trapping lines me and Ellen [Charlie's wife] put on our snowshoes and went to visit them and one family was gone out to Hope Dale for Christmas, and the family was there could not talk english Ellen could understand them a little they were awful glad to see us and when we went to leave them they wanted to give us something so they took a partridge out of the pot they had cooking on the stove and give it to us so that was the first people I saw since august. . . .

The partridge, however, became the return gift for the visit, not the opener for a series of exchanges, and the interchange seems to end there: a brief, tentative touch across the chasm.

In 1942 an air base was built at Goose Bay, in the interior of Hamilton Inlet, and Jim Goudie went to work there, building a house in the nearby town of Happy Valley that Elizabeth Goudie was still living in when she wrote her life story. The transition to a life centered on wage labor mixed the welcome and the painful.

I think the people of Labrador weren't not prepared for such a change in such a short time they did not know how to cope . . . I have been here about 20 years and I have saw the change that have taken place . . . I have a family of my own a part of them grew up here a part of them grew up in the old life of Labrador I have suffered more sorrows with the latter part of my family than I did with the first 4 that was Born before the Base . . . many little children [now] have had lots of milk and good food and clothing which the children of the past did not have I have looked at the nice clothing and thought back to my own little ones how proud I would have been if only I could have had a little of all the good things for my little ones

My first four children was brought up as trappers but they could all do most any work . . . and my 3 girls learned also about cooking and making their own clothes. I learned them all what I knew about house keeping to the best of my knowledge and Jim done the best he could with Horace . . . If I had to live my life over again I would chose the trappers life. I cant explain the life but my little children was happy and we were happy and at Peace with our neighbor it was a good life believe me and now I am trying to live a different life trying to keep up with the times as much as I can . . . I will never keep up with it all and I don't think I will try . . . I have a electric washer and an iron. I used my hands all my life until Joe [her son] got to work and he bought a washer. Jim had all he could do to build the house and pay the Bills so through the fifties we lost all our girls. They got married and left home and I was left with all the boys so I was no better off then because I had to do all the work my self and I wasent getting any younger

Near the end of her manuscript ethnicity and gender, and her sense of history, merge together as she reflects upon, and restates, some of the central points of her life:

after I grew up old enough to get married I married in the Goudie family and there the family got Indian blood John Goudie went up Hudson Bay and got his wife she was a half Cree and half Scotch John Goudie was a Scotch men so our family have quite a mixture Eskmou English French Scotch & Indian my children are proud of their Indian and Scotch Blood. Now this trappers life is behind us but I am proud I had the chance to live such a life because the trappers and their wives learned not by books but By experience and the wife of trappers played a great Part in it because she had to live as a man 5 months of the year she had to use her gun and she had to know how to set nets to catch fish and also how to judge the right distance for the shore to cut her fish holes [in the ice] . . . as I learned all of this the Hard way and many others like me that was the outdoors life indoors if you was a mother you had to cook and make clothes for the family boots and often you had to act as a Doctor or nurse and I am not ashamed of it because that kind of life fit our country at that time there was no other way out and I am proud that I could be part of that life . . . now things are changed even the name of Grand River to Churchill Falls many of us didn't like it when we heard it because Grand River was its name since the 1800 hundreds and to the trappers it was their Home and I would say their birth Right I have nothing against the name Churchill but he was a good man too but no one was ask if they were satisfied to have it changed if Joe Smallwood [Newfoundland and Labrador's Premier] saw the trappers return from (Grand River) with their Frost Bitten faces and half starved and exhausted he might have thought twice before he changed it but that is beside the point now but for many old timers it is still (Grand River) but for the younger generation it will be (Churchill) and I hope they will treat it with respect . . . people in the past they made there own laws among the trappers and they respected each others laws and they were carried out to the best of their ability this I know because my whole life was a trappers life

## IV

The evidence here is scant, and subject to misreading. When the texts come from only two women, the possibility that we are dealing with personal style and with personality rather than socially based variation in situation is substantial. But I think these texts in their historical context can be read as illustrative of several fundamental and interconnected transformations: in domesticity, gender, ethnicity, and ethnohistory.

The transition between the kind of life led by Lydia Campbell and that of Elizabeth Goudie is marked by two massive changes: the increasing hardship of trappers' work, and the increasing "presence" in Labrador of Euro-Canadian customs and at least the shell of certain European institutions.

The decline of commercially valuable fur-bearing animals near the coast, coupled with the declining relative worth of furs measured against the commodities residents needed to purchase, meant that by the early twentieth century men had to journey far into the interior to trap, living in "tilts" or cabins in the interior five or six months a year, with a one-month break at home in the middle of the winter. The family went from two households— summer and winter—to three, and the third, the trapline "tilt," separated adult men from women and children for a substantial part of the year.

At the same time that life was becoming physically and perhaps also emotionally more difficult, certain Euro-Canadian customs and institutions were materializing in Labrador—Santa Claus, churches, missionary pastors, some medical services, and so forth: all were changing from being ideas, or elements of the stories told by parents who came from Great Britain or Canada, to being present in the landscape. New developments, such as radios that missionaries supplied to trappers and their families near the time of World War II, markedly diminished the isolation of trappers and their families from each other, from the world at large, and from centers of power and domination. Elizabeth Goudie mentioned, several times when talking about her engagement to Jim, how it was months after World War I ended that the people in her area heard the news.

The emerging presence of European culture, customs, and institutions in Labrador had complex effects. Both the sense and the reality of increasing participation in a larger world alleviated some of the increasing hardship of trapping families. Improved medical services, radio contact with the outside world, and the radio messages that missionaries relayed from families to trappers in the interior were all spoken of as substantial gains. But these radio messages to the isolated trappers, which the men could receive but not directly respond to, were a symbolic example of a larger set of processes— processes summed up in Elizabeth Goudie's comments on the Newfoundland government changing the name of the river along which her husband and her son trapped. Participation and powerlessness came together, and did so in a manner reminiscent of "King and crowd" riots in early modern European history ("if the King only knew . . . "). Elizabeth Goudie thought that the suffering of the trappers and their families would, or might, constitute a claim of the past upon the present: "if Joe Smallwood saw the trappers return with their Frost Bitten faces and half starved and exhausted he might have thought twice before he changed it." To the contrary, however: their suffering, when it drew any notice at all, was used to deny their claims— in the name of "progress" and "development."

We can see the household, particularly the woman-centered winter household, emerging as a separate social domain in this context—a domain of loneliness and of increasingly separate men's and women's work, where ordinary women become almost as dependent upon their husbands, and perhaps less sure of their skills, as the blind and paralytic women of earlier generations: contrast elderly Hannah and her husband, a family whose well-being depended on both their skills, with the semi-starving aunt that Elizabeth Goudie describes, whose husband could not trap well. Moreover, as a woman Elizabeth Goudie comes to define herself by, and even to merge herself in, her husband's trade, and through her husband to connect herself to the overarching domination of Hudson's Bay Company—"my whole life was a trappers life"—creating and denying herself simultaneously.

For Lydia Campbell, what we would call her "gender" is, for her, not her status but simply her life history—her marriages, her children, her present and past participation in the work of the family. Elizabeth Goudie is more "gender-conscious" in our sense of the term: "for 5 months of the year we had to do men's work," she wrote—when in fact it was more usually six, as a simple examination of trapper's schedules will show. But by making it five she is hanging on to her notion of herself as primarily a woman, with a woman's role and women's tasks. Thus also she describes her work as making clothes and preparing food, when in fact she also hunted, fished, and prepared seal skins for sale.

As the household increasingly emerged as a distinct and submerged social sphere, both gender and ethnicity took on new meanings as well. The changes both in women's gender-consciousness and in the place of the household in daily and productive life (from the center to a partially subordinate position) are closely interwoven, and both seem as if they occurred simply in reaction to the increasing physical difficulty of trapping, and the increasing subservience of trappers and their families to the demands and price schedules of the Hudson's Bay Company. But related changes in the area of social life that we call "ethnicity" indicate a more complex set of underlying forces at work.

In contrast with Lydia Campbell's intimacy with Innu and Inuit people—an intimacy that both her criticism and her sympathy for their plight expresses and more subtly also denies, for in both criticism and sympathy they remain the other; the other engaged—we can note the more totalizing distance that seems to emerge between Elizabeth Goudie and both her Inuit past and her Inuit contemporaries, who are literally her distant cousins being made even more distant when Elizabeth and her husband camp out upon, and poke around in, their graves.

The distances that open up in the course of the history of Euro-Canadian settlement in Labrador—from the actual physical distance between men's work and women's work to the actual genealogical distance between Indian and Inuit on the one hand, and Euro-Canadians on the other—take on a symbolic dynamic in the increasingly separate gender differentiation, the increasingly separate domestic sphere, and the increasing symbolic (or, more generally, "cultural") distancing from Inuit and Indian. With this, the sense of history changes.

In contrast with the concrete, materially focused ethnohistory of Lydia Campbell, Elizabeth Goudie's history often invokes rules and expectations—for example, "that was expected of the average Labrador girl at that time." What was called "custom" by Lydia Campbell was the framework and habits of her life. She went hunting with her children, when she was upset, "not for want or hunger but for custom." Custom is here neither thoughtless nor simply routine, but a self-conscious style of living. With

Elizabeth Goudie the work aspect of custom is more prominent, and custom becomes, in part, the demands one lives up to, even if willingly: "The custom of trappers wifes are to have something cooked for them when they come home." In these rules and expectations, and in these demands, there is a subtle sense that Elizabeth Goudie has become somewhat distanced from herself and her own feelings—a distance that was made more poignant when it culminated in having the trapping way of life, and its history as embedded in place-names with their local associations, torn from the trappers and their families by larger economic, social, and cultural forces, and all they were left with was their own feelings.

## V

I hold Elizabeth Goudie in immense respect, no less at all than Lydia Campbell. These are women—people—who accomplished a very great deal with very little apart from their skills and resources. With this respect and admiration, and also with the experience I have had working with Indians and Blacks in the southeastern United States, which taught the lesson that a critical and oppositional culture holds a substantial potential for easing the plight of dominated peoples, the question in this instance is all the more urgent: what happened in Newfoundland and Labrador that an oppositional folk culture did not form and flourish? By way of conclusion some theoretical suggestions will be made, suggestions that are speculative and not intended as an answer but an opening.

The term "relations of production" is used in different ways both by Marx and by marxists. Broadly speaking, it means the social relations that people must enter into in order to produce the conditions of their existence. Without an extended discussion of this term, which is not relevant here, what is relevant both for a historical anthropology and for this discussion is that the term "relations of production" has, throughout its various uses, a *double* meaning: (1) the social processes through which *work* is organized to produce goods, and simultaneously, (2) the processes through which surpluses are formed, transferred out of the control of the producers, and transformed, by those who have the power, into a wide range of economic, political, and cultural "values."

In this double sense of "relations of production" people in hunting and gathering societies, who are not dominated for surplus extraction, do not have social relations of production in the usual sense of the term, for they form no surpluses that pass out of the producer's control and influence. The term is, even if broadly, historically specific; moreover, I doubt that it is useful to make a simple either/or distinction: hunters and gatherers do not have relations of production; class societies do. While such a distinction is technically correct, I think it is more useful to say that relations of production emerge and intensify as social life comes to be increasingly pervasively dominated by surplus extraction, and by extension, that they can subside and decline, or that people can more or less successfully form areas of social life where the dominant relations of production are challenged, their grip diminished, and a domain of increasingly autonomous social relations develops.

Europeans came, or were brought, to Labrador to trap furs to create wealth. But in the early nineteenth century their whole lives did not seem dominated by this, so long as home life and work remained conjoined (although, simultaneously, this same conjunction of home life and work made the potential threat, and at times the reality, of domination all the more total). As trapping became more difficult with the decline of fur-bearing animals, and as the price spread between the sale of furs and the purchase of consumption goods and production supplies became increasingly unfavorable to trappers, it could well be argued that domination became more intense, more onerous, and certainly more apparent.

But however increasingly severe, the domination associated with the flourishing and consolidating relations of production of Labrador trapping was not total. There were still substantial areas of social life where, however pervaded by the demands of the trapping life, people sought to live their own lives on much their own terms, and thought of themselves as doing so. The areas of social life that we term the "domestic," "gender," and "ethnicity" are all forms of conjoining and separating people that are particularly crucial in this, for they are social forms that participate both in the social relations of production and also in the social relations of daily life and work—the central ways in which people relate to one another and to themselves outside of the demands of the relations of production, as well as in terms of those demands.

*Since the relations of production combine and separate people in the context of domination and surplus extraction, it would seem that the areas of social life where these relations could be most powerfully opposed are those areas where people feel themselves to be combining, separating, and distinguishing themselves and one another on their own terms— that is, in the concepts and practices of being male and female, the relations within and between domestic groups, the differences that are asserted or denied between ethnic groups: precisely the domains in which the ethnohistories of Lydia Campbell and Elizabeth Goudie were formed and developed.* What went wrong? Why was there not a more fully developed oppositional culture in Labrador, where people were treated so badly?

To begin: the isolation of families made it unlikely that collective action of any kind could develop, and in the absence of collective action a collective consciousness is not likely to develop (Thompson 1978a).[6] But Elizabeth Goudie wrote after twenty years of living in the town of Happy Valley, twenty years of her husband's wage work, and there is still little more than hints at a developed collective consciousness, class or ethnohistorical.

To pursue this point we must distinguish between class consciousness and class culture, and pursue the concept of ethnohistory in this context.

A class culture is, in simple terms, the culture of a class: its forms of discourse and of connectedness, antagonistic to or in alliance both with those who are seen as belonging to the class and with other classes—and the content conveyed by these connections, from the playful to the tragic. Class consciousness differs from class culture in two fundamental ways: first, it must specifically include consciousness of the situation of other classes, of the presence of one's own class, antagonistically, within the life and work of other classes, and of their presence within one's own class—a multiple consciousness that is simultaneously incorporative and distancing (the Gramscian notion of hegemony points to the surface of this intensely paradoxical process): second, class consciousness is, necessarily, consciousness of the antagonisms *within* classes—the antagonisms that must be taken into account in even the smallest, most ordinary forms of resistance, claim and counterclaim. The most important lesson I have learned from my years of work in southern United States civil rights struggles is that class consciousness, which is ultimately a consciousness for and about struggle, either includes consciousness of the tensions and oppositions *within* the dominated classes which emerge in the context of the imposed or chosen struggles, or it dissolves into individualistic fantasies. Class cultures can be reflexive, and can mediate this reflexivity through a sense of how one seems to the other; class consciousness contains, beyond this, a sense of the potential and actual costs of the connectedness to the other.

Marx indirectly and suggestively pointed toward the antagonistic internal differentiation that forms the sine qua non of class, and hence of class consciousness, in his famous "sack of potatoes" discussion of the smallholding French peasantry, which he saw in the mid-nineteenth century as

> an immense mass, the members of which live in the same situation but do not enter into manifold relationships with each other. Their mode of operation isolates them instead of bringing them into mutual intercourse. . . . Their place of operation, the smallholding, permits no division of labour in its cultivation, no application of science and therefore no diversity of development, variety of talent, or wealth of social relationships. Each individual peasant family is almost self sufficient. . . . In so far as millions of families live under economic conditions of existence that separate their mode of life, their interests and their cultural formation from those of the other classes and bring them into conflict with those classes, they form a class. In so far as these small peasant proprietors are merely connected on a local basis, and the identity of their interests fails to produce a feeling of community, national links or a political organization, they do not form a class. (Marx 1974 [1852]:238, 239)

Among the many very significant implications of this illustration is that it is the organization of work and of production in such manner as to generate *diversity within* a similarly situated, dominated people that engenders class. This diversity must in some ways be constrained: the internal antagonisms and alliances must be sufficient to bind people together, and not so explosive as to take primacy over the antagonisms to other classes. Further, and of central importance to the case at hand, the diverse groupings among a dominated people must continually and directly press a wide range of claims upon one another, including claims that cannot possibly be satisfied—for such claims can clarify more basic antagonisms.

We have seen, in the formation and development of these two ethnohistories (or, taken together, this ethnohistory), a subtle but profound separation and intensification of social differentiation among the dominated people of Labrador: separations of gender, of the domestic sphere from productive life, of ethnicity. What kept these separations from being reunited into a form of class consciousness—a politically more assertive ethnohistory?

I suggest that above and beyond the substantial isolation of people, and the fragmentation created by their production processes and by the competition between Euro-Canadians, Innu, and Inuit for the same resources, it was the absence of assertive, even aggressive claims upon one another (including claims between Euro-Canadians, Innu, and Inuit) which further depoliticized the "traditional" culture of Euro-Canadian Labrador. The most clearly expressed claims come in the domain of gender, but even here they were diffused into the demands of custom.

The cultures we, and often the participants also, term "traditional" are not, basically, about ways of dressing, or styles of housing or eating. They are, rather, ways that people form relationships to, or against, one another that, I think often specifically and quite consciously, all together—the alliances and the enmities—distance people from the imposed forms of domination and the social relations that serve domination and exploitation. While "traditional" cultures can be in collusion with external domination, and elaborate their own forms of domination and exploitation as well, even at such times they often convey the mystique, if not the reality, of a partial and critical distancing from external domination, a distance that perhaps is most consciously constructed and expressed in the domains of ethnohistory, custom, play, and the senses of humor and tragedy. "Traditional" cultures, in sum, often contain—although in surprisingly different forms—what we would elsewhere call "class consciousness." As with class consciousness the self-consciousness of traditional cultures can become either liberating or self-defeating: both ordinarily conjoin self-assertion and collective self-destruction so pervasively that it is difficult to distinguish the two even conceptually[7]—frostbitten faces on half-starved, exhausted men express both their amazing power to survive at all and their near-total powerlessness.

In this perspective I am suggesting that "what happened" in Labrador to block the formation of a critical, assertive, or even substantially autonomous folk culture was the emergence of domesticity, gender differentiation, and ethnic differentiation in a way that further fragmented the social ties of daily and working life, to the point where the social-relational basis for the development of an oppositional culture was severely diminished. In such contexts folk "culture" takes on much of its coloration from the social relations of production, rather than constituting a partly separate sphere of social life, with its own social and historical dynamic.

My earlier work on Newfoundland (Sider 1986) concluded with the assertion, "It is the strategic purpose of this analysis to suggest that developing the collective [political] intentionality requires first developing the linkages between people in daily life and production. . . ." Here, still wrestling with the problem of how most effectively to participate in politically organizing marginal, dominated hinterland peoples, I conclude with a suggestion at once less romantic and more specific: it is through the formation of claims upon one another, including directly expressed antagonistic claims, that the increasingly diverse sectors of a dominated people would come to understand their history in new, and newly productive, ways.

## NOTES

1. The explorer Jacques Cartier, in 1534: "the land [now called Labrador, or by the people of the area, "the Labrador"] should not be called the New Land, being composed of stones and horrible rugged rocks. [It] is the land God gave to Cain."

The first draft of this paper was presented in April 1986 at the American Ethnological Society meetings, a second draft in July 1986 at the Fifth Roundtable Conference in History and Anthropology, "The Production of History," cosponsored by the Maison des Sciences de l'Homme and the Max-Planck-Institut für Geschichte, and a third version in 1987 at Memorial University of Newfoundland. Special thanks are due to Anne Hart, chief librarian of the Newfoundland Collection at Memorial University of Newfoundland, for calling my attention—forcefully and perceptively—to the autobiographies discussed here and to the Honorable D. J. Goudie, for permission to use the manuscript, rather than the published, version of Elizabeth Goudie's autobiography. This essay has been through several drafts over the past several years, and has benefited substantially from the friendly intermixture of encouragement and assault, gently called advice, of several people, including especially Andrea Bardfeld, Geraldine Casey, Rex Clark, Maria Lagos, Alf Luedtke, Hans Medick, William Roseberry, and Gavin Smith.

2. This historical and geographic sketch of Labrador relies primarily on Zimmerly (1975) and Fitzhugh (1972), supplemented by Cartwright (1792) and Junek (1937). Lydia Campbell's and Elizabeth Goudie's autobiographies, cited in the text, give the fullest sense of the land and landscape.

3. When paraphrasing Lydia Campbell and Elizabeth Goudie I follow their usage of "Eskimo" and "Indian" to facilitate shifting from quote to paraphrase.

4. I have changed the spelling to make it more "standard," particularly in places likely to give difficulty to those whose first language is not English. The punctuation and the capitalization are as in the original.

5. This instance is further discussed in Sider (1986:158–161).

6. E. P. Thompson (1978*a*) perceptively discusses the rootedness of both class and class consciousness in struggle.

7. On the intermixing of self-assertion and self-destruction in the context of domination see Luedtke (1985).

TEN

# Habits of the Cumbered Heart: Ethnic Community and Women's Culture as American Invented Traditions

*Micaela di Leonardo*

## INTRODUCTION

Recent literature on the American temperament portrays United States citizens as a people without traditions, except perhaps the tradition of invented and individualizing social orders. Thus Frances Fitzgerald (1986) chooses recently established communities with narrow membership criteria—an affluent white retirement development, a Christian cult, San Francisco's gay neighborhoods—as exemplars of a broad-scale and continuous American turn against both the past and the larger society in attempts to establish utopian orders for a narrow elect. Allan Bloom (1988) excoriates American popular culture, and thus America's young, as vulgar, traditionless, and, not coincidentally, subject to the illogical and unnatural "fads" of leftist and feminist thought and action. On the other end of the political spectrum, Russell Jacoby (1987) deplores the dying off of early-to-mid-twentieth-century traditions of American public intellectual life and the retreat of radical intellectuals into an arid and hermetic scholasticism. Finally, and most instructively, Robert Bellah and his coauthors in their multiple interview study *Habits of the Heart* (1985) determine that Americans primarily conceive the self as unencumbered by dependent others, by community obligations, by history. These authors' analysis underscores current images of protean American individualism.

*Habits* typifies recent evaluations of American cultural perceptions in other ways as well. The unencumbered selves—such as those making use of "therapeutic" or "managerial" modes of apprehending reality—with which the authors find their informants struggling, and which the authors wish to adjure us to discard—significantly are white, male, and middle-class. This narrow conception of American selfhood is unsurprising when we consider

234

both the authors' demographically skewed choice of interviewees and the prototypically elite historical "American Studies" texts to which they turn to flesh out their interviewees' hesitant statements. Indeed, if we shift the focus to include all Americans, both as agents and as objects of the cultural construction of the self, we perceive instead an American landscape littered with images of very cumbered selves. While the myth of the nineteenth-century pioneer or frontiersman lives on, it has been joined by those of rebellious black slaves, the planners and sojourners on the Underground Railroad, and the cooperative and contentious struggles of the Suffragists. And present-day images reflected in mass-media treatment include more than the unencumbered (white, middle-class, and largely male) urban and economic "pioneers"—gentrifiers in inner cities and entrepreneurs in new industries. They also include the cumbered poor, mixed-sex groups of recent Latin, Caribbean, and Asian migrants to the United States who are financed by and arrive as kinspeople, gain jobs through and work with kin and compatriots, and live doubled and tripled up in apartments and homes on the East, West, and South Coasts of the country. Even those migrants who travel to the United States alone and work in isolation from their kin and compatriots, such as the many thousands of Caribbean and Latin American women working as childminders and domestic servants, find themselves very cumbered with their largely live-in status and the emotionally intense nature of child care and household labor for others.

Despite the fact that the very notion of an unencumbered self is, as Bellah et al. point out, a traditional American invention, scholars and popular cultural commentators associate "tradition" in the United States with *Gemeinschaft*, groupness, interdependence, responsibility—with the state of cumberedness.[1] Two American groups have popular cultural "traditions" in this sense: foreign peasantry and their descendants, and women. In this piece, I examine the two current, competing, and related images uniting these two population groups and notions of a cumbered self: ethnic community and women's culture. I shall first locate each construct historically as an invented tradition, and then consider the relations of these images to each other and to other key images, most particularly those which arose in the 1960s and 1970s with the civil rights and black power movements. In so doing I shall suggest not only that there are multiple inventions of tradition in American life and many versions of the self, but also that all invented traditions, as Barth noted in 1969 concerning ethnicity, are constructed on the boundaries of group membership. Even (or especially) the various mainstream notions of a white, male unencumbered self exist in unadmitted relation to raced, classed, and gendered others and in contexts of power and domination. Male frontiersmen relied on wifely help and displaced and expropriated land from male and female Native Americans. The new white male entrepreneurs of, say, Silicon Valley rely on a vast army of white female clerical labor and of Third World female factory labor both inside and outside the United States. The myth of the unencumbered self is thus a myth that exists in part to disguise material realities, and we need to consider, as Bellah et al. do not, the political-economic foundations of invented traditions.

But images of cumbered selves are not themselves free of mystifying functions, nor do they operate monolithically. Notions of ethnic communities and of nurturing women are used by many cultural agents (the general population, commercial interests) for diverse purposes. And, as Roseberry and O'Brien note in the Introduction to this volume, the process of inventing traditions is deeply intertwined with anthropological and, indeed, Western intellectual history.

These contemporary invented traditions of ethnic community and women's culture, as used by different social actors, implicate two related themes in Western social thought: the nature/nurture dichotomy and the ambiguous functions and meanings of human community. Women and ethnic-racial others, in fact, inhabit, in related and contradictory ways, the pole representing the past in Roseberry and O'Brien's sketch of our recurrent use of oppositional past/present modeling. They (we) are primitive, traditional, folk, natural, and underdeveloped. While these points have been made before, both for women and ethnic and racial others, it is my purpose here to consider more carefully their interrelationship and their specific connections to larger intellectual and political debates in the contemporary United States.

## WHITE ETHNIC COMMUNITY

While certain popular works (such as *Streetcorner Society* [1943] and *The Urban Villagers* [1962]) foreshadowed it, the American concept of the white ethnic community coalesced in the early 1970s, the period in which the term "white ethnic" itself gained currency. A "white ethnic," of course, exists in contradistinction to those ethnics defined as nonwhites, and thus white ethnics came into existence as a labeled group in response to the civil rights/black power movements and the allied organizing of Latinos, Asians, and Native Americans.

Populations we now label white ethnic—those whose antecedents arrived from (largely southeastern) Europe from the 1840s and increasingly after the 1880s—were subject to intensive, largely deprecating or patronizing, public scrutiny throughout the Reform and Depression eras. Popular representations of Irish, Italians, Poles, Jews, and others as mentally deficient, diseased, and/or innately criminal were widespread, and there is no need to recapitulate that popular cultural story here. It is important to note, though, that these populations were the first American groups classically defined as "urban poor," both by the nascent reform movement and by the developing field of urban sociology in the 1920s and 1930s.[2] As such, they were heirs to a profound Enlightenment ambivalence about the nature of communities. Since at least the time of Rousseau and his critics, "community" has explicitly or implicitly contained both the images of equality, order, and civility and those of ignorance, hidebound tradition, and narrowness. This dichotomy was first inscribed as a country/city contrast and was transposed, in the urban American context, into a contradictory vision of the functioning of newly arrived European peasantry in United States cities. Thus the work of the Chicago School sociologists could describe migrants to the city both as the inheritors of *Gemeinschaft*—the simple humanly satisfying, face-to-face, traditional rural world that was giving way to the complex, anomic, modern urban world of strangers—and as rude, uncivilized peasants who must modernize, assimilate, Americanize in order to rise to the level of work and social life in the new industrial city.

With the coming of World War II and through the 1950s, there was a general hiatus in both scholarly and popular attention to the non-American origins of this large segment of the American population. This was in part an epiphenomenon of restrictive immigration legislation in 1924; by the end of World War II most immigrants had been resident in the United States at least twenty years and had children and often grandchildren. It was also in part a result of the conscious efforts (assisted, of course, by capital and state) of migrants and their children to "modernize" and "Americanize." As well, it was in part the result of social scientists' interests in the changing physical features of the postwar American landscape, such as increasing suburbanization (*The Levittowners*), and in emerging social types and characteristic social relations related to the maturation of corporate capitalism (*The Organization Man* [1956], *Workingman's Wife* [1959], *Blue-Collar Marriage* [1962], *The Lonely Crowd* [1950]). Even research specifically concerned with ethnic and racial life in the United States during this period (such as Milton Gordon's *Assimilation in American Life* [1964]) continued to use the Progressive Era melting-pot metaphor and was more concerned with negative than with positive aspects of "unmelted" populations.

This era of public and scholarly quiescence ended abruptly in the early 1970s as white ethnicity suddenly became a topic of key national concern. Across the nation, moribund ethnic voluntary associations revived and countless new ones were formed; popular books celebrating white ethnic experience, such as Glazer and Moynihan's *Beyond the Melting Pot* (1970), Michael Novak's *The Rise of the Unmeltable Ethnics* (1971), and Richard Gambino's *Blood of My Blood* (1974), became best-sellers; and a stream of scholarly books and articles began to flow from the academy. Journalistic and scholarly accounts alike parlayed the notions that white ethnics were an unjustly [repressed, maligned, ignored—take your pick] segment of the

American population, were just beginning to rediscover their own histories and cultures, and deserved respect and attention in the public arena. Michael Novak, among many others, threw down the white ethnic gauntlet:

> In the country clubs, as city executives, established families, industrialists, owners, lawyers, masters of etiquette, college presidents, dominators of the military, fund raisers, members of blue ribbon communities, realtors, brokers, deans, sheriffs—it is the cumulative power and distinctive styles of WASPS that the rest of us have had to learn in order to survive. WASPS have never had to celebrate Columbus Day or march down Fifth Avenue wearing green. Every day has been their day in America. No more. (1971:136)

Tied to these notions of the nature of white ethnic Americans was the construct of the white ethnic community, which journalists, academics, and individual white ethnics themselves proclaimed as an endangered but surviving inner-city institution. White ethnic communities were characterized in terms reminiscent of Chicago School interpretations of 1930s immigrant populations—with the negative end of the pole removed.

> Social life in white ethnic neighborhoods is largely rooted in the family. . . . Most people know or at least recognize one another. There is a sense of community integrity and group identity. (Seifer 1973:8)

> The pattern of Italian-American life is continuous with that of their ancestors. Its verities continue to demonstrate that family, community and work mean survival and that outsiders are threats to neighborhood stability which is necessary to the close-knit life and culture of the people. (Gambino 1974:343)

> Within the geographic boundaries of the Italian Quarters the *connazionali* gave life to a closely woven community within which the Italian way of life flourished. (Gumina 1978:37)

As I have argued elsewhere, these claims concerning white ethnic communities rest upon unexamined presuppositions that there *were* in fact such discrete phenomena: long-term, self-reproducing, ethnically homogeneous inner-city neighborhoods (1984:47–151). In reality, American white ethnic populations throughout the nineteenth and twentieth centuries lived in ethnically heterogeneous and shifting urban neighborhoods—and moved often. They also took flight to the suburbs in concert with their urban WASP neighbors. Thus, for example, by the mid-1970s, in the height of white ethnic renaissance publicity, the prototypical California Italian-American "community," San Francisco's North Beach, had more than 90 percent Chinese residents, and California's Italian-American population was in reality scattered far and wide across the state's urban, suburban, and rural areas.

If such popular claims about white ethnic communities were untrue, were, in fact, a newly invented tradition, what was the purpose and meaning of this ideological construct? Clearly the assertion of self-worth had psychological benefits for individual white ethnics, but why did these assertions arise at that particular historical moment, and why were they so attentively heeded? In other words, how did the rise of white ethnic community ideology inter- sect with other contemporary political, economic, and cultural forces? Why did the various social actors who made use of it find it salient?

The period of the late 1960s and early 1970s in the United States was characterized by continuing economic expansion, the ongoing war in Viet- nam, and a linked set of social movements directly related to these two key political-economic realities: civil rights/black power, the antiwar movement, the student/youth movement, and the revived feminist movement.[3] The con- nections among these social movements and their links to larger political- economic realities have been exhaustively documented, but in brief: both the prospect of partaking in the benefits of postwar economic expansion and anger at the disproportionate induction of black youth for war service helped to fuel black power activism. The antiwar and feminist movements drew inspiration and personnel from contemporary black movements. Economic expansion and the demographic bulge of a 1960s college-age cohort laid the material basis for college- and then high-school-located youth rebellion— including civil rights, antiwar, and feminist protests but also involving demands for increased autonomy and sexual freedom. Finally, postwar economic expansion led to American capital's greatly increased demands for labor, and thus American women's rising labor-force participation rate. The very possibility of supporting themselves without reliance on father or husband allowed many women to challenge male societal dominance, while the low pay, low status, and minimal prospects for advancement that char- acterized most "women's jobs" in that era stimulated feminist reaction.

These multiple movements for reform and liberation challenged both the federal, state, and institutional structures—such as those of colleges and universities—and individuals who perceived themselves to be threatened by particular demands for social change. The Nixon Administration in particu- lar sought to exploit and enhance these social divisions through the use of the polarizing discourse of the Silent Majority—as opposed to the protesting anti-Administration "minority." Between Administration rhetoric and media response, an image grew of this stipulated entity: the Silent Majority were white—implicitly white ethnic—largely male, blue-collar workers. They were held to be "patriotic" and to live in "traditional" families—ones in which males ruled, women did not work outside the home for pay, and parents controlled their children.

This media image, of course, did not reflect an aggregate social reality. This was the era, after all, in which married working-class women were en- tering the labor force at record rates, and in which their additions to family income maintained working-class living standards in the face of declining real incomes. And sexual adventurism and drug use in the late 1960s and

early 1970s were the property of working-class no less than middle-class
youth. Nevertheless, as a media construct, as a symbol of the hemorrhaging
of Democratic voters to the Republican Party, the conservative white ethnic
blue-collar worker gained salience in this period. This salience was much
enhanced by the shifting populations and power relations in American
cities.[4]

In the 1960s, poor black Americans became newly visible, and newly defined as a social problem in Northern cities. The two great waves of black
migration from the South, during the First and Second World Wars, had
each resulted in cohorts of permanent Northern black urban residents. These
men and women had come north (often through employer recruitment) to
take advantage of lucrative war jobs, and had then often been laid off, and
largely had become part of a permanent army of reserve labor. Urban renewal projects in the 1950s and 1960s destroyed countless urban black neighborhoods, replaced them with office blocks and sports complexes, and shifted
and concentrated the poor black population in areas dominated by inhospi-
table, poorly built government housing projects. Big-city governments refused
to shift budgetary resources to basic services for these impoverished areas.
Neighborhood deterioration, increased crime, and urban uprisings stimulated the establishment of highly visible federal Great Society programs. At
the same time, a small cohort of socially mobile blacks, emboldened by the
civil rights movement, attempted to buy homes in formerly white urban and
suburban neighborhoods. The resulting "white flight" greatly enriched the
real estate speculators who fanned its flames and exacerbated inner-city
white racism. Black (and Latin) struggles for higher-quality public education, neighborhood services, and civil service and union jobs led to increased
friction between white, often white ethnic, and minority citizens in Northern
urban environments, friction only furthered by the newly oppositional rhetorical style of black power advocacy. The first scattered fringe of desubur-
banizing bourgeois whites entered into this polarized and often dangerous
environment, benefiting, of course, from its resulting low real estate values.

Thus the white ethnic community construct arose from an extraordinarily
complex historical ground, and this complexity was reflected in its multiple
expressions and political uses. Key to all expressions and uses, though, was
its reliance upon the basic ideological tropes of the civil rights and black
cultural nationalist movements as structural templates, and thus its posture
of competition through emulation. This ideology posited that blacks were a
unitary, identifiable group who had experienced and were experiencing extreme forms of discrimination, and who therefore were entitled not only to
cessation of discriminatory laws and behaviors but also to financial and other
sorts of recompense (affirmative action, Head Start, CETA, etc.). Thus, ironically, key expressions of white ethnic resentment were couched in language
consciously and unconsciously copied from blacks themselves. Notions, for

example, of the strength and richness of white ethnic cultures and their repression by WASPS mimicked black cultural nationalist (and white scholars'—see Stack 1974; Gutman 1976; Levine 1977) celebrations of black culture's endurance despite white domination. When I was doing fieldwork among California Italian-Americans in the mid-1970s, for example, several informants identified my documentation of their and their antecedents' life histories as "our Roots," after the book and television film series on a Southern black family's history.

Deliberate denigration of blacks vis-à-vis white ethnics relied as well on the ideological frame of entitlement used by black Americans. Both popular journalistic accounts and grass roots white ethnic discourse, for example, focused on the strength and unity of white ethnic families as opposed to those of black Americans—whose popular image had been shaped in the early 1960s as a "tangle of pathology" by the Moynihan Report. Many of my own informants' racist expressions against blacks focused on inferior black family behavior as both explaining and justifying widespread black poverty. Thus the argument that, as the undeserving poor, blacks were not entitled to the largesse of Great Society programs, which should instead flow to "deserving" white ethnics:

> The ethnics believe that they chose one route to moderate success in America; namely, loyalty, hard work, family discipline, and gradual self-development. They tend to believe that some blacks, admittedly more deeply injured and penalized in America, want to jump, *via* revolutionary militance, from a largely rural base of skills and habits over the heads of lower-class whites. Instead of forming a coalition of the black and white lower classes, black militants seem to prefer coalition with intellectual elites. Campus and urban disorders witness a similarity of violence, disorder, rhetoric, ideology, and style. (Novak 1971:30)

This relative entitlement frame is attached, as I have argued elsewhere, to a "report card mentality": a model of shifting American class divisions as caused by proper and improper ethnic/racial family and economic behavior rather than by the differential incorporation of immigrant and resident populations in American capitalism's evolving class structure (1984:96–112). And proper and improper behaviors are related to notions of cumbered and unencumbered selfhood. The "cumberedness" that Chicago School social scientists saw Southeastern European immigrants as inevitably losing in the *Gesellschaft* of modernizing urban America was rediscovered in the 1970s as a surviving feature of white ethnic selfhood. Scholarship, journalism, and grass roots expressions celebrated white ethnics for their family loyalties and neighborhood ties. In fact, advertising in this period began to exploit white ethnic imagery: the pizza-baking grandmother, the extended family at the laden dinner table—in order to invest frozen and canned foods with the cachet of the *Gemeinschaft*.

This *Gemeinschaft*, cumberedness—this community—was delineated as an
urban phenomenon existing alongside of and in opposition to urban black
populations. In fact, there is the distinct flavor of a "three bears" analogy in
much 1970s rhetoric on white ethnicity. While WASPs were "too cold"—
bloodless, modern, and unencumbered—and blacks "too hot"—wild, primitive, and overcumbered—white ethnics were "just right." They could and
did claim to represent the golden historical mean between the overwhelming
ancientness and primitiveness of *Gemeinschaft* and the etiolated modernism of
*Gesellschaft*.

This new vision of white ethnics as the proper urban residents, those who
maintain stable neighborhoods that nevertheless have "character"—ethnic
restaurants, delicatessens, and other small businesses—was a major ideological component of growing gentrification. Ironically, of course, the more
urban professionals were attracted to inner-city neighborhoods, the more
real estate prices rose and the less could *any* working-class urban residents
and shopkeepers, white ethnic, black, or other, continue to afford to live or to
do business in those neighborhoods.

Central to the new construction of white ethnic community has been the
Madonna-like image of the white ethnic woman. Early 1970s popular writers
extolled her devotion to home and family, and many of my more conservative
Italian-American informants in the late 1970s echoed this fusion of ethnic
chauvinism and antifeminism. Clelia Cipolla, a middle-aged civil servant,
said, in describing her elaborate cooking for family holidays: "I've always
thought of Thanksgiving as the only holiday the American wife really cooks
for. . . maybe that's a wrong idea of it, but that's the way my feelings are"
(1984:222). Part of the appeal to women and men of this construction was the
notion that white ethnic mothers, unlike "selfish" WASP and "lazy" black
mothers, could control their children and thus were exempt from blame for
the current youth protests. Clelia Cipolla exclaimed to me in response to my
narration of a recent Thanksgiving holiday's activities: "You mean Mommy
and Daddy *allowed* you to have Thanksgiving away from home?" (1984:37).

But in fact, white ethnic women were no less subject to the pressures and
opportunities of the shifting American political economy of the 1970s, and
many more of my women informants actively altered or rejected the popular
image of the self-sacrificing, kitchen-bound ethnic mother. What is important to note is not whether or not white ethnic women fit the model—by and
large, they did and do not—but that the model has been so hegemonic as to
command belief and to influence the construction of identity. Linda Mornese,
for example, judged her own immigrant grandmother as insufficiently ethnic
because she did not conform to the nurturant peasant model:

> I remember my aunt's mother, she was really the old Italian: white hair, never
> any makeup, the old dresses, wine barrels in the basement. I always thought:
> there's a *real* Italian lady. I don't see an Italian lady as one with her hair done.

My grandmother's always kept herself, she's always dressed very well, she puts her jewelry on—she's better at it than I am! (1984:181)

In an era of rising feminist activism, the sudden celebration of a group of women who theretofore had been socially labeled as backward, stolid, and possessive wives and mothers functioned very clearly as antifeminist— particularly anti–women's work-force participation—rhetoric. As well, in focusing on women's "duties" to husband and children, it worked against prevalent civil rights imagery of heroic black movement women whose perceived duties lay in the public sphere. But like all symbols, the white ethnic woman is polyvalent and was and is subject to feminist and progressive interpretation, witness the following description:

> As Barbara Mikulski of Baltimore points out, the white ethnic woman in America is not a dingbat, however warm and humanistic may be the character of Edith Bunker, nor is she limited to "tacky clothes," "plastic flowers," *True Confessions*, and an "IQ of 47." Rather, she is Maria Fava and Ann Giordano, who travelled to Albany to express parent and community concern over limitations on day care. She is Rosemarie Reed, who attended a Washington conference on community organizing. She is Marie Anastasi, who is working with senior citizens as well as a "mothers' morning out" group. She is one of dozens of women who have joined with Monsignor Genno Baroni of the National Center for Urban Ethnic Affairs to deal with housing, redlining by banks, and neighborhood preservation. (Kennedy 1979:241–242)

Many feminist scholars have attempted to celebrate the strength and endurance of "traditional" ethnic women and to use, for example, narratives of past union and strike activities, or consumer protests, to construct a vision of innately progressive, rebellious ethnic womanhood (see Gutman 1977: Smith 1978). This attempt to wrest the white ethnic woman from the antifeminist Right overlapped with another prominent invented tradition of the same period, the notion of women's culture.

## WOMEN'S CULTURE

In 1975, American historian Carroll Smith-Rosenberg published "The Female World of Love and Ritual: Relations between Women in Nineteenth-Century America" in the first issue of the feminist scholarly journal *Signs*. In this article, with the use of extracts from letters between female friends and kinswomen, Smith-Rosenberg contended that American women in this period constituted a mutually supportive society separate from the world of their fathers, brothers, and husbands. Smith-Rosenberg's larger point was a critique of our reductionist Western visions of sexuality. Her letters between women provided evidence of passionately romantic relations among schoolgirl friends that lasted lifetimes and were unaffected by the women's heterosexual courtships and marriages.

Smith-Rosenberg's article was to prove to be part of a highly influential trend in burgeoning American feminist scholarship. Historians, literary critics, and social scientists began to focus more on relations between women, tipping the balance over from work on relations between women and men, the prime concern of early second-wave feminist scholarship.

The focus on women's relations with one another and its attendant assumptions of female nurturance and cooperativeness reflected a growing phenomenon not only among feminist scholars but also feminist activists, lesbian feminists, and feminist entrepreneurs (not mutually exclusive categories by any means), a phenomenon I label women's culture.[5] While actual expressions of women's culture ideology vary greatly, the following is an ideal-typical description. There is an entity, women's culture, which represents an *Ur*-form of women's nature and has the same characteristics across time and space. These characteristics include moral superiority to men; cooperative rather than competitive social relations; selfless maternality; and benevolent sexuality. Thus women's culture embodies the notion that there is an authentic feminine selfhood that has been distorted, accreted over by male domination. While many of these tenets are parallel to those said to be characteristic of radical or cultural feminism, I would distinguish between women's culture and these theoretical strands in feminism. Women's culture is not a political or theoretical perspective but a protean set of claims that may be (and are, as I shall demonstrate) used to construct varying arguments concerning women's rights and duties.

Feminist scholars across many disciplines from the mid-1970s into the present have taken to the notion of women's culture. Consider the following extracts:

Literary criticism:

[W]omen's culture forms a collective experience within the cultural whole, an experience that binds women writers to each other over time and space. (Showalter 1982:27)

Political theory:

There is always a women's culture within every culture. (Moschkovich 1981:82)

Social theory:

[T]he bedrock of women's consciousness is the obligation to preserve life. Now as in the past, women judge themselves and one another on how well they do work associated with being female. (Kaplan 1982:543)

Political history:

Women's culture is the ground upon which women stand in their resistance to patriarchal domination and their assertion of their own creativity in sharing society. (Lerner 1980:53)

Psychology:

Women not only define themselves in a context of human relationship but also judge themselves in terms of their ability to care. (Gilligan 1982:17)

Among feminist activists as well during this period there sprang up widespread adoption of women's culture themes. Consider, for example, the popular feminist antimilitarist slogan: "Take the toys away from the boys." The implicit meaning is that morally superior, maternal women will discipline male warriors who are responsible for world militarism. Or, consider the popular T-shirt and bumper sticker slogan, "When God created man, He was only practicing." Even more important to women's culture imagery have been a series of popular works that claim the existence of prehistoric matriarchies often associated with the worship of female supernatural beings. Books such as *When God Was a Woman* and *The First Sex* have fueled popular feminist constructions of a prior perfect state, not unlike the pristine ethnic community of the white ethnic renaissance's imagination and the superior precolonial societies of Africa evoked in black cultural nationalism.

Women's culture ideology, like white ethnic community ideology, makes claims that are simply counterfactual. It denies the reality of female participation in theft, torture, murder, the abandonment of children—activities that have been carried on by at least some women in most past and present societies, and activities that are not necessarily explained away by prevalent male domination. And it denies the realities of women's self-seeking strategizing *within* their "nurturant," "unselfish" activities of caring for home and children. Children, after all, until very recently in the industrialized West, labored for their parents and as adults owed them—often especially their mothers—loyalty, labor, and cash.

Clearly, the women's culture concept exists in complex relation to recent political-economic shifts and the ideological constructions of contemporary political movements. "Women's culture" responds to antifeminist accusations that feminists are selfish—that they do not, in other words, accept their proper load of cumberedness—through embracing an a priori moral high ground. All women are innately morally superior to all men because they are naturally cooperative and nurturant. They are automatically cumbered, but by responsibility for other women and children, not necessarily for men. This feminist essentialist stance, as Janet Sayers (1982) labels it, by appeal to biological or near-biological differences between the sexes, neatly preempts accusations that feminists and/or lesbians have lost their femininity. They cannot lose that which is innately theirs, which is ascribed, not achieved.

Women's culture also exists within an ideological landscape that contains images of female difference: of differing women, and women's lives across class, color, nationality, sexual identity, and historical era. Some feminists deal with difference by abolishing it through sleight of pen, as does Adrienne Rich in the well-known 1980 essay "Compulsory Heterosexuality and the

Lesbian Existence.'' Rich envisions all women everywhere as forced into sub-
mission to men and to heterosexuality; she perceives all evidences of male
activity against women and of women's lower social status across time and
space as proof of the pan-male activity of "gynocide," and thus labels all
unconventional female activities everywhere—whether the practice of witch-
craft or the planning of a demonstration—as lesbian.

The women's culture construct, then, is structurally related to the white
ethnic community construct in two ways. First, it attempts to take over a
preexisting polarized notion of its subject (warm versus primitive and insular
European migrants, Madonnas versus harridans and sluts) by chopping off
and denying the existence of the negative pole. This operation has been relatively successful for the white ethnic community construct. The historical
version of the negative pole—the stolid, backward, socially immobile ethnic
community—has been superseded in the public mind by the black and
brown poor whose social immobility is presumed to be self-caused. The more
recent historically negative vision, that of the racist, conservative white
ethnic community, has not been revived, despite, for example, the prevalence
of Italian surnames among the Howard Beach and Bensonhurst adolescents
and others guilty of recent unprovoked and murderous attacks against blacks
and Latinos in New York City; and despite the fact that white ethnic leaders
in Yonkers risked bankrupting the city in 1988 in order to continue their
four-decades-long segregationist tradition.

The negative pole of women's culture, in contrast, is alive and kicking in
popular culture. Recent journalistic coverage—not to mention the behavior
of courts and police—of reproductive issues such as surrogate motherhood
and prenatal care have tended toward automatic blame of women caught in
difficult circumstances. Thus women who agree to be surrogates are deemed
selfish, as was the woman who agreed and then wished to back out of her
agreement. And pregnant women who do not follow doctors' orders have
been arrested and charged. Negative stereotypes of women abound in popular culture, from the psychotic rejected woman in *Fatal Attraction* to the evil
upper-class boss in *Working Girl* to selfish, unmaternal bourgeois witches of
John Updike's recent fiction. American popular-press coverage of "rich
bitches" such as Ivana Trump, Imelda Marcos, and Leona Helmsley—the
consuming wives of far richer and more directly evil men—is characterized
by a populist venom not aimed at wealthy or powerful men since Nixon and
Watergate.

There are a number of obvious reasons for the relative failure of women's
culture ideology. The first is that it is easier to maintain a counterfactual
vision of an elusive ephemeral community—particular neighborhoods and
individuals can be labeled inauthentic—than of half the human race. As
well, the social base for anti–white ethnic community sentiment is small. The
Nixon era is long over, and Reagan and Bush's three electoral victories cannot be ascribed to crossover white ethnics alone. In contrast, the key main-

stream feminist goal of the 1980s—ratification of the ERA—failed, and anti-feminist ideologies have been strongly represented in the 1980s from the White House down. It is in the current interests of a large number of politically active groups to blame some population of American women—those seeking abortions, those who leave husbands, those on welfare, those in the labor force, those who put their children in day care—for all social ills.

The second relation between women's culture and white ethnic community is not emulation but annexation. In the 1970s context of rising feminism and the first antifeminist construct of the white ethnic woman, feminists responded, as I have noted, by claiming the white ethnic woman for themselves and their discourse. But the women's culture construct also emulates the white ethnic community's annexation of the symbolic structures of the civil rights movement, "swallowing" not only the beleaguered white ethnic Madonna but the oppressed, heroic women of color.

This phenomenon was structured within and in response to American political, economic, and cultural landscape in the 1970s and 1980s. The mid-1970s energy crisis was the first of a series of shocks to the economy that helped to usher in the new public ideology that we had entered an "era of limits." During the Carter Administration, rapidly escalating inflation, particularly in the rising speculative real estate market, set the stage for the dismantling of Great Society programs that were newly seen as "too expensive." Welfare cutbacks under Carter became wholesale shrinkage of the federal social welfare budget under Reagan. Concomitant recession drove unemployment figures into double digits. Numbers of individuals and families made homeless by unemployment, real estate speculation, and the federal abandonment of low-cost housing programs grew rapidly (Piven and Cloward 1982; Block et al. 1987).

With the economic recovery of the middle and late 1980s, unemployment has shrunk to early-1970s levels, but it has shrunk less for minority Americans, and of those now reemployed, many work part-time or at jobs with lower status and pay. As a combination of these shifts and regressive tax legislation, over the Reagan years both the numbers of very poor and very rich have risen (Levy 1988). Despite local grass-roots organizing against obvious inequities such as plant shutdowns, farm foreclosures, and continuously increasing homeless populations, popular political discourse has shifted distinctly rightward over the past decade. Civil rights, women's, gay, and labor groups are labeled "special interests." Public discourse on the poor, particularly poor blacks and Latins, has turned nearly hegemonically to automatic deprecation and "blame the victim" rhetoric. Welfare mothers—deemed to be nearly all young blacks despite the fact that black teenage pregnancy rates have been declining for two decades—are stigmatized even by black scholars as the source of disorder, drug use, and urban crime (see Reed 1988*b*). The rise of AIDS and the increase of drug-related street crime have been used rhetorically to further homophobic and racist discourse.

Right-wing think tanks, such as the Heritage Foundation and the American Enterprise Institute, have grown and are given a respectful hearing in the mass media. Individual minority and female scholars and administrators, such as Clarence Pendleton, Thomas Sowell, Linda Chavez, and Gertrude Himmelfarb take distinctly anti–civil rights and antifeminist stands and are rewarded with government posts and academic respectability.

It is in this context that the linked phenomena of feminist academic work and popular feminist cultural production have taken on a distinctive shape and thrust. American universities, by default, as Russell Jacoby has noted, have become in the recent conservative era important havens for progressive social thought. Faculty in explicitly new, interdisciplinary programs, such as women's and Afro-American studies, have often evolved a beleaguered circle-the-wagons perspective. This defensiveness is often justified, given the stalled feminist and civil rights agendas in the larger society, and recent eruptions of racist and sexist behavior on American campuses.

Such a beleaguered sensibility, combined with evidences of aggregate male danger and irresponsibility (high rates of violence against women, little change in indices of occupational segregation by sex, aggregate male failure to pay child support) enhance cultural feminist interpretations of women's common lot irrespective of their differences, and also encourage the presumption of female moral superiority upon which the construction of women's culture rests. Thus the tendency of women's culture writers to annex the construct of the heroic "triply oppressed" woman of color—which is of course the obverse of the hegemonic popular cultural vision of the feckless welfare-dependent, drug-taking black or Latina teenage mother.

This tendency to illogical inclusion has not gone uncriticized within feminism. Nancy Hewitt (1985) has incisively noted the ways in which scholars' accounts of nineteenth-century "women's culture" do not account for the realities of nineteenth-century black women's lives. Phyllis Palmer (1983) has criticized the tendency of white feminists to rely on the heroic images of such past black women activists as Sojourner Truth without acknowledging the financial gap, exacerbated by prevalent race endogamy, between black and white women today. And more impressionistic, "literary" women writers of color have indicted white feminists' race-blind inclusionary stance.


## DISCUSSION

American culture, contrary to the assumptions of *Habits of the Heart*, has historically abounded in visions of cumbered selves. Two of these, the white ethnic woman and women's culture, have salience and sufficient institutional impedimenta—books, journals, festivals, associations—to constitute full-blown invented traditions. How do these cultural constructs function today in the contested space of the national political arena?

White ethnic community, in the 1980s, is no longer a hot topic for academic papers and popular cultural accounts. Festivals and meetings of ethnic historical associations and social groups do not receive the public attention they once did. In Andy Warhol's phrase, white ethnicity had its fifteen minutes of fame in the mid-1970s, and other social groups and issues have since captured the public stage.

Nevertheless, the transformed construction of white ethnic community remains "on hold"—Bellah et al., for example, pay it lip service before hurrying on to their (presumably nonethnic) interviewees. To switch the metaphor back, white ethnic community stands backstage, ready to reenter stage left or right at a given cue. Recently, for example, a series of Democratic politicians have attempted to make use of notions of family, stability, and tradition now associated with white ethnicity to bolster their appeal to the electorate. This strategy backfired for Geraldine Ferraro, of course, when both her husband and son fell afoul of the law, but it has been quite successful to date for both Mario Cuomo and was one of the few winning elements of Michael Dukakis's ill-fared presidential campaign.

Women's culture, in contrast, is of more recent vintage and has never gained broad popular appeal, remaining an invented tradition in use only within sections of college and nonacademic feminist populations. Among this group, however, and despite intragroup criticism, militant belief makes up for small numbers. A steady stream of books reflecting women's culture or near–women's culture assumptions flows from the mainstream and alternative presses. In 1985, for example, St. Martin's published Elinor Lenz and Barbara Meyerhoff's *The Feminization of America*, which argued that "women's values" were taking over American culture and promised a "bright and peaceable future." In 1986, Basic Books published the multiple-authored *Women's Ways of Knowing*, which claimed that all women experienced male domination as "silencing" and thus perceived "male" schooling entirely differently from males and had unique modes of learning. In 1988, New Society Publishers brought out Pam McAllister's *You Can't Kill the Spirit*, which narrates "inspiring stories" of women's nonviolent action going back to "thirteenth-century-B.C. Egypt."

The most important political application of women's culture in the past decade, however, was feminist historian Rosalind Rosenberg's expert testimony on behalf of Sears Roebuck in the 1985 EEOC affirmative action case. Rosenberg argued that American women had established a separate women's culture in the nineteenth century based on nurturance and cooperation, and that commitment to those values has limited their desires and attempts to be competitive in the American labor market into the present. (Sears Roebuck won the case, although, it is argued, not on grounds of expert testimony.)[6]

Thus women's culture, which is based upon our inheritance of nineteenth-century constructions of moral motherhood, is vulnerable to a politics that reduces women to beings morally responsible for children and home and thus not worthy of equal treatment in the workplace. But as I have noted, both white ethnic community and women's culture are highly reliant on prior cultural constructs, most particularly those of the civil rights movement, and it is to the issue of Western historical constructs of the self and other that I now turn.

White ethnic community and women's culture share in common the claims of unjust oppression, moral superiority (to the oppressor group and/or others), and the possession of unique and valuable cultural heritage. These characteristics were borrowed from black cultural nationalism and ultimately from the history of modern nationalist movements. (A key distinction between nationalism and cultural nationalism is the absence of a claim to territory, except for such symbolic intrastate sovereignty claims as the Chicano renaming of the American Southwest as Aztlan or the creation of "women-only" spaces in concerts, demonstrations, bookstores, or houses.)

Modern nationalism, as Benedict Anderson (1983) notes, is an "invention of community" that, once constructed in a number of European states, provided a new ideological template which native elites in colonized and semicolonized Third World territories could borrow. The rise of European nationalism was a complex process involving multiple constructions of self and other: the nation versus other European states, versus Third World colonies, and national populations vis-à-vis one another. Most particularly, European (and later Third World) nationalisms relied—and still rely, to some extent—on constructed notions of national peasantries and on distinctive images of vulnerable national womanhood.

In European state after state, national enthusiasts discovered the unique characteristics of "their" countrypeople. The "folk" had particular customs of dress, food, dancing, and music that reflected specific national virtues and must be selected, documented, and if possible preserved. Thus the founding of the discipline of folklore—in journals such as Britain's *Notes and Queries*, collections such as the Brothers Grimm's *Kinder und Hausmarchen*, and in historical folk museums from Wales to central Europe to Greece—arose in concert with European nationalisms (Hobsbawm and Ranger 1983; Herzfeld 1987).

Women in this era were newly defined as more traditional ("priest-ridden" in the French Revolutionary rhetoric) than men. They were thus often seen as the most folk of the folk, natural, outside history in their housebound maternality, needing both the modernizing guidance and the preservationist protection of "their" men (Jordanova 1980; Bloch and Bloch 1980; Mosse 1985). This cultural phenomenon continued in the rhetoric and reality of Third World nationalisms: male nationalists in state after state determined that some female customs must be sacrificed for an appearance of modernity in tune with national aspirations while others, particularly those relating to women's wifely and maternal duties, must be preserved to embody national distinctiveness and worth (Jayawardena 1986).

Thus white ethnic community and women's culture stand in ironic relation to the historic crucible of modern nationalism. Their models of human social reality mimic the structures and characteristics of historic claims to national recognition and fealty. At the same time, their very subjects—the descendants of European peasants and "natural" womanhood—are constructs formed by that same historical process, and formed not for the purposes of peasant and female liberation but in the furtherance of male bourgeois and aristocratic political objectives.

Invented traditions, whether of nation, economy, race, neighborhood, family, or self, involve epochal thinking—constructed dichotomies of past and present—and notions of differentially moral self and other. *Habits of the Heart*'s unencumbered American selves are always in a *dialogue in absentia* with those whom they refuse consciously to acknowledge—and so are the book's authors. Thus their summary criticism of American culture also should stand as a self-criticism:

> We believe that much of the thinking about the self of educated Americans, thinking that has become almost hegemonic in our universities and much of the middle class, is based on inadequate social science, impoverished philosophy, and vacuous theology. There are truths we do not see when we adopt the language of radical individualism. We find ourselves not independently of other people and institutions but through them. We never get to the bottom of ourselves on our own. We discover who we are face to face and side by side with others in work, love and learning. (Bellah et al 1985:84)

Precisely. And thus we must consider the enormous impact of perceptions of social difference—by gender, race/ethnicity, and class, and by those above or below these lines of stratification—on American perceptions of self, other, past and present, and the meaning of social life. *Habits* listens to the soliloquies of white, middle-class, largely male actors, ignoring the other actors on the stage and the rest of the play. Addressing three key sets of questions about prevalent constructions of self and other helps to set the true partners in dialogue on the same stage and to sketch in the *mise en scène*.

The first question pertains simply to the verification of actual empirical realities. To what extent are the claims of invented traditions accurate? Upon what slender threads do they attempt to braid visions of social reality? We have seen the counterfactual claims of the white ethnic community and women's culture constructs, based, nevertheless, on the partial realities of temporary ethnic agglomerations in inner-city neighborhoods and on women's historic responsibilities for household and children.

The second inquiry is the Marxist Occam's razor: *cui bono*—who benefits? By whom and in whose interests are traditions invented? In some cases, such as the deliberate creation of national festivities and the manufacture of imperial traditions in British India, the author and the beneficiary are clear; but in many others, as we have seen with white ethnicity and women's culture, the tradition is actually a multiply constructed, highly contested symbolic space, and those who benefit may shift over time. In all cases, the question of material interest entails the inclusion of an analysis of the current political economy and social hierarchy and of the ways in which relevant social groups are embedded within them.

Finally, how do invented traditions under consideration rely upon or transform historical cultural constructs? All cultural production is parasitic upon the past, but very different pasts can be chosen for scavenging. Thus the intellectual genealogies of constructs, such as those I have attempted to sketch for white ethnic community and women's culture, can redound upon questions of empirical fact and of material interest. But structures them-selves—epochal thinking, morally weighted differential constructions of self and other—enforce their own tyrannies, and it is useful to investigate the ways in which they mold successive invented traditions. Of course, unbudg-ing political-economic realities, such as ongoing racial/ethnic economic strat-ification and gender-based social responsibilities and vulnerabilities to sex-ual violence, contribute to the tyrannizing potential of cognitive structures. The informant voices in *Habits of the Heart*, like those we hear in popular culture, and from Washington, D.C., and other centers of power, articulate visions of the self that are both provoked by such political-economic realities (the managerial self) and that attempt to disguise them (the therapeutic self). Our task is not to reproduce this pattern, not to invent new traditions, but to articulate the ideological and historical forces that joust to dominate our perceptions of ourselves as American—and of only particular kinds of Amer-icans as legitimate spokespeople, as authentic bearers of the meanings of authentic American selves, American community.

## NOTES

1. Individualism, of course, is a major strand in the history of Western political and social theory. See Macpherson (1962).

2. See di Leonardo (1984:129–135) for a more extensive critique of the commu-nity myth. (See also Persons 1987; Higham 1981; Handlin 1951.)

3. The following discussion relies on Evans (1979); Reed (1986); Miller (1987).

4. Reed (1988) lays out both the political-economic backdrop and black-and-white response schematically rendered in the following passage. (See also Shefter 1985; Fainstein 1987; Lieberson 1980; Brown 1988.)

5. See my extended discussion of women's culture, forthcoming. See also Echols's history of the devolution of radical feminism into cultural feminism (Echols 1989), unfortunately not yet in print when this paper went to press.

6. On the politics of this case, see Weiner (1985); Rosenberg (1986); Kessler-Harris (1986).

# References Cited

Adams, William Y.
    1977    *Nubia: Corridor to Africa*. Princeton: Princeton University Press.

Alberti, Georgio, and Enrique Mayer
    1974    Reciprocidad andina: ayer y hoy. In *Reciprocidad e intercambio en Los Andes peruanos*, ed. Giorgio Alberti and Enrique Mayer, 13–33. Lima: Instituto de Estudios Peruanos.

Alexander, Franz G., and Sheldon T. Selesnick
    1966    *The History of Psychiatry*. New York: Harper and Row.

Ali, Taisier, and Jay O'Brien
    1984    Labor, Community and Protest in Sudanese Agriculture. In *The Politics of Agriculture in Tropical Africa*, ed. Jonathan Barker, 205–238. Beverly Hills, Calif.: Sage.

'Allush, Naji
    1978    *Al-haraka al-wataniya al-Filastiniya 'amam al-yahud wa-al-sahyuniya 1882–1948* (The Palestinian national movement in the face of the Jews and Zionism 1882–1948). 2d printing. Beirut: Dar al-Tali'a.

Alonso, Ana Maria
    1988    The Effects of Truth: Re-presentations of the Past and the 'Imaging' of Community. *Journal of Historical Sociology* 1:33–57.

Alvarez, Elena
    1980    *Política agraria y estancamiento de la agricultura, 1969–1977*. Lima: Instituto de Estudios Peruanos.

    1983    *Política económica y agricultura en el Peru, 1969–1979*. Lima: Instituto de Estudios Peruanos.

Amin, Samir
    1976    *Unequal Development*. New York: Monthly Review Press.

Anderson, Benedict
    1983    *Imagined Communities: Reflections on the Origin and Spread of Nationalism*. London: Verso.

Anderson, Perry
    1977    The Antinomies of Antonio Gramsci. *New Left Review* 100:5–78.
Anonymous
    1876    *Algunas cuestiones sociales con motivo de los disturbios de Huancane.* Lima: J. M. Moterola.
Appleby, Gordon
    1976    The Role of Urban Food Needs in the Regional Development of Puno, Peru. In *Regional Analysis*, ed. Carol A. Smith, 1:147–178. New York: Academic Press.
    1978    Exploration and Its Aftermath: The Spatioeconomic Evolution of the Regional Marketing System in Highland Puno, Peru. Ph.D. diss., Anthropology Department, Stanford University.
    1980    Markets and the Marketing System in the Southern Sierra. Paper presented at the Symposium on Andean Peasant Economics and Pastoralism, Columbia, Mo.
Arkell, A. J.
    1961    *A History of the Sudan from the Earliest Times to 1821.* London: Athlone Press.
Arnon-Ohanna, Yuval
    1981    The Bands in the Palestinian Arab Revolt, 1936–39: Structure and Organization. *Asian and African Studies* 15:229–247.
Asad, Talal
    1970    *The Kababish Arabs.* London: C. Hurst.
    1987    Are There Histories of Peoples without Europe? *Comparative Studies in Society and History* 29:594–607.
Asad, Talal, ed.
    1973    *Anthropology and the Colonial Encounter.* London: Ithaca Press.
Ashrawi, Hanan Mikhail
    1978    The Contemporary Palestinian Poetry of Occupation. *Journal of Palestine Studies* 7(3):77–101.
Bakie, Margaret
    1983?    *Labrador Memories: Reflections at Mulligan.* Happy Valley, Labrador: Them Days Press. (Original 1917–18.)
Banton, Michael
    1970    The Concept of Racism. In *Race and Racialism*, ed. Sami Zubaida, 17–34. London: Tavistock Publications.
Barth, Fredrik, ed.
    1969    *Ethnic Groups and Boundaries: The Social Organization of Cultural Difference.* Boston: Little, Brown.
Bastien, Joseph
    1978    *Mountain of the Condor.* American Ethnological Society Monograph no. 64. St. Paul: West.
Bauer, Yehuda
    1966    The Arab Revolt of 1936. *New Outlook* 9(6):49–57; 9(7):21–28.
Beckett, J. W.
    1977    English Landownership in the Later Seventeenth and Eighteenth Centuries: The Debate and the Problems. *Economic History Review*, 2d ser., 30(4):567–581.

1982          The Decline of the Small Landowner in Eighteenth- and Nineteenth-
              Century England: Some Regional Considerations. *Agricultural History Re-
              view* 18:148–177.
Behar, Ruth
1986          *Santa Maria del Monte*. Princeton: Princeton University Press.
Beier, A. L.
1974          Vagrants and the Social Order in Elizabethan England. *Past and Present*
              (64):3–29.
Bejar, Hector
1970          *Peru 1965: Notes on a Guerrilla Experience*. New York: Monthly Review
              Press.
Belenky, Mary F., et al.
1986          *Women's Ways of Knowing*. New York: Basic Books.
Bellah, Robert N., Richard Madsen, William M. Sullivan, Ann Swidler, and Steven
Tipton
1985          *Habits of the Heart: Individualism and Commitment in American Life*. New
              York: Harper and Row.
Benjamin, Walter
1969          *Illuminations*. Ed. Hannah Arendt. Trans. Harry Zohn. New York:
              Schocken Books.
Benjelloun-Ollivier, Nadia
1983          Israel-Palestine: Le nombre et l'espace. *Herodote* 29/30:83–94.
Benvenisti, Meron
1983          *Israeli Censorship of Arab Publications*. New York: Fund for Free Expression.
1984          *The West Bank Data Project. A Survey of Israel's Policies*. Washington: Amer-
              ican Enterprise Institute.
1986          *1986 Report: Demographic, Economic, Legal, Social and Political Developments in
              the West Bank*. Boulder, Colo.: Westview Press.
Berkner, Lutz
1972          The Stem Family and the Developmental Cycle of the Peasant House-
              hold: An Eighteenth-Century Austrian Example. *American Historical Re-
              view* 77:398–418.
Bernard, Paul B.
1979          *The Limits of the Enlightenment: Joseph II and the Law*. Urbana: University of
              Illinois Press.
Bernstein, Henry
1979          African Peasantries: A Theoretical Framework. *Journal of Peasant Studies*
              6(4):421–443.
1990          Taking the Part of the Peasants? In *The Food Question*, ed. H. Bernstein,
              B. Crow, M. Mackintosh, and C. Martin. New York: Monthly Review
              Press.
Bhabha, Homi
1986          The Other Question: Difference, Discrimination, and the Discourse of
              Colonialism. In *Literature, Politics, and Theory*, ed. Francis Barker et al.,
              148–172. London: Methuen.
Bloch, Ernst
1968          *Über Karl Marx*. Frankfurt: Suhrkamp.

Bloch, Marc
1966      *French Rural History*. Berkeley and Los Angeles: University of California Press. (Original 1931.)
Bloch, Maurice
1975      Property and the End of Affinity. In *Marxist Analyses and Social Anthropology*, ed. M. Bloch, 203–222. London: Malaby.
Bloch, Maurice, and Jean L. Bloch
1980      Women and the Dialectics of Nature in Eighteenth-Century French Thought. In *Nature, Culture and Gender*, ed. Carol MacCormack and Marilyn Strathern, 25–41. Cambridge: Cambridge University Press.
Block, Fred, Richard A. Cloward, Barbara Ehrenreich, and Frances Fox Piven
1987      *The Mean Season: The Attack on the Welfare State*. New York: Pantheon.
Bloom, Allan
1988      *The Closing of the American Mind*. New York: Touchstone.
Blum, Jerome
1948      *Noble Landowners and Agriculture in Austria, 1815–1848*. Baltimore: Johns Hopkins University Press.
1981      English Parliamentary Enclosure. *Journal of Modern History* 53:477–504.
Bog, Ingomar
1969      Mercantilism in Germany. In *Revisions in Mercantilism*, ed. D. C. Coleman, 162–189. London: Methuen.
Bohannon, Paul, and George Dalton, eds.
1962      *Markets in Africa*. Evanston, Ill.: Northwestern University Press.
Bommes, Michael, and Patrick Wright
1982      Charms of Residence. In *Making Histories*, ed. Richard Johnson et al., 253–301. Minneapolis: University of Minnesota Press.
Bourricaud, François
1967      *Cambios en Puno*. Mexico City: Instituto Indigenista Interamericano.
Bradby, Barbara
1975      The Destruction of Natural Economy. *Economy and Society* 4:127–161.
1982      "Resistance to Capitalism" in the Peruvian Andes. In *Ecology and Exchange in the Andes*, ed. David Lehmann, 97–122. Cambridge: Cambridge University Press.
Brass, Tom
1983      Of Human Bondage: Campesinos, Coffee, and Capitalism on the Peruvian Frontier. *Journal of Peasant Studies* 11(1):76–88.
1985      Review of *Ecology and Exchange in the Andes*, ed David Lehmann, and *Capitalist Development and the Peasant Economy in Peru*, by Adolfo Figueroa. *Journal of Peasant Studies* 12(4):122–128.
Braudel, Fernand
1972      History and the Social Sciences. In *Economy and Society in Early Modern Europe: Essays from the Annales*, ed. Peter Burke, 11–42. New York: Harper and Row.
1984      *The Perspective of the World*. New York: Harper and Row.
Braun, Rudolf
1960      *Industrialisierung und Volksleben*. Stuttgart: Erlenbach-Zurich.

1975    Taxation, Sociopolitical Structure, and State-Building: Great Britain and Brandenburg-Prussia. In *The Formation of National States in Western Europe*, ed. C. Tilly, 243–327. Princeton: Princeton University Press.

Brenner, Robert

1976    Agrarian Class Structure and Economic Development in Pre-Industrial Europe. *Past and Present* (70):30–75.

1982    The Agrarian Roots of European Capitalism. *Past and Present* (97):16–113.

Brow, James

1990a    Notes on Community, Hegemony, and the Uses of the Past. *Anthropological Quarterly* 63:1–5.

1990b    The Incorporation of a Marginal Community within the Sinhalese Nation. *Anthropological Quarterly* 63:6–17.

Browman, David

1987    Pastoralism in Highland Peru and Bolivia. In *Arid Land Use Strategies and Risk Management in the Andes*, ed. David Browman, 121–150. Boulder, Colo.: Westview Press.

Brown, Michael

1988    The Segmented Welfare System: Distributive Conflict and Retrenchment in the United States, 1968–84. In *Remaking the Welfare State: Retrenchment and Social Policy in America and Europe*, ed. Michael Brown, 182–210. Philadelphia: Temple University Press.

Bruckmüller, Ernst

1984    *Nation Österreich*. Vienna: Bohlau.

Brunner, Otto

1968    Das 'ganze Haus' und die alteuropäische 'Ökonomik,' In *Neue Wege der Verfassungs- und Sozialgeschichte*, 2d ed., 103–127. Göttingen: Vandenhoeck und Ruprecht.

Bucher, Karl

1967    *Industrial Evolution*. New York: Burt Franklin. (Original 1900.)

Buci-Glucksman, Christine

1982    Hegemony and Consent. In *Approaches to Gramsci*, ed. Ann Showstack Sassoon, 116–126. London: Readers and Writers.

Buechler, Hans, and Judith M. Buechler

1971    *The Bolivian Aymara*. New York: Holt, Rinehart, and Winston.

Byres, T. J.

1979    Of Neo-Populist Pipedreams: Daedalus in the Third World and the Myth of Urban Bias. *Journal of Peasant Studies* 6(1):210–244.

Caballero, Jose Maria

1981    *Economía agraria de la sierra peruana antes de la reforma agraria de 1969*. Lima: Instituto de Estudios Peruanos.

1984    Agriculture and the Peasantry under Industrialization Pressures: Lessons from the Peruvian Experience. *Latin American Research Review* 19:3–41.

Cabral, Amilcar

1973    *Return to the Source*. New York: Monthly Review Press.

Caceres, Andres Avelino
  1973    *La guerra de 79: Sus campañas.* Lima: Editorial Milla Bartes.
Campbell, B. M. S.
  1980    Population Change and the Genesis of Commonfields on a Norfolk
          Manor. *Economic History Review,* 2d ser., 33(2):174–192.
  1981    The Regional Uniqueness of English Field Systems? Some Evidence
          from Eastern Norfolk. *Agricultural History Review* 29(1):16–28.
Campbell, Lydia
  1894–95 Sketches of Labrador Life by a Labrador Woman. Ed. Rev. A. C.
          Waghorne. *Evening Herald,* St. John's (Newfoundland) 3 December
          1894–6 February 1895.
Cartwright, George
  1792    *A Journal of Transactions and Events, during a Residence of Nearly Sixteen Years
          on the Coast of Labrador.* 3 vols. Newark: Notts.
Castro Pozo, Hildebrando
  1924    *Nuestra comunidad indigena.* Lima: n.p.
  1936    *Del ayllu al cooperativismo socialista.* Lima. P. Barrantes Castro.
Celati, Gianni
  1986    Thoughts of a Storyteller on a Happy Ending. *Granta* 18:14–16.
Chambers, J. D., and G. E. Mingay
  1966    *The Agricultural Revolution, 1750–1880.* New York: Schocken.
Chatterjee, Partha
  1986    *Nationalist Thought and the Colonial World—A Derivative Discourse.* London:
          Zed Press.
Chayanov, A. V.
  1966    *The Theory of Peasant Economy.* Homewood, Ill.: Richard Irwin. (Original
          1925.)
Chevalier, François
  1970    Official 'Indigenismo' in Peru in 1920: Origins, Significance, and
          Socioeconomic Scope. In *Race and Class in Latin America,* ed. Magnus
          Morner. New York: Columbia University Press.
Church, Jonathan T.
  1990    Confabulations of Community: The Hamefarins and Political Discourse
          on Shetland. *Anthropological Quarterly* 63:31–42.
Cole, Jeffrey A.
  1984    Viceregal Persistence versus Indian Mobility: The Impact of the Duque
          de la Palata's Reform Program in Alto Peru, 1681–1692. *Latin American
          Research Review* 19(1):37–56.
Coleman, D. C.
  1955–56 Labour in the English Economy of the Seventeenth Century. *Economic
          History Review,* 2d ser., 8:280–295.
Collins, Jane L.
  1984    The Maintenance of Peasant Coffee Production in a Peruvian Valley.
          *American Ethnologist* 11(3):413–438.
  1988    *Unseasonal Migrations: The Effects of Rural Labor Scarcity in Peru.* Princeton:
          Princeton University Press.

Collins, Robert O.
  1983    *Shadows in the Grass: Britain in the Southern Sudan, 1918–1956.* New Haven: Yale University Press.
Colson, Elizabeth
  1968    Contemporary Tribes and the Development of Nationalism. In *Essays on the Problem of the Tribe*, ed. June Helm, 201–206. Seattle: University of Washington Press.
Cooper, J. P.
  1967    The Social Division of Land and Men in England, 1436–1700. *Economic History Review*, 2d ser., 20(3):419–440.
Coquery-Vidrovitch, Catherine
  1978    Research on an African Mode of Production. In *Relations of Production*, ed. David Seddon, 261–288. London: Frank Cass.
Crain, Mary
  1990    The Social Construction of National Identity in Highland Ecuador. *Anthropological Quarterly* 63:43–59.
Crawford, O. G. S.
  1948    People without History. *Antiquity* 85:8–12.
  1951    *The Fung Kingdom of Sennar.* Gloucester: John Bellows.
Cunnison, Ian
  1966    *The Baggara Arabs.* Oxford: Clarendon Press.
da Matta, Roberto
  1986    Review of Chevalier and Taussig. *Social Analysis* 19:57–63.
Davies, E.
  1927    The Small Landowner 1780–1832, in the Light of the Land Tax Assessments. *Economic History Review*, o.s., 1:87–113.
Davies, W. H. A.
  1843    Notes on Esquimaux Bay and the Surrounding Country. *Transactions of the Literary and Historical Society of Quebec.*
de Certeau, Michel
  1986    *Heterologies.* Trans. Brian Massumi. Minneapolis: University of Minnesota Press.
Deere, Carman Diana, and Alain de Janvry
  1981    Demographic and Social Differentiation among Northern Peruvian Peasants. *Journal of Peasant Studies* 8(3):335–366.
Dew Edward
  1969    *Politics in the Altiplano: The Dynamics of Change in Rural Peru.* Austin: University of Texas Press.
di Leonardo, Micaela
  1984    *The Varieties of Ethnic Experience: Kinship, Class and Gender among California Italian-Americans.* Ithaca, N.Y.: Cornell University Press.
  1990    Women's Culture and its Discontents. In *The Politics of Culture*, ed. Brett Williams. Washington, D.C.: Smithsonian Institution Press.
Dodgshon, Robert
  1975    The Landholding Foundations of the Open-Field system. *Past and Present* (67):1–29.

Donham, Donald, and Wendy James, eds.
   1986     *The Southern Marches of Imperial Ethiopia*. Cambridge: Cambridge University Press.
Doughty, Paul L.
   1968     *Huaylas: An Andean District in Search of Progress*. Ithaca, N.Y.: Cornell University Press.
Dreitzel, Hans-Peter
   1968     *Die gesellschaftlichen Leiden und das Leiden an der Gesellschaft*. Stuttgart: Klett.
Duffield, Mark
   1979     Hausa and Fulani Settlement and the Development of Capitalism in Sudan. Ph.D. diss., Center of West African Studies, University of Birmingham.
   1981     *Maiurno: Capitalism and Rural Life in Sudan*. London: Ithaca.
   1983     Change among West African Settlers in Northern Sudan. *Review of African Political Economy* 26:45–59.
Dyer, Christopher
   1980     *Lords and Peasants in a Changing Economy*. Cambridge: Cambridge University Press.
Echols, Alice
   1989     *Daring to Be Bad: Radical Feminism in America, 1967–1975*. Minneapolis: University of Minnesota Press.
Elpeleg, Tsvi
   1978     The 1936–39 Disturbances: Riot or Rebellion? *The Wiener Library Bulletin* 45/46:40–51.
Elster, John
   1986     *An Introduction to Karl Marx*. Cambridge: Cambridge University Press.
Epstein, Bill
   1990     Counter-Intelligence, Cold War Criticism and Eighteenth Century Studies. *Elh* 57:63–99.
Epstein, Klaus
   1966     *The Genesis of German Conservatism*. Princeton: Princeton University Press.
Esculies Larrabure, Oscar, Marcial Rubio Correa, and Veronica Gonzales del Castillo
   1977     *Comercialización de alimentos*. Lima: Desco.
Evans, Sara
   1979     *Personal Politics: The Roots of Women's Liberation in the Civil Rights Movement and the New Left*. New York: Random House.
Everitt, Alan
   1966     Social Mobility in Early Modern England. *Past and Present* (33):56–73.
   1967     Farm Labourers. In *The Agrarian History of England and Wales*, vol. 4 (1500–1640), ed. Joan Thirsk. Cambridge: Cambridge University Press.
Fabian, Johannes
   1983     *Time and the Other: How Anthropology Makes Its Object*. New York: Columbia University Press.
Fainstein, Norman
   1987     The Underclass/Mismatch Hypothesis as an Explanation for Black Economic Deprivation. *Politics and Society* 4:1–29.

Figueroa, Adolfo
  1979    Política de precios agropecuarios e ingresos rurales en el Peru. *Allpanchis Phuturinga* 8:25–50.
  1982    Production and Market Exchange in Peasant Economies: The Case of the Southern Highlands in Peru. In *Ecology and Exchange in the Andes*, ed. David Lehmann, 122–156. Cambridge: Cambridge University Press.
  1984    *Capitalist Development and the Peasant Economy in Peru.* Cambridge: Cambridge University Press.
Fischer, Wolfram, and Peter Lundgreen
  1975    The Recruitment and Training of Administrative Personnel. In *The Formation of National States in Western Europe*, ed. Charles Tilly, 456–561. Princeton: Princeton University Press.
Fitzgerald, Frances
  1986    *Cities on a Hill.* New York: Simon and Schuster.
Fitzhugh, William W.
  1972    Environmental Archeology and Cultural Systems in Hamilton Inlet, Labrador. Smithsonian Contributions to Anthropology, no. 16. Washington, D.C.: Smithsonian Institution Press.
Flapan, Simcha
  1987    *The Birth of Israel: Myths and Realities.* New York: Pantheon.
Foucault, Michel
  1980    *Power/Knowledge.* Ed. Colin Gordon. New York: Pantheon Books.
  1989    Film and Popular Memory. In *Foucault Live*, 89–106. New York: Semiotext(e).
Frangi, Abdallah
  1983    *The PLO and Palestine.* Trans. Paul Knight. London: Zed Press.
Frank, Andre Gunder
  1969    Sociology of Development and Underdevelopment of Sociology. In *Latin America: Underdevelopment or Revolution*, 21–94. New York: Monthly Review Press.
  1978    *World Accumulation, 1492–1789.* New York: Monthly Review Press.
Freccero, John
  1986    Autobiography and Narrative. In *Reconstructing Individualism*, ed. Thomas C. Heller et al., 16–29. Stanford: Stanford University Press.
Freud, Sigmund
  1965    *The Interpretation of Dreams.* Trans. James Strachey. New York: Avon Books. (Original 1913.)
  1967    *Moses and Monotheism.* Trans. Katherine Jones. New York: Avon Books. (Original 1939.)
Friedmann, Harriet
  1980    Household Production and the National Economy: Concepts for the Analysis of Agrarian Formations. *Journal of Peasant Studies* 7(2):158–184.
Furani, Fathi
  1984    *Difa'an 'an al-judhur* (Defending the roots). Nazareth: Al-matba' al-sha'biyya.
Galeski, Boguslaw
  1972    *Basic Concepts of Rural Sociology.* Manchester: Manchester University Press.

Gallegos, Luis
    n.d.      *Wancho Lima*. Unpublished ms., files of Michael Painter.
Gambino, Richard
    1974      *Blood of My Blood: The Dilemma of the Italian-Americans*. New York: Anchor
              Books.
Gans, Herbert
    1962      *Urban Villagers: Group and Class in the Life of Italian-Americans*. New York:
              Free Press.
    1967      *The Levittowners: Ways of Life and Politics in a New Suburban Community*. New
              York: Random House.
al-Ghazali, Said
    1986      Bir Zeit Center Revives the Memory of Ein Houd. *Al-Fajr*, 28 Feb.
Gilligan, Carol
    1982      *In a Different Voice: Psychological Theory and Women's Development*. Cam-
              bridge, Mass.: Harvard University Press.
Ginat, Joseph
    1982      *Women in Muslim Rural Society*. New Brunswick, N.J.: Transaction Books.
Glazer, Nathan and Daniel Patrick Moynihan
    1970      *Beyond the Melting Pot: The Negroes, Puerto Ricans, Jews, Italians, and Irish of
              New York City*, 2nd ed. Cambridge, MA: MIT Press.
Glockner, Hermann
    1968      *Die europäische Philosophie von den Anfängen bis zur Gegenwart*. Stuttgart: Re-
              clam.
Golte, Jürgen, and Marisol de la Cadena
    1983      *La co-determinación de la reproducción social andina*. Lima: Instituto de Estu-
              dios Peruanos. Mimeographed.
Gonner, E. C. K.
    1912      *Common Land and Inclosure*. London: Macmillan.
Gonzalez, Michael J.
    1985      *Plantation Agriculture and Social Control in Northern Peru, 1875–1933*. Austin:
              University of Texas Press.
Gordon, Henry
    1974      *A Winter in Labrador*. In *By Great Waters*, ed. Peter Neary and Patrick
              O'Flaherty. Toronto: University of Toronto Press. (Original 1920.)
Gordon, Milton
    1964      *Assimilation in American Life: The Role of Race, Religion, and National Origins*.
              New York: Oxford University Press.
Goudie, Elizabeth
    1983      *Woman of Labrador*. Ed. David Zimmerly. Toronto: Book Society of
              Canada.
Graham-Brown, Sarah
    1983      The Economic Consequences of the Occupation. In *Occupation: Israel over
              Palestine*, ed. Naseer Aruri, 167–222. Belmont, Mass.: Association of
              Arab-American University Graduates.
    1984      *Education, Repression and Liberation: Palestinians*. London: World University
              Service (UK).
Gramsci, Antonio
    1971      *Selections from the Prison Notebooks*. Ed. Quintin Hoare. Trans. Geoffrey

Nowell Smith. New York: International Publishers. (Original 1929–35.)
1985   *Selections from Cultural Writings.* Trans. William Boelhower. Cambridge, Mass.: Harvard University Press.

Gregory, Chris
1986   On Taussig on Aristotle and Chevalier on Everyone. *Social Analysis* 19:64–69.

Gresh, Alain
1985   *The PLO: The Struggle Within.* Trans. A. M. Berrett. London: Zed Books.

Grüll, Georg
1955   *Weinberg: Die Enstehungsgeschichte einer Mühlviertler Wirtschaftscherrschaft.* Graz: Böhlau.
1957   Die Herrschaftsschichtungen in Österreich ob der Enns. *Mitteilungen des Oberösterreichischen Landearchivs* 5.

Gudmundson, Lowell
1986   *Costa Rica before Coffee: Society and Economy on the Eve of the Export Boom.* Baton Rouge: Louisiana State University Press.

Guha, Ranajit
1983   *Elementary Aspects of Peasant Insurgency in Colonial India.* Delhi: Oxford University Press.

Gumina, Deanna Paoli
1978   *The Italians of San Francisco, 1850–1930.* New York: Center for Migration Studies.

Gutman, Herbert
1976   *The Black Family in Slavery and Freedom, 1750–1825.* New York: Pantheon.
1977   *Work, Culture and Society in Industrializing America: Essays in American Working-Class and Social History.* New York: Random House.

Habakkuk, H. J.
1940   English Landownership, 1680–1740. *Economic History Review,* o.s., 10(1):2–17.
1965   La disparition du paysan anglais. *Annales: Economies, sociétés, civilisations.* 20(2):649–663.

Hall, Marjorie, and Bakhita Amin Ismail
1981   *Sisters under the Sun: The Story of Sudanese Women.* London: Longman.

Hall, Stuart, et al.
1977   Politics and Ideology: Gramsci. *Working Papers in Cultural Staudies* 10:45–76.
1979   Culture, the Media and the Ideological Effect. In *Mass Communication Society,* ed. James Curran et al., 315–348. Beverly Hills, Calif.: Sage Publications.
1980   Race, Articulation and Societies Structured in Dominance. In *Sociological Theories: Race and Colonialism,* 305–345. Paris: UNESCO Press.

Hamacher, Werner
1986   Disgregation of the Will: Nietzsche on the Individual and Individuality. In *Reconstructing Individualism,* ed. Thomas C. Heller et al., 106–139. Stanford: Stanford University Press.

Hammond, J. L., and Barbara Hammond
1970   *The Village Labourer, 1760–1832.* New York: Harper and Row. (Original 1911.)

Handlin, Oscar
1951    *The Uprooted.* Boston: Little, Brown.
Harris, Marvin
1964    *Patterns of Race in the Americas.* New York: W. W. Norton.
Harrison, Mark
1977    The Peasant Mode of Production in the Work of A. V. Chayanov. *Journal of Peasant Studies* 4(4):323–336.
1979    Chayanov and the Marxists. *Journal of Peasant Studies* 7(1):86–100.
Haya de la Torre, Victor Raul
1935    *¿Adonde va indoamérica?* Santiago: Ediciones Ercilla.
Hazen, Dan
1974    *The Awakening of Puno: Government Policy and the Indian Problem in Southern Peru, 1900–1955.* PhD Thesis, Department of History, Yale University.
Heidegger, Martin
1971    *Poetry, Language, Thought.* Trans. Albert Hofstadter. New York: Harper and Row.
Herzfeld, Michael
1987    *Ours Once More: Folklore, Ideology and the Making of Modern Greece.* New York: Pella Publications.
Hewitt, Nancy
1985    Beyond the Search for Sisterhood: American Women's History in the 1980s. *Social History* 10(1):299–321.
Hickman, John M.
1963    The Aymara of Chinchera, Peru: Persistence and Change in a Bicultural Context. Ph.D. diss., Anthropology Department, Cornell University, Ithaca, N.Y.
Hickman, John M., and William T. Stuart
1977    Descent, Alliance, and Moiety in Chucuito, Peru: An Explanatory Sketch of Aymara Social Organization. In *Andean Kinship and Marriage*, ed. Ralph Bolton and Enrique Mayer, 43–59. Washington, D.C.: American Anthropological Association.
Higham, John
1981    *Strangers in the Land: Patterns of American Nativism, 1860–1925.* New York: Atheneum.
Hill, Polly
1972    *Rural Hausa.* Cambridge: Cambridge University Press.
1977    *Population, Prosperity, and Poverty.* Cambridge: Cambridge University Press.
Hilton, R. H.
1954    Medieval Agrarian History. In *Victoria County History, Leicestershire* 2:145–198.
1973    *Bond Men Made Free.* New York: Viking.
Hintze, Otto
1975    *The Historical Essays of Otto Hintze.* Ed. Felix Gilbert. New York: Oxford University Press.
Hobsbawn, E. J.
1964    Custom, Wages, and Work-load. In *Labouring Men*, 344–370. New York: Basic Books.

1973    Peasants and Politics. *Journal of Peasant Studies* 1(1):3–22.
1974    Peasant Land Occupations. *Past and Present* (62):120–152.
Hobsbawn, E. J., and Terence Ranger, eds.
1983    *The Invention of Tradition.* Cambridge: Cambridge University Press.
Hoffman, Richard C.
1975    Medieval Origins of the Common Fields. In *European Peasants and Their Markets*, ed. William Parker and Eric Jones, 23–71. Princeton: Princeton University Press.
Hoffmann, Alfred
1952    *Werden, Wachsen, Reifen.* Vol. 1 of *Wirtschaftsgeschichte des Landes Oberösterreich*, ed. Vinzenz Kotzina. Salzburg: Müller.
Hohberg, Wolfgang Helmhard von
1715    *Georgica Curiosa Aucta.* 5th ed. Nuremberg: Endters.
Holt, P. M.
1965a   *The Study of Modern Arab History.* London: School of Oriental and African Studies.
1965b   Fundj. In *The Encyclopaedia of Islam*, ed. Bernard Lewis et al., 2d ed., 2:943–945. Leiden: Brill.
1966    *A Modern History of the Sudan.* New York: Praeger.
1970    The Nilotic Sudan. In *The Cambridge History of Islam*, ed. P. M. Holt et al., 2:327–344. Cambridge: Cambridge University Press.
1973    *Studies in the History of the Near East.* London: Frank Cass.
1975    Egypt, the Funj and Darfur. In *The Cambridge History of Africa*, ed. Richard Gray, 4:14–57. Cambridge: Cambridge University Press.
1986    A Muslim Monarchy. *Journal of African History* 27(3):565–566.
Holt, P. M., and M. W. Daly
1979    *The History of the Sudan from the Coming of Islam to the Present Day.* 3d ed. Boulder, Colo.: Westview Press.
1988    *The History of the Sudan from the Coming of Islam to the Present Day.* 4th ed. London: Longman.
Homans, George C.
1953    The Rural Sociology of Medieval England. *Past and Present* (4):32–43.
Hörnigk, Philipp Wilhelm von
1964    *Österreich über alles, wenn (wann) es nur will.* Ed. Gustav Otruba. Vienna: Bergland.
Hoskins, W. G.
1950    The Leicestershire Farmer in the Sixteenth Century. In *Essays in Leicestershire History*, 123–183. Liverpool: Liverpool University Press.
1951    The Leicestershire Farmer in the Seventeenth Century. *Agricultural History* 25:10–20.
1957    *The Midland Peasant.* London: Macmillan.
Howell, Ciceley
1983    *Land, Family and Inheritance in Transition.* Cambridge: Cambridge University Press.
Huizinga, Johan
1934    *The Waning of the Middle Ages.* London: Edward Arnold.
Humphreys, S. C.
1983    *Anthropology and the Greeks.* London: Routledge & Kegan Paul.

Isbell, Billie Jean
   1978    *To Defend Ourselves: Ecology and Ritual in an Andean Village.* Austin: University of Texas Press.
Jackson, H. C.
   1912    *Tooth of Fire.* Oxford: B. H. Blackwell.
Jacoby, Russell
   1987    *The Last Intellectuals: American Culture in the Age of Academe.* New York: Basic Books.
Janik, Allan, and Stephen Toulmin
   1973    *Wittgenstein's Vienna.* New York: Simon and Schuster.
Jay, Martin
   1988    Mass Culture and Aesthetic Redemption: The Debate between Max Horkheimer and Siegfried Kracauer. In *Fin de Siècle Socialism and Other Essays,* 82–94. New York: Routledge.
Jayawardena, Kumari
   1986    *Feminism and Nationalism in the Third World.* London: Zed Press.
Jenks, William A.
   1976    *Vienna and the Young Hitler.* New York: Octagon.
Jiryis, Sabri
   1976    *The Arabs in Israel.* Trans. Anaed Bushnaq. New York: Monthly Review Press.
Johnson, Arthur Henry
   1909    *The Disappearance of the Small Landowner.* Oxford: Clarendon Press.
Johnston, William
   1981    Cultural Criticism as a Neglected Topic in Austrian Studies. In *Austrian Philosophy: Studies and Texts,* ed. J. C. Nyiri, 31–42. Munich: Philosophia.
Jordanova, L. J.
   1980    Natural Facts: A Historical Perspective on Science and Sexuality. In *Nature, Culture and Gender,* ed. Carol MacCormack and Marilyn Strathern, 42–69. Cambridge: Cambridge University Press.
Junek, Oscar
   1937    *Isolated Communities: A Study of a Labrador Fishing Village.* New York: American Book Co.
Justi, J. H. G. von
   1758    *Staatswirthschaft.* Leipzig: Breitkopf.
Kahn, Joel
   1980    *Miñangkabau Social Formations: Indonesian Peasants and the World-Economy.* Cambridge: Cambridge University Press.
   1981    Marxist Anthropology and Segmented Societies: A Review of the Literature. In *The Anthropology of Pre-Capitalist Societies,* ed. J. Kahn and J. Llobera, 57–88. London: Macmillan.
Kann, Robert A.
   1960    *A Study in Austrian Intellectual History: From Late Baroque to Romanticism.* New York: Praeger.
Kaplan, Temma
   1982    Female Consciousness and Collective Action: The Case of Barcelona, 1910–1918. *Signs* 7(3):545–566.

Kayyali, A. W.
1978    *Palestine: A Modern History.* London: Croom Helm.
Kellenbenz, Hermann
1965    Rural Industries in the West: From the End of the Middle Ages to the 18th Century. In *Essays in European Economic History*, ed. Peter Earle, 45–88. Oxford: Oxford University Press.
Kennedy, Susan Estabrook
1979    *If All We Did Was Weep at Home: A History of White Working-Class Women in America.* Bloomington: Indiana University Press.
Kerridge, Eric
1968    *The Agricultural Revolution.* New York: Augustus M. Kelley.
1969    *Agrarian Problems of the Sixteenth Century and After.* London: George Allen and Unwin.
Kessler-Harris, Alice
1986    Equal Employment Opportunity Commission vs. Sears Roebuck and Company: A Personal Account. *Radical History Review* 35 (April):57–79.
Khalili, Ali
1980    Palestinian Folklore. *Al-Fajr*, 11 May.
Kitching, Gavin
1983    *Development and Underdevelopment in Historical Perspective: Populism, Nationalism and Industrialisation.* London: Methuen.
Klein, Herbert S.
1982    *Bolivia, The Evolution of a Multi-Ethnic Society.* New York: Oxford University Press
Kocke, Jasper
1979    Some Early German Contributions to Economic Anthropology. *Research in Economic Anthropology* 2:119–167.
Komarovsky, Mirra
1962    *Blue Collar Marriage.* New York: Vintage.
Kondylis, Panajotis
1987    *Marx und die griechische Antike: Zwei Studien.* Heidelberg: Manutius.
Kracauer, Siegfried
1966    Time and History. In *History and the Concept of Time*, 65–78. *History and Theory*, Beiheft 6.
Kraemer, Horst
1974    *Der deutsche Kleinstaat des 17. Jahrhunderts im Spiegel von Seckendorffs' Teutschem Fürstenstaat.* Darmstadt: Wissenschaftliche Buchgesellschaft.
Kriedte, Peter
1983    *Peasants, Landlords and Merchant Capitalists: Europe and the World Economy, 1500–1800.* Cambridge: Cambridge University Press.
Krieger, Leonard
1972    *The German Idea of Freedom: History of a Political Tradition.* Chicago: University of Chicago Press.
Kuczynski-Godard, Maximo
1945    *Estudios medico-sociales en las minas de Puno con anotaciones sobre las migraciones indigenas.* Lima.
Lacan, Jacques
1981    *The Four Fundamental Concepts of Psychoanalysis.* New York: W. W. Norton.

LaCapra, Dominick
1985    *History and Criticism*. Ithaca, N.Y.: Cornell University Press.
Lacey, W. K.
1968    *The Family in Classical Greece*. Ithaca, N.Y.: Cornell University Press.
Lachman, Shai
1982    Arab Rebellion and Terrorism in Palestine 1929–39: The Case of Sheikh Izz al-Din al-Qassam and His Movement. In *Zionism and Arabism in Palestine and Israel*, ed. Elie Kedourie and Sylvia G. Haim, 52–99. London: Frank Cass.
Laclau, Ernesto
1977    *Politics and Ideology in Marxist Theory*. London: New Left Books.
Larson, Brooke
1988    *Colonialism and Agrarian Transformation in Bolivia: Cochabamba, 1550–1900*. Princeton: Princeton University Press.
Layoun, Mary N.
1988    Fictional Formations and Deformations of National Culture. *South Atlantic Quarterly* 87(1):53–73.
Lazarsfeld, Paul
1983    Die Psychologie in Hendrik de Mans Marxkritik. In *Austromarxistische Positionen*, ed. Gerald Mozetic, 421–427. Vienna: Böhlau.
Lears, Jackson
1985    The Concept of Cultural Hegemony. *American Historical Review* 90:567–593.
Lenin, V. I.
1974    *The Development of Capitalism in Russia*. Moscow: Progress Publishers.
Lennihan, Louise
1982    Rights in Men and Rights in Land. *Slavery and Abolition* 3(2):113–121.
1983    The Origins and Development of Agricultural Wage Labor in Northern Nigeria. Ph.D. diss., Department of Anthropology, Columbia University.
1986    Agricultural Wage Labor in Northern Nigeria. In *State and Agriculture in Nigeria*, ed. M. Watts. Berkeley, Los Angeles, London: University of California Press.
1988    Wages of Change: The Unseen Transition in Northern Nigerian Agriculture. *Human Organization* 47(2):119–126.
Lenz, Elinor, and Barbara Meyerhoff
1985    *The Feminization of America*. New York: St. Martin's Press.
Lerner, Gerda
1980    Politics and Culture in Women's History: A Symposium. *Feminist Studies* 6(1):26–64.
Levine, Lawrence
1977    *Black Culture and Black Consciousness: Afro-American Folk Thought from Slavery to Freedom*. New York: Oxford University Press.
Levy, Frank
1988    *Dollars and Dreams: The Changing American Income Distribution*. New York: W. W. Norton.
Lewellen, Ted.
1978    *Peasants in Transition: The Changing Economy of the Peruvian Aymara: General Systems Approach*. Boulder, Colo.: Westview Press.

Lieberson, Stanley
1988    *Dollars and Dreams: The Changing American Income Distribution.* New York: W. W. Norton.
Lewellen, Ted.
1978    *Peasants in Transition: The Changing Economy of the Peruvian Aymara: General Systems Approach.* Boulder, Colo.: Westview Press.
Liberson, Stanley
1980    *A Piece of the Pie: Blacks and White Immigrants since 1880.* Berkeley, Los Angeles, London: University of California Press.
Lloyd-Jones, Hugh
1983    *The Justice of Zeus.* Berkeley, Los Angeles, London: University of California Press.
Lofgren, Orvar
1984    Family and Household: Image and Realities: Cultural Change in Swedish Society. In *Households: Comparative and Historical Studies of the Domestic Group*, ed. Robert M. Netting, Richard R. Wilk, and Eric Arnould, 446–469. Berkeley, Los Angeles, London: University of California Press.
Lomnitz, Claudio
1987    Cultural Relations in Regional Spaces: An Exploration in Theory and Method for the Study of National Culture in Mexico. Ph.D. diss., Anthropology Department, Stanford University.
Long, Norman, and Bryan Roberts, eds.
1978    *Peasant Cooperation and Capitalist Expansion in Peru.* Institute of Latin American Studies. Austin: University of Texas Press.
1984    *Miners, Peasants and Entrepreneurs: Regional Development in the Central Highlands of Peru.* Cambridge Latin American Studies, 48. Cambridge: Cambridge University Press.
Luedtke, Alf
1985    Organizational Order or *Eigensinn*? Workers' Privacy and Workers' Politics in Imperial Germany. In *Rites of Power: Symbolism, Ritual, and Politics since the Middle Ages*, ed. Sean Wilentz, 303–333. Philadelphia: University of Pennsylvania Press.
Luhmann, Niklas
1986    The Individuality of the Individual: Historical Meanings and Contemporary Problems. In *Reconstructing Individualism*, ed. Thomas C. Heller et al., 313–325. Stanford: Stanford University Press.
McAllister, Pam
1988    *You Can't Kill the Spirit.* Philadelphia: New Society Publishers.
McCloskey, Donald
1975    The Economics of Enclosure: A Market Analysis. In *European Peasants and Their Markets*, ed. William Parker and Eric Jones, 123–176. Princeton: Princeton University Press.
McEachern, Charmaine, and Peter Mayer
1986    The Children of Bronze and the Children of Gold: The Apolitical Anthropology of the Peasant. *Social Analysis* 19:70–77.
Macfarlane, Alan
1978    *The Origins of English Individualism.* Cambridge: Cambridge University Press.

MacGaffey, Wyatt.
  1966      Concepts of Race in the Historiography of Northeast Africa. *Journal of African History* 7(1):1–17.
Macherey, Pierre
  1978      *A Theory of Literary Production.* Trans. Geoffrey Wall. London: Routledge & Kegan Paul.
Mack, John, and Peter Robershaw, eds.
  1982      *Culture History in the Southern Sudan: Archaeology, Linguistics and Ethnohistory.* Nairobi: British Institute in Eastern Africa.
MacMichael, H. A.
  1912      *The Tribes of Northern and Central Kordofan.* Cambridge: Cambridge University Press.
  1922      *A History of the Arabs in the Sudan.* 2 vols. Cambridge: Cambridge University Press.
  1934      *The Anglo-Egyptian Sudan.* London: Faber and Faber.
  1954      *The Sudan.* London: Benn.
Macpherson, C. B.
  1962      *The Political Theory of Possessive Individualism.* New York: Oxford University Press.
Malcolm, Janet
  1982      *Psychoanalysis: The Impossible Profession.* New York: Vintage.
Manrique, Nelson
  1981      *Las guerrillas indígenas en la guerra con Chile.* Lima: Centro de Investigación y Capacitación; Editora Ital Peru.
Marcus, George, and Dick Cushman
  1982      Ethnographies as Texts. *Annual Review of Anthropology* (11):29–69.
Marcus, George, and Michael Fischer
  1986      *Anthropology as Cultural Critique.* Chicago: University of Chicago Press.
Mariátegui, Jose Carlos
  1928      *Siete ensayos de interpretacion de la realidad peruana.* Lima: Ediciones Amauta.
Martinez, Hector
  1969      *Las migraciones altiplanicas y la colonización del Tambopata.* Lima: Centro de Estudios de Población y Desarrollo.
  1980      Las empresas asociativas agrícolas peruanas. In *Realidad del campo Peruano después de la reforma agraria,* 105–153. Lima: Centro de Investigación y Capacitación; Editora Ital Peru.
Marx, Karl
  1967      *Capital.* Vol. 1. New York: International Publishers. (Original 1867.)
  1973      *Grundrisse.* New York: Vintage. (Original 1857–58.)
  1974      The Eighteenth Brumaire of Louis Bonaparte. In *Surveys from Exile,* ed. David Fernbach, 143–249. New York: Vintage. (Original 1852.)
  1977      *Capital.* Vol. 1. New York: Vintage. (Original 1867.)
Marx, Karl, and Frederick Engels
  1970      *The German Ideology.* New York: International. (Original 1846.)
Mathias, Peter, and Patrick O'Brien
  1976      Taxation in Britain and France, 1715–1810: A Comparison of the Social and Economic Incidence of Taxes Collected from the Central Government. *Journal of European Economic History* 5:601–650.

Medick, Hans
1981    The Proto-Industrial Family Economy. In Peter Kriedte, Hans Medick, and Jürgen Schlumbohm, *Industrialization before Industrialization*, 36–73. Cambridge: Cambridge University Press.

Miller, James
1987    *Democracy Is in the Streets: From Port Huron to the Siege of Chicago.* New York: Simon and Schuster.

Mingay, G. E.
1963    *English Landed Society in the Eighteenth Century.* London: Routledge & Kegan Paul.
1968    *Enclosure and the Small Farmer in the Age of the Industrial Revolution.* London: Macmillan.

Mitterauer, Michael
n.d.    Lebensformen und Lebensverhältnisse ländlicher Unterschichten. Typescript, Institut für Wirtschafts- und Sozialgeschichte, University of Vienna.
1982    Auswirkungen der Agrarrevolution auf die bäurliche Familienstruktur in Österreich. In *Historische Familienforschung*, ed. M. Mitterauer and R. Sieder, 241–270. Frankfurt: Suhrkamp.

Moore, Barrington
1966    *The Social Origins of Dictatorship and Democracy.* Boston: Beacon.

Mortimore, M. J., and J. Wilson
1965    *Land and People in the Kano Closed-Settled Zone.* Zaria, Nigeria: Department of Geography, Ahmadu Bello University.

Morton, Geoffrey
1957    *Just the Job.* London: Hodder and Stoughton.

Moschkovich, Judith
1981    —But I Know You, American Woman. In *This Bridge Called My Back: Writings by Radical Women of Color*, ed. Cherrie Moraga and Gloria Anzaldua, 79–84. Watertown, Mass.: Persephone Press.

Mosse, George L.
1985    *Nationalism and Sexuality: Middle-Class Morality and Sexual Norms in Modern Europe.* Madison: University of Wisconsin Press.

Mouffe, Chantal
1981    Hegemony and the Integral State in Gramsci: Towards a New Concept of Politics. In *Silver Linings*, ed. George Bridges and Rosalind Brunt, 167–187. London: Lawrence and Wishart.

Müller, Jan-Dirk
1982    *Gedechtnus: Literatur und Hofgesellschaft um Maximilian I.* Munich: Wilhelm Fink.

Murra, John
1972    El control vertical de un máximo de pisos ecológicos en la economía de las sociedades andinas. In *Visita hecha a la Provincia de Leon de Huanuco de Inigo de Ortiz de Zuniga en 1562*, ed. John Murra, 429–476. Huanuco, Peru: Universidad Nacional Hermilio Valdizan.

Murra, John V., and Nathan Wachtel
1986    Introduction. In *Anthropological History of Andean Polities*, ed. John V. Murra, Nathan Wachtel, and Jacques Revel, 1–8. Cambridge: Cambridge University Press.

Nairn, Tom
1981    *The Break-up of Britain.* 2d ed. London: Verso.
Nash, June
1979    *We Eat the Mines and the Mines Eat Us.* New York: Columbia University Press.
Naujoks, Eberhard
1958    *Obrigkeitsgedanke, Zunftverfassung, und Reformation.* Stuttgart: Kohlhammer.
Newsome, Linda A.
1985    Indian Population Patterns in Colonial Spanish America. *Latin American Research Review* 20(3):41–74.
Nicholas, David M.
1970    New Paths of Social History and Old Paths of Historical Romanticism. *Journal of Modern History* 3.
Nietzsche, Friedrich
1969    *On the Genealogy of Morals; Ecce Homo.* Trans. Walter Kaufmann. New York: Vintage Books.
Norman, David W.
1972    *An Economic Study of Three Villages in Zaria Province: Land and Labour Relationships.* Samaru Miscellaneous Paper, 9. Samaru, Nigeria: Institute of Agricultural Research.
Novak, Michael
1971    *The Rise of the Unmeltable Ethnics: Politics and Culture in the Seventies.* New York: Macmillan.
O'Brien, J.
1980    Agricultural Labor and Development in Sudan. Ph.D. diss., Anthropology Department, University of Connecticut.
1983    The Formation of the Agricultural Labor Force in Sudan. *Review of African Political Economy* 26:15–34.
1984    The Political Economy of Semi-proletarianisation under Colonialism: Sudan 1925–50. In *Proletarianisation in the Third World*, ed. Barry Munslow and Henry Finch, 121–147. London: Croom Helm.
Oestreich, Gerhard
1982    *Neostoicism and the Early Modern State.* Cambridge: Cambridge University Press.
Orlove, Benjamin S.
1977    *Alpacas, Sheep, and Men.* New York: Academic Press.
1978    Systems of Production and Indian Peasant Insurrections: A General Discussion of Three Specific Cases. In *Actes du XLIIe Congrès international des américanistes*, vol. 3. Paris: Société des américanistes.
Ortner, Sherry
1984    Anthropological Theory since the Sixties. *Comparative Studies in Society and History* 26(1):126–166.
Paas, Margaret White
1981    *Population Change, Labor Supply, and Agriculture in Augsburg, 1480–1618.* New York: Arno.
Painter, Michael
1981    The Political Economy of Food Production: An Example of an Aymara-

speaking Region of Peru. Ph.D. diss., Anthropology Department, University of Florida, Gainesville.

1983    The Political Economy of Food Production in Peru. *Studies in Comparative International Development* 18(4):34–52.

1986    The Value of Peasant Labour Power in a Prolonged Transition to Capitalism. *Journal of Peasant Studies* 13(4):221–239.

Palmer, Phyllis
1983    White Women/Black Women: The Dualism of Female Identity and Experience in the United States. *Feminist Studies* 9(1):151–170.

Parmentier, Barbara
1984    Toward a Geography of Home: Palestinian Literature and the Sense of Place. M.A. thesis, Department of Geography, University of Texas at Austin.

Parry, J. H.
1963    *The Age of Discovery*. Cleveland and New York: World Publishing.

Persons, Stow
1987    *Ethnic Studies at Chicago, 1905–45*. Urbana: University of Illinois Press.

Peters, Joan
1984    *From Time Immemorial*. New York: Harper and Row.

Piven, Frances, and Richard A. Cloward
1982    *The New Class War: Reagan's Attack on the Welfare State and Its Consequences*. New York: Pantheon Books.

Platt, Tristan
1982    The Role of the Andean "Ayllu" in the Reproduction of the Petty Commodity Regime in Northern Potosi (Bolivia). In *Ecology and Exchange in the Andes*, ed. David Lehmann, 27–69. Cambridge: Cambridge University Press.

1986    Mirrors and Maize: Concept of "Yanantin" among the Macha of Bolivia. In *Anthropological History of Andean Polities*, ed. John V. Murra, Nathan Wachtel, and Jacques Revel, 229–259. Cambridge: Cambridge University Press.

Polanyi, Karl
1944    *The Great Transformation*. Boston: Beacon.

Polier, Nicole, and William Roseberry
1989    Tristes Tropes: Post-Modern Anthropologists Encounter the Other and Discover Themselves. *Economy and Society* 18(2):245–264.

Popular Memory Group
1982    Popular Memory: Theory, Politics, Method. In *Making Histories*, ed. Richard Johnson et al., 205–252. Minneapolis: University of Minnesota Press.

Porath, Yehoshua
1974    *The Emergence of the Palestinian Arab National Movement, 1918–1929*. London: Frank Cass.

1977    *The Palestinian Arab National Movement: From Riots to Rebellion*. London: Frank Cass.

Post, Ken
1986    Can One Have an Historical Anthropology? Some Reactions to Taussig and Chevalier. *Social Analysis* 19:78–84.

Poulantzas, Nicos
   1980      *State, Power, Socialism.* Trans. Patrick Camiller. London: New Left Books.
Pribram, Karl
   1983      *A History of Economic Reasoning.* Baltimore: Johns Hopkins University Press.
Raeff, Marc
   1983      *The Well-Ordered Police State: Social and Institutional Change through Law in the Germanies and Russia, 1600–1800.* New Haven: Yale University Press.
Rainwater, Lee, et al.
   1959      *Workingman's Wife: Her Personality, World and Life Style.* New York: Ayer Company.
Rebel, Hermann
   1983      *Peasant Classes: The Bureaucratization of Property and Family Relations under Early Habsburg Absolutism, 1511–1636.* Princeton: Princeton University Press.
   1988      Why Not "Old Marie" . . . or Someone Very Much Like Her? A Reassessment of the Question about the Grimms' Contributors from a Social Historical Perspective. *Social History* 13:1–24.
   1989      Cultural Hegemony and Class Experience: A Critical Reading of Recent Ethnological-Historical Approaches. *American Ethnologist* 16:117–136, 350–365.
Reddy, William
   1984      *The Rise of Market Culture: The Textile Trade and French Society, 1750–1900.* New York: Cambridge University Press.
Reed, Adolph L., Jr.
   1988a     The Black Urban Regime: Structural Origins and Constraints. *Comparative Urban and Community Research* 1.
   1988b     The Liberal Technocrat: Review of William Julius Wilson's *The Truly Disadvantaged. The Nation,* 6 February.
Reed, Adolph, Jr., ed.
   1986      *Race, Politics, and Culture: Critical Essays on the Radicalism of the 1960s.* New York: Greenwood Press.
Relaciones Geográficas de Indias
   1965      Información sobre las minas de Carabuco. In *Relaciones Geográficas de Indias—Peru,* vol. 2. Madrid: Altas. (Original 1572).
Rénique, Jose Luis
   1987      Estado, partidos políticos y lucha por la tierra en Puno. *Debate Agrario* 1(1):55–76.
Rich, Adrienne
   1980      Compulsory Heterosexuality and the Lesbian Existence. *Signs* 5(4):631–660.
Riesman, David
   1950      *The Lonely Crowd.* New Haven: Yale University Press.
Röd, Wolfgang
   1974      *Dialektische Philosophie der Neuzeit.* Vol. 1. Munich: Beck.
Rodinson, Maxime
   1973      *Israel: A Colonial Settler State?* Trans. David Thorstad. New York: Monad Press.

Rondinelli, Dennis A.
1981    Administrative Decentralization and Economic Development: The Sudan's Experiment with Devolution. *Journal of Modern African Studies* 19(4):595–624.

Rosaldo, Renato
1989    "Imperialist Nostalgia." In *Culture and Truth*. Boston: Beacon.

Rose, Gillian
1984    *Dialectic of Nihilism: Post-Structuralism and Law*. Oxford: Basil Blackwell.

Roseberry, William
1983    *Coffee and Capitalism in the Venezuelan Andes*. Austin: University of Texas Press.
1986    The Ideology of Domestic Production. *Labour, Capital and Society* 19:70–93.
1988    Domestic Modes, Domesticated Models. *Journal of Historical Sociology* 1(4):423–430.
1989    *Anthropologies and Histories: Essays in Culture, History, and Political Economy*. New Brunswick, N.J.: Rutgers University Press.

Rosenberg, Hans
1966    *Bureaucracy, Aristocracy, and Autocracy: The Prussian Experience, 1660–1815*. Boston: Beacon.
1967    *Grosse Depression und Bismarckzeit: Wirtschaftsablauf, Gesellschaft und Politik in Mitteleuropa*. Berlin: Walter de Gruyter.

Rosenberg, Rosalind
1986    What Harms Women in the Workplace. *New York Times*, 27 February.

Sabean, David
1972    *Landbesitz und Gesellschaft am Vorabend des Bauernkriegs*. Stuttgart: Fischer.
1984    *Power in the Blood: Popular Culture and Village Discourse in Early Modern Germany*. New York: Cambridge University Press.

Sahlins, Marshall
1972    *Stone Age Economics*. Chicago: Aldine.

Said, Edward W.
1978    *Orientalism*. New York: Vintage Books.
1979    *The Question of Palestine*. New York: Times Books.
1981    *Covering Islam*. New York: Pantheon Books.
1984    Permission to Narrate. *Journal of Palestine Studies* 13(3):27–48.
1986    *After the Last Sky*. New York: Pantheon.

Saignes, Thierry
1978    De la filiation à la residence: Les ethnies dans les vallées de Larecaja. *Annales: Economies, sociétés, civilisations* 33:1160–1181.

Salomon, Frank
1982    Andean Ethnology in the 1970s: A Retrospective. *Latin American Research Review* 17(2):75–128.

Sanbar, Elias
1984    *Palestine 1948: L'expulsion*. Paris: Revue d'études palestiniennes.

Sanchez-Albornoz, Nicolas
1978    *Indios y Tributos en el Alto Peru*. Lima: Instituto de Estudios Peruanos.

Sanchez, Rodrigo
1982    The Andean Economic System and Capitalism. In *Ecology and Exchange in*

*the Andes*, ed. David Lehmann, 157–190. Cambridge: Cambridge University Press.

Sayers, Janet
  1982    *Biological Politics*: *Feminist and Antifeminist Perspectives*. New York: Tavistock.

Sayigh, Rosemary
  1979    *Palestinians*: *From Peasants to Revolutionaries*. London: Zed Press.

Schaedel, Richard P.
  1967    *La demografía y los recursos humanos del sur del Peru*. Mexico City: Instituto Indigenista Interamericano.

Schorske, Carl
  1980    *Fin-de-Siècle Vienna*. New York: Knopf.

Schremmer, Eckhart
  1972    Agrarverfassung und Wirtschaftsstruktur: Die Südostdeutsche Hofmark, eine Wirtschaftsherrschaft? *Zeitschrift fur Agrargeschichte und Agrarsoziologie* 20.

Scott, Alison MacEwen, ed.
  1986    *Rethinking Petty Commodity Production. Social Analysis*, Special Issue, 20.

Scott, James C.
  1972    The Erosion of Patron-Client Bonds and Social Change in Rural Southeast Asia. *Journal of Asian Studies* 32(1):5–37
  1985    *Weapons of the Weak*: *Everyday Forms of Peasant Resistance*. New Haven: Yale University Press.
  1986    Everyday Forms of Resistance. In *Everyday Forms of Peasant Resistance in South-East Asia*, ed. Scott and Benedict J. Tria Kerkvliet. Special issue of *Journal of Peasant Studies* 13(2).

Seeley, John R., R. Alexander Sim, and Elizabeth W. Loosley
  1963    *Crestwood Heights*: *A Study of the Culture of Suburban Life*. New York: John Wiley and Sons.

Seifer, Nancy
  1973    *Absent from the Majority*: *Working Class Women in America*. New York: National Project on Ethnic America, American Jewish Committee.

Sharpe, Jennifer
  1987    Scenes of an Encounter: A Double Discourse of Colonialism and Nationalism. Ph.D. diss., Department of Comparative Literature, University of Texas at Austin.

Shefter, Martin
  1985    *Political Crisis/Fiscal Crisis*: *The Collapse and Revival of New York City*. New York: Basic Books.

Shehadeh, Raja
  1982    *The Third Way*. London: Quartet Books.

Shenton, Robert W.
  1986    *The Development of Capitalism in Northern Nigeria*. Toronto: University of Toronto Press.

Shenton, Robert W., and L. Lennihan
  1981    Capital and Class: Peasant Differentiation in Northern Nigeria. *Journal of Peasant Studies* 9(1):47–70.

Showalter, Elaine
    1982    Feminist Criticism in the Wilderness. In *Writing and Sexual Difference*, ed. Elizabeth Abel, 9–36. Chicago: University of Chicago Press.

Sider, Gerald
    1986    *Culture and Class in Anthropology and History: A Newfoundland Illustration.* Cambridge: Cambridge University Press.
    1987    When Parrots Learn to Talk, and Why They Can't: Domination, Deception, and Self-Deception in Indian-White Relationships. *Comparative Studies in Society and History* 29:3–23.

Skar, Sarah Lund
    1984    Interhousehold Co-operation in Peru's Southern Andes: A Case of Multiple Sibling-Group Marriage. In *Family and Work in Rural Societies: Perspective on Non-wage Labour*, ed. Norman Long, 83–98. London: Tavistock Publications.

Smith, Gavin
    1975    The Account of Don Victor. *Journal of Peasant Studies* 2(3).
    1977    Contemporary Peasant Folk History: Some Preliminary Observations. *Bulletin of the Society for Latin American Studies* 3(3).
    1979    Socio-Economic Differentiation and the Social Relations of Production among Petty Commodity Producers in Central Peru 1880–1970. *Journal of Peasant Studies* 6(3).
    1984    Confederations of Households: Extended Domestic Enterprises in City and Country. In *Miners, Peasants and Entrepreneurs: Regional Development in the Central Highlands of Peru*, ed. Norman Long and Bryan Roberts. Cambridge: Cambridge University Press.
    1985    Reflections on the Social Relations of Simple Commodity Production. *Journal of Peasant Studies* 13(1):99–108.
    1989    *Livelihood and Resistance: Peasants and the Politics of Land in Peru.* Berkeley, Los Angeles, London: University of California Press.

Smith, Judith E.
    1978    Our Own Kind: Family and Community Networks. *Radical History Review* 17:99–120.

Smith, Mary
    1954    *Baba of Karo.* London: Faber.

Smith-Rosenberg, Carroll
    1975    The Female World of Love and Ritual: Relations between Women in Nineteenth-Century America. *Signs* 1(1):1–29.

Solomon, Susan G.
    1975    *The Soviet Agrarian Debate.* Boulder, Colo.: Westview Press.

Sombart, Werner
    1923    Hausindustrie. In *Handwörterbuch der Staatswissenschaften*, 4th ed. Jena: G. Fischer.

Sommer, Louise
    1930    Cameralism. In *Encyclopedia of the Social Sciences*. New York: Macmillan.

Spaulding, Jay
    1985    *The Heroic Age in Sinnar.* East Lansing: African Studies Center, Michigan State University.

Spence, Donald P.
  1982      *Narrative Truth and Historical Truth*. New York: W. W. Norton.
Spivak, Gayatri Chakravorty
  1985      Three Women's Texts and a Critique of Imperialism. *Critical Inquiry*
            12(1):243–262.
Spufford, Margaret
  1974      *Contrasting Communities: English Villagers in the Sixteenth and Seventeenth Cen-*
            *turies*. Cambridge: Cambridge University Press.
Stack, Carol B.
  1974      *All Our Kin: Strategies for Survival in a Black Community*. New York: Harper
            & Row.
Stein, William
  1984      The Practice of Economic Anthropology in the Peruvian Andes: Com-
            munity, Household, and Relations of Production. Paper presented at the
            Annual Meeting of the American Anthropological Association, Denver,
            Colo.
Stekl, Hannes
  1978      *Österreichs Zucht- und Arbeitshäuser, 1671–1920*. Vienna: Verlag für Ges-
            chichte und Politik.
Stoler, Ann
  1985      *Capitalism and Confrontation in Sumatra's Plantation Belt*. New Haven: Yale
            University Press.
Stone, Lawrence
  1965      *The Crisis of the Aristocracy, 1558–1641*. Oxford: Clarendon Press.
Swedenburg, Ted
  1987      Al-Qassam Remembered. *Alif: Journal of Comparative Poetics* 7:9–24.
  1988      The Role of the Palestinian Peasantry in the Great Revolt (1936–39). In
            *Islam, Politics, and Social Movements*, ed. Edmund Burke, III, and Ira M.
            Lapidus, 169–203. Berkeley, Los Angeles, London: University of Cali-
            fornia Press.
  1990      The Palestinian Peasant as National Signifier. *Anthropological Quarterly*
            63:18–30.
Tamari, Selim
  1981      Building Other Peoples' Homes. The Palestinian Peasant's Household
            and Work in Israel. *Journal Palestine Studies* 12(1):31–36.
Tate, W. E.
  1952–53  The Cost of Parliamentary Enclosure in England (with Special Refer-
            ence to the County of Oxford). *Economic History Review*, 2d ser., 5:258–
            265.
  1967      *The English Village Community and the Enclosure Movements*. London: Victor
            Gollancz.
Taussig, Michael
  1978      Peasant Economics and the Development of Capitalist Agriculture in the
            Cauca Valley, Colombia. *Latin American Perspectives* 5:62–91.
  1980      *The Devil and Commodity Fetishism in South America*. Chapel Hill: University
            of North Carolina Press.
  1987      The Rise and Fall of Marxist Anthropology. *Social Analysis* 21:101–113.

Tawney, R. H.
1912    *The Agrarian Problem of the Sixteenth Century.* London: Longmans, Green and Co.
1941    The Rise of the Gentry. *Economic History Review,* o.s., 11:1–38.
1954    The Rise of the Gentry: A Postscript. *Economic History Review,* 2d ser., 7:91–97.

Taylor, Lewis
n.d.    *Bandits and Politics in Peru: Landlord and Peasant Violence in Hualgayoc, 1900–30.* Center of Latin American Studies, University of Cambridge.

Taylor, Peter, and Hermann Rebel
1981    Hessian Peasant Women, Their Families, and the Draft: A Sociohistorical Interpretation of Four Tales from the Grimm Collection. *Journal of Family History* 6:347–378.

Terdiman, Richard
1985    Deconstructing Memory: On Representing the Past and Theorizing Culture in France since the Revolution. *Diacritics* 15(4):13–36.

Thirsk, Joan
1957    *English Peasant Farming.* London: Routledge & Kegan Paul.
1961    Industries in the Countryside. In *Essays in the Economic and Social History of Tudor and Stuart England,* ed. F. J. Fisher, 70–78. Cambridge: Cambridge University Press.
1964    The Common Fields. *Past and Present* (29):3–25.
1966    The Origin of the Common Fields. *Past and Present* (33):142–147.
1967    Enclosing and Engrossing. In *The Agrarian History of England and Wales,* vol. 4 (1500–1640), ed. Joan Thirsk, 200–255. Cambridge: Cambridge University Press.
1970    Seventeenth-Century Agriculture and Social Change. In *Land, Church, and People,* ed. Joan Thirsk, 148–177. Supplement to vol. 18 of *Agricultural History Review.* Reading, Berks: Museum of English Rural Life.

Thomas, Michael
1987    *Edmund Husserl: Zur Genesis einer spätbürgerlichen Philosophie.* Berlin: Akademie Verlag.

Thompson, Edward P.
1963    *The Making of the English Working Class.* New York: Vintage.
1967    Time, Work Discipline, and Industrial Capitalism. *Past and Present* (38):56–98.
1974    Patrician Society, Plebeian Culture. *Journal of Social History* 7(4):382–405.
1976    The Grid of Inheritance: A Comment. In *Family and Inheritance: Rural Society in Western Europe 1200–1800,* ed. Jack Goody, Joan Thirsk, and E. P. Thompson, 328–360. Cambridge: Cambridge University Press.
1978a   Eighteenth-Century English Society: Class Struggle without Class? *Social History* 3(2):133–165.
1978b   *The Poverty of Theory and Other Essays.* New York: Monthly Review Press.

Thompson, F. M. L.
1966    The Social Distribution of Landed Property in England since the Sixteenth Century. *Economic History Review,* 2d ser., 19(3):505–517.

Tilly, Charles
1986    *The Contentious French*. Cambridge: Belknap, Harvard University Press.
Tilly, Louise, and Joan Scott
1978    *Women, Work, and Family*. New York: Holt, Rinehart, and Winston.
Titow, J. Z.
1965    Medieval England and the Open-Field System. *Past and Present* (32):86–102.
Toledo, Francisco de
1975    *Tasa de la visita general de Toledo*. Lima: n.p. (Original 1575.)
Torres Juarez, Dionisio
1962    Monografía de la provincia de San Roman. Arequipa: Offset Acosta.
Totah, Dr. Khalil
1938    Memo, enclosed in Consul General of Jerusalem to Secretary of State, 19 Sept. National Archives, Washington, D.C., 867 N.4016/64.
Trevor-Roper, H. R.
1953    *The Gentry, 1540–1640. Economic History Review*, supplement no, 1,
Trimingham, J. S.
1949    *Islam in the Sudan*. Oxford: Oxford University Press.
1969    The Expansion of Islam. In *Islam in Africa*, ed. James Kritzeck and William H. Lewis, 13–34. New York: Van Nostrand-Reinhold.
Trouillot, Michel-Rolph
1986    The Price of Indulgence. *Social Analysis* 19:85–90.
Tschopik, Harry
1951    The Aymara of Chucuito, Peru. *Anthropological Papers of the American Museum of Natural History* (New York) 44(2).
Turner, Terence
1986    Production, Exploitation, and Social Consciousness in the "Peripheral Situation." *Social Analysis* 19:91–115.
Uris, Leon
1984    *The Haj*. New York: Doubleday.
Vargas Llosa, Mario
1983    Inquest in the Andes: A Latin American Writer Explores the Political Lessons of a Peruvian Massacre. *New York Times Magazine*, 31 July.
Vasquez, Emilio
1976    *La rebelion de Juan Bustamante*. Lima: Editorial Juan Mejia Baca.
Velásquez Rodríguez, Marco Gustavo
1978    Análisis de la estructura comercial de la ciudad de Juliaca. Licenciatura Thesis, Programa Académico de Ingenería Económica, Universidad Nacional Técnica del Altiplano, Puno, Peru.
Vierhaus, Rudolf
1988    *Germany in the Age of Absolutism*. Cambridge: Cambridge University Press.
Voll, John O., and Sarah P. Voll
1985    *The Sudan: Unity and Diversity in a Multicultural State*. London: Croom Helm.
Walker, Mack
1971    *German Hometowns: Community, State, and Estate, 1648–1871*. Ithaca, N.Y.: Cornell University Press.

Wallerstein, Immanuel
1974    *The Modern World-System.* New York: Academic.
Walser, Martin
1964    *Lügengeschichten.* Frankfurt: Suhrkamp.
Wangermann, Ernst
1973    *The Austrian Achievement, 1700–1800.* New York: Harcourt Brace Jovanovich.
Watts, Michael J.
1983    *Silent Violence.* Berkeley, Los Angeles, London: University of California Press.
Weiner, Jon
1985    Women's History on Trial. *The Nation,* 7 September, 161, 176, 178–180.
White, Hayden
1981    The Value of Narrativity in the Representation of Reality. In *On Narrative,* ed. W. J. T. Mitchell, 1–23. Chicago: University of Chicago Press.
Whyte, William Foote
1943    *Streetcorner Society: The Social Structure of an Italian Slum.* Chicago: University of Chicago Press.
Whyte, William H., Jr.
1956    *The Organization Man.* New York: Simon and Schuster.
Williams, Gavin
1988    Why Is There No Agrarian Capitalism in Northern Nigeria? *Journal of Historical Sociology* 1(4):345–398.
Williams, Raymond
1976    *Keywords: A Vocabulary of Culture and Society.* London: Fontana.
Wilson, Patricia, and Patricia Wise
1986    The Regional Implications of Public Investment in Peru, 1968–1983. *Latin American Research Review* 21(2):93–116.
Wilmsen, Edwin
1989    *Land Filled with Flies: A Political Economy of the Kalahari.* Chicago: University of Chicago Press.
Winnicott, D. W.
1982    *Playing and Reality.* London: Tavistock.
Wobst, H. Martin
1978    The Archaeo-Ethnology of Hunter-Gatherers or the Tyranny of the Ethnographic Record in Archaeology. *American Antiquity* 43:303–309.
Wolf, Eric
1955    Types of Latin American Peasantries: A Preliminary Discussion. *American Anthropologist* 57:457–471.
1957    Closed Corporate Communities in Mesoamerica and Central Java. *Southwestern Journal of Anthropology* 13(1):1–18.
1969    *Peasant Wars of the Twentieth Century.* New York: Harper and Row.
1982    *Europe and the People without History.* Berkeley, Los Angeles, London: University of California Press.
1987    On Peasant Rebellions. In *Peasants and Peasant Societies,* 2d ed., ed. Teodor Shanin. Oxford: Basil Blackwell. (Originally published in *International Social Science Journal* 21 [1969].)

Wordie, J. R.
  1983     The Chronology of English Enclosure, 1500–1914. *Economic History Review*, 2d ser., 36(4):483–505.
Worsley, Peter
  1984*a*     A Landmark in Anthropology. *American Enthnologist* 11.
  1984*b*     *The Three Worlds*. Chicago: University of Chicago Press.
Wright, Patrick
  1985     *On Living in an Old Country: The National Past in Contemporary Britain*. London: Verso.
Yapita Moya, Juan de Dios
  1981     The Aymara Alphabet: Linguistics for Indigenous Communities. In *The Aymara Language in Its Social and Cultural Context*, ed. M. J. Hardman, 262–270. Gainesville: University Presses of Florida.
Yasin, 'Abd al-Qadir
  1975     *Kifah al-sha'b al-Filastini qabl al-'am 1948* (The struggle of the Palestinian people before 1948). Beirut: PLO Research Center.
Zauner, Alois
  1971     *Vöcklabruck und der Attergau*. Vienna: Böhlau.
Zimmerly, David William
  1975     *Cain's Land Revisited*. St. John's: Institute of Social and Economic Research, Memorial University of Newfoundland.
Zu'aytir, Akram
  1955     *Al-gadiya al-Filastiniya* (The Palestine Question). Cairo: Dar al-Ma'arif.

# INDEX